Peter Barnes

# Peter Barnes

## Collected Plays

*With Barnes' People:*
*Seven Monologues*
*and*
*an Introduction*

**HEINEMANN**
London

Heinemann Educational Books Ltd
22 Bedford Square, London WC1B 3HH

LONDON    EDINBURGH    MELBOURNE    AUCKLAND
HONG KONG    SINGAPORE    KUALA LUMPUR    NEW DELHI
NAIROBI    JOHANNESBURG    IBADAN    KINGSTON
EXETER (NH)    PORT OF SPAIN

**British Library Cataloguing in Publication Data**

Barnes, Peter, 1931–    200  307  322  NOT
   Collected plays.
   I. Title
   822'.914        PR6052.A668

   ISBN 0–435–18281–1        822 BARN

Printed and bound in Great Britain by
Biddles Ltd, Guildford, Surrey

# Contents

# Introduction to
# the Collected Plays

## Peter Barnes

This introduction is something of a problem. It should be
personal to some extent. But I have always seen the world of
the strictly personal as shallow, tending to break life up into
little closed cells. I have therefore tried, as far as possible, to
keep any conscious autobiographical element out of my plays.

I can remember being evacuated to the country during the
war and waiting outside our cottage, for my father to come
home from night work at a nearby factory. He would come
up the hill coughing loudly in the cold morning light and
have two eggs for breakfast. It has no significance; it's just
personal history. What is important in my life will not
necessarily be so for an audience. Write what you know is
good advice for journalists. I write what I imagine, believe,
fear, think.

If there is one certain way of achieving absolute unpopularity
it is by writing against the prevailing modes and pieties. With
each new play I presented to disinterested parties I felt I was
always starting from scratch. Here, the fact one may have
written a number of major plays over the years counts for
very little. I always had to persuade theatre directors,
producers and agents that I knew what I was doing. They did
not know. For them the theatre was a job, not their lives.
Unfortunately I am passionate about it. And it *is* unfortunate.
Fish trust the water and are cooked in it, sometimes I'm not
smart enough to be an idiot. Passion is an emotion you must
never show if you want to be effective in England. Play it
cool, understate, pretend to be an amateur who has just

wandered into the arts by mistake. It is what puts the damp in walls and white hair on old men.

At the start I believed that it was enough to write well, everything would follow. It is not enough and it never has been. Few know what a well-written page is, with all the words looking in the same direction.

So what was I trying to do in these plays? I wanted to write a roller-coaster drama of hairpin bends; a drama of expertise and ecstasy balanced on a tight-rope between the comic and tragic with a multi-faceted fly-like vision where every line was dramatic and every scene a play in itself; a drama with a language so exact it could describe what the flame of a candle looked like after the candle had been blown out and so high-powered it could fuse telephone wires and have a direct impact on reality; a drama that made the surreal real, that went to the limit, then further, with no dead time, but with the speed of a seismograph recording an earthquake; a drama of 'The Garden of Earthly Delights' where a Lion, a Tinman and a Scarecrow are always looking for a girl with ruby slippers; a drama glorifying differences, condemning hierarchies, that would rouse the dead to fight, always in the forefront of the struggle for the happiness of all mankind; an anti-boss drama for the shorn not the shearers.

The theatre is a thermometer of life but our theatre is a theatre without size or daring; a theatre without communion. It contains no miracles. The bread is never changed into flesh or the wine into blood. It is a theatre of carpet-slippers.

'Well, change it then! Nothing's impossible.'

'Have you tried juggling soot?'

There is no creativity only discovery. If I return again and again to the same themes, like a child to the fire, it is because they are essential and I still owe them something. But whatever forms I use, whether it is the drama or the song lyric it is still, above all, *information*.

To strike out, to launch repeated bayonet attacks on naturalism, to write rigorously against the prevailing mode, requires courage. What courage I have I put into my work and I have none left for my life. The word must act for me. Like others I want to help create a people who are sceptical, rational, critical, not impressed or fooled. In a word, free, and in the literal sense, ungovernable. Of course that is not very practical but it is not unthinkable. It says something about our inadequacies and limitations, rather than the bizarreness of the idea itself. However, I who advocate freedom and boldness remain in my life, clinging to routine and habit like the most conforming bourgeoisie, in order to write. But, please, always believe the song not the singer.

At times I feel I could not track an elephant in six feet of snow, but at least I have provided a good home for scores of old jokes who had nowhere else to go. I have laughed a lot when I did not feel a lot like laughing and of course I have made a mess of my life, but then I have made a mess of all my shirts. I write hoping to make the world a little better and perhaps to be remembered. The latter part of that statement is foolish, as I can see, quite plainly, the time when this planet grows cold and the Universe leaks away into another Universe and the Cosmos finally dies and there is nothing but night and nothing. It's the end, but that is never a good enough reason for not going on. A writer who does not write corrupts the soul. Besides, it is absurd to sit around sniffing wild flowers when you can invent them, and new worlds.

# The Ruling Class

*With an Introduction by Harold Hobson*

## THE CHARACTERS

13TH EARL OF GURNEY
TOASTMASTER
DANIEL TUCKER
BISHOP LAMPTON
SIR CHARLES GURNEY
DINSDALE GURNEY
LADY CLAIRE GURNEY
MATTHEW PEAKE
14TH EARL OF GURNEY
DR PAUL HERDER
MRS TREADWELL

MRS PIGGOT-JONES
GRACE SHELLEY
MCKYLE
MCKYLE'S ASSISTANT
KELSO TRUSCOTT, Q.C.
GIRL
DETECTIVE INSPECTOR BROCKETT
DETECTIVE SERGEANT FRASER
FIRST LORD
SECOND LORD
THIRD LORD

# Introduction
## by Harold Hobson

The most exciting thing that can happen to a dramatic critic is when he is suddenly and unexpectedly faced with the explosive blaze of an entirely new talent of a very high order. This happens very rarely. In twenty years of reviewing plays it has happened to me, for example, only four times. The first was the original production at the Arts Theatre in 1955 of Samuel Beckett's *Waiting for Godot*. The second, John Osborne's *Look Back in Anger* at the Royal Court a year later. The third was Harold Pinter's *The Birthday Party* at the Lyric, Hammersmith, in 1958; and the fourth Peter Barnes's *The Ruling Class* at the Nottingham Playhouse, directed by Stuart Burge, in the autumn of 1968.

The peculiar impact of such an experience is that one is taken completely by surprise. To see John Gielgud in *The Importance of Being Earnest*, or Laurence Olivier in *Macbeth*, his finest Shakespeare creation, is a memorable experience. In a certain sense, too, it holds the unexpected, but not altogether the unforeseen. Before one sees it one cannot tell what particular aspect of humanity Olivier will derive from his performance of Macbeth. Until he had played Macbeth one did not know that he would heartrendingly present a man who had so ordered his life that when he came to the end of it he had no friends, and no man who owed loyalty to him. But one did know before hand that in all probability the performance would be fine and moving, even revelatory. One knew this for the simple reason that one had seen Olivier on many other occasions, and had come to recognise in him the possession of transcendent abilities.

That amazing evening at Nottingham, towards the close of 1968, however, to its other joys and triumphs, added those of astonishment and discovery. Before the curtain rose on *The Ruling Class* no one appeared to have heard of its author, Peter

Barnes. Nobody in the theatre appeared to know whether he had been to university, had written any other plays, was a stripling in his last year at school, or an old gentleman of ninety. It was hazarded to me that Mr Barnes was not a member of the aristocracy, but this was only a deduction from the fact that *The Ruling Class* is hostile to the nobility. As such, the deduction might easily have been wrong. For the production, if not the play, has firm connections with the upper classes that it derides. One of its most charmingly unintelligent characters, Dinsdale, the thirteenth Earl of Gurney's nephew, has been played by two extremely bright young aristocrats, first, by Peter Eyre, whose grandfather was Lord Acton, and later, when Mr Eyre had contractual obligations elsewhere, by Jonathan Cecil, the grandson of the Marquis of Salisbury. Mr Barnes, however, is not himself an offshoot of Debrett, though privately he is very good-humoured about those who are. He has, I later found out, written other plays, and is an assiduous worker in that forcing house of revolution, the Reading Room of the British Museum. Even this information does not amount to very much. But it is more than I could discover on the opening night of *The Ruling Class*.

At that performance the play struck me like a revelation. Prudently I had expected nothing, and overwhelmingly I was given all: wit, pathos, exciting melodrama, brilliant satire, double-edged philosophy, horror, cynicism, and sentiment, all combined in a perfect unity in the theatrical world of Mr Barnes's extraordinary and idiosyncratic creation. Baudelaire, in discussing a nineteenth-century actor, says that the primary condition of a work of art, without which it cannot exist, is energy or life. *The Ruling Class* throbs with life and energy all through. Whatever else it is, it is not dead. From the unfortunate hanging of the twelfth Earl, through the crucifixion of the thirteenth, the disputable miracle and the battle of rival gods, the episode of Jack the Ripper and the striptease of Marguerite Gautier, it flashes all along with life. Paradoxically, the culminating scene in the House of Lords, with their Lordships cobwebbed, somnolent, and seemingly on the point of dissolution, is almost the most alive of all.

At a time when a great deal of theatrical energy is concentrated on forcing plays which no one wants to see on the sort of audiences that do not want to see any play at all it came as an immense delight to discover a drama which was not only thoughtful, but also exciting and amusing. For many years now incident and plot have been driven out of our theatre; Mr Barnes brings them back with both gusto and skill. The *coup de théâtre* by which the Lady of the Camelias is brought on to the stage, prompt on cue, is in itself a little marvel of stagecraft. It gives the kind of pleasure we have not had in the theatre for more than a decade. The moment one heard the thirteenth Earl's reply to the question what made him think that he was God, one knew that a new wit had been born in the theatre; and all through the play one has the delightful thrill, which one felt had gone from the theatre for ever, of actually feeling that one wants to know what is going to happen next.

*The Ruling Class*, then, is immensely entertaining, but it is admirably philosophic, too. It mounts a lively and vigorous attack, not only on the upper echelons of society, but also on all of us who rate cruelty higher than compassion, and consider violence more sane than peace. It brings us into contact with a mind of poise and depth and power; it combines rumbustiousness with delicacy, and in doing so is likely to prove a turning point in the drama of the second half of the twentieth century.

# FOR CHARLOTTE

*The Ruling Class* was first presented at Nottingham Playhouse on 6 November 1968 and was subsequently transferred to The Piccadilly Theatre, London, on 26 February 1969. The play was presented by Gene Persson and Richard Pilbrow with the following cast:

| | |
|---|---|
| 13TH EARL OF GURNEY | *Peter Whitbread* |
| TOASTMASTER | *Robert Robertson* |
| DANIEL TUCKER | *Dudley Jones* |
| BISHOP LAMPTON | *Ronald Magill* |
| SIR CHARLES GURNEY | *David Dodimead* |
| DINSDALE GURNEY | *Jonathan Cecil* |
| LADY CLAIRE GURNEY | *Irene Hamilton* |
| MATTHEW PEAKE | *Brown Derby* |
| 14TH EARL OF GURNEY | *Derek Godfrey* |
| DR PAUL HERDER | *David Neal* |
| MRS TREADWELL | *Ann Heffernan* |
| MRS PIGGOT-JONES | *Elizabeth Tyrrell* |
| GRACE SHELLEY | *Vivienne Martin* |
| MCKYLE | *Ken Hutchison* |
| MCKYLE'S ASSISTANT | *Terence Ratcliffe* |
| KELSO TRUSCOTT, Q.C. | *Laurence Harrington* |
| GIRL | *Vicky Clayton* |
| DETECTIVE INSPECTOR BROCKETT | *Peter Whitbread* |
| DETECTIVE SERGEANT FRASER | *Robert Robertson* |
| FIRST LORD | *C. Denier Warren* |
| SECOND LORD | *Brown Derby* |
| THIRD LORD | *Timothy Welsh* |

*The Play directed by* STUART BURGE

*Designed by* JOHN NAPIER

*Lighting by* ROBERT ORNBO

# THE RULING CLASS

# PROLOGUE

*Three distinct raps. Curtain rises. Spot Down Stage Centre. The*
13TH EARL OF GURNEY *stands in full evening dress and medals at*
*a banqueting table. On it a silver coffee pot and a half-filled wine*
*glass.*
A TOASTMASTER *in scarlet jacket and sash stands beside him;*
*he has just rapped his gavel for silence.*

13TH EARL OF GURNEY: The aim of the Society of St George
Is to keep green the memory of England
And what England means to her sons and daughters.
I say the fabric holds, though families fly apart.
Once the rulers of the greatest Empire
The world has ever known,
Ruled not by superior force or skill
But by sheer presence. (*Raises glass in a toast.*)
This teeming womb of privilege, this feudal state,
Whose shores beat back the turbulent sea of foreign anarchy.
This ancient fortress, still commanded by the noblest
Of our royal blood; this ancient land of ritual.
This precious stone set in a silver sea.
TOASTMASTER: My Lords, Ladies and Gentlemen. The toast is—
England. This precious stone set in a silver sea.
13TH EARL OF GURNEY AND VOICES: England. Set in a
silver sea.

> *He drinks. The National Anthem plays over as his* LORDSHIP
> *comes rigidly to attention, whilst behind him, the* TOASTMASTER
> *exits, and the table is taken off. The Anthem ends.*
> *Lights up on his Lordship's bedroom. An ornate four-poster*
> *bed Stage Centre, and a wardrobe near a door Stage Left. Dressed*
> *in a traditional butler's uniform,* DANIEL TUCKER, *his Lordship's*

*aged manservant, creakingly lays out his master's dressing-gown on
the bed, whilst his* LORDSHIP *undresses.*

TUCKER: How was your speech, sir?

13TH EARL OF GURNEY (*dropping jacket absently on floor*): Went
well, Tuck. Englishmen like to hear the truth about themselves.

   TUCKER *painfully picks up the jacket, whilst his* LORDSHIP
*sits on the edge of the bed.*

The Guv'nor loved this bed.

TUCKER: Wouldn't sleep anywhere else, sir.

13TH EARL OF GURNEY: Took it all over the world, Delhi,
Cairo, Hong Kong. Devilish great man, the Guv'nor. Superb
shot.

TUCKER (*kneeling to take off his Lordship's shoes*): Did wonderful needlework too, sir. 'Petit-Point'.

13TH EARL OF GURNEY (*undoing his trousers*): Tuck, I'm getting
married again.

TUCKER: Yes, my Lord.

13TH EARL OF GURNEY: Miss Grace Shelley. Charles is right.
Sake of the family. Gurney name. Been putting it off. Only
Jack left.

TUCKER: This house used to be full of mischief . . . mischief . . .

13TH EARL OF GURNEY: Four young devils. Thought I was safe
enough.

TUCKER: Master Paul would have been the 14th Earl.

13TH EARL OF GURNEY: District Officer at twenty-one. Dead
at twenty-three. Beri-beri. Picked it up off some scruffy
fuzzy-wuzzy in a dressing-gown, shouldn't wonder.

TUCKER (*getting up slowly*): Young Richard used to play the
xylophone.

13TH EARL OF GURNEY: And young Raymond killed in
Malaya. Not one of 'em buried in England. Never seen their
graves.

TUCKER (*crossing to the wardrobe with clothes*): You could do that
on your honeymoon, your Lordship.

13TH EARL OF GURNEY: There's still Jack. (*They look at each other*.) It's all based on land, Tuck. Can't have those knaves from Whitehall moving in. So it's Miss Grace Shelley.

TUCKER: Is she anyone, sir?

13TH EARL OF GURNEY: No one. But Charles recommends her as good breeding stock. Family foals well. Sires mostly. There's always room at the top for brains, money or a good pair of titties.

TUCKER: Miss Shelley seems well-endowed, sir.

TUCKER *comes back with a flat leather case from the wardrobe. He opens it for his* LORDSHIP, *who is deep in thought. Inside are four coils of rope, each eight feet long, made of silk, nylon, hemp and cord respectively.*

Your Lordship?

13TH EARL OF GURNEY: What? Eh? (*Looking*.) Yes, I suppose so. Hard day. Need to relax.

TUCKER: May I suggest silk tonight, sir?

13TH EARL OF GURNEY: Good idea, Tuck. For St George.

TUCKER *takes the silk rope and goes round to a pair of steps. He places them under a cross-beam at the corner of the bed and climbs up with the rope.*

13TH EARL OF GURNEY: Ah, Tuck, there's no end to duty. Every day's like climbing a mountain. How did Tiberius do it at his age?

TUCKER: Will-power, sir.

13TH EARL OF GURNEY: The Law's been my life, Tuck. And the reason is the soul of the Law. A judge can't be unreasonable. So how can he be a lover, eh? Ours is a damned dry world, Tuck.

TUCKER: A long life, and a grey one, your Lordship.

13TH EARL OF GURNEY (*musing*): The power of life and death. No need of other vices. If you've once put on the black cap, everything else tastes like wax fruit.

TUCKER *ties the rope to a hook on the cross-beam. The rope hangs down in a noose. His* LORDSHIP *peers up.*

Noose a bit high, Tuck. Pull the knot down half an inch. That's it.

TUCKER *comes down.*

TUCKER: Will that be all, your Lordship?

13TH EARL OF GURNEY: Whisky and soda in about five minutes as usual. Oh, Tuck, tell Cook the trial ends tomorrow. She knows I don't like passing sentence on an empty stomach.

TUCKER: Very good, my Lord.

*TUCKER exits Stage Left. Humming to himself, his* LORDSHIP *goes to the wardrobe and brings out a three-cornered cocked hat, a sword in a scabbard and a white tutu ballet skirt.*

13TH EARL OF GURNEY: Nothing like a good English breakfast. Big meal of the day for the Guv'nor. Always sat at the head of the table. All the mail in front of him. He'd pass it out to the rest of us. Same with the newspapers. Always read *The Times* through first, in case there was anything too disturbing in it. Mother didn't know what the word 'Socialist' meant till she was past fifty. Remember standing at the foot of this bed here, telling him I wanted to be a painter. 'The Gurneys have never been slackers,' he said. 'Pulled their weight. Earned their privileges.' Great concession letting me study law. Not the Gurney tradition. Always the Army. (*He puts the tutu on, delicately flouncing it out.*) The smell of cordite. The clash of steel. Feet, feet, feet, the boys are marching! A little more grape-shot Captain Bragg! Give 'em the cold steel, boys.' (*He straps the sword to his side and puts on the three-cornered hat.*)

*Now dressed in three-cornered hat, ballet skirt, long underwear and sword, the* 13TH EARL OF GURNEY *curtseys and moves towards the steps, trembling slightly in anticipation.*

Close. I can feel her hot breath. Wonderful. One slip. The worms have the best of it. They dine off the tenderest joints. Juicy breasts, white thighs, red hair colour of rust . . . the worms have the best of it. (*He climbs up the steps, stands under the noose and comes to attention.*) It is a far, far better thing I do

now, than I have ever done. (*He slips the noose over his head,*
*trembling.*) No, Sir. No bandage. Die my dear doctor? That's the
last thing I shall do. Is that you, my love? Now, come darling
. . . to me . . . ha! . . .

*Stepping off the top of the steps, he dangles for a few seconds and*
*begins to twitch and jump. He puts his feet back on the top of the*
*steps. Gasping, he loosens the noose.*
(*Trembling hoarsely.*) Touched him, saw her, towers of death
and silence, angels of fire and ice. Saw Alexander covered
with honey and beeswax in his tomb and felt the flowers
growing over me. A man must have his visions. How else
could an English judge and peer of the realm take moonlight
trips to Marrakesh and Ponders End? See six vestal virgins
smoking cigars? Moses in bedroom slippers? Naked bosoms
floating past Formosa? Desperate diseases need desperate
remedies. (*Glancing towards the door.*) Just time for a quick one.
(*Reverently places noose over his head again.*) Be of good cheer,
Master Ridley, and play the man. There's plenty of time to
win this game, and thrash the Spaniards too. (*Excitedly draws*
*his sword.*) Form squares men! Smash the Mahdi, and Binnie
Barnes!

*With a lustful gurgle he steps off. But this time he knocks over the*
*steps. Dangling helpless for a second he drops the sword and tries*
*to tear the noose free, gesturing frantically. Every muscle begins to*
*tremble. His legs jack-knife up to his stomach; they jack-knife*
*again and again with increasing speed and violence. The spasms*
*reach a climax, then stop suddenly. The body goes limp and sways*
*gently at the end of the rope. A discreet knock on door Stage Left.*
TUCKER (*voice off*): Your Lordship? Are you ready?
*The door opens slightly.* TUCKER *shuffles in carrying a tray*
*with whisky and soda. He sees his* LORDSHIP.
Bleeding bloody hell!
*Blackout.*

                         CURTAIN

*Act One*

# SCENE ONE

*A great church organ thunders out 'The Dead March from Saul'. The curtain parts enough to reveal the imposing figure of* BISHOP BERTRAM LAMPTON, *magnificently dressed in red cope, surplice, embroidered stole and mitre.* FOUR PALL BEARERS *in top-hats and morning-coats slowly cross Down Stage, bearing a coffin, draped with the Gurney banner.*

BISHOP LAMPTON (*chanting*): I am the Resurrection and the Life, saith the Lord; he that believeth in me though he were dead, yet shall he live: and whosoever liveth and believeth in me shall never die.
Gilead is mine, and Manasses is mine: Ephraim also is the strength of my head; Judah is my lawgiver,
Moab is my washpot; over Edom will I cast out my shoe: Philistria, triumph thou because of me.
Who will lead me onto the strong city: who will bring me into Edom?

*The* PALL BEARERS *exit Right. The curtain opens behind the* BISHOP *to show his Lordship's relatives dressed in black, standing grouped in the drawing room of the Gurney country house.*

BISHOP LAMPTON *and* RELATIVES (*singing*): 'All things bright and beautiful. All creatures great and small. All things wise and wonderful, the Lord God made them all. The rich man in his castle, the poor man at his gate. God made them high and lowly, and ordered their estate . . .'

*As they sing* BISHOP LAMPTON *disrobes, handing his cope, surplice and mitre to* TUCKER. *The* BISHOP *has shrunk to a small, bald-headed, asthmatic old man in dog-collar and gaiters. As the last note of the hymn dies away and* TUCKER *staggers off Wings Left with the robes, he smooths down his non-existent hair and waddles Up Stage to join the others.*

# SCENE TWO

*The large drawing room of Gurney Manor. It is seventeenth century, except for the high double french-windows, now heavily curtained, Stage Right. Running the length of the back wall Up Stage is a narrow gallery: small stairways, Up Stage Left and Right, lead up to it. On the wall above the gallery are portraits of past Earls. Up Stage Centre, below the gallery, is a wide double-doorway leading to the hall. Just above it the Gurney crest. Door, Down Stage Left, and alongside, a bell-rope. Sofa and chairs Centre Stage. Desk, chair and coffee table adjacent to the windows.*

LADY CLAIRE GURNEY *is on the sofa: long black cigarette holder, long black velvet gloves.* SIR CHARLES GURNEY *stands ramrod stiff, his legs slightly apart, whilst* DINSDALE GURNEY *lounges on the arm of the sofa, elegantly picking his nose.* BISHOP LAMPTON *joins them.*

SIR CHARLES: Excellent service, Bertie. Created exactly the right impression.

DINSDALE: Damned if I could understand a word of it.

BISHOP LAMPTON (*asthmatically*): Hardly expected you to, young man. It was a Church service. A service, Charles, I might add, I could not have conducted for someone who may have lain violent hands upon himself. A disturbing rumour has reached my ears. Did Ralph commit suicide?

SIR CHARLES (*slightly exasperated*): Suicide? Tucker found Ralph hanging in the bedroom dressed in a cocked hat, underpants and a ballet skirt. Does that *sound* like suicide?

DINSDALE: I'm sure if Uncle Ralph had wanted to do anything foolish he'd have done it decently. Bullet through the head, always the Gurney way.

SIR CHARLES: No idea how these malicious rumours get

started. The Coroner's verdict is clear enough. Accident brought on by the strain of overwork.

BISHOP LAMPTON (*sitting*): Had to be sure. He's buried in consecrated ground.

DINSDALE (*thoughtfully*): Still, you know, I must say it's odd, Uncle Ralph found hanging around like that in a ballet skirt.

CLAIRE (*maliciously*): Charles didn't you say Ralph always was rather artistic?

SIR CHARLES: He was wilful, stubborn, and this time he went too far. But he was my brother—well, half-brother. I won't have you calling him *artistic*.

BISHOP LAMPTON (*between gasps: puzzled*): Cocked hat? Why was he wearing a cocked hat?

SIR CHARLES: Trying it on for size obviously. I told him not to stay a widower. The Guv'nor didn't. Understood his duty to the family. Had to start breeding again. Not pleasant, I grant you, for a man of Ralph's age. But it was something he had to get on top of.

BISHOP LAMPTON: Underpants? Why was he in his underpants?

SIR CHARLES: Why not? Going to bed wasn't he? Thought our troubles were over when he took a fancy to young Grace Shelley. That would have solved everything.

CLAIRE: Yes, wouldn't it just.

DINSDALE: Frankly, I don't understand all the plother. Uncle Ralph has an heir—Jack, the 14th Earl of Gurney.

SIR CHARLES (*stroking his moustache*): Yes . . . It's going to be awkward. Damned awkward.

CLAIRE: Ralph was aware of the situation. I'm sure he's made proper arrangements. A matter of finding out who he's appointed guardian of the estate.

BISHOP LAMPTON (*sitting up*): But what was he doing in a *ballet-skirt*? Answer me that!

> TUCKER *enters Up Stage Centre.*

TUCKER: Mr Matthew Peake to see you, Sir Charles.

SIR CHARLES: Right. Show him in.

*TUCKER steps aside, and* MATTHEW PEAKE, *solicitor, enters and gives him his trilby. He is a dessicated, deferential man with round shoulders, winged collar and a briefcase.*

SIR CHARLES: I believe you know everyone here, Peake.

PEAKE: I have had that honour, Sir Charles.

SIR CHARLES: All right, Tucker, that'll be all. We're not to be disturbed.

PEAKE: Sir Charles, might I suggest Tucker stays. (*Taps briefcase significantly.*)

SIR CHARLES: What? Oh quite. Well, Tucker, seems you're going to hear something to your advantage.

TUCKER: Yes, sir.

*He stands discreetly in the background, holding* PEAKE'S *trilby.*

PEAKE: May I take this opportunity to express my condolences.

CLAIRE: Tucker, *do* sit down.

TUCKER: Thank you, madam.

*He sits on the edge of a chair, whilst* PEAKE *crosses to the desk, and takes out some legal documents.*

PEAKE: Hmmm, may I say, Sir Charles, how refreshing it is to meet with such restraint. Usually I'm afraid these occasions are so . . . (*purses lips in distaste*) emotional.

SIR CHARLES: Do get on with it.

PEAKE: But, Sir Charles, shouldn't we wait? His Lordship's heir . . .

SIR CHARLES: Jack's been notified. Wasn't able to get away for the funeral. Not likely to come now.

PEAKE: Very well, Sir Charles. I'll inform him later.

*All eyes now on* PEAKE *as he puts on horn-rimmed spectacles, and reads in a dry monotone.*

(*Reading.*) 'I, Ralph, Douglas, Christopher, Alexander, Gurney, of Gurney House in the county of Bedfordshire, hereby revoke all former Wills and Codicils and declare this to be my last Will. I appoint Mr Matthew Peake of 17 Brownlow Gardens, Bedfordshire, to be the sole executor of this my

Will. I give and bequeath unto my manservant, Daniel Tucker, the sum of twenty thousand pounds free of duty.'

*Murmurs of surprise from the listeners. But no reaction from* TUCKER *himself.*

There follow a number of bequests to various charities, which his Lordship was interested in. I'll run through them briefly. 'I bequeth the sum of five thousand pounds to the Tailwavers Registered National Charity. Three thousand pounds to the Bankers Beneficent Society Ltd.' . . .

TUCKER: Yippee! (*Shoots off the chair.*) *Twenty thousand! Twenty thousand smackers! Yawee!*

*Jumping clumsily into the air, and clicking his heels together, he flicks* PEAKE's *trilby on to his head and gleefully capers forward.* (*Singing in a croak.*) 'I'm Gilbert the Filbert the Knut with a "K". (*Gives gouty high kick.*) The pride of Piccadilly, the blase roué. Oh Hades! The Ladies (*ogles* CLAIRE) who leave their wooden huts, For Gilbert the Filbert, the Colonel of the Knuts.' Yah!

*Flinging open the door Up Stage he leaps raggedly out, arms held high. There is a crash off as he hits something followed by a cackle of laughter. Silence in the room.*

DINSDALE: Tucker seems het up.

BISHOP LAMPTON: 'So are the ways of everyone that is greedy of gain'. What about the Zambesi Mission, Peake? And the Overseas Bishoprics Fund?

SIR CHARLES: Never mind that, Bertie. What about the estate?

PEAKE (*continues reading*): 'I devise and bequeath all the remainder of my estate both real and personal whatsoever and wheresoever to which I might be entitled or over which I have any disposing at the time of my death, to my beloved son, Jack, Arnold, Alexander, Tancred, Gurney, the 14th Earl of Gurney, for his own use absolutely.'

SIR CHARLES (*repeating slowly*): 'For his own use absolutely.' But who's been appointed legal guardian?

PEAKE: No one.

BISHOP LAMPTON: 'By the rivers of Babylon there we sat down, yea, we wept when we remembered Zion.'

SIR CHARLES (*stunned*): You mean Jack is free to run the estate... and everything . . .?

CLAIRE: Think of Jack in the Royal Enclosure.

BISHOP LAMPTON: Jack in the *Athenæum*.

SIR CHARLES (*grimly*): It's obvious Ralph has let his personal feelings come before his duty to his family. We'll have to fight. Awkward. Scandal an'all. But we've no choice.

PEAKE (*diffidently reading*): 'If this my Will is contested, the whole of my estate, both real and personal, is bequeathed to the charities named herewith: The Earl Haig Fund, Lord Wharton's . . .'

*The rest is drowned out as all start shouting angrily. They are too busy yelling to notice* TUCKER *appear in the doorway Up Stage Centre smoking a cigar. He disappears for a second, re-appearing immediately carrying a large hall vase. Holding it up, he deliberately drops it on the floor. It smashes with a loud crash. The shouting stops. They all turn in astonishment.* TUCKER *takes the cigar out of his mouth and makes the announcement in his usual calm, respectful tone.*

TUCKER: Ladies and gentlemen. The Queen's Right Trusty and Well Beloved Cousin—Jack, Arnold, Alexander, Tancred, Gurney, the 14th Earl of Gurney.

*Surprised gasps.* TUCKER *steps to one side. The sound of approaching footsteps. All eyes on the door.* BISHOP LAMPTON'S *asthma becomes painfully pronounced as the tension mounts. His breathing turns into a thin, high-pitched screech as the new* EARL OF GURNEY *finally appears in the doorway: a Franciscan monk of the Capuchi Order. His habit is a coarse, brown tunic, cord, girdle, pointed cowl, bare feet in sandals. Tall and ascetic, the* EARL *has a sensitive face, fair beard and a magnetic personality.*

EARL OF GURNEY (*gently*): Hello . . . (*Hands clasped in his large sleeves, he crosses Down Stage.*) I'm sorry I wasn't here before but I only received the news yesterday. I'm afraid our little community is somewhat cut off. I hope you'll forgive me. I know he would. My sorrow isn't less, or the pain. I've just been to his grave. Thank you, Uncle Charles, for making all the arrangements.

SIR CHARLES *looks uncomfortable.*

Aunt Claire, it's been so long. You haven't changed.

CLAIRE: Nor you.

EARL OF GURNEY: You must be Dinsdale?

DINSDALE: Er—yes, I must. How do you do, sir.

EARL OF GURNEY (*turning to* BISHOP LAMPTON): Are you still angry with me, Bishop?

*But speechless with asthma,* BISHOP LAMPTON *can only wave him away feebly.*

First let me put your minds at rest. The choice has been made. I've come back to take my proper place in the world. The monastic ideal isn't easy. I've had many broken nights. But I've come back refreshed. (*He smiles.*) Though hardly equipped for society. I shall need your help, Uncle Charles. We're all one family. Let's wash away the old sores. If the Bishop doesn't mind. I think we should pray.

SIR CHARLES: Pray?

EARL OF GURNEY: For love and understanding. Surely you pray for love and understanding?

CLAIRE (*looking at* SIR CHARLES): Every night. Without success.

PEAKE *moves silently towards the door.*

EARL OF GURNEY: You too, Mr Peake.

PEAKE: I'm Methodist.

EARL OF GURNEY: I'm sure you're still a Christian. (*Gestures gently.*) Come, for me.

PEAKE: Yes, my lord.

*Embarrassed, he begins awkwardly to kneel.* CLAIRE *smiles slightly and joins* PEAKE *and* TUCKER *on her knees.* SIR CHARLES *is about to protest but then thinks better of it. Clenching his jaw he follows pulling* DINSDALE *down with him.* BISHOP LAMPTON *fights off a violent asthma attack with an inhaler whilst the others kneel round the* EARL. *The lights start to dim down to a Spot on them as he holds out his hand in blessing.*

EARL OF GURNEY: A prayer should rise up like incense. For you are acknowledging the power and goodness of God. It's an act of faith and a union. A prayer is not a request, but an appeal. To pray means to ask, to beg, to plead. A prayer is a message to Heaven. You are talking directly to God . . . express your desires freely, don't be afraid, I know them already. (*They all look up at him in horror.*) For I am the Creator and ruler of the Universe, Khoda, the One Supreme Being and Infinite Personal Being, Yaweh, Shangri-Ti and El, the First Immovable Mover, Yea, I am the Absolute Unknowable Righteous Eternal, the Lord of Hosts, the King of Kings, Lord of Lords, the Father, Son and Holy Ghost, the one True God, the God of Love, the Naz!

*A strangled cry from* BISHOP LAMPTON *as he slips off his chair and thuds unconscious on to the floor in the darkness.*

# SCENE THREE

*A plain white backing lowered immediately Down Stage Centre into the spot, cutting the* EARL OF GURNEY *from view.* SIR CHARLES *and* DR PAUL HERDER, *a thin man with a cold manner, enter from Wings Left and stand in front of it.*

DR HERDER: His lordship is a paranoid-schizophrenic.

SIR CHARLES: But he's a *Gurney*.

DR HERDER: Then he's a paranoid-schizophrenic-Gurney who believes he's God.

SIR CHARLES: But we've always been Church of England.

DR HERDER: In paranoid-schizophrenia the patient's relationship with reality is disturbed. His idea of the world we live in is determined solely by his feelings. What he feels is—*is*.

SIR CHARLES: If my nephew's bonkers, why the blazes did you let him out?

DR HERDER: He's a voluntary patient in a private clinic, free to leave when he chooses. His father insisted on no official certification. If you want him permanently detained here, bring him before the Board of Control or get the Master in Lunacy to sign an order.

SIR CHARLES (*quickly*): Er—later, when we've got a few things settled.

DR HERDER: From the medical point of view a plunge into the waking world won't do the Earl any harm.

SIR CHARLES: Won't do him any harm. What about the rest of us?

DR HERDER: He's not dangerous. Provided he's left relatively secluded it shouldn't be too difficult. It'll be a very interesting experiment. A harsh dose of reality can sometimes help towards a cure.

SIR CHARLES: Cure! You've had him here for seven years already, and look at him. What've you been doing?

DR HERDER: Exercising patience and understanding. Something he'll need from his family.

SIR CHARLES (*testily*): Yes, yes, but why haven't you used the knife?

DR HERDER: Because labotomy is irrelevant and dangerous in this case. He showed classic schizophrenic symptoms by withdrawing from his environment. Then, of course, he never forgot being brutally rejected by his mother and father at the age of eleven. They sent him away, alone, into a primitive community of licensed bullies and pederasts.

SIR CHARLES: You mean he went to Public School.

HERDER *nods and they begin to walk slowly to the Wings Left, Spot follows them, whilst another Spot remains on the white backing, which is taken up to show the* EARL OF GURNEY *standing in exactly the same place as before, Centre Stage.*

DR HERDER: You must realize the Earl's strange position. It's what makes him such an interesting case. Remember, he's suffering from delusions of *grandeur*. In reality he's an Earl, an English aristocrat, a peer of the realm, a member of the ruling class. Naturally, he's come to believe there's only one person grander than that—the Lord God Almighty Himself.

SIR CHARLES (*suspiciously*): Are you English?

DR HERDER: No.

SIR CHARLES: Ahhh ...

*They exit.*

# SCENE FOUR

*Spot on the* EARL, *Stage Centre, remains.*

EARL OF GURNEY (*looking after them*): Q.E.D. If I saw a man eating grass I'd say he was hungry. They'd have him certified. They claim snow is only percipitation and not candied dew, and the single heart-beat only the contraction and dilation of the central organ of the vascular system. *Whroom.* (*He makes a circular motion with his right hand.*) I'm always thinking so fast. Could a rooster forget he was a rooster and lay an egg? *Whroom.* Space and time only exist within the walls of my brain. What I'm trying to say is, if the words sound queer or funny to your ear, a little bit jumbled and jivy, sing mares eat oats and does eat oats and little lambs eat ivy. Ivy? Who's Ivy? . . . I . . .

*Lights come up to show* CLAIRE *listening attentively on sofa.*

I am that Lord Jesus come again in my body to save the sick, the troubled, the ignorant. I am He that liveth and behold I am alive for everyone. (*Opens his arms mimicking American night-club entertainer Ted Lewis.*) Is everybody happy? Now hear this, I come to proclaim the new Dispensation. The Gospel Dispensation promised only salvation for the soul, my new Dispensation of Love gives it to the *body* as well. J. Christ Mark I suffered to redeem the spirit and left the body separated from God, so Satan found a place in man, and formed in him a false consciousness, a false love, a love of self. EXPLODE only FEEL, LOVE, and sin no more. Most everything you see, touch and FEEL glorifies my love. (*Mimes putting on a hat.*) The top hat is my mitre and the walking stick my rod. (*Twirls imaginary stick.*) I'm sorry. I really must apologise. Once I get started I find it damnable difficult to stop. They diagnose it as arbitrary discharge from the speech centre. Diarrhoea of the mouth. Nobody else gets much of a look-in.

CLAIRE: It's fascinating.

EARL OF GURNEY: If there's anything you'd like me to explain, fire away.

CLAIRE: How do you know you're . . . God?

EARL OF GURNEY: Simple. When I pray to Him I find I'm talking to myself.

CLAIRE: I see. How did it happen? How did you come to be in this state . . . of grace?

EARL OF GURNEY: Like every prophet I saw visions, heard voices. I ran but the voices of St Francis, Socrates, General Gordon, and Tim O'Leary the Jewish Buddha all told me I was God. Pretty reliable witnesses—agreed? It was Sunday August 25th at 3.32 standard British Summer Time. I heard with my outward ear a terrible thunder clap and I saw a great body of light like the light from the sun, and red as fire, in the form of a drum. I clapped my hands and cried Amen! Hallelujah! Hallelujah! Amen! I cried out, Lord what will you do? But the light vanished . . . a blackness of darkness until a great brush dipped in light swept across the sky. And I saw the distinction, diversity, variety, all clearly rolled up into the unity of Universal Love.

CLAIRE: Where did all this happen?

EARL OF GURNEY: East Acton. Outside the public urinal.

CLAIRE: What does it feel like to be God?

EARL OF GURNEY: Like a river flowing over everything. I pick up a newspaper and I'm everywhere, conducting a Summit Conference, dying of hunger in a Peruvian gutter, accepting the Nobel Prize for Literature, raping a nun in Sumatra.

CLAIRE: You don't look any different.

EARL OF GURNEY (*starts taking off his monk's habit*): When a parasite called the Sacculina attacks the common shore crab, it bores a tiny hole through the crab's protective outer shell. Once in the body it spreads like a root devouring the tissues and turning the flesh to pulp. It's no longer crab's flesh but Sacculina. The crab is transformed, even its sex changes. The outer shell remains unaltered, but inside is a new creature. (*He is dressed underneath in a loose-fitting white tropical suit and Eton tie: his hair cascades over his shoulder.*) I was devoured by the Divine Sacculina, it hollowed me out. Under this protective shell I'm God-filled.

> TUCKER *stands in the doorway Up Stage Centre.* SIR CHARLES, *with a briefcase under his arm, comes in behind him.*

TUCKER: Your lordship, Sir . . .

> As SIR CHARLES *impatiently brushes past,* TUCKER *grabs the bottom of his jacket and jerks him back.*

SIR CHARLES: What in . . . ?

TUCKER: I *haven't* finished yet, Sir Charles. (*Continuing unruffled.*) Your lordship, Sir Charles Gurney.

> TUCKER *steps aside, lets the furious* SIR CHARLES *into the room, then exits.*

SIR CHARLES: Insolent clown!

TUCKER (*reappearing*): I *heard* that, sir.

> *He disappears again.*

SIR CHARLES: The world's gone mad. He'll have to go.

CLAIRE: Hadn't we better wait till things get sorted out? Someone new might not understand the situation.

SIR CHARLES (*opening his briefcase on desk*): How come he's still here anyway, with twenty thousand in the bank? Why's he hanging on?

EARL OF GURNEY: Out of love. He knows he's needed.

SIR CHARLES (*taking out a document*): Love? Tucker? Rot. Now, m'boy, certain matters concerning the estate need clearing up. Nothing important. Just needs your signature. Gives me power to handle odd things.

EARL OF GURNEY: Of course, Uncle. (*Crosses to him, putting on glasses.*)

SIR CHARLES (*hastily*): You don't have to read it. Just take my word.

EARL OF GURNEY: I take your word. I put on my glasses because I feel cold. Need one of Dr Jaegers' Sanitary Woollens to keep my soul-duft in. Where do I sign?

SIR CHARLES: Just there.

> The EARL *signs with a flourish.* SIR CHARLES *glances triumphantly at* CLAIRE.

Excellent. Excellent. Easily done, eh? (*Reads.*) 'I the undersigned . . . Mycroft *Holmes*? Who's Mycroft Holmes?

TUCKER (*entering carrying robes and coronet*): Brother of Sherlock Holmes, illiterate oaf!

SIR CHARLES: But your name's Jack!

EARL OF GURNEY (*fiercely*): Never call me that! (*Strokes forehead.*) Jack's a word I reject absolutely. It's a word I put into my galvanized pressure-cooker, whrr . . .

CLAIRE: Your pressure-cooker?

EARL OF GURNEY: I don't mince words. I prefer them parboiled fried or scrambled. Jack's dead! It's my old shell-name— a sham name.

CLAIRE: All right, what should we call you then?

EARL OF GURNEY: Any of the nine billion names of God. My lordship will do, or J.C., Eric, Bert, Barney Entwistle. I don't need to cling to one name. I know exactly who I am.

TUCKER (*indicating robes*): You asked for these, my Lord.

EARL OF GURNEY: Burn 'em, Mr Tucker. Burn 'em.

SIR CHARLES: What? Great Scott, man, these are your coronation robes! Marks of our elevation.

TUCKER: Lot of tradition here, your lordship.

EARL OF GURNEY: The axe must be laid to the root. Pomp and riches, pride and property will have to be lopped off. All men are brothers. Love makes all equal. The mighty must bow down before the pricks of the louse-ridden rogues. (*Suddenly warmly embraces* SIR CHARLES.) I love you dearly, Uncle Charles. (*Gestures to robes.*) Keep them if you feel so lost. But soon you will abandon everything to follow me. Come, Mr Tucker, join me in a constitutional before lunch.

TUCKER *dumps the robes and they move to french-windows Stage Right.*

Enjoy yourself whilst I'm gone. Relax. Have sex.

*He exits with* TUCKER. CLAIRE *and* SIR CHARLES *look after him.*

SIR CHARLES (*exploding*): My God!

EARL GURNEY (*popping his head back*): Yes?

CLAIRE: No, no. Nothing.

*The* EARL *exits again.*

Well, you heard what he said, Charles.

SIR CHARLES (*trembling with rage*): I did . . . bowing before rogues . . . destroying property . . . all men equal . . . (*Pointing after* EARL.) My God, Claire, he's not only *mad*, he's *Bolshie!*

*Lights down.*

# SCENE FIVE

*Spot up immediately on a metal sun lowered from Flies, Down Stage Centre, Footlights up as* TUCKER *and the* EARL OF GURNEY *enter Wings Right.*

EARL OF GURNEY: Just smell that soul-duft from the lawns and hedgerows. What a beautiful day I've made. Look—Soft Thistle and Nigella. (*Crouches down.*) My sweet poetics. (*Ear to imaginary flower.*) What? No water in days. I can't be expected to think of everything. I'll see to it. Remember the Sunday picnics here, Mr Tucker, in my old shell-days? The world was all top hats and white lace.

TUCKER (*taking out a hip-flask*): And the best heavy silverware. A snort, your lordship?

EARL OF GURNEY: Not during Yom Kippur.

TUCKER: You mind if I partake?

EARL OF GURNEY: Go ahead. I'm God-intoxicated. If only I knew then who I was now. (*Stretching out hand.*) Ah, Mr Grasshopper, of course I bless you, my chirrup, along with General de Gaulle.

TUCKER (*drinking*): First chance I've had of speaking to you alone, your lordship. Be on guard, sir.

EARL OF GURNEY (*straightening up*): Mr Tucker, I'm puzzled.

TUCKER: The family. I've seen 'em at work a'fore. They got the power and they made the rules. They're back there plotting against you like mad.

EARL OF GURNEY: Love cannot doubt nor faith the mustard seed, no more plotting, Mr Tucker, please. It's negativism. Plotting's a word I put into my pressure-cooker, whrrr. It's gone. Feeling persecuted's one of the signs of paranoid schizophrenia. Many poor wretches in Dr Herder's Dancing Academy suffered from same. But I am being watched they said. Everybody is against me they cried. (*Shakes himself vigorously.*) You've set up profound negative disturbances with your Kremlin plots, Mr Tucker, I'm going in. (*Turns abruptly and walks Upstage Centre.*) Resist it, Mr Tucker, that way madness lies.

*He disappears into the darkness.* TUCKER *looks after him, swaying slightly.*

TUCKER: That's the thanks you get. He's the same as all the rest, what he doesn't want to be so just *isn't* so. Tried to help, you stupid old fool. No skin off my nose. My twenty thousand's safe—and I deserve every last penny of it, and more, more, more! Why should I worry—villa in the South of France, and a bit o' golden crumpet every day, breast and buttocks done to a turn. (*He cackles.*) Just pack a tooth-brush and a French letter and you're away Daniel Tucker. What's keeping you then, Dan? You've got the scratch. (*Drinks, gloomily.*) Fear. Be honest now, Daniel. Fear and habit. You get into the habit of serving. Born a servant, see, son of a servant. Family of servants. From a nation of servants. Very first thing an Englishman does, straight from his mother's womb is touch his forelock. That's how they can tell the wrinkled little bastard's English. *Me*, this tired old creeping servant, I'm the real England, not beef-eating Johnny Bullshit. I know my history. Masters and servants, that's the way of it. Didn't think I was like that, eh? A lot yer don't know about Daniel Tucker. Just old faithful Tucker. Give doggy boney. Just 'ere for comic relief. Know who I really am? (*Beckons confidentially.*) Alexei Kronstadt. Number 243. Anarchist—Trotskyist—Communist—Revolutionary. I'm a cell! All these years I've been working for the Revolution, spitting in the hot soup, peeing on the Wedgwood dinner plates. (*Coming to attention and singing.*) 'Then raise the scarlet standard high! Within its shade we'll live or die; Tho' cowards flinch and traitors sneer, We'll keep the red flag flying here.'

*Spot out. He exits.*

# SCENE SIX

*Lights up to show* EARL OF GURNEY *crucified on a wooden cross, leaning against the far wall to the right of the centre doorway. The cross-beam is above the gallery.* TUCKER *is still heard singing faintly off. Lights up to show* CLAIRE, *by the sofa, smoking nervously and staring up at the* EARL *on the cross.*

CLAIRE: J.C.? . . . Bert? . . . my lord? . . . Barney Entwistle?
> *Still no response from the* EARL. TUCKER *comes in Up Stage, pushing a tea-trolley. He crosses to* CLAIRE, *wincing at every sound, obviously suffering from a bad hangover.*

TUCKER: Tea, madam?

CLAIRE: Oh, yes. What was that you were singing just now, Tucker?

TUCKER: An old German hymn, madam—Tannenbaum. Lemon or milk, madam?

CLAIRE: Lemon.
> *He pours shakily as a flustered* DINSDALE *enters Up Stage.*

DINSDALE: I say, where's the Guv'nor? Is that tea? Just the job, Tucker.

CLAIRE: Your father's in town. Another meeting with Sir Humphrey Spens trying to find a way round this mess.

DINSDALE: When's he back?

CLAIRE: Any time now if he doesn't drop in on his mistress first.
> DINSDALE *shoots a sidelong glance at* TUCKER, *who is too busy pouring and shuddering with nausea, to react.*

DINSDALE: Ah, hmm. Hope he gets things settled soon. It's already getting awkward. They're used to us Gurneys being in everything. Mrs Piggot-Jones and Mrs Treadwell and the

other old girls thought it'd be a splendid idea for the new
Earl to open the Fête, Sunday week.

CLAIRE: Naturally you told them it was impossible.

TUCKER: Milk or lemon, sir?

DINSDALE: Lemon, Tucker. But dammit I am prospective
Parliamentary candidate for the division. Had to watch my
step with 'em. Couldn't say he was 'non-compis'.

CLAIRE: If you're going to be a successful Conservative poli-
tician, you'll have to learn to make convincing excuses.

DINSDALE: Where is he now?

    TUCKER *hands him his tea.*

CLAIRE (*gesturing behind him*): Up there.

DINSDALE (*turning*): Oh . . . Ah!

    *He gives an involuntary cry of fright at his first sight of the*
    EARL *on the cross and spills some tea.*

TUCKER (*tetchily*): Now look what you've done. (*Wipes
carpet with foot.*) Never get tea-stains out. Show some
consideration.

DINSDALE: Is it Yogi or something?

    TUCKER *has walked Up Stage to the cross.*

TUCKER: Tea, my lord?

CLAIRE: It's no good, Tucker, I've tried. He's asleep; dead to
the world.

EARL OF GURNEY: His Body sleeps but his Divinity is always
watching. Yes, Mr Tucker. Milk please. Any toasted muffins?

TUCKER: Yes, sir. Shall I bring them up?

EARL OF GURNEY: No thanks. I'll be right down.

    *The* EARL *twists round, and clambers off the cross.*

DINSDALE: It's Yogi, isn't it? A form of Yogi?

CLAIRE: Don't give me another headache, Dinsdale.

EARL OF GURNEY (*puts his hands together, Indian style*): Welcome,
Dinsdale.

DINSDALE: Oh, ah, yes. How are you?

EARL OF GURNEY: Sometimes my spirit sinks below the high
watermark in Palestine, but I'm adjusting gradually.

TUCKER *uncovers a dish of muffins and sways slightly.*
Mr Tucker, you look ill. Bed, Mr Tucker. Right now.
TUCKER: Thank you, my lord.
EARL OF GURNEY: Take a cup of Dr Langley's Root and Herb
   Bitters. It acts directly on the bowels and blood, eradicates
   all liver disorders, dyspepsia, dizziness, heartburn . . .
TUCKER (*exiting*): Yes, sir.
EARL OF GURNEY (*calling*): . . . foul stomach and *piles.*
   TUCKER *is heard muttering agreement off.*
For what I am about to receive may I make myself truly
thankful. (*Eats muffin.*) I must soon be moving on. Sail to
Wigan, Wrexham, Port Said and Crewe.
   CLAIRE *and* DINSDALE *exchange uneasy glances.*
First I shall command the Pope to consecrate a planeload of
light-weight contraceptives for the priest-ridden Irish. (*Mimes
blessing.*) ' Pax et benedíctio . . . adjutorium nostrum. Dóminus
vobíscum'. (*Chanting.*) Arise, shine for my light is come and
the glory of the Lord is risen upon thee . . . (*Singing with
actions.*) 'Here is the Drag, See how it goes; Down on the
heels; Up on the toes. That's the way to the Varsity Drag.'
(*He dances round in exuberant ragtime.*) 'Hotter than hot,
Newer than new! Meaner than mean, Bluer than blue. Gets
as much applause as waving the flag!'
   TUCKER *appears in doorway Up Stage Centre with two solid,
   middle-aged* WOMEN *in grotesque hats.* CLAIRE *glares angrily at
   a horrified* DINSDALE.
TUCKER: Mrs Piggot-Jones—Mrs Treadwell.
EARL OF GURNEY (*singing at newcomers*): . . . 'You can pass
   many a class whether you're dumb or wise. If you all answer
   the call, when your professor cries . . .'
   *Suddenly, despite themselves,* MRS PIGGOT-JONES, MRS
   TREADWELL *and* TUCKER *sweep irresistibly Down Stage with
   the Earl, in an all-singing, all-dancing chorus line.*
EARL OF GURNEY, TWO WOMEN *and* TUCKER (*singing*):
   'Everybody down on the heels, up on the toes, stay after

school, learn how it goes: Everybody do the Varsity . . . Everybody do the Varsity . . . Everybody do the Varsity Drag!'

*They finish in line Down Stage, arms outstretched to the audience, puzzled.*

EARL OF GURNEY (*without pause*): Welcome, ladies. I'm the new Lord.

MRS TREADWELL, *a dumpy woman in straw hat decorated with wax fruit, gives a dazed smile, whilst the boney* MRS PIGGOT-JONES, *in tweeds and trilby, lets out a bewildered grunt. Clutching his head,* TUCKER *weaves his way out.*

You know Lady Claire and my cousin Dinsdale?

DINSDALE: This is a surprise. Delightful though, delightful.

MRS TREADWELL (*recovering her natural obsequiousness*): Dear Mr Dinsdale, do forgive us, but we've come to try and persuade his lordship to open our little Church Fête. Do say yes, my lord.

EARL OF GURNEY: I always say yes, yes, whatever the question.

MRS TREADWELL (*delighted*): Your lordship.

MRS PIGGOT-JONES: Splendid!

CLAIRE: Now ladies, if you'll excuse us, we have a lot to do.

EARL OF GURNEY: Stay for tea. (*To* MRS TREADWELL.) You be mother.

*Gurgles of delight from the two women. Whilst* MRS TREADWELL *pours,* DINSDALE *looks uncertain, and* CLAIRE *watches with increasing tension.*

CLAIRE (*low*): Dinsdale, see if your father's come back.

DINSDALE *hurries out.*

EARL OF GURNEY: Now ladies, tell me my part in this gala opening. Do I charm bracelets, swing lead, break wind, pass water?

MRS TREADWELL: No, you make a speech.

EARL OF GURNEY: On what text, Mother Superior?

MRS PIGGOT-JONES: We leave that to the speaker. It can be any topic of general interest. Hanging, Immigration, the Stranglehold of the Unions. Anything . . .

MRS TREADWELL: So long as it isn't political.

EARL OF GURNEY: Nat-ur-ally.

MRS PIGGOT-JONES: As the fête *is* in aid of the British Legion I've always felt the speeches should be something about Britain and our way of life.

EARL OF GURNEY (*off-handed*): Britain is an imaginary island off the continent of Europe, covering 93,982 square miles, with a population of over 52 million, lying in a westerly wind belt. A fly-blown speck in the North Sea, a country of cosmic unimportance in my sight. (*Sadly at them.*) You can't kick the natives in the back streets of Calcutta any more.

MRS TREADWELL (*giggling*): He's joking again. Aren't you, my lord?

MRS PIGGOT-JONES: I am not laughing, Pamela. I'm afraid we can't stay here, Lady Claire.

CLAIRE: Then for Christ's sake, go!

EARL OF GURNEY: Please don't go for my sake. (*Casually takes a bunch of imitation wax grapes from* MRS TREADWELL'S *hat and starts eating them.*) Hmm, delicious. Home-grown?

MRS TREADWELL: No, I bought them, I mean . . .

EARL OF GURNEY: I've decided to begin my second ministry at your gathering. Last time I preached the Word in Holy Galilee I spoke in parables. MISTAKE. Now I must speak plain. (*Crosses hands on chest.*) God is love.

MRS TREADWELL (*frightened*): Love?

EARL OF GURNEY: God is love as water is wet as jade is green as bread is life so God is love.

    MRS TREADWELL *and* MRS PIGGOT JONES *begin to back towards the door Up Stage Centre.* DINSDALE *is heard calling off beyond the french windows.*

EARL OF GURNEY (*advancing after them*): Mrs Pamela Treadwell, can you love? Can your blood bubble, flesh melt, thighs twitch, heart burst for love?

MRS TREADWELL: Your lordship, I'm a married woman.

EARL OF GURNEY: Sexual perversion is no sin.

DINSDALE (*voice off*): I say, have you seen my father?

EARL OF GURNEY (*advancing*): Remember the commandment I gave you, love one another as I loved you.

MRS PIGGOT-JONES (*retreating*): Stay back! My husband is a Master of Hounds!

EARL OF GURNEY: Fill your hearts, let your eyes sparkle, your soul dance. Be *bird-happy*!

MRS PIGGOT-JONES: Ahh!
MRS TREADWELL:

*Their nerve breaks. They turn and plunge for the door, but are frozen in mid-flight as they see the cross for the first time.*

MRS PIGGOT-JONES: What is it?

EARL OF GURNEY: A Watusi walking-stick! Big people the Watusis. Listen, ladies.

*But with cries of fear the two women rush Up Stage Centre.* SIR CHARLES *appears in the doorway and is flattened by them as they charge out into the passage, followed by the* EARL, *who is heard calling:*

EARL OF GURNEY (*voice off*): Don't be frightened. Hear the word of the Lord.

SIR CHARLES (*picking himself up*): Treadwell . . . Piggot . . . What the blazes are they doing here? Great Scott, who's the idiot responsible?

DINSDALE (*voice off*): I say, I say, have you seen my father?

CLAIRE *gestures expressively.*

SIR CHARLES: Oh. Dinsdale.

CLAIRE: You'll have to do something about that boy.

SIR CHARLES: He'll soon be off our hands. Old Barrington-Cochran's on his last legs. That means a by-election.

CLAIRE: Dinsdale's such a fool.

SIR CHARLES: One time thought of bringing him into the business, but it's too risky. Can't have Dinsdale messing about with money. He's proved disappointing.

DINSDALE *re-enters.*

DINSDALE: Oh, there you are.

CLAIRE: What did Sir Humphrey say?

SIR CHARLES: Gave me a lot o' expensive legal fal-de-roll. As it stands, there's no chance of breaking the Will. Only one possible solution. A male heir.

CLAIRE: A what?

SIR CHARLES: If Jack had a son, Sir Humphrey says we could have him certified quietly, because everything could then pass to the heir. We'd administer the estate till the boy came of age. That way everything'd remain in the family.

CLAIRE (*sarcastically*): Oh, brilliant. A small point, but before he can have an heir, our lunatic nephew has to be married.

SIR CHARLES: Exactly. And the sooner the better!

*The* EARL *enters Up Stage Centre playing a flute.*

EARL OF GURNEY: Married?

SIR CHARLES: Yes, J.C., you should take a wife.

EARL OF GURNEY: Who from?

CLAIRE: I'm sure we'll be able to find you a suitable young goddess.

SIR CHARLES: Most appropriate, eh-eh?

*They chuckle to themselves.*

EARL OF GURNEY: But I can't marry a second time.

*They immediately stop chuckling.*

SIR CHARLES: A second . . .

CLAIRE (*sceptically*): Second wife? You believe you're already married?

EARL OF GURNEY: On August 28th in the year of me, 1961.

SIR CHARLES *looks across doubtfully at* CLAIRE *who shakes her head.*

Somerset House records will confirm. Father wanted it kept secret for some reason.

*He walks away to Wings Right playing the 'Drinking Song' from 'La Traviata' on the flute.*

SIR CHARLES: This wife of yours? What's her name?

EARL OF GURNEY: Marguerite Gautier.

SIR CHARLES: French.

DINSDALE (*slowly*): Marguerite Gautier? . . . Gautier? . . .
I say, isn't that the 'Lady of the Camelias'?
EARL OF GURNEY: You know her too? Wonderful!
    *He exits playing the aria.* DINSDALE *and* SIR CHARLES
*exchange looks and rush after him. Blackout.*

# SCENE SEVEN

*Spot up on white screen lowered Down Stage Left to show* CLAIRE *and* DR HERDER *talking.*

DR HERDER: Of course there's no question of marriage. He has no wife, but he believes he has, which is the same thing.

CLAIRE: Why did he pick on Marguerite Gautier?

DR HERDER: Another martyr for love. His delusions are of a piece. Marguerite is the only person he trusts.

CLAIRE: Why does he keep on about love?

DR HERDER: Because he hasn't had any. Or wasn't shown any, which is just as bad. He wants us all to love goodness. To love goodness is to love God, to love God is to love the 14th Earl of Gurney.

CLAIRE: That's very clever. Is it the truth?

DR HERDER: Lady Claire, don't come to me for the truth, only explanations.

CLAIRE: Does any of his talk mean anything?

DR HERDER: To him, yes. Your nephew suffers from the delusion that the world we live in is based on the fact that God is love.

CLAIRE: Can't he see what the world's really like?

DR HERDER: No. But he will, when he's cured.

CLAIRE: Can I ask one more question?

DR HERDER: If it's as revealing as the others.

CLAIRE: Why does he hate being called Jack?

DR HERDER: Because it's his real name. Naturally he rejects it violently. If he ever answers to the name of Jack, he'll be on the road to sanity.

CLAIRE: How are my questions revealing?

DR HERDER: The first one you asked me was about love.

*White screen taken up and lights up as they move into the drawing-room of Gurney Manor where* TUCKER *is pouring drinks.*

CLAIRE: This is our own Tucker, Dr Herder. He's been with the family for over forty years.

TUCKER: Man and snivelling boy, sir.

DR HERDER: Really. How do you find the new Earl, Tucker?

TUCKER: By sniffing. He's a Gurney, sir. A real Gurney.

DR HERDER (*puzzled*): You don't find him odd?

TUCKER: Odd? Soda, sir?

DR HERDER: Please. Yes, odd. Peculiar.

TUCKER: Oh, you mean *nutty*. Yes, he's a nut-case all right, but then so are most of these titled flea-bags. Rich nobs and privileged arse-holes can afford to be bonkers. Living in a dream world, aren't they, sir? Don't know what time o' day it is. Life's made too easy for 'em. Don't have to earn a living so they can do just what they want to. Most of us'd look pretty cracked if we went round doing just what we wanted to, eh, sir?

DR HERDER (*bewildered*): Yes, I suppose . . .

CLAIRE (*smiling*): The late Earl left Tucker twenty thousand pounds. Since then he's been very outspoken.

TUCKER *hands a drink to* DR HERDER *and another to* CLAIRE.

CLAIRE: Not for me, Tucker.

TUCKER: Waste not want not. (*He drinks.*) Doctor, you might take a look at my back. The ol' lumbago's acting up again.

SIR CHARLES *and* DINSDALE *enter arguing with the* EARL OF GURNEY.

DINSDALE (*gesturing with the book*): But I've shown you it's in here. *The Lady of the Camelias* by Alexandre Dumas. *Camille.* The opera by Verdi *La Traviata*. Same woman. A figure of romance.

EARL OF GURNEY: My dear chap, you prove my point ipso

facto, a divine figure of romance. Paul, what a pleasant surprise.

DR HERDER: How are you?

EARL OF GURNEY: In the middle of a debate on the existence of my wife Marguerite. With passions roused and intellects sharpened, pray continue, Dinsdale Gurney.

SIR CHARLES: I give up. You did say it'd be impossible to convince him, doctor.

DR HERDER: Impossible. But you can try.

　　CLAIRE *takes the book from* DINSDALE, *opens it and shows it to the* EARL.

CLAIRE: Look. It's a play, *The Lady of the Camelias.* Fiction.

EARL OF GURNEY (*taking book*): Ah, yes, a biography of my Marguerite—affectionately known as La Dame Aux Camelias. (*Sternly.*) Dinsdale, this book looks tired from over-reading. You should let it out more.

CLAIRE: You aren't married. The woman doesn't exist.

EARL OF GURNEY: Come, come, you exaggerate unduly. (*Makes circular movement with right hand.*) You'll be saying I'm not God, Jesus, and the Holy Ghost next.

CLAIRE: You're not! God wouldn't be so ridiculous waving his arms like a maniac dressed in a white suit and carnation.

EARL OF GURNEY: The prophet Ezekiel lay three hundred days on his left side and forty days on his right. He cut his hair and divided it into three parts. The first part he burnt, the second he chopped into pieces, the third he scattered into the wind. Ridiculous, mad, certifiable. It was all merely a sign of something more important. God teaches by signs as well as words.

DR HERDER (*with satisfaction*): He can defend his beliefs with great skill.

DINSDALE: All right, if you're God, reveal your Godhead.

　　*The* EARL *immediately starts to unzip his flies.*

　　No, no. A miracle. Show us a miracle.

EARL OF GURNEY: A miracle. (*Holds out his hand.*) Here's a miracle.

DINSDALE: Where?

EARL OF GURNEY: This hand. This city network of tissues, nerves, muscles, ligaments, carpals, metacarpals and phalanges. And what about the hairy-nosed wombat?

DINSDALE: Not that sort. A miracle like the making of loaves and fishes.

EARL OF GURNEY: Oh, those. You see ten billion million miracles a day, yet you want your conjuring tricks, your pretty flim-flams, from the incense burners. I can't raise Lazarus again, he's decomposed, so bring me that table.

CLAIRE: What are you going to do?

EARL OF GURNEY: A grade-one Galilee miracle.

CLAIRE *starts to say something but* DR HERDER *gestures. He nods to* DINSDALE, *who drags the coffee table to Stage Centre, and steps back uncertainly. They are all roughly grouped behind it.*

EARL OF GURNEY: Instead of raising Laz, I'll raise yon table.

SIR CHARLES: That table?

EARL OF GURNEY: Ten feet. Not by mirrors or crippled midgets behind black curtains, but by the power of love.

CLAIRE: Just love?

EARL OF GURNEY: It moves mountains, and makes the puny weed split the rock. Look.

*All eyes now sceptically on the table. The* EARL *stretches out his hands, palms upwards. As he slowly starts to raise them, lights imperceptibly begin to dim.*

Believe in me, in love, in loving goodness, raise yourself up . . . Rise, up, up. See, see . . . slowly, slowly. One foot, two feet, three, four . . . slowly up . . . five, six, seven . . . rise, rise up . . . Eight, nine, ten. (*His arms are now above his head.*) There! The table floats ten feet in space.

TUCKER (*pointing up excitedly*): Ahhh! Look, I see it! Up there! (*He lurches forward, grasping a half-empty whisky decanter.*) Sh-miracle, sh-miracle, halleluja sh-miracle. Praise the Lord and pass t' ammunition.

SIR CHARLES: Drunken lout!

TUCKER *collapses in a stupor in a chair. The spell is broken.* CLAIRE *crosses angrily to the table.*

CLAIRE: It didn't rise. (*Raps it.*) Here it is.

EARL OF GURNEY (*making circle with hand*): Tucker saw, believed, yeees.

CLAIRE: Did you see it, doctor?

DR HERDER: No.

SIR CHARLES: 'Course not. Damned rot.

EARL OF GURNEY (*shakes his head*): Into any platinum pressure-cooker, grrh grrhh shurhh . . .

CLAIRE: There's no miracle. No wife. She doesn't exist. She's fiction. Part of a play. An opera. She's not flesh and blood. Not real.

EARL OF GURNEY (*flapping hands, disturbed*): Gross gree crull craaah . . .

DR HERDER: Shhh. Listen.

*From the corridor beyond the darkened room comes the sound of a woman singing. 'Go diam fie—ga-ca-e-ra-pi-do—e il gan dio dell 'a-mo-re . . .' It grows louder. We can hear the rustle of crinoline. They turn towards the doorway. Up Stage Centre: The Lady of the Camelias stands there, in a Spot, carrying a camelia and singing the 'Drinking Song' from 'La Traviata'.*

LA DAME AUX CAMELIAS (*singing*): 'Eun fior che na—see e muo—re, ne, piu si puv go-der—Go-diam c-In-vi-ta, c'in-vi-taun, fervi do-ae-cen-to-la-sin-gheer . . .'

EARL OF GURNEY: Marguerite!

*Blackout.*

# SCENE EIGHT

*Lights up on the Drawing Room of Gurney Manor where* CLAIRE
*and* SIR CHARLES *are arguing with measured ferocity.*

CLAIRE: How *dare* you bring that woman here?

SIR CHARLES: You should be grateful to Miss Shelley.

CLAIRE: Grace Shelley is your mistress. Hairs on the collar,
stains on the sheets, I know you.

SIR CHARLES: And I know you. Miss Shelley's just a hard-
working girl.

CLAIRE: Only on her back. First you try and palm her off on to
your own brother.

SIR CHARLES: Ralph needed a wife. He took a fancy to Miss
Shelley.

CLAIRE: That didn't work, so now you try her for the son.
It's incestuous.

SIR CHARLES: Don't talk to me about incest. I remember
young Jeremy Gore. You knew his father and I went to
school together. But you went ahead and seduced his son.
That's incest, madam.

CLAIRE (*wearily*): What's the use? It isn't worth raising one's
voice. But why the devil didn't you warn us?

SIR CHARLES: No time. After what that 'Trick-Cyclist'
chappie told me I knew we'd never convince Jack he wasn't
married and this Marguerite filly didn't exist. So I 'phoned
Grace and explained the position. She got dressed up in some
theatrical togs and came down. Put me on a first-rate show, I
thought.

CLAIRE: It had impact.

SIR CHARLES: Anyway, Jack believes she's Marguerite. All

she has to do now is convince him he has to marry her again. Shouldn't be difficult.

CLAIRE: Dr Herder'll object.

SIR CHARLES: Object? He's got no right to object to anything, he's not family.

CLAIRE: He could make things difficult by having Jack declared insane before he's produced an heir for you.

SIR CHARLES: Damn kraut! You'd better keep an eye on him, my dear. I'll have my hands full getting Grace married and pregnant.

GRACE SHELLEY *comes in Up Stage Centre, a blonde, still dressed in a low-cut ball gown, she gestures with the camelia.*

GRACE: *What an entrance.* Beautiful, *but* beautiful. The look on your faces. I should have stuck to the classics. I was trained for it y'know—Mrs Phoebe Giavanno, 27A Brixton Hill. She sang with Caruso. Grand old lady. 'From the diaphragm dear, from the diaphragm.' Always said I had the voice. Let's face it, Bert Bacharach is great but he's not in the same class as Giuseppi Verdi. Phew, this dress's tight. How did they breathe? I feel constipated. (*Notices cross by the door for the first time.*) *Christy O'Connor,* what's that? Is the roof falling in or something?

CLAIRE: Any minute now. (*Moving Up Stage.*) Your flower's wilting, my dear.

GRACE (*waving it cheerfully*): Can't be. It's wax.

CLAIRE: Careful your husband-to-be doesn't eat it for breakfast. *She exits.*

GRACE: You're right, Charlie Boy. She's an ice-cold Biddy.

SIR CHARLES: Too clever by half, that woman. But I get things done my way. She doesn't know what she wants.

GRACE: But I do, Charlie Boy. Lady Grace, Lady Grace Gurney, the Countess of Gurney.

SIR CHARLES: Now look here, Grace, you mustn't call me Charlie Boy. We have to be careful.

GRACE: If that's what you want.

SIR CHARLES: It's not what I want. It's what has to be. I'm very fond of you, m'dear, you know that.

GRACE: You've a funny way of showing it. First you push me into the arms of your half-dead half-brother, and then on to his looney son.

SIR CHARLES: I'd make any sacrifice for the sake of the family. You sure you can handle the situation? Tricky an' all, marrying a man who thinks he's God.

GRACE: It happens all the time. (*Crossing to french windows.*) On certain nights. In front of the right audience. When the magic works. I've known what it's like to be a God too. (*Sees someone outside.*) Ah, there he is on the lawn. Let's get the show on the road. Damn, where's my lousy camelia. (SIR CHARLES *hands it to her, she hitches up her dress.*) I'll be glad to get out of this clobber. (*Pats bare bosom.*) No wonder she was dying of consumption. (*Coughs hoarsely.*)

SIR CHARLES: Careful now.

GRACE: Trust me, Charlie B . . . Charles. I've got too much at stake to blow it.

    *Holding the camelia modestly across her chest, and smiling wanly, she glides out.* SIR CHARLES *looks at the audience.*

SIR CHARLES: Damned plucky filly.

    DINSDALE *enters Up Stage Centre.*

DINSDALE: I say, Mother's just told me this Lady-of-the-Camelia-woman's a fake. I know J.C.'s as batty as a moor-hen, sir, but this isn't playing the game.

SIR CHARLES: Game? What game? It's no game, Sir! This is real.

    *Blackout.*

# SCENE NINE

*Footlights up immediately. A metal sun lowered from Flies. The*
*EARL lying Down Stage Right, rouses himself as GRACE enters*
*Wings Left.*

EARL OF GURNEY: My dreams made flesh or a reasonable
facsimile thereforeto. (*Gets up, bows politely.*) Eh—bien,
comment allez-vous, madame?

GRACE: Sorry, I don't speak French.

EARL OF GURNEY: German? Italian? Albanian? Yiddish?

GRACE: No. English.

EARL OF GURNEY: English. Why didn't you say so before?
Nothing to be ashamed of, hard language to master. But we
can't play this love-scene with mere words, be they English,
Japanese or Serbo-Croat.

GRACE: Love scene? What now?

EARL OF GURNEY: Love isn't just for one season. (*Smiles,*
*flapping arms like a bird.*) Hweet, hweep.

GRACE: Hweet?

EARL OF GURNEY (*arms quivering*): Tsiff-tsiff-tsiff. (*Hopping.*)
Chiff-chaff-chaff-chaff.

GRACE (*laughing*): Oh, well. (*Flaps arms.*) Chiff-chaff.
*They circle round each other with tiny bird movements; GRACE*
*bending forward and hopping, the EARL bobbing his head and*
*making low loping sweeps.*

EARL OF GURNEY (*long drawn-out, high-pitched*): Pioo . . .
pioo . . . pioo.

GRACE: Cuckoo!

EARL OF GURNEY (*crescendo*): Pioo.

GRACE (*breathless*): I'll bet even Ludovic Koch wasn't made
love to with bird cries.

EARL OF GURNEY: What else would you like? The Grand Canyon? A musical teacup? A hundred pre-sold holy wafers? A disused banana factory? Absolution?

GRACE: A white wedding.

EARL OF GURNEY: Will next Tuesday suit you?

GRACE: You deserve a big kiss.

EARL OF GURNEY: Not here in the garden. Last time I was kissed in a garden—it turned out rather awkward.

GRACE: Ah, but Judas was a man.

EARL OF GURNEY (*nodding*): Hmm, yes, a strange business. (GRACE *laughs*.) Who are you?

GRACE: A woman.

EARL OF GURNEY: Descended from Eve.

GRACE: No, a doorstep. I'm an orphan.

EARL OF GURNEY: Then we'll be orphans together, Marguerite.

GRACE: Call me Grace, as I don't speak French.

EARL OF GURNEY: A good name. It means a gift of faith.

GRACE: Which is what I have in you. I'm holding you to that wedding.

EARL OF GURNEY: Hold hard. You'll be my Queen of Queens.

GRACE: I'll be satisfied with Lady Gurney.

EARL OF GURNEY (*takes her hands*): And I say unto you, thou shall love the Lord thy God with all thy heart and with all thy soul and with all thy mind.

GRACE: I do.

EARL OF GURNEY: I want to show you the bottom drawer of my soul. (*Suddenly joyful.*) Oh, but I'm happy, I'm the sunshine-man, the driver of the gravy-train, chu-chu-chu. (GRACE *laughs*.) It's all so simple, for me. Paradise is just a smiling face. What's it for you?

GRACE: Me? Paradise? Oh, a fireplace. A cosy room.

EARL OF GURNEY (*nodding*): A little nest . . .

*Hand in hand they go into a dance routine to Wings Right.*

GRACE (*singing*): 'That nestles where the roses bloom.'

EARL OF GURNEY (*singing; indicating partner*): 'Sweet Gracey and me . . .'

GRACE (*singing: looking at him*): 'And a baby makes three.'

GRACE (*singing*):
EARL OF GURNEY (*singing*):     'We're going to our blue heaven.'

    GRACE *kisses him, exits Wings Right. The* EARL *takes out a pocket telescope, opens it out and stares after her as* DINSDALE *enters sulkily.*

DINSDALE: What are you looking at?

EARL OF GURNEY (*handing him telescope*): Beauty in motion.

DINSDALE (*looking*): I can't see a thing.

EARL OF GURNEY: Because you're not looking with the eyes of love.

DINSDALE (*coming to a decision*): Hang it all, whatever else you are, you're still a Gurney. That Camelia woman's really Grace Shelley. Close friend of my father's. He's put her up to it.

    *The* EARL *stops humming.*

Got her to dress like that. Absolutely ridiculous.

    *The* EARL *shivers with cold.*

He wants you married off.

    *The* EARL *puts his hand to his face; when he takes it away his features are covered with white make-up.*

Mother's in it too. Shouldn't be surprised if even old Tuck knew. Everybody but me.

EARL OF GURNEY (*shrinking miserably*): Stop! You're making me a crippled dwarf, a deformed midget, a crippled newt!

DINSDALE (*sees the* EARL *with bent knees, now half-size*): What're you doing?

    *Stage Lights Up.*

EARL OF GURNEY: It's your negative insinuendo.

DINSDALE: Insinuendo?

EARL OF GURNEY (*making circle with right hand*): Insinuendo is insinuation towards innuendo, brought on by increased negativism out of a negative reaction to your father's positivism. (*Takes out glasses, breaks them, puts half frame over one eye, peers up at* DINSDALE.) Your negativism is fully charged. I see by the Habeas Corpus parchment round your neck.

DINSDALE: I don't know what the devil you're on about, but I resent your attitude. I only told you about Grace Shelley . . .

EARL OF GURNEY (*tearing off his jacket and shirt*): She's my Righteous-Ideal-Planned-Wife. Don't forget, besides being God, Christ and the Holy Ghost, I'm also a San D., B.F.C. and D.A.C.—Doctor of Sanitation, Bachelor of Family Life, and Doctor of Air Conditioning. Please remember that you're dealing with the Big One. I've told aged Tucker. Injecting me with his Kremlin-plot negative-microbes. I said verbatim. Feeling persecuted is paranoid schizophrenia-wretches. Dr H. suffered from it. But watched they said against me . . . one of the signs. Many poor 'erders' Dancing Academy. I *am* being EVERYBODY they CRIED . . . whrr! rr! . . . rrr! Krr-krr-krek!

*He scuttles absurdly Up Stage and clambers on to the cross. On the back of his vest are painted the words 'God is Love'.* DINSDALE *exits as the* EARL *clings to the cross, his painful, metallic cries growing louder and louder. The lights dim down. The cries stop abruptly.*

# SCENE TEN

*Lights Up as* BISHOP LAMPTON *and* SIR CHARLES *enter Up Stage Centre glancing with distaste at the* EARL, *stretched out on the cross.*

BISHOP LAMPTON: I will not solemnize any marriage, even of my own nephew, during the period from Advent Sunday till eight days after Epiphany. So it must be on Tuesday the 12th. Eight a.m. Private Chapel. Ordinary Licence. But I have grave misgivings, Charles. Grave misgivings.

SIR CHARLES: Misgivings? About Jack?

BISHOP LAMPTON: No, about the bride, Miss Shelley. Who is she? What is she? I fear she may be using this marriage merely to advance her social position. I hear she's an 'entertainer'.

SIR CHARLES: I'll vouch for Grace Shelley.

BISHOP LAMPTON: No doubt. I hear she's a most handsome woman. I venture you've been dazzled by her charms. 'A woman whose heart is snares and nets.' I, however, due to my cloth—and age—can take a more dispassionate view of her character and motives.

SIR CHARLES: Dash it all, Bertie, you know the position. We can't be fussy. Grace—Miss Shelley—is the best we can come up with. This is a crisis.

BISHOP LAMPTON: Even so, we shouldn't be too hasty. God in his infinite wisdom has clouded our nephew's senses. But it can only be temporary. I take it as a sure sign of hope that his delusions are at least of a *religious* nature. Consider the consequences of this mis-mating, Charles. When he recovers, he'll find himself married to a woman who is frankly not suitable. And he *will* recover. God is merciful.

SIR CHARLES: Can't wait on God's mercy, Bertie, everything's going to pot. Dr Herder agrees.

BISHOP LAMPTON: Dr Herder? 'Herder'? Is he English?

SIR CHARLES: No.

BISHOP LAMPTON: Ahh . . .

SIR CHARLES: Mark my words, this'll be the making of Jack.

BISHOP LAMPTON (*sagely*): It's true, there's nothing like marriage to bring a fella' to his senses.

*They exit Up Stage as Spot Up Down Stage Left on DR HERDER and CLAIRE standing in front of a white backing lowered from the Flies. A couch to Left.*

CLAIRE: My husband's an idiot.

DR HERDER (*icily*): I've no idea what he's playing at, and it's not strictly my concern. The Earl's no longer under my care. But that charade with Miss Shelley made me feel an absolute fool, and I don't care to underestimate myself.

CLAIRE: I apologise. Charles has some idea Jack might accept her if she dressed up as the Lady of the Camelias.

DR HERDER: Sometimes it's very easy to forget that outside this comedy Sir Charles occupies a position of responsibility and power. I just learned he's on the Board of the Guggenheim Research Foundation. Extraordinary.

CLAIRE: Ah, yes, he mentioned you were asking for a grant. You won't have any trouble.

DR HERDER: It's only a nominal 130,000. For the study of paranoid schizophrenic rats.

CLAIRE (*sitting on couch*): Sounds fascinating.

DR HERDER: I should have said electrically controlled paranoid rats.

CLAIRE: Electrically?

DR HERDER: We insert very fine silver wires into the rat's mid-brain. The rat's behaviour is controlled by the strength of the current passed through them. By pressing a button and stimulating one area in its mid-brain, the rat is made to feel threatened. It attacks any rat in sight. There's really no threat, but the mid-brain can't tell the difference. Roughly the same thing happens with a human paranoid. No silver wires, but an unknown area of his brain is stimulated, and he feels threatened without cause. Naturally, men aren't rats.

CLAIRE: Only a man would say so.

DR HERDER (*smiling*): I'm speaking biologically. Eventually we'll have to conduct similar experiments on the human brain.

CLAIRE: Today rats. Tomorrow the world. Who will you wire for visions?

DR HERDER: First of all myself, naturally.

CLAIRE (*taking off glove*): I see. Then if I press a button, you'd limp for me, feel fear and love . . .

DR HERDER: Love? No. Desire, yes.

CLAIRE: By pressing a button? (*Raises finger and mimes pressing.*)

DR HERDER (*covers her hand*): Not too hard. I might get over-stimulated and lose control.

CLAIRE: You, lose control? Think of the risk, doctor.

DR HERDER: There's only one commandment a doctor need ever worry about. 'Thou shalt not advertise.'

DR HERDER *kisses* CLAIRE'S *hand. Spot out.*

# SCENE ELEVEN

*Lights Up. The* EARL *stops jerking on the cross.*

EARL OF GURNEY: My heart rises with the sun. I'm purged of doubts and negative innuendos. Today I want to bless everything! Bless the crawfish that has a scuttling walk, bless the trout, the pilchard and periwinkle. Bless Ted Smoothey of 22 East Hackney Road—with a name like that he needs blessing. Bless the mealy-redpole, the black-gloved wallaby and W. C. Fields, who's dead but lives on. Bless the skunk, bless the red-bellied lemur, bless 'Judo' Al Hayes and Ski-Hi-Lee. Bless the snotty-nosed giraffe, bless the buffalo, bless the Society of Women Engineers, bless the wild yak, bless the Piccadilly Match King, bless the pygmy hippo, bless the weasel, bless the mighty cockroach, bless me. Today's my wedding day!
   *Wedding bells peal out.*

# SCENE TWELVE

*Screen lowered immediately Down Stage Centre, cutting out the cross from view. On it, a photo-collage of Society weddings.* BISHOP LAMPTON *enters imposingly, Wings Right, in full regalia, followed by* CLAIRE *and* DINSDALE. TUCKER *hobbles in from Wings Left. They cross slowly Down Stage Centre. With* CLAIRE *and* DINSDALE *on his right, and* TUCKER *on his left.* LAMPTON *turns and faces the audience.*

*The bells stop ringing. An organ plays 'The Wedding March' as* GRACE *in a white wedding dress and an apprehensive* SIR CHARLES *enter Wings Right. They all wait for the groom. The* EARL *scampers in Wings Right in a cut-away jacket, no shirt and broken glasses and flute hanging from his chest.* BISHOP LAMPTON *shudders.*

BISHOP LAMPTON (*reading from prayer book*): 'Dearly beloved, we are gathered together here in the sight of God . . .'

    *The* EARL *clasps his hands above his head and shakes them triumphantly.*

'. . . and in the face of this company to join together this man and this woman in Holy Matrimony, which is an honourable estate.'

EARL OF GURNEY: Instituted by me in the time of man's innocence.

    GRACE *puts her fingers to his lips.*

BISHOP LAMPTON (*looking up warningly*): 'Therefore if anyone can show just cause why they may not be lawfully joined together, let him now speak, or else hereafter forever hold his peace.'

    CLAIRE, DINSDALE *and* SIR CHARLES *stare deliberately at the audience. Silence.*

TUCKER: Load o' British jelly-meat whiskers! Stand up on your tea-soaked haunches and stop it. Piddling, half-dead helots.

SIR CHARLES: Quiet, man. Show some respect.

TUCKER (*indignantly*): I'm always respectful. S'what I'm paid for. No one can say I'm not respectful. (*Removes his false teeth.*) There.

BISHOP LAMPTON: 'I require and charge you both that if either of you have any impediment why ye may not be lawfully joined together in matrimony ye do now confess it.'

EARL OF GURNEY (*quietly*): Yes, I'm afraid I do know an impediment.

*His family glance anxiously at each other.*

CLAIRE: It's only a rhetorical question, like all the others in the wedding service.

EARL OF GURNEY: 'Tis no good glossing o'er the facts. Certain R.C. knackers think I'm already married to the Virgin Mary.

SIR CHARLES We're not concerned with what other people think.

BISHOP LAMPTON: Especially not Roman Catholics. 'Wilt thou have this woman to thy wedded wife, to live together after God's ordinance in the holy state of matrimony? Wilt thou love her . . .'

EARL OF GURNEY: From the bottom of my soul to the tip of my penis, like the sun in its brightness, the moon in its beauty, the heavens in their emptiness, streams in their gentleness, no breeze stirs that doesn't bear my love.

BISHOP LAMPTON: Blasphemous . . .!

GRACE: But will you love *me*?

EARL OF GURNEY: I will.

BISHOP LAMPTON (*quickly, to* GRACE): 'Wilt thou have this man to thy wedded husband, to live together after God's ordinance.'

GRACE: I will.

BISHOP LAMPTON: Who gives this woman to this man?

SIR CHARLES: I do.

BISHOP LAMPTON (*to* EARL): Repeat after me. I, J.C., take thee Grace Shelley to my wedded wife . . .

EARL OF GURNEY: I, J.C. the Holy Flying Roller, the Morning Star, known to his intimates as the Naz, take thee Marguerite, called Grace Shelley because she doesn't speak French.

BISHOP LAMPTON *shudders and plunges on.*

BISHOP LAMPTON (*to* GRACE): Repeat after me.

GRACE: I know the lines. I, Grace Shelley, take thee J.C. to my wedded husband to have and to hold from this day forward, for better for worse, for richer for poorer, in sickness and in health, to love and to cherish till death do us part, according to God's holy ordinance and thereto I give thee my troth.

SIR CHARLES *steps forward with the ring and hurriedly puts it on* GRACE'S *finger.*

BISHOP LAMPTON (*with increasing speed*): 'For as much as these two persons have consented together in holy wedlock, I pronounce that they be man and wife together. In-the-name-of-the-Father-and-of-the-Son-and-of-the-Holy-Ghost-whom-God-hath-joined-together-let-no-man-put-asunder . . .' (*One last effort.*) Lord have mercy upon us!

ALL: Christ have mercy upon us.

BISHOP LAMPTON: Lord have mercy upon us!

BISHOP LAMPTON *sinks to the floor exhausted, but* DINSDALE *and* SIR CHARLES *jerk him up as the bells peal and the organ booms.*

# SCENE THIRTEEN

*Bells and organ fade down. The screen is taken up to show a small buffet has been laid out—drinks, sandwiches, and a wedding cake. The* EARL *picks up* GRACE *and carries her laughing into the drawing-room.*

DINSDALE (*to* BISHOP LAMPTON): Frankly, I thought it was going to be a jolly sight worse.

BISHOP LAMPTON (*being helped out of his vestments by* TUCKER): Worse? How could it have been worse? When that woman entered in *white* I knew. (*Shudders.*) An actress, married in white, *white*.

GRACE: Hildegarde! This is a bit tatty. No reception, no guests, a few curled sandwiches and a deformed wedding cake. William Hickey won't give us a mention.

TUCKER: It's not my fault, your ladyship.

GRACE: 'Your ladyship.' (*Brightening.*) That's better. Now watch 'em creep and crawl at Harrods.

BISHOP LAMPTON *slumps down on a chair whilst the* EARL *hands* SIR CHARLES *and* DINSDALE *paper hats and coloured balloons. They put on the hats.*

SIR CHARLES (*to* GRACE): We thought you'd prefer a quiet affair.

GRACE: It's like a wet Monday in Warrington. What about a toast to the newly-weds or something? Let's try and keep it a bit trad.

SIR CHARLES: Oh, very well. Ladies and gentlemen—to the long life, prosperity and happiness of the bride and groom. *They drink.*

EARL OF GURNEY (*picking up knife*): Thank you, ladies and gentlemen, in reply I name this ship 'Loving Kindness'.

May I keep her and all who sail in her. (*Cuts wedding cake.*)

TUCKER: Ah, your ladyship, you should have seen the late Earl's wedding. Over five hundred guests. The créme de menthe. Wastrels all! Lords of conspicuous consumption.

    SIR CHARLES *has taken* GRACE *aside.*

SIR CHARLES (*low*): Can't say I fancy the idea of you alone with him.

GRACE (*low, angry*): Everything's still yours, even if you've given it away.

EARL OF GURNEY: Good. Let's have a minute's silence.

CLAIRE: What for?

EARL OF GURNEY: For all the dead books of World War I. For Mr Moto, the Cisco Kid and Me. Muffle the drums, beat the retreat. Quiet, sshh, silence . . .

    *The sudden silence is physical. Even after only a few seconds the tension grows. The strain is too much. All burst out at once—* 'Why the devil . . .' 'I say . . .' 'Hell . . .!'

(*Sadly.*) Terrible, isn't it? That's why I have to talk, sing, dance.

GRACE (*glancing at* SIR CHARLES): And make love?

TUCKER (*singing in hoarse croak*): 'Oh, how we danced on the night we were wed . . .'

    *While he cavorts around,* GRACE *takes the* EARL'S *arm and they slip away Up Stage Centre.*

'We pledged our true love and a word wasn't said.' My mother loved that song. Mammy! Mammy! You weighed twenty stone but you were my little Mammy.

SIR CHARLES: Tucker!

TUCKER: I'm sorry, sir. I thought you might wish me to liven up this wake.

SIR CHARLES (*noticing bride and groom are missing*): Where have they gone?

CLAIRE: Upstairs.

DINSDALE: Must say I wouldn't much like to be in her shoes tonight.

TUCKER: Not her shoes he'll be in, Master Dinsdale, sir.

BISHOP LAMPTON (*shuddering*): *White* . . .

SIR CHARLES (*angrily*): You never stop talking, Bertie. All of you sneering, sniggering. (*Lights dim down.*) We've got to pull together in this. Families like ours set the tone. Doesn't help poking and prying into personal lives. The strength of the English people lies in their inhibitions. What are they doing up there? (*He now stands in Single Spot Down Stage Left, still wearing a paper hat with a tiny bell at the end.*) You go to any foreign country and see the difference. There's always some scruffy chappie on a street corner who wants to tell you all about his love life, and sell you a strip of dirty postcards. What are they doing up there? Sacrifices must be made. Nothing more to be said. (*Looks up.*) *What* . . . *are* . . . *they* . . . *doing* . . . *up* . . . *there?*

　　　*Spot out.*

# SCENE FOURTEEN

*Spot up immediately on the four-poster bed and a chair.* GRACE
*is stripping to music played softly over. Her movements are pro-
vocative, but utterly unselfconscious. Stepping out of her wedding
dress,* GRACE *bends to pick it up. She drapes it over the chair.*

GRACE: I always get first night nerves. Any good performer does.
You have to be keyed up to give a good show. I've done it
all, from Stanislavski to Strip. Never think I once worked as
a stripper, would you? It's true, as God is my witness—no,
you weren't there, were you, J.C.? Greasy make-up towels,
cracked mirrors, rhinestones and beads. What a world.
(*Takes off stocking and throws it absently into audience.*) I
sang 'This Can't Be Love'. Funny, I did the same act
later at the 'Pigalle' for twice the money without remov-
ing a stitch. (*Proudly.*) Of course, some women can strip
without taking their clothes off. (*She sits on a chair and
takes off other stocking.*) Nobody could call me undersexed,
but I could never get worked up watching some man strip
down to his suspenders and jockstrap. Where's the fun? I
suppose some people just enjoy the smell of a steak better
than the steak itself. (*Throws stocking into audience.*) If my
mother could see me now—it's what she always wanted for
me—the Big Time. She never forgave Dad for being born
in Clapham. Guess she found it hard to settle down to civilian
life after being in a touring company of *Chu Chin Chow.*
Nobody need worry about me fitting in. (*Walks momentarily
into darkness, left.*) All I have to do is play it cool. (*Reappears
into Spot, in black nightdress, miming drinking tea with finger
cocked up.*) I can cock my little finger with the best. (*Calls
Wings Right.*) What you doing in there, Honey?

*She stares as the* EARL *enters unsteadily from Wings Right, in white pyjamas and riding a one-wheel bicycle.*

It's ridiculous! It's not dignified!

EARL OF GURNEY (*wobbling*): Dignity has nothing to do with divinity.

GRACE (*sudden panic*): Not here! Not now! A *bike?* You're mad.

EARL OF GURNEY: Don't be frightened.

GRACE (*recovering*): I'm not frightened. But I didn't expect to see my husband riding a one-wheel bike on his wedding night.

EARL OF GURNEY: It's the only way to travel. (*Jumps off bike.*) Remember, God loves you, God wants you, God needs you. Let's to bed.

*Spot fades out. Music swells up. From out of the darkness the beating of giant wings as a great bird hovers overhead, followed by the sound of rain falling heavily.*

# SCENE FIFTEEN

*Lights up on drawing-room to show* SIR CHARLES *standing by the french-windows staring out moodily at the rain.* GRACE *enters.*

GRACE: It was a damn long night. I'm starving.

SIR CHARLES: What happened?

GRACE: Happened?

SIR CHARLES (*impatiently*): Last night. What did he do?

GRACE: Rode around on a one-wheel bicycle.

SIR CHARLES: Filthy beast! . . . That must be the Guv'nor's old bike. The attic's full of his junk. So he just rode around all night, then?

GRACE: First the bike, then me.

SIR CHARLES: Oh.

GRACE: His mind may be wonky but there's nothing wrong with the rest of his anatomy.

SIR CHARLES (*gloomily*): We Gurneys have always been damnably virile.

GRACE: I thought you'd be delighted to find he's not impotent.

SIR CHARLES (*frowning*): I am. I am. Delighted.

 CLAIRE *enters briskly.* SIR CHARLES *quickly lets go of* GRACE'S *hand.*

CLAIRE: 'morning. Well, what happened last night? Was it successful?

GRACE: I should have sold tickets.

SIR CHARLES: Really, Claire, how can you ask a question like that?

CLAIRE: Why not? This is your idea, remember? If your nephew's incapable, then somebody else may have to step into the breach for him.

GRACE: Charles, tell her to keep her sharp tongue and low mind to herself.

CLAIRE: She has claws.

GRACE: This is my pad now. If you want to keep kibbitzing here, belt up on the snide remarks or you'll find yourself horizontal.

CLAIRE: Horizontal's more your position than mine, dear.

GRACE: Listen you Black Witch of the North.

*There is the sound of a commotion from the corridor.* TUCKER *comes in arguing with* DR HERDER.

TUCKER: Why can't you look at my back? It's 'cause I'm on the National Health, isn't it? Damn money-grubbers, you and your Hypocrite's Oath . . . Your ladyship, Dr Paul Herder. Lunch is ready, Madam.

TUCKER *shuffles out.* DR HERDER *faces* CLAIRE, GRACE *and* SIR CHARLES, *who instinctively unite against him, their internal quarrel forgotten.*

DR HERDER: I've come to offer my congratulations, if that's the right word.

SIR CHARLES: This is Dr Herder, Lady Gurney.

GRACE: How do you do, Doctor. So nice to meet you at last. You'll stay for lunch. I want to talk to you about my husband. I'm sorry you weren't told about the wedding, but it was done in such a rush we didn't have time to invite anybody except the close family. Besides, you would have tried to talk me out of it. It wouldn't have done any good . . . (*ironically*) you see, I love him!

*She exits.*

DR HERDER: You should have consulted me before you went ahead. It's madness.

SIR CHARLES: Come, come, Doctor. You said he needed a harsh dose of reality. You can't have a harsher dose of the stuff than marriage.

DR HERDER: It can't even be legal.

SIR CHARLES: It's legal. My brother-in-law conducted the

service. He's a Bishop, and a Bishop would never do anything that wasn't legal.

*He exits.*

DR HERDER: And what do you say, Lady Claire.

CLAIRE: Congratulations.

DR HERDER: Congratulations?

CLAIRE: On getting your Guggenheim Grant.

DR HERDER: You made love to me to make sure I didn't cause any trouble.

CLAIRE: You seduced me to make sure of that 130,000 for your schizophrenic rats. Don't be tiresome.

DR HERDER: I don't like being made a fool of, Claire.

CLAIRE: You haven't been. Charles would have gone ahead with the marriage anyway. The Gurneys must have an heir. As soon as there is one Charles will have J.C. committed. The only way you would change the plot is by making the 14th Earl of Gurney sane like the rest of us. And you haven't got much time. Lady Grace Shelley isn't the type to survive the rabbit test for long.

DR HERDER (*quiet hate*): Verdammt. Verdammt. Verdammt.

*Blackout.*

# SCENE SIXTEEN

*A roll of thunder. Spot up on* GRACE *framed in the doorway Up Stage Centre. She is nine months pregnant. Lights full up to show* DR HERDER, CLAIRE *and* SIR CHARLES *watching her waddle in. The* EARL *comes in behind her, with the same heavy tread, leaning on a shepherd's crook, as if he, too, is carrying.*

GRACE: Can you beat it, J.C.'s got labour pains too.

DR HERDER: It's called 'couvade'. Sympathetic illness. Psychosomatic. Not at all unusual.

SIR CHARLES: Hmm. I never felt a thing when Lady Claire here was pregnant.

CLAIRE: I'm sure you didn't.

EARL OF GURNEY (*helping* GRACE *into chair, she winces and the* EARL *clutches his stomach*): Ooo-ah, Mighty Mouse is roaring.

DR HERDER: What are you going to call the child?

SIR CHARLES: Vincent, after the Guv'nor.

EARL OF GURNEY (*firmly*): No shell name. We'll call the little beggar Bussay d'Ambois, the UNO Boy-Wonder. And if it's a girl, Capucine.

SIR CHARLES: Capucine? You can't call anyone Capucine?

    TUCKER *enters.*

TUCKER: Dr Herder. Mr McKyle is here.

DR HERDER: Show them straight in.

TUCKER: Certainly, sir, I'll lay down on the doorstep and let 'em walk over me.

    *He exits.*

CLAIRE: Do you need us?

DR HERDER: Yes. But whatever happens, please don't interfere or interrupt, unless I ask.

CLAIRE: What are you going to do?

DR HERDER (*picks up tape-recorder*): Prove it's impossible for two objects to occupy the same space at the same time. A colleague of mine, Dr Sackstead, has agreed to send me some help as a personal favour.

SIR CHARLES: All these damned experiments. Look at the last one with the lie-detector. You asked him if he was God, he grinned, said 'No' and the damn fool machine said he was lying.

DR HERDER: You've forced me to risk the unorthodox. (*Takes the* EARL'S *arm.*) I'm going to show you the world in the hard light of Truth.

EARL OF GURNEY: I am the Light of Truth, the Light of the World.

DR HERDER (*into tape-recorder*): This is experiment fifteen.

SIR CHARLES: All these damned experiments.

> TUCKER *enters.*

TUCKER: Dr Herder. Mr McKyle . . .

> MCKYLE *enters, brushing past him impatiently, followed by a burly* ASSISTANT.

Oh, charming.

> *He exits.*

MCKYLE (*gesturing*): Mae assistant, Mr Shape.

> MCKYLE *is a powerful gaunt man, with an iron-grey beard and brusque manner. He is still wearing gloves.*

ASSISTANT: Dr Sackstead was held up. He hopes to be along later.

MCKYLE: Shall we gie on wi' it?

DR HERDER: Let me introduce you.

MCKYLE: No need. I'm sure they a' ken me here. (*The others look puzzled; he takes off right-hand glove, extends fingers.*) Ach, who else has electricity streaming fraw his fingers and eyeballs? I'm the High Voltage Messiah.

CLAIRE: The who?

MCKYLE: The Electric Christ, the AC/DC God. You look

fused. Cannae y'see the wall plug in mae forehead? Here, here. The booster converter. Takes everything I eats and drinks and converts it into watts and kilowatts.

*All stare except* ASSISTANT *and* DR HERDER. SIR CHARLES *and* CLAIRE *are about to protest.* DR HERDER *gestures to them to keep quiet and flicks on the tape-recorder.*

DR HERDER: Are you saying you're God too?

MCKYLE: God 1, 2, 3, 4, 5, 6, 7, 8, 9, 10. AC/DC. Havenae' y' seen God a'fore?

EARL OF GURNEY (*quietly*): They have, Sir. Your remarks are in extreme bad taste. I'm God.

MCKYLE (*focussing on him for the first time*): Yer' nae God. Yer' what mae snot-rag's made of. (*Plugs deaf-aid in ear.*) I've obliterated hundreds o' dupe-Messiahs in mae time.

EARL OF GURNEY (*begins to circle slowly clock-wise*): You think I'd go around saying I was God if I could help it? Mental hospitals are full of chaps saying they're God.

MCKYLE (*moving slowly around in opposite direction*): It's a bit much o' Sackstead sending me twenty million miles through Galactic space and the interplanetary dust piled two feet thick outside the windows, to bandy words wi' a poxy moon-looney who thinks he's me.

EARL OF GURNEY: I'm here. You're there.

MCKYLE: Ach, I'm here and I'm there too. (*Opposite each other again.*) Dinnae trifle wi' me. I'm Jehovah o' the Old Testament, the Vengeful God. Awae or you'll be *dropped.*

DR HERDER: You can't both be God.

MCKYLE: He's only a bleery-eyed blooster, an English pinhead, the hollowed out son o' a Cameronian brothel-keeper.

EARL OF GURNEY: That's because I'm not myself today. (*To* DR HERDER.) You're trying to split my mind with his tongue.

MCKYLE: Awae home, laddie, afore I burn you to a crispy noodle.

EARL OF GURNEY: You can't touch me. I'm the Rock.

(*Becomes square, massive.*) And the Vine. (*Stretching arms up.*) The goat. (*Springs into chair, fingers as horns.*) The East Wind. (*Blows.*) The Sacred Bug. (*Jumps down, scuttles along.*) The Upright Testicle. (*Jerks upright.*) The Bull.

*As they watch him paw and bellow, fascinated,* MCKYLE *picks up the empty brandy glass from table and before the* ASSISTANT *can stop him takes a bite out of it. Having recaptured their horrified attention, he continues talking with his mouth full of blood.*

MCKYLE: I saw mae son Jamie dei. He had cancer at the base of his spine and one in his head. They used the black spider treatment on him. It crawled all over, using its feelers, cracking the body vermin and germs wi' its nippers. (*Suddenly to* GRACE.) I can cure yer bursting. Fire a laser beam doon into yer eye, let a black spider crawl down to clear away the sick puss the sack o' pus, the white puss, the deid . . .

GRACE *rises, shaken.*

But first I'll deal wi' yon Irishman. (*Stands on one leg.*) I'm earthed. (*Whipping off glove he suddenly whirls round and stabs forefinger at the* EARL'S *stomach.*) Zzzzzzzzz . . .

*The* EARL *tries to protect himself with his hands but slowly doubles up, letting out a long groan which turns into a cry of pain as* GRACE, *who has staggered to her feet, collapses on the floor clutching her stomach.*

DR HERDER: Damn!

SIR CHARLES: Grace. Grace.

CLAIRE (*hurrying to the door*): Tucker!

SIR CHARLES (*to* DR HERDER *bending down to* GRACE): Your responsibility, Sir. Damn you.

TUCKER *appears in doorway.*

DR HERDER: Tucker—Nurse Brice. And tell the midwife to be ready!

MCKYLE (*taking bulb out of standard lamp*): I'm *dead*! (*sticks finger into the socket, shakes violently.*) Re-ch-a-r-ge!

DR HERDER: Get her upstairs.

SIR CHARLES (*picking* GRACE *up*): If we lose this child . . .

*They move Up Stage to the door.*

MCKYLE (*shaking*): B-B-Burn-n-n-n a f-f-f-eath-e-e-e-e-er
o-o-o-n-d-d-er her n-n-nose!

DINSDALE *rushes in excitedly.*

DINSDALE: Super news! Old Barrington-Cochrain's dying.
It'll mean a by-election.

CLAIRE: Not now, Dinsdale!

EARL OF GURNEY: *Paul, Paul, why persecutest thou me?*

*All look round and up to the* EARL *who has, in the confusion,
climbed up to the gallery and is now spread out on the cross.*
SIR CHARLES *hurries out with* GRACE *in his arms.* CLAIRE
*quickly follows as* TUCKER *reappears in doorway.*

DR HERDER (*to* ASSISTANT): Don't let 'em leave!

*He exits.*

TUCKER: Don't worry, Doctor. I'm a Brown Belt. Fifth Dan.
(*Assumes Judo stance, with loud grunts.*) Ho—Ha!

DINSDALE: Will somebody please tell me what's going on?

TUCKER (*pouring drink*): Life, Master Dinsdale, sir. The rich
moth-eaten tapestry of life.

DR HERDER *re-enters with* CLAIRE.

DR HERDER: Mrs Grant's a fully qualified midwife. She'd
resent me interfering professionally. Anyway, I'll be extremely
busy down here.

CLAIRE: You're not going on with this?

DR HERDER: It's our last chance. Sackstead will never agree to
let McKyle out again.

DINSDALE: Where's father?

CLAIRE: Pacing the corridor upstairs.

DR HERDER: Come, McKyle, get your finger out. (*Up at cross.*)
Gentlemen, it's important to know which of you is telling
the truth. If one of you is God, the other must be somebody
else.

MCKYLE: Your Worship, Ladies and Gentlemen o' the Jury.
I stand accused o' nae being who I am: to wit, the aforesaid,
after-mentioned, hereafter-named, uncontested GOD. These

are facts. I made the world in mae image. I'm a holy terror. Sae that accoonts fer the bloody mess it's in. Gi' up y' windy wa's McNaughton and plead insanity.

EARL OF GURNEY: If it's facts you want, the Great Peacock is a Moth which only lives two days. With no mouth to eat or drink it flies miles to love, breed and die. Consider a life o' love without one selfish act, members of the Jury.

MCKYLE: Ach, and they put me awae fer seventeen years. Only the sick wi' spiders webs round their brains clack o' about lo'e and goodness. I'm a braw God fer bashing bairns' heads on rocks, a God for strong stomachs.

EARL OF GURNEY: You're one of the Fu Manchu gang. (*Gestures at audience.*) They're children of condensed sunlight.

MCKYLE: The children o' licht you ken, are far awa'. This is Earth. An early failure o' mine. Earth is where I dump the excrement o' the Universe, the privy o' the Cosmos.

EARL OF GURNEY: I'm too full of Grace to listen. People care for love—love for everything that's necessary for the continuation of life.

TUCKER (*lurching forward*): We don't want love, we want a fat slice o' revenge. Kiss me arse!

DINSDALE (*indignantly*): Tucker, you're an unmitigated stinker.

DR HERDER: No God of *love* made this world. I've seen a girl of four's nails had been torn out by her father. I've seen the mountains of gold teeth and hair and the millions boiled down for soap.

EARL OF GURNEY (*he stumbles desperately off the cross, putting sticking plaster over his eyes*): S-S-some-times G-G-God turns his b-b-back on his p-p-people . . .

MCKYLE: And breaks wind and the stench clouds the globe! That's settled the verdict 'tween twa' poor Scottish loons. I'm the High Voltage Man, nearer to God than yon senti-mental clishmac-laverer.

EARL OF GURNEY: There's a light of truth inside as well as a light of truth outside.

DR HERDER (*violently*): Here's the truth! (*Rips sticking plaster from the* EARL'S *eyes.*) You're *Jack Gurney*, the 14th Earl of Gurney.

> *Roll of thunder.*

MCKYLE: I'm Cock o' the North, mae boys. Oh. I'm Cock o' the North. (*Breaks* EARL'S *staff across knee.*)

EARL OF GURNEY (*writhing as if in labour*): ELOI ELOI.

DR HERDER: Your loving family tricked you into marriage because they want an heir.

EARL OF GURNEY: Pater-Noster-Pater-Noster-Pater-Noster . . .

DR.HERDER: If the baby turns out to be a boy they'll have you certified, committed, and in a strait-jacket before you can say another Pater-Noster.

EARL OF GURNEY (*in great pain*): I am the Father. Cherish the worm. Errsh . . . I'm splitting. I tear. Torn. (*Writhing.*) Crowned. Coming out crowned. BORN . . . I *AM* THE FATHER.

> *A clap of thunder.* CLAIRE *jumps up.*

CLAIRE (*shouting, putting hands to head like horns*): You're the father of nothing! You're Jack—Jack the *Cuckold*!

MCKYLE (*firing with both hands at* EARL): Zzzzzzzzzzz . . .

> *The* EARL *lets out an extraordinary deep-throated cry, careering backwards, bucking and twisting from the force of the imaginary electrical charge. He crashes against the recorder on the table, starting it playing back at high speed. Simultaneously, there is a clap of thunder, the french-windows fly open and with a rush of cold wind a monstrous eight-feet beast bursts in. It walks upright like a man, covered with thick black hair swept out from each side of its face like a gigantic guinea-pig, and is dressed incongruously in high Victorian fashion: morning coat and top hat. None of the others see the beast, which grabs the* EARL *and shakes him violently, to the accompaniment of high-speed jabber from the tape-recorder, thunder-claps and* MCKYLE'S *harsh chants 'two million volts zzzzz three million zzzzzzzzzz'.*
>
> *The* EARL *wrestles in an epileptic fit, saliva dribbling from his*

*mouth.* CLAIRE *and* DINSDALE *watch with well-bred revulsion,* DR HERDER *and* ASSISTANT *with clinical interest while pushing the heavy furniture out of the way as the beast pummels his victim in a series of vicious wrestling holds. The* EARL'S *legs and arms are twisted, and his face forced back by a heavy paw. He struggles, but his strength soon leaves him. As the background noise reaches a crescendo, the beast slams him down across its knee, tosses him onto the floor and then looking down at the unconscious man, raises its hat, grunts and lurches out the way it came in.*

*The* EARL *lies still, Stage Centre, one leg twisted under his body.* MCKYLE *stops chanting, and* CLAIRE *switches off the tape-recorder, whilst* DINSDALE *and* TUCKER *close the french-windows. Silence. There is the distinct sound of a single slap and a baby begins to cry faintly. The* ASSISTANT *straightens the* EARL'S *leg whilst* DR HERDER *bends down and lifts his head. The* EARL'S *eyes open.*

EARL OF GURNEY (*feebly*): Jack.

DR HERDER: What?

EARL OF GURNET: Jack. My name . . .

DR HERDER (*dawning realization*): Yes, Jack. That's right, your name's Jack. (*Looks up at others.*) It's worked!

MCKYLE: Cowl the Minnie! Hallelujah! Hallelujah!

DINSDALE: Oh, well done.

EARL OF GURNEY: Jack. My name's Jack . . .

SIR CHARLES *enters Up Stage Centre, a bundle in his arms.*

SIR CHARLES (*holding up bundle triumphantly*): It's a boy!

EARL OF GURNEY: Jack. I'm Jack. I'm Jack. I'm Jack!

*The baby starts to cry.*

**CURTAIN**

*Act Two*

# SCENE ONE

*'Oh for the Wings of a Dove' played over, then out of the darkness*
BISHOP LAMPTON'S *voice intones:*

BISHOP LAMPTON (*over*): Vincent, Henry, Edward, Ralph
Gurney, I baptize thee in the name of the Father and of the
Son and of the Holy Ghost.

*Baby cries. Photographer's flash momentarily lights a christening
group of* SIR CHARLES, CLAIRE, DINSDALE, DR HERDER,
TUCKER *and* BISHOP LAMPTON, *grouped around* GRACE *with
the child.*

*Then lights up on the drawing-room, now containing pieces of
Victorian furniture and bric-a-brac. The cross has gone.* TUCKER
*pulls off the* BISHOP'S *robes.*

GRACE: What a pair of lungs. The little devil up-staged everybody. He's a trouper.

SIR CHARLES (*jovially, at baby*): Coochy-coochy. He's a splendid
fella, eh, Bertie?

BISHOP LAMPTON: A vessel newly filled with the Holy
Spirit, but I fear regrettably leaky.

GRACE: Leaky or not, he's saved you Gurneys from becoming
extinct.

*She exits.*

SIR CHARLES: Things are beginning to get back to normal.

DR HERDER: What are we going to do about his lordship?

SIR CHARLES: The family came to a decision some time ago,
that after certain matters had been cleared up he'd be put
away. Permanently this time. For his own good.

CLAIRE: That was before, Charles. The situation's changed.

BISHOP LAMPTON: I gather he's improved. But we can't be
sure he won't sink back into darkness and shadow.

DINSDALE: Sometimes it's worse than when he was completely potty. I mean, we're all just waiting for him to go off again, tick-tick-tick-tick-*boom*. We've been darned lucky up to now but with a possible by-election in the offing, it's too risky.

SIR CHARLES: Can't say I'm the sensitive type, but the strain of the last few months is beginning to tell. I think it's best all round if Jack were put away. (*Notices* TUCKER *staggering off with the vestments.*) And he's not the only one we can say goodbye to.

TUCKER *scowls darkly at him, as* GRACE *comes back in.*

GRACE: Nothing like a couple of nursemaids to take the curse out of having kids.

CLAIRE: We were talking about Jack.

GRACE: He's a helluva problem. What do you say, Doctor?

DR HERDER (*drily*): Thank you for asking. You must realize that the battle between the God of Love and the Electric Messiah was a tremendous breakthrough.

GRACE: Is he cured?

DR HERDER: He's on the way to recovery. His behaviour is nearer the acceptable norm. I don't know whether it's permanent. I do know, you mustn't have him committed. I've got a full schedule of research lined up, but I'm taking valuable time out for this therapy. This case could become a classic of psychology—Freud's Anna O., now Herder's Earl of Gurney.

EARL OF GURNEY: Call me Jack.

The EARL *stands in the doorway Up Stage Centre with an ancient shotgun levelled at them. Before they can react he pulls the trigger and says 'click'; nothing happens. He has changed; no beard, his hair is short, and he wears an old-fashioned dark suit with waistcoat and stiff collar. His words and gestures are still slightly out of 'synch'.*

It's a pleasant name. (*Imitating bell.*) J-J-Jack, J-J-Jack, J-J-Jack.

*Using his shotgun as a temporary crutch he crosses Stage Centre with a peculiar loping hop.*

SIR CHARLES: And he's recovering? (*To the* EARL.) Why are
you walking like that?

   *The* EARL *pulls off his right shoe, feels inside, and takes out a*
   *large pebble. He shows it to* SIR CHARLES *by way of reply.*
   (*Disappointed.*) Oh. A stone.

CLAIRE: Reasonable.

EARL OF GURNEY (*gesturing with gun*): I found it in the attic.

GRACE: Why aren't you resting?

EARL OF GURNEY: I wanted to apologize for not being at my
own son's christening.

GRACE: The little devil stole the show.

EARL OF GURNEY: I must be sure before I make my first
public appearance. Very important to leave the right impression. When I g-g- huitment, re-return dunt d-d- impression of overall superiority and volatile farts the shadow
of it is sludge ghoul of a whore, whoredom's bloddy network.
(*Struggles fiercely to regain control.*) *Hold Sir, hold hold hold*
*hold Sir.* (*Recovering, to* DINSDALE.) A relative who said he
was Christ could hardly be a political asset for you, Dinsdale.

DR HERDER: I don't know. The Tory Leader's the son of a
carpenter, after all.

EARL OF GURNEY (*surprised*): Lord Salisbury's a carpenter's
son. Really?

CLAIRE: How are you feeling?

EARL OF GURNEY: Lazarus felt like I feel. Odour of dung.
Duat d' d' s'muss bed sores the executioners arrive for Nijinsky
the liquid streets unstable my wooden leg needs morphine.
(*Struggling, sweating.*) *Back, Sir. Back, Sir. Back.* (*Controlled.*)
Be patient, I'll learn the rules of the game.

DR HERDER: We know you will.

CLAIRE: You've changed already.

   TUCKER *enters carrying a cape and deerstalker cap.*

TUCKER: You wished to take a constitutional at noon, my
lord.

EARL OF GURNEY: Thank you, Tuck. Invaluable man, Tuck.

TUCKER: There's some 'ere who don't think so, your lordship. (*Darkly at* SIR CHARLES.) No names, no pack-drill. I know they're waiting to give me the boot.

EARL OF GURNEY (*sadly*): You and me both, Tuck. We must give 'em no cause, no cause.

GRACE (*helping him on with the cape*): Don't stay out too long, Jack.

EARL OF GURNEY: Just want to get the feel of terra firma. I must learn to keep my mouth shut, bowels open and never volunteer. Come, Tuck.

*They exit through french-windows.*

CLAIRE: Well? Has he changed or hasn't he? I agreed with you before, Charles, he was hopeless and the sooner we put him away the better. Now it'd be stupid. I know he'll recover.

GRACE: And if he does? Where does that leave us? He mightn't understand what we did.

DINSDALE: I say, aren't you all jumping the gun? Look at the way he suddenly goes off. 'Volatile farts a' a' duat.' What's all that then?

DR HERDER: Paralalia—speech disturbance. It would be simpler if a man was paranoid one moment and cured the next. Unfortunately, it takes time.

DINSDALE: There's all this Victorian bric-a-brac stuff he's got everywhere. And what about him thinking the leader of the Conservative Party was the Marquis of Salisbury?

DR HERDER: Sicilian peasants thought Churchill was a kind of tomato. Thousands of Indians have never heard of Gandhi. Political ignorance is not a symptom of psychosis. It might even be considered a sign of mental health.

CLAIRE: Bertie, you haven't seen much of Jack lately. What's your opinion?

BISHOP LAMPTON: The acid test still is, would he pass muster in the Athenæum? Could he be introduced to members without raising eyebrows?

DR HERDER: In the end it's really her ladyship's decision.

GRACE: Oh, hell. Thanks a lot. I don't know. There's the baby
. . . What if he suddenly . . .? Have I got to right now? Jeez,
I can't make up my mind.

SIR CHARLES: You don't have to. It's done. I've already asked
the Master in Lunacy to come down and certify Jack's insane.

*A single shot, off Right, breaks the stunned silence.* CLAIRE,
DR HERDER *and* GRACE *look at each other, then rush out of the
french-windows.*

SIR CHARLES (*hopefully, to* DINSDALE): Do you think Jack's
done the decent thing at last?

BISHOP LAMPTON *crosses himself.*

*Lights down.*

# SCENE TWO

*Spot up on metal sun hanging Down Stage Centre: some white feathers float down. Footlights up to show the EARL standing with TUCKER, Down Stage Right, looking blankly at his smoking shotgun, a dead dove at his feet. Voices are heard calling off.*

TUCKER (*shakily*): That's how accidents happen. That could have been me, your lordship. You've been waving that gun all over the place. (*Takes out hip-flask.*) Not that anyone'd have cared much. No one to weep for poor creeping Tucker. (*Drinks.*) But I'm not ready for stoking the fiery furnace yet. I've got an awful lot of living to do. Girls by the hundreds to name only a few . . .

> GRACE, CLAIRE *and* DR HERDER *rush anxiously on Wings Right.*

GRACE: What happened? You all right?

TUCKER: As rain, your ladyship. Just a little accident. The gun went off. But Ironside never flinched.

CLAIRE: You're not hurt, Jack?

EARL OF GURNEY (*indicating dove, takes off hat*): R.I.P.

GRACE: Where the devil were you, Jeeves?

CLAIRE: Guzzling! Your job's to look after his lordship, Tucker.

TUCKER: I know my job, Lady Claire, and my place. And that's indoors. It's f-f-freezing.

> *With the exception of the* EARL *the others are already feeling cold. They shift from one foot to the other to keep warm during the rest of the scene.* SIR CHARLES *hurries on, Wings Right.*

SIR CHARLES (*sees* EARL): Oh. Still in one piece?

CLAIRE: Disappointed?

EARL OF GURNEY: I was trying to do what's expected. I recall it's a sign of normalcy in our circle to slaughter anything that moves. All I did was . . .

*He aims the shotgun up at the Flies off Left, and pulls the trigger. To everyone's horror, the second barrel fires. There is a bellow of pain from the Flies, a cry 'Ahhhhh . . .' followed by a crash as someone hits the ground.*

SIR CHARLES: Poachers! Damn poachers! (*Grabs the* EARL'S *gun.*) Come on, Tucker. After him!

SIR CHARLES *rushes off with a reluctant* TUCKER. DINSDALE *can be heard calling 'I say, where is everybody? H-e-ll-ooo', as* CLAIRE, DR HERDER *and* GRACE *look suspiciously at the* EARL.

EARL OF GURNEY: I had a stone in my shoe and an accident with an old gun, so you still think I'm insane. I know a man who hated the sight of his wrinkled socks, so he wore his girl friend's girdle to keep 'em up. Now she's his wife. (*Fiercely.*) I've got to stop talking. (*Takes* GRACE'S *hand.*) Just give me time.

DR HERDER (*deliberately*): Sir Charles has asked the Master in Lunacy to come here to commit you to an institution.

EARL *lets go of* GRACE'S *hand; he becomes rigid and sways.*
Naturally I'll oppose any commitment. But in the end it depends on how you act.

EARL OF GURNEY (*stops swaying*): Perhaps it's for the best. If I satisfy the Lunatic Master, I'll be officially sane, and I'll have a certificate to prove it. (*Quietly.*) But Charles has been unwise. (*All shiver.*) You'll catch your deaths out here. Odd expression.

DR HERDER: L-L-Let's get in then. We've got work to do.

EARL OF GURNEY: I'll stay a moment and compose myself.

DR HERDER *nods and exits briskly Wings Right, with* CLAIRE.

GRACE: What a family. Enough to drive anyone round the bend. Will you be all right, Jack?

EARL OF GURNEY (*arm around her*): The only sensible thing I've done in the last seven years was to marry you.

GRACE (*touched*): There now. There now. Don't stay out too

long, Honey. (*Moves off, shivering.*) Charles is a bloody moron. I'll have his guts for garters.

*As she exits Wings Left, the metal sun is taken up.*

EARL OF GURNEY (*softly*): Soft. Softly. Down, down, down, oh, let me keep it down, pianissimo, damp down, damp down. Down. (*Voice rises despite himself.*) I'm a soft grub unun-duuulating. They'll rip me open. (*Trembling.*) Nail my brain to my skull. Strom, strom, grunk, grok, *Crunk.* Fug. That means you. *Fug. Fug. Fug.* Silence when you speak S-i-l-e-n-c-e. Steady the Buffs, waiter, I say, waiter, there's a moustache in my soup. (*Violently.*) Kerr-un-crrrr. KORKSHIST—KORK-SHIST—KUK-KUK-KUK-KUK-KUK-KUK . . .

*Unable to stop he takes out two strips of sticky-tape and sticks them across his mouth. Now he can't speak and his savage struggle to control himself can only be expressed in abrupt body movements. He starts leaping, spreading out his cape; higher and higher, till a last climactic leap, and he lands, crouching in a ball, Down Stage Centre. Dim Lights Up Stage Centre, to show a dark shadowy figure waiting in the drawing-room behind him: it is the* MASTER IN LUNACY.

# SCENE THREE

*Lights up on the* MASTER, KELSO TRUSCOTT, Q.C., *in the
drawing-room, which now contains more Victorian bric-a-brac:
stuffed pheasants, wax fruit under glass, and a red-plush sofa. The*
EARL *straightens up resolutely and is joined by* TUCKER. *The* EARL
*hands him his hat and cape and* TUCKER *gives him 'The Times'
newspaper in return. The* EARL *puts it under his arm and sticks
a briar pipe firmly in his mouth. Turning sharply on his heels, he
squares his shoulders and marches purposefully Up Stage to join*
TRUSCOTT, *a big hard-faced man who is looking through some
documents.*

TRUSCOTT: Where did you spring from?

EARL OF GURNEY: You must be Truscott, the Lunatic fella.

TRUSCOTT (*frowning*): I'm the Master of the Court of Protection.
The title 'Master in Lunacy' isn't used nowadays.

*It is obvious* TRUSCOTT *is scrutinizing the* EARL *closely.*

EARL OF GURNEY: How about a snifter? No? All right then,
Tuck.

TUCKER: Very good, sir. Watch yourself now. He looks a
fishy-eyed, light-fingered gent to me. (*Glaring at* TRUSCOTT.)
I know the price of everything in this room. So if there's
anything missing we shall know where to look.

*He exits Up Stage Centre.* TRUSCOTT *stares after him.*

EARL OF GURNEY: Splendid fella. Very loyal.

TRUSCOTT: Hmmm. You know why I'm here?

EARL OF GURNEY: I'd better introduce myself first. Jack
Gurney. (*With slightest emphasis.*) The Earl of Gurney.
I believe Charles considers me incapable and you're here to
commit me officially.

TRUSCOTT: Not exactly, my lord. I make a recommendation

to a Nominated Judge and he does the actual committing. My main concern is property and its proper administration. This investigation, however, is rather informal. A favour to Charles. (*Takes out silver snuff box.*) Yours is a confusing case. (*Taps the snuff box three times and takes snuff.*) Two doctors recommend you to be put under care, but Dr Herder says you're nearly back to normal. Of course, he *is* a foreigner and his idea of normal may not be mine.

*Despite himself the* EARL'*s hand trembles, as he fills his pipe.* TRUSCOTT *watches closely.*

EARL OF GURNEY: How do you find out?

TRUSCOTT: You talk. I listen.

EARL OF GURNEY (*sits on sofa*): Ah, yes, talk. Judas talk t-t-t-t-talk . . . (*Tails off miserably.*)

TRUSCOTT (*glances at file*): Do you still believe you're Christ, my lord? (*No reply.*) Are you God? (*No reply.*) Come, sir, are you the God of Love?

*The* EARL *stares into space, deep in thought, then slowly rises and points at him.*

EARL OF GURNEY: Harrow may be more clever.

TRUSCOTT (*incredulously*): What!?

EARL OF GURNEY (*singing*): 'Rugby may make more row. But we'll row, row for ever. Steady from stroke to bow. And nothing in life shall sever the chain that is round us now . . .'

TRUSCOTT *crosses grimly to the* EARL, *stares at him, and then, without warning joins in, in a barber-shop duet.*

TRUSCOTT and EARL OF GURNEY: 'Others will fill our places, dressed in the old light blue. We'll recollect our races. We'll to the flag be true.' (*They mime rowing.*) 'But we'll still swing together. And swear by the best of schools. But we'll still swing together and swear by the best of schools!'

EARL OF GURNEY: I didn't realize—you're *Kelso* Truscott. *The* Kelso Truscott who scored that double century at Lords.

TRUSCOTT (*modestly*): A long time ago.

EARL OF GURNEY: Of course, I was pretty low down the school when you were in your glory, Truscott. They said when you got back after the Lords match dressed in a kilt, you debagged the Chaplain and hit the local constable over the head with an ebony shelalee.

TRUSCOTT (*chuckling*): Ah, schooldays, schooldays. It's all ahead of you then . . . You realize, your lordship, the fact that we're both Old Etonians can have no possible influence on my recommendation. (*Taps snuff box.*) Of course, I find it even harder to believe now. Etonians aren't exactly noted for their grey matter, but I've always found them perfectly adjusted to society. (*Sniffs.*) Now, are you the God of Love?

EARL OF GURNEY (*fiercely*): He no longer exists. I was wild with too much jubilating. I've been raving for seven years, Truscott. But everyone's entitled to one mistake.

TRUSCOTT: Seven years. That accounts for your not being at any of the Old Boys' Reunion Dinners.

EARL OF GURNEY (*bitterly*): I went around saying the Lord loooooves you LOOOOOVES. Tch. Grrk. (*Bites hard on pipe.*) Sorry there, Truscott. It's embarrassing for a fella to remember what a spectacle he made of himself. Naturally I get tongue-tied. Bit shame-faced, don't y'know.

TRUSCOTT: You seem right enough to me, but these things are deceptive. Is there anything you feel strongly about, your lordship?

EARL OF GURNEY: My w-w-wasted years. I woke up the other day and I had grey hairs. Grey hairs and duty neglected. Our country's being destroyed before our e-e-eyes. You're MOCKED in the Strand if you speak of patriotism and the old Queen. Discipline's gone. They're sapping the foundations of our society with their adultery and fornication!

TRUSCOTT *crosses Down Stage Left and pulls bell-rope.*

The barbarians are waiting outside with their chaos, anarchy, homosexuality and worse!

SIR CHARLES, CLAIRE, GRACE *and* DR HERDER *hurry in Up Stage Centre.*

GRACE: Well?

TRUSCOTT (*putting papers into the briefcase*): Dr Herder you said you thought his lordship was on the road to recovery. I can't agree.

SIR CHARLES: *There.*

TRUSCOTT: You're too cautious. For my money he's recovered.

   GRACE *kisses the* EARL *impulsively.*

GRACE: We're grateful to you, Mr Truscott.

TRUSCOTT: Thank you, your ladyship. (*To the* EARL.) We'll expect you at the next Reunion Dinner, my lord. Lady Claire, a pleasure. Dr Herder, congratulations. Splendid achievement. (*To* SIR CHARLES.) You're lucky this was only a friendly investigation, old boy. We take a dim view of frivolous complaints.

   *He exits.*

SIR CHARLES: Truscott's a damn ass. Can't he see I'm right?

GRACE: Right? I've had enough of your right. You've stuck your aristocratic schnozzle into my affairs for the last time. Right? Jack's changed. Right? Everything's changed—you, me, us, them. It's a new deal all round. Right? You know what I mean. Right? *Right!*

   *She exits.*

SIR CHARLES: Did what I thought best.

DR HERDER: The best you can do now is to leave Jack alone. He's made a spectacular breakthrough. We're in the process of making a new man.

CLAIRE: I'm always on the lookout for new men.

   SIR CHARLES *exits.*

   You did it, Jack. Wonderful.

DR HERDER: Leave him, he's been under a great strain. I didn't think he was ready for that blockhead Truscott.

CLAIRE: Blockhead or not, he brought in the right verdict.

DR HERDER: I suspect the Earl's behaviour just happened to

coincide with his idea of sanity. Your nephew needs very
delicate handling at this stage. And if possible, a little love.

CLAIRE: That shouldn't be too difficult.

DR HERDER: You helped Sir Charles crucify him.

CLAIRE: Jack's changed. He's strong now.

DR HERDER: What about us?

CLAIRE: We're too much alike. Ice on ice. I wanna' feel *alive*.

DR HERDER: And you think Jack'll perform that miracle?

CLAIRE: Oh, rats to you.

   *Lights dim to a Spot on the* EARL *as they exit.*

## SCENE FOUR

*The* EARL *hunches his right shoulder and drags his left leg.*

EARL OF GURNEY: Deformed, unfinished, sent before me time, those eminent doctors of Divinity, Professors McKyle and Herder cured me of paranoid delusions fantasy obsessions of love, that's where it ended, a solvental of inner and outer tensions. No more inter-stage friction. See how I marshal words. That's the secret of being normal. (*He pulls the words out of his mouth.*) 'I'—straighten up there. 'AM'—close up, close up with 'I' you 'orrible little word. 'GOD' . . . I AM GOD. Not the God of Love but God Almighty. God the Law-Giver, Chastiser and Judge. For I massacred the Amalekites and the Seven Nations of Canaan, I hacked Agag to pieces and blasted the barren fig-tree. I will tread them in mine anger and trample them in my fury, and their blood shall be sprinkled upon my garments. For the day of vengeance is in my heart! Hats off for the God of Justice, the God of Love is dead. Oh, you lunar jackass. *She betrayed you.* Lust muscles tighten over plexus. Guilty, guilty, guilty. The punishment is death. I've finally been processed into right-thinking power. They made me adjust to modern times. This is 1888 isn't it? I knew I was Jack. Hats off. I said Jack. I'm Jack, cunning Jack, quiet Jack, Jack's my name. (*Produces knife, flicks it open.*) Jack whose sword never sleeps. Hats off I'm Jack, not the Good Shepherd, not the Prince of Peace. I'm Red Jack, Springheeled Jack, Saucy Jack, Jack from Hell, trade-name Jack the Ripper! . . . Mary, Annie, Elizabeth, Catherine, Marie Kelly. (*Sings.*) 'Six little whores glad to be alive, one sidles up to Jack, then there were five.'
*He exits Wings Left, slashing the air with his knife.*

# SCENE FIVE

*Lights up to show* GRACE *and* DINSDALE *talking in the drawing-room, now completely furnished in authentic Victorian style.*

DINSDALE: How could you have asked 'em? What about my career?

GRACE: Politics is no career for a healthy young chap. You should go out to work like the rest of us.

DINSDALE: But look what happened last time.

GRACE: That's why I got 'em to come again. When they see how Jack's changed they'll spread the word. Everybody'll know he's back to normal.

DINSDALE: I don't think he is.

GRACE: You're just siding with your father. He won't admit Jack's cured because it doesn't suit him.

DINSDALE: I don't know how you persuaded 'em to come.

GRACE: I'm her ladyship. Sixty miles outside London an awful lot of cap tugging and forelock touching still goes on. You couldn't keep 'em away.

    TUCKER *enters.*

TUCKER: Mrs Treadwell and Mrs Piggot-Jones, your ladyship. *Two heads, topped with absurd hats, peer round the door.*

MRS TREADWELL *and* MRS PIGGOT-JONES *edge their way apprehensively into the room. Though relieved to see the cross has gone they keep close together for protection.*

GRACE: Welcome, ladies. You can serve tea now, Jeeves.

    TUCKER *crosses to the tea-trolley.*

MRS TREADWELL (*nervously*): Everything's changed.

GRACE: Yes his Nibs—Jack's just crazy about this Victorian stuff.

MRS PIGGOT-JONES: It's very hard-wearing.

GRACE: I hear the atmosphere was a trifle strained on your last visit.

MRS TREADWELL: Well, it was our first meeting with his Lordship. Neither Mrs Piggot-Jones nor myself knew him personally. Though of course we knew his father.

GRACE: I never knew mine. But my mother knew Lloyd George.

DINSDALE: He wasn't himself, don't y'know. Bit unsettled. Didn't have a wife and family then.

MRS TREADWELL: How is the Right Honourable Lord Vincent, your ladyship?

GRACE (*laughing*): 'The Honourable Lord Vince.' Oh, he's fine, just like his dad.

*The two women look startled.*

(*Quickly.*) I know Jack wants to explain about last time.

TUCKER *serves tea.*

MRS TREADWELL (*tentatively*): He asked me if I loved. Your manservant heard him.

TUCKER (*cupping right ear*): What's that? Speak up, missus.

MRS TREADWELL: Why did he say God is love?

EARL OF GURNEY: Because he was mad. Mad with grief. His father had just died.

*A sombrely dressed* EARL OF GURNEY *enters smiling, with* CLAIRE. *He is quiet, self-possessed.* CLAIRE *sits on the sofa, fascinated.*

GRACE: Talk of the devil. Darling, you remember Mrs Piggot-Jones and Mrs Treadwell?

EARL OF GURNEY: Tucker, why are those table legs uncovered? Stark naked wooden legs in mixed company—it's not decent. Curved and fluted, too. Don't you agree, Mrs Treadwell?

MRS TREADWELL: Well, I do think young girls nowadays show too much. After all, the main purpose of legs isn't seduction.

EARL OF GURNEY: Cover 'em with calico or cotton, Tucker.

TUCKER: Yes, sir, no, sir, three bags full, sir. I'm a 104-year-old Creep and I 'ave to do everything.

*He exits, mumbling.*

EARL OF GURNEY: Now ladies, when did we meet?

MRS TREADWELL: Remember you asked me if I loved?

EARL OF GURNEY: *Please*, not in front of women and children.

MRS PIGGOT-JONES: I've told Pamela not to brood about it.

EARL OF GURNEY: Let's have no talk of bestial orgasms, erotic tongueings. It burns small high-voltage holes in the brain. It's been proved in oscillographs.

GRACE: My husband hates anything suggestive.

MRS PIGGOT-JONES: So do I. I find the whole subject distressing. I can't understand why the Good Lord chose such a disgusting way of reproducing human-beings.

EARL OF GURNEY: Anything more refined would be too good for producing such two-legged, front-facing Hairies.

CLAIRE: Who did you finally get as Guest Speaker for your Church Fête?

MRS TREADWELL: Sir Barrington-Cochran. That was just before he became ill.

MRS PIGGOT-JONES: Made a splendid speech, didn't he, Pamela, about the rise of crime and socialism.

DINSDALE: I intend to campaign actively, for the reintroduction of the death penalty.

EARL OF GURNEY (*trembling*): You mean there's no death penalty in England's green and pleasant?

MRS TREADWELL: Surely you knew, your lordship?

GRACE: We're a bit out of touch. My husband only reads *Punch*.

EARL OF GURNEY: Is nothing sacred? Why, the Hangman holds society together. He is the symbol of the Great Chastiser. He built this world on punishment and fear.

MRS TREADWELL *and* MRS PIGGOT-JONES *nod vigorously.* Snuff out fear and see what discords follow. Sons strike their doddering dads, young girls show their bosoms and ankles and say rude things about the Queen. Anything goes and they do it openly in the streets and frighten the horses.

MRS PIGGOT-JONES: It's the times we live in. But what can one do?

EARL OF GURNEY: Bring back fear. In the old days the Executioner kept the forelock-touching ranks in order. When he stood on the gallows, stripped to the waist, tight breeches, black hood, you knew God was in his heaven, all's right with the world. The punishment for blaspheming was to be broken on the wheel. First the fibula. (*Mimes bringing down an iron bar.*) Cr-a-a-ck. Then the tibia, patella and femur. *Crack. crack, crack.* The corpus, ulna and radius, *crack.* 'Disconnect dem bones, dem dry bones, Disconnect dem bones dem dry bones. Now hear the word of the Lord.'

*Irresistibly the two women join in.*

EARL OF GURNEY, MRS PIGGOT-JONES and MRS TREADWELL (*singing*): 'When your head bone's connected from your neck bone, your neck bone's connected from your shoulder bone, your shoulder bone's connected from your backbone. Now hear the word of the Lord. Dem bones dem bones dem dry bones. Now hear the word of the Lord . . .'

EARL OF GURNEY: We understand each other perfectly. But that's only to be expected. Breeding speaks to breeding.

MRS PIGGOT-JONES (*flushing with pleasure*): How splendid, your lordship.

MRS TREADWELL: I've always believed I'm descended from the Kings of Munster, even though my family originally came from Wimbledon.

MRS PIGGOT-JONES: Forgive me for saying so, my lord, but this is so different from our last visit. Such an unfortunate misunderstanding.

EARL OF GURNEY: Don't give it another thought, madam. I don't hold it against you. I'm sure I forgot it the moment you left. (*Crosses to desk.*) Now forgive me, I have so much to do. (*To* GRACE.) My dear, why don't you show our guests round the estate?

GRACE: Fine. Give us a hand, Dinsdale.

EARL OF GURNEY: Don't forget to show these good ladies my coronation robes, the mantle of crimson velvet lined with white taffeta, edged with miniver. Good day, ladies. You may withdraw.

*He dismisses them with a regal wave of his hand.* MRS PIGGOT-JONES *and* MRS TREADWELL *find themselves curtseying. The* EARL *turns away and picks up some letters from his desk.*

MRS PIGGOT-JONES (*low*): He's so impressive, your ladyship, such natural dignity.

GRACE: He's still a bit eccentric.

MRS PIGGOT-JONES: Runs in the family. But it's only on the surface. Deep down one knows he's sound.

*They stop in the doorway and look back at the* EARL *calmly slitting open a letter with a paper-knife.*

MRS TREADWELL: He's so like his father. He gets more like him every day, it's frightening.

*As they exit* DINSDALE *turns, gives a delighted thumbs-up sign and hurries after them.*

GRACE: Claire . . .

CLAIRE: I'll stay and keep Jack company.

GRACE: You seem to be doing a lot of company keeping lately. Don't put yourself to so much trouble.

CLAIRE: No trouble. It's a pleasure.

GRACE: We're going to miss you when you leave.

*She exits.* CLAIRE *watches the* EARL *deftly slitting open envelopes one after the other.*

# SCENE SIX

*The* EARL *puts down the paper-knife and smiles. Throughout the scene the lights imperceptibly fade down as dusk falls.*

CLAIRE: Good. That leaves the two of us.

EARL OF GURNEY: I'm still not word perfect. That talk of bestial orgasms, erotic tongueings—was very unfortunate.

CLAIRE: They didn't mind much what you said. Your manner won 'em over. Just the right blend of God-given arrogance and condescension.

EARL OF GURNEY: I stand outside myself watching myself watching myself. (*Pulls up the corners of his mouth.*) I smile, I smile, I smile.

CLAIRE: I like your smile. Before I was only sorry for you.

EARL OF GURNEY: Ah, before, madam. Before I was a mass of light. Mad, you see. Nothing was fast enough to match my inner speed. Now I'm sane. The world sweats into my brain, madam.

CLAIRE: Don't keep calling me madam.

EARL OF GURNEY: It's hard to look at people from down-wind. They smell, they stink, they stench of stale greens, wet nappies. It's terrible but it's the real thing.

CLAIRE: I've always wanted to find the real thing. Do you remember our first talk together after you came back?

EARL OF GURNEY: I remember nothing.

CLAIRE: Explode, only feel, you said. Poor Jack. You didn't know how impossible it was for our sort to feel.

EARL OF GURNEY: Why do you remember now what I said then, when I can't remember myself?

CLAIRE: Because you're so different. I keep thinking about something that happened at my last term at Roedean. There'd

been reports of a prowler in the grounds, probably a Peeping
Tom. Something woke me about 2 a.m. and I went to the
window and looked out. There was a shadow in the shadows.
Somebody was watching me. It was a hot night but I started
shivering and shaking. It was *marvellous*.

EARL OF GURNEY: Yea, I say unto you, fear Him. I'm no
shadow. I'm flesh and blood. Touch.

CLAIRE (*touching his cheek*): Perhaps I'm not really dead, only
sleeping. Wake me with a kiss.

EARL OF GURNEY (*takes her hand away*): Remember our
common consanguinity.

CLAIRE: Don't be ridiculous. I'm married to your father's
half-brother for my sins. That makes us practically strangers,
bloodwise.

*He attempts to move away. She steps in front of him.*

EARL OF GURNEY (*smiling*): Are you accosting me?

CLAIRE (*playing up*): That's right, ducks. 'Ow's about it?

*They come close in the half-light. She kisses him on the mouth.
The Set begins to change to a nineteenth-century slum street in
Whitechapel. A gauze lowered Up Stage, shows a dark huddle of
filthy houses, broken doors, windows stuffed with paper. Beyond,
an impression of dark alleys, low arches, row upon row of lodging
houses. It is dank and foggy. Stage Left, a single flickering street
lamp. Stage Right a filthy brick wall with the name of the street:
'Buck's Row'. Drunken singing and street cries can be heard off:
'Apple-a-pound-pears, whelks, they're lovely' and the clip-clop of
a horse-drawn van over cobbles.*

*The overall effect is of a furnished room in the middle of a London
street.*

*Moonlight shines through the french-windows as the* EARL *and*
CLAIRE *cross the street to the sofa.*

We'll be alone here. They're all out except Tucker and he's
drunk. Listen . . .

*They listen to a drunk singing in the distance.*

You don't seem surprised this has happened to us, Jack?

EARL OF GURNEY: We were destined to meet.

CLAIRE: That sounds romantic. More please.

EARL OF GURNEY (*low, passionate*): Suuuuuck. GRAHHH. Spinnkk. The flesh lusteth against the spirit, against God. Labia, foreskin, testicles, scrotum.

CLAIRE: *That's* romantic?

EARL OF GURNEY: Orgasm, coitus, copulation, fornication. Gangrened shoulder of sex. If it offends. (*Softly into her ear.*) Tear. Tear. Spill the seed, gut-slime.

CLAIRE: I know some women like being stimulated with dirty words, filthy talk. I don't.
    *She starts taking off his jacket, waistcoat and shirt.*

EARL OF GURNEY: You want maggots crawling through black grass.

CLAIRE: I want to hear you say you love me, even if it isn't true.

EARL OF GURNEY: I've seen three thousand houses collapse exposing their privees to the naked eye. *Oh, run, Mary. RUN.*

CLAIRE: You're talking nonsense again, Jack.

EARL OF GURNEY (*softly*): If thy eye offends thee pluck it out. You'll be nicked down to your bloody membrane, Mary.

CLAIRE: I want to hear how beautiful you think I am.

EARL OF GURNEY: You want two seconds of DRIPPING SIN to fertilize sodomized idiots.

CLAIRE: Say something soft and tender.

EARL OF GURNEY (*tenderly*): You want gullet and rack. Gugged SHAARK.

CLAIRE: Tell me I'm fairer than the evening star. Clad in the beauty of a thousand nights.

EARL OF GURNEY (*now stripped to the waist, she caresses him*): Cut-price lumps of flesh: three and six an hour. Calves paunches, tender tongue, ear-lobes, e-e-ar-lobe-sss, hearts, bladders, teats, nippllezzz.

CLAIRE (*shivering*): Lover.

EARL OF GURNEY: The sword of the Lord is filled with blood.

CLAIRE (*trembling violently*): Stop talking, Jack, and make me immortal with a kiss.

*Putting his left arm around her waist he pulls her close, forcing her head back with a kiss. Taking out his knife, he flicks it open, and plunges it into her stomach. Bucking and writhing with the great knife thrust,* CLAIRE *can only let out a muffled cry as the* EARL'S *mouth is still clamped over hers in a kiss. She writhes, twists and moans under two more powerful stabs. He lets her go.* AHHHRREEEE. I'M ALIVE. ALIVE.

*She falls and dies. The* EARL *stands listening for a second, puts his knife away, picks up his clothes crosses Stage Right and leaves silently by the french-windows. Even as he does so, the Set begins to change back to the drawing-room interior, the gauze and street lamp are taken up as the noises off grow louder. Someone is heard yelling: 'Help! Police!' Sounds of men running. A police whistle blows shrilly, followed by a jumble of panic-stricken cries. These merge into a Newsboy shouting 'Read all about it' 'Orrible Murder. Murder and Mutilation in White-Chapel. Maniac claims another victim. Mary Ann Nichols found murdered in Buck's Row. Read all about it!' The drawing-room set is now completely restored. The hysterical hubbub dies down to a solitary drunk singing incoherently: 'Come Into the Garden Maud'. It grows louder as he comes closer.* TUCKER *enters swaying and singing.*

TUCKER: 'Come into the sh' garden Maudy.' Did you s' ring? (*Blinks, sees* CLAIRE *on the floor.*) S'Lady Claire . . . are you comfortable? Stoned, eh? (*Stumbles over.*) Can I be of . . . aeeeehh.

*He gives a great rasping intake of breath at the sight and stands mumbling in shock. Then he shakes all over. But not from fear.* (*Gleefully.*) One less! One less! Praise the Lord. *Hallelujah.*

*Convulsed with glee he capers creakingly round the corpse in a wierd dance. He freezes in mid-gesture as voices are heard off.* SIR CHARLES, DINSDALE *and* DR HERDER *and* GRACE *come in.*

SIR CHARLES: No lights, Tucker?

DINSDALE *switches on the lights.*

DR HERDER: My God!
*They rush over.* GRACE *puts her hand to her mouth in horror.
Appalled,* DR HERDER *bends to examine the corpse whilst* SIR
CHARLES *stares in disbelief, unable to find words to express
himself. Finally he turns and explodes indignantly at the audience:*
SIR CHARLES: All right, who's the impudent clown responsible
for this?
*Blackout.*

# SCENE SEVEN

*A great church organ plays, and a choir sings the 'Dies Irae'. As the last note of the terrifying hymn dies away, lights up on the drawing-room to show* DETECTIVE INSPECTOR BROCKETT, *a middle-aged man with tired face, feeling his stomach, whilst his assistant,* DETECTIVE SERGEANT FRASER, *checks through some notes. The carpet by the sofa has been pulled back and there is a cardboard outline of Claire's body on the floor.*

FRASER (*reads quickly*): 'Five-inch gash under right ear to centre of throat severing windpipe. Three stab wounds in lower abdomen. Two knife wounds, one veering to right slitting the groin and passing over the lower left hip, and the other straight up along the centre of the body to the breast-bone. Severe bruising round the mouth. The pathologist thinks the murderer must have had some medical knowledge.' Reminds me of the Drayhurst killing, sir.

BROCKETT: Not really. Martha Drayhurst was found all over the place. Arms and legs in Woolwich, trunk in Euston Station, and the rest of her turned up in Penge. Old Sam Drayhurst had a quirky sense of humour for a butcher. At least Lady Claire was all in one piece.

> *Footsteps outside.*

They're back. Bishop Lampton'll be with 'em. How do you address a bishop?

FRASER: Bishop, sir.

BROCKETT: Bishop, Bishop.

> BISHOP LAMPTON *enters supported by* SIR CHARLES *and* DINSDALE. *They have just come from the funeral.*

BISHOP LAMPTON: This house is doomed, Charles. I should

never have allowed my poor sister to marry into this accursed family. It's another House of Usher.

*Carefully avoiding the outline on the floor they half-carry him Down Stage Left and drop him into a chair, gasping.*

SIR CHARLES: Don't talk rubbish, Bertie. Terrible business, but we mustn't lose our heads.

DINSDALE: How could anything like this happen to us? What was mother thinking of?

SIR CHARLES (*urgently*): Not in front of strangers, Dinsdale. Brockett, why aren't you running this animal to earth?

BROCKETT: Don't you worry, sir, we'll get him. But there's still a few points I'd like to clear up. We know the butler found the body just after the killer left by the french-windows. When you came in a moment later, whereabouts was he standing?

SIR CHARLES: Who, Tucker?

*GRACE enters.*

GRACE: The baby's asleep. What are you lot doing?

SIR CHARLES: Brockett, this is her ladyship. He wants to know how we found Tucker beside Claire's body.

GRACE: Oh, here.

*She stands beside the outline, puts her left foot out and raises both her arms.*

Like the Hokey-Cokey.

BROCKETT: Why would he be doing anything like the Hokey-Cokey?

DINSDALE: He was drunk and he had his teeth out.

BROCKETT: I'd better have another word with Tucker. Run a double check on him, Sergeant.

SIR CHARLES: Senile old fool should have been booted out years ago. Not the only one you should re-check. What about my nephew?

GRACE (*deliberately*): You've been through a lot, Charles, but I warn you.

DINSDALE: That's rather disgraceful, Father.

BISHOP LAMPTON: Uncalled for, Jack's behaved splendidly.

SIR CHARLES: I'm not saying he's involved but . . .

GRACE: *But*. I'll give you *but*.

BROCKETT: We have the medical reports on his lordship. But if you have something to add.

GRACE: Charles isn't doing this 'cause of what happened to Claire. He's jealous 'cause I love my husband. Charles and me were lovers! I was this randy old goat's mistress!

BISHOP LAMPTON (*wailing*): Aeeeh. Cleanse your hands, you sinner.

SIR CHARLES: Madam, you'll *never* be a Gurney.

GRACE: I'd rather be dead.

DINSDALE (*stricken*): Mother knew, she knew before she died. Father, I have to say this. You've proved a big disappointment to me.

SIR CHARLES: It's *mutual*, sir.

BROCKETT: Does his lordship know about the relationship, Lady Grace?

GRACE: No, and he's not going to unless somebody blabs. (*Looks round at* BROCKETT.) Anyway, it's none of your business, Copper!

BISHOP LAMPTON: Private matters, sir. A gentleman would have left!

> As the family are suddenly conscious again of the two policemen and start yelling at them, the EARL enters, a commanding figure in black carrying a black silver-top cane.

EARL OF GURNEY: Is this the way to act in the presence of death? (*They stop shouting.*) Remember where you are and what happened here.

> He pauses by the outline on the floor. Embarrassed, the others clear their throats.

BISHOP LAMPTON: Forgive them, they know not what they do.

EARL OF GURNEY: Oh, Dinsdale, you should answer those messages of condolence. Even if you don't feel like it.

SIR CHARLES: Nonsense. Let 'em wait.

DINSDALE (*defiantly*): You're right, Jack. Create a good impression. It'll take my mind off things. Been a bad day for me what with one thing and another.

*He exits Up Stage Centre.* GRACE *moves round beside the* EARL.

BROCKETT: My lord, there are still a few details I'd like to clear up. On the night of the murder you talked with Lady Claire till 11.30. How was she when you left her?

EARL OF GURNEY: Unhappy.

BROCKETT: Why's that?

GRACE (*pointedly*): What with one thing and another, she had plenty of reasons, don't you think.

SIR CHARLES: Dammit, Brockett, what the devil does it matter how my wife was feeling.

BROCKETT (*sighing*): You went straight up to bed and heard nothing.

EARL OF GURNEY: Thought I heard Tucker singing.

BROCKETT: Hmm, but he said he didn't leave the kitchen till 12. Odd. Important question, my lord. Think hard now. Has anything unusual happened here recently; anything out of the ordinary?

*The* EARL *thinks, shakes his head.*

Bishop? Your ladyship?

*They shake their heads.*

Sir Charles?

TUCKER *is heard singing off.* BROCKETT *turns swiftly.*

Get him, Fraser!

FRASER *rushes out Up Stage Centre and reappears dragging* TUCKER *who is dressed in a striped jacket, bow-tie and straw hat; he carries a battered suitcase festooned with foreign labels.*

TUCKER: What's the idea? I got a plane to catch.

BROCKETT: You going somewhere, Tucker?

TUCKER: *Mr* Tucker, *Flatfoot.* Looks like it don't it. It's cockles and champagne for yours truly, gay Paree where all the girls say oui oui.

GRACE: Bit sudden isn't it?

TUCKER: I'm a creature o' impulse, your ladyship. (*Singing melodiously as he shuffles to exit with suitcase.*) 'Goodbye, I wish you all a last . . . g-o-o-d-b-y-e.'

*As he gestures farewell* FRASER *pulls him back into the room.*

BROCKETT: You're not going anywhere, Tucker, me lad. I've got questions I want answering.

TUCKER: I told you all I know.

BROCKETT: Have you? . . . Daniel Tucker alias Alexei Kronstadt Communist Party Member Number 243!

SIR CHARLES: Murdering swine!

TUCKER *gives a frightened cry and rushes for the exit Up Stage Centre, but the* EARL OF GURNEY *bars the way.*

TUCKER: Let me pass, let me pass!

*As* FRASER *pulls* TUCKER *back amid excited shouts,* DINSDALE *hurries in.*

DINSDALE: What's going on?

GRACE: They say old Jeeves is a Bolshie.

EARL OF GURNEY: T-U-C-K-E-R. Are you a low-life leveller? An East End agitator?

TUCKER: How can I be an agitator. I've got a weak chest. (*Suddenly defiant.*) What if I am? You don't know what it's like being a servant, picking up the droppings of these Titled Turds. Everybody has to have secrets. What's it to you how I spend my leisure time, Flatfoot?

BROCKETT: You're a suspect in a murder case. You concealed certain facts about yourself. What else are you hiding, Tucker?

TUCKER (*agitated*): Suspect? Suspect? I don't *do* anything. I just pays me dues to the Party and they send me pamphlets, under plain covers. And every year I get a Christmas card from Mr Palme Dutt.

BROCKETT (*sticks out leg and raises arms*): Why were you standing like this beside the body? EH? EH? You told me you discovered her dead just before the others came back. But his lordship swears he heard you down here in this room, a *half-hour* earlier.

TUCKER (*frightened*): You got it wrong, my lord. I wasn't here. This is ol' Tuck, your lordship. (*Jigs up and down.*) All talk, no action. (*Sobbing.*) I couldn't do a crime even if I wanted. Not the type.

*As he takes out a handkerchief to wipe his eyes, a half-dozen silver spoons fall out of his pocket with a clatter.*

GRACE: Jeeves!

SIR CHARLES: You brainwashed thug!

BROCKETT *puts the silverware on to a chair and gestures impatiently for* TUCKER *to disgorge.*

TUCKER: Hope there's no misunderstanding. Just a few little keepsakes. (*Brings out a handful of knives and forks from a bulging pocket.*) Mementoes of my 107 happy years with the Gurney family. (*Produces complete silver cruet set.*) I took 'em for their sentimental value. They call me Mr Softee. (*Produces jewel-encrusted snuff box.*) A few worthless trinkets to help keep the memory green when I'm swanning on the Cote de Jour. (*Finally adds gold bowl from the back of his trousers.*)

BROCKETT: You forgotten something?

TUCKER: No, that's the lot. Oh, goodness me . . . (*Removes hat with feigned surprise and takes out a small silver dinner-plate hidden in the crown.*) Tell you what, your lordship, I'll keep these instead of the two weeks money you owe me in lieu of notice.

DINSDALE: I say, look here, Inspector.

*He and* FRASER *have opened* TUCKER'S *suitcase. All the others move over except the* EARL.

BROCKETT (*bringing out books*): Lenin's 'Complete Revolutionary'. Mao Tse-Tung's 'Selected Writings'.

FRASER (*discovering pile of photographs*): Look at these, sir.

BROCKETT (*looks at them slowly*): Dis-gus-ting . . .

*Shocked gasp from* SIR CHARLES *and* DINSDALE *as they*

*glance over his shoulder.* GRACE *takes a photograph and turns it round and round.*

GRACE: How the devil did she get into that position.

BROCKETT: We'll keep this as evidence.

TUCKER *staggers over to the* EARL *who stands dark, implacable.*

TUCKER: Your lordship, say something fer me. You're the only one who can help. You always was my favourite, Master Jack. You always was my favourite. (*Sobbing.*) Before he died the old Earl, s'bless him, said look after that feeble-minded idiot Master Jack fer me, Tuck. I could have gone but I stayed.

EARL OF GURNEY: If thy hand offends thee, cut it off. Tuck, Tuck, you rot the air with your sexual filth. And there's an innocent baby upstairs. It was you, spawned out of envy, hate, revenge. *You* killed her. *Oh, Dan, Dan, you dirty old man.* (*Lifts* TUCKER *up bodily by his armpits and drops him in front of* BROCKETT.) Take him away, Inspector.

BROCKETT: Daniel Tucker, I must ask you . . .

TUCKER (*at the* EARL): Judas Jack Iscariot! You've sold me down the sewer, hard-hearted, stony-hearted, like the rest. And I knows s'why. You did it. You and Sir Charles, standing there like a pickled walrus. You Gurneys don't draw the line at murder. (*Suddenly exploding with rage and fear.*) Upper-class excrement, you wanna' do me dirt 'cause I know too much. I know one percent of the population owns half the property in England. That vomity 'one per cent' needs kosher killing, hung up so the blue blood drains out slow and easy. Aristocratic carcasses hung up like kosher beef *drip-drip-drip.*

FRASER *grabs him as he lurches forward. The* EARL *whispers to* DINSDALE *who helps* FRASER *pick* TUCKER *up. As they carry him out, stiff and horizontal Up Stage he starts bawling:*

TUCKER: 'Then comrades come rally. And the last fight let us face. The International Army, Unites the human race.' (*Passing* GRACE *he tips his hat.*) 'I'm only a strolling vagabond, so good night, pretty maiden, *good night.*'

GRACE: What an exit.

BROCKETT: Sorry you heard all that, your ladyship, but I had to let him rave on. The more they talk, the more they convict themselves.

GRACE: At least, Inspector, this destroys any doubts anyone might have had about Jack.

BROCKETT: Of course, my lady.

SIR CHARLES: Good work, Inspector. Let me show you out.

BROCKETT (*to the* EARL): My lord, I'd just like to say what a pleasure it's been meeting you. It couldn't 'ave been easy. But you realized I was only doing my job. You've shown me what 'noblesse oblige' really means.

*He gives a slight bow and exits, with* SIR CHARLES

BISHOP LAMPTON (*looking down at the outline*): She was beautiful as Tirzah, comely as Jerusalem, the darling of her mother, flawless to her that loved her. Dead now. Gone, down, down, down, down.

EARL OF GURNEY: Up, up, up, up, she flies. Her soul flies up. Surely you believe she's gone to another place to enjoy even greater privileges than she had on earth?

BISHOP LAMPTON: I have to. I'm a bishop. Forgive an old man's wavering. I remember her fondly, such a terrible death.

EARL OF GURNEY: Lean on me. Trust God's judgment.

BISHOP LAMPTON: You make an old man ashamed. You've become a great source of strength to me, Jack. (*Grasps his arm.*) I won't forget what you've done, Jack. You were the instrument that restored my faith. I feel reborn. I've found the way. Now let me walk humbly with my God.

*The* EARL *walks with him Up Stage, then hands him to* GRACE *and the two exit.*

# SCENE EIGHT

*The* EARL *takes out a pair of binoculars from the desk as cries are heard off.*

TUCKER'S VOICE (*hysterical*): I done nothing! I want justice!

BROCKETT'S VOICE: Justice is what you're going to get, Tucker. If he gives you any trouble, Fraser, break his arm. Now, MARCH!

TUCKER'S VOICE: I'm another Dreyfus case!

*The* EARL *leans on his cane and looks out of the french-windows through the binoculars.*

EARL OF GURNEY: Left-right, left-right, left-right, left-right, left-right.

DR HERDER, *tired and sick, enters with the aid of a walking stick. He stares at the* EARL, *crosses, and stops beside Claire's outline on the floor.*

DR HERDER: Mir ist es winterlich im Leibe. She was cut up like meat.

EARL OF GURNEY: Left-right, left-right, left-right.

DR HERDER (*looks across at* EARL): It's not possible. I cured you. You could never turn violent. It's not in your illness. If I'd failed I'd know it. You'd retreat back into delusion. You haven't. You've accepted the world on its own terms. You believe more or less what other people believe.

EARL OF GURNEY (*turns, raising cane in salute*): En guarde. Your job's done, Herr Doktor. I'm adjusted to my environment. I brush my teeth twice daily. And smile. You trepanned me, opened my brain, telephoned the truth direct into my skull, as it were.

DR HERDER: Let me be the judge of that.

EARL OF GURNEY: There's only one Judge here. (*Looks at him through the wrong end of the binoculars.*) You've shrunk to a teutonic midget.

DR HERDER: You call that being adjusted?

EARL OF GURNEY: Behaviour which would be considered insanity in a tradesman is looked on as mild eccentricity in a lord. I'm allowed a certain lat-i-tude. (*He lunges at* DR HERDER.)

DR HERDER (*involuntarily parrying stroke with his stick*): I want to know about Claire.

EARL OF GURNEY: An irreversible rearrangement of her structural molecules has taken place, Doctor. She's dead. One of the facts of life.

DR HERDER: I know that.

EARL OF GURNEY: She lies stinking. Algo mortis, rigor mortis, livor mortis. She's turning to slime, Doctor. She's puss, Doctor, stinking puss, Doctor!

DR HERDER: I don't wish to know that!

EARL OF GURNEY: Then kindly leave the stage. (*Lunges.*) These are scientific facts.

DR HERDER (*parrying*): You killed her.

EARL OF GURNEY: A touch.

DR HERDER: You killed heeeeeeeeer.

*He leaps at the* EARL, *flailing wildly with his stick.*

EARL OF GURNEY (*parrying the stroke*): Ha, a swordsman worthy of me steel. Didn't we meet at Heidelberg?

DR HERDER: You killed her!

EARL OF GURNEY (*driving him back*): You were fornicating lovers. Sperm dancers.

DR HERDER: It's a lie. Lady Claire meant nothing to me.

EARL OF GURNEY: Cock-a-doodle-do!

DR HERDER (*lashes out*): *You* killed her.

EARL OF GURNEY (*beating off the attack*): I'm cured, Herr Doktor, M.D., Ph.D. You cured me. I was a pale lovesick straw-in-the-air moon-looney. You changed me into a murderer, is that what you're saying?

DR HERDER (*attacking wildly*): Yes. No. Yes. May God forgive me.

EARL OF GURNEY: *Never.* What proof have you?

DR HERDER: I don't need proof, I *know.*

EARL OF GURNEY (*parrying with contemptuous ease*): Physician heal thyself. Don't you recognize the symptoms? You suddenly *know* against all the evidence. You don't need proof from anybody or anything. This monstrous belief of yours that I'm guilty is a clear case of paranoia. I've heard of 'transference', Doctor, but this is ridiculous! . . . If they ask about me at the trial, tell them the truth.

DR HERDER: What truth?

EARL OF GURNEY: That I'm a hundred per cent normal. (*He lunges and hits* DR HERDER, *who sits with a bump.*) Touché, Herr Doktor.

*Clicking his heels, he salutes with his cane and crosses Up Stage Right.* DR HERDER *remains on the floor. The lights dim slightly as he punches the ground in frustration.*

DR HERDER: He's right. He is normal. It's only a feeling. (*Shudders.*) I can't rely on feelings. Everything he's done confirms to a classic recovery pattern. His occasional paralalia is normal. Even his trying to blackmail me into saying he's completely normal, is normal. Natural I should have doubts. This is pioneer work. Claire's death, one of those terrible ironies—nothing to do with the case. Unpleasant as he is, the good lord's himself again . . . My head's splitting. I've had an abdomen full of the upper classes. Claire, Claire, I should have specialized in heart diseases. (*Suddenly trembling with rage.*) *Cock-a-doodle-do.* Scheisshund! He made me deny you. (*He picks up and clasps cardboard outline tenderly.*) *Cock-a-doodle-do. Cock-a-doodle-do. Cock-a-doodle-do.*

*He exits crowing with the cardboard outline.*

# SCENE NINE

SIR CHARLES *and* GRACE *enter Up Stage Centre.*

SIR CHARLES: *There.* It's what I've always said. You simply can't give the working-class money.

GRACE (*to the* EARL): It must have been a terrible shock for you, Sweet. Someone like Jeeves—someone you've known all your life turning out to be a killer. I was proud of you.

SIR CHARLES: Yes, Jack, this time you behaved like a Gurney should.

GRACE: You might apologize for all the stinking things you've said about him.

SIR CHARLES: Jack understands. I did what I had to.

EARL OF GURNEY: I won't forget what you did, Charles. (*Arm round* GRACE'S *shoulder.*) Or you, my dear.

GRACE (*eagerly*): Jack, let's take off. It's been hell here. We need a holiday.

EARL OF GURNEY: No. Here I stand. Now our little local difficulty has been solved I must show myself. It'll be the perfect story-book ending.

    DINSDALE *enters carrying the* EARL'S *Parliamentary robes.*
I'm taking my seat in the House of Lords.

SIR CHARLES: What . . .?

GRACE (*disturbed*): What, now? So soon after your illness? I mean, are you ready for them?

EARL OF GURNEY: Are *they* ready for me, madam?

DINSDALE: We're going to work as a team once I get elected. Jack in the Lords, me in the 'other place'. We think alike on lots of things.

    DINSDALE *helps the* EARL *on with his Parliamentary robes.*

SIR CHARLES: It's asking for trouble. What happens if you have a relapse? Fine spectacle you'd make, gibbering in the Upper House.

GRACE: You're so bloody tactful, Charles. (*Helps* DINSDALE.) If Jack thinks he's ready, then he's ready and I'm with him all the way.

SIR CHARLES: It's out of the question.

EARL OF GURNEY: Who asked you a question, pray? Did anybody here ask him a question?
*They shake their heads.*
Nobody asked a question so I'll ask a question. Who's the legit head of the family Gurney-cum-Gurney?

SIR CHARLES: You are, Jack, but . . .

EARL OF GURNEY: Don't let me hear you answering unasked questions again.

DINSDALE: Don't make a complete ass of yourself, Father.

GRACE: From now on just keep quiet, Charles.

EARL OF GURNEY: Your days of hard manipulating are over. Your brain's silting, Charles!

SIR CHARLES (*starts to grow old, his limbs shake slightly*): Don't talk to me like that! After all I've done. (*Voice quavers.*) Where'd you be without me? No wife, no Gurney heir without me—answer me, Sir! (*Passes hands over hair and moustache: they turn white.*) I'm giving you the benefit of my experience, years of . . .
DINSDALE *sniggers.*

SIR CHARLES (*petulantly*): What are you sniggering at, you young pup?

DINSDALE: I wasn't sniggering.

SIR CHARLES: You were sniggering too. I know sniggering when I hear it, I'm not deaf. You've got nothing to snigger about. It'll happen to you one day. You'll be standing there and then suddenly nobody's taking any notice. You start coughing and coughing. Skin goes dry and the veins show through. Everything turns watery. It dribbles away, bowels, eyes, ears, nose . . . hmm. The hard thing is you're still twenty-one inside, but outside your feet go *flop, flop, flop, flop,* nothing you can do, *flop, flop, flop* . . .

*The* EARL *points to* SIR CHARLES. DINSDALE *nods and leads him firmly Up Stage.*

DINSDALE: That's enough, Father. You've had a long innings. It's beddy-byes and milk-rusks for you now.

GRACE (*carefully adjusting the* EARL'S *robe*): He's getting tiresome, but I feel obligated. He did introduce us, Honey. Luckily Dinsdale can handle him. That boy's come on. He worships you, you know.

EARL OF GURNEY: Splendid fella', Dinsdale.

GRACE: Guess we've all changed. You're more than just cured, Jack. People look up to you now. You've got something extra. What we used to call star quality!

EARL OF GURNEY: Ek, ek, ek, ek. It's going to be a triumphant climax.

GRACE: Talking about climaxes, we must get together again. We were more loving when you were batty. (*Closer to him.*) Now it should be even better. Do you love me, Jack?

EARL OF GURNEY: Y'know, in Roman times it was always the women who turned down their thumbs when defeated gladiators asked for mercy, Annie.

GRACE (*laughing*): Annie? Why Annie?

EARL OF GURNEY: Mary, Annie, Elizabeth, Catherine, Marie Kelly—a name by any other name would smell as sweet.

GRACE (*anxiously*): Jack, you're not going off again?

EARL OF GURNEY: It's nothing m'dear. Don't forget I've a big day ahead of me. I'm speaking in the House of Lords.

GRACE (*relieved*): Oh, you've got first-night nerves. Don't worry, you'll kill 'em.

EARL OF GURNEY: In time. Perhaps.

GRACE: I know it. Then you'll get around to me, I hope. Promise?

*The* EARL *nods, smiling.*

Jack, Jack, you're so attractive when you smile like that. (*Kisses him.*) Jack, Jack . . .

EARL OF GURNEY: Must get my grunch thoughts in order, marshal my facts, prepare my argument, pro and contra.

GRACE: You don't have to worry. After all, you're one of 'em, only more so. Be your own sweet self and they'll adore you as I adore you, Jack. (*Kissing him again and moving Up Stage.*) I just love happy endings.

  *The lights dim. The 'Pomp and Circumstance March' is played softly over.*

# SCENE TEN

*The image of the* EARL *in his Parliamentary robes Down Stage Centre is menacing as he hunches his shoulder and drags his leg.*

EARL OF GURNEY (*softly*): Tash t'ur tshh t'aigh, s'ssssh kkk? Freee 'eee u Me Me Me epeeeeee . . . tita a-a-a grahhh scrk Khraht! (*Sounds now coming from back of throat, rising intensely.*) Grak GRACK. Graaa gruuuuuuaaKK ka-ka-ka-ka-ka. YU. OOOO. YU. (*Arm jerks out convulsively at audience, his leg twists under him.*) YU. Screee. Fuuuuuth, CRUUUKK-aa-K. (*Grinds heel into ground, face contorted with rage.*) HRRRUUUR TRUGHUUUK. (*As if bringing up phlegm, the cries now come from the pit of the stomach.*) Ha-CH-U-UR-UR. URRR. GoooooaRCH. TROKK! EK-K-Y. Arri-Bra-K-Yi-Skiiii, Arrk-ar-rk ARR ARR K-K-K-K, YIT YIT TRUGHUUGH ARK KKKK A-A-A-A-A-A-KRUTK! aaaaaaaaaaaaAAA-ARRRRRR!

# SCENE ELEVEN

*Even as the scream dies away a backcloth with a blow-up photograph of Westminster captioned 'House of Lords' is lowered, Stage Centre. On either side of it massive purple drapes. The 'Pomp and Circumstance March' is loud now as two tiers of mouldering dummies dressed as Lords and covered with cobwebs are pushed on either side, Stage Right and Left. Smothered in age-old dust, three goitred* LORDS *with bloated stomachs and skull-like faces crawl on stage groaning, to take their places beside the dummies and the* EARL OF GURNEY. *One of them drags a skeleton behind him. The music stops as the* FIRST LORD *hauls himself as upright as his twisted body allows.*

1ST LORD (*croaking*): My Lords, I wish to draw attention to the grave disquiet felt throughout the country at the increase in immorality.

2ND LORD (*wheezing*): I must support the noble Lord. For thirteen years there has been no flogging, and there has been a steadily rising volume of crime, lawlessness and thuggery. I believe the cissy treatment of young thugs and hooligans is utterly wrong.

3RD LORD: My Lord, we must step up the penalties by making hanging and flogging the punishments for certain State crimes. In order to protect the public the criminal must be treated as an animal.

> *The* EARL OF GURNEY *jerks up. All eyes on him.* DINSDALE *and* SIR CHARLES *hobbling on two walking sticks, enter Wings Left.*

EARL OF GURNEY: My Lords, I had doubts about speaking here but after what I've heard, I realize this is where I belong. My Lords, these are grave times, killing times.

Stars collapse, universes shrink daily, but the natural order is still crime—guilt—punishment. Without pause. There is no love without fear. By His hand, sword, pike and grappling-hook, God, the Crowbar of the World, flays, stabs, bludgeons, mutilates. Just as I was—is—have been—flayed, bludgeoned . . . (*Recovering.*) You've forgotten how to punish, my noble Lords. The strong MUST manipulate the weak. That's the first law of the Universe—was and ever shall be world without end. The weak would hand this planet back to the crabs and primeval slime. The Hard survive, the Soft quickly turn to corruption. (*Shuddering.*) *God the Son* wants nothing only to give freely in love and gentleness. It's loathsome, a foul perversion of life! And must be rooted out. *God the Father* demands, orders, controls, crushes. We must follow Him, my noble Lords. This is a call to greatness . . . On, on you noblest English.
I see you stand like greyhounds in the slips
Straining upon the start. The game's afoot
Follow your spirit; and upon this charge
Cry, God for Jack, England and Saint George.
    *A pause, then all burst into spontaneous shouts of 'hear-hear', 'bravo', as the excited* PEERS, *waving order-papers, stumble over to congratulate the* EARL.

DINSDALE: Bravo! Bravo! You see, Father, you see. He's capable of anything!

SIR CHARLES (*waving stick excitedly*): *He's one of us at last!*
    *They all exit except the* EARL, *singing exultantly.*

ALL (*singing*): 'Let us now praise famous men
                And our fathers that begat us.
                Such as did there rule in their kingdoms
                Men renowned for their power.'

# EPILOGUE

*The* EARL *is alone amongst the dummies. The chorus fades down with the lights.* GRACE *enters Up Stage Centre singing, in a black night-dress.*

GRACE (*singing*): 'Along came Jack, not my type at all . . .
You'd meet him on the street and never notice him . . .
But his form and face, his manly grace. Makes me—*thrill* . . .
I love him . . .'
   *He stands smiling as she circles him sensually.*
'I love him, because he's . . . wond-er-ful . . .'
   *She yields as he pulls her close.*
'Because he's just my Jack.'
   *Faint street-cries are heard over and they kiss passionately. As the* EARL *envelops her in his Parliamentary robes, his hand reaches for his pocket. The lights fade down slowly, then, out of the darkness, a single scream of fear and agony.*

CURTAIN

# Leonardo's Last Supper

*With an Introduction by the Author*

## THE CHARACTERS

LASCA
MARIA
ALPHONSO
LEONARDO

## THE SCENE

AMBOIS CHARNEL HOUSE
2 MAY 1519

# Introduction
## by the Author

And so the aim is to create, by means of soliloquy, rhetoric, formalized ritual, slapstick, songs and dances, a comic theatre of contrasting moods and opposites, where everything is simultaneously tragic and ridiculous.

Every play is a problem of language. With *Leonardo's Last Supper* and *Noonday Demons* one had to find, in each case, a live theatrical language which had the feel of a historical period (Renaissance and AD 395), yet could be understood by a contemporary audience. This artificial vernacular had to have historical weight yet be flexible enough to incorporate modern songs and jokes. For such deliberate anachronisms can only work fully if they spring out of an acceptable period texture. So I pillaged; everything, from Elizabeth argot to the Bible.

I can vouch for the authenticity of the facts in these plays – except the biggest. Mother Midnight could have been found guilty of witchcraft the moment she swore she was not a witch; the goldsmiths did beat out gold along the Canto di Vacchereccia; the Chancellor of Hungary did have a billygoat tied to his sickbed to absorb the plague; the desert saints did live on black olives, dry bread and muddy water, practised elevation and 'even' elongation and watered dry sticks in the desert. And, yes, according to the records, the smell from privies was supposed to be a protection from the plague.

The more bizarre the fact, the more certain one can be that it happened, sometime, somewhere, to someone.

Nothing a writer can imagine is as surrealistic as the reality. Everything has happened. The difficulty is finding the record of it.

Of course, historical truth is no guarantee of dramatic truth.

But it makes for a certain confidence between author and audience; a reassuring feeling of firm ground under the feet.

A word about the playing of these pieces. The meaning is in the lines, not between them. Absolute precision is essential; the words must be hit dead-centre. No 'fluting', with the actor enjoying the sound of the words rather than their meaning.

Precision and speed. Not necessarily in the delivery of the dialogue, but speed of thought and reaction. There are no rest periods, no place where the actor can coast.

*Noonday Demons* is particularly demanding in this respect but I was lucky in my interpreters. As St Pior, Mr David Neal, an incisively intelligent actor, had already appeared in a previous play of mine and knew the required Barnesonian style, whilst Mr Joe Melia, as St Eusebius, had a natural rapier astringency.

It was interesting to compare Mr Melia's acting technique with that of Mr Derek Godfrey – the 13th Earl of Gurney in *The Ruling Class*. Both performed with absolute fidelity to the play. Mr Melia, however, possessed the text and made it his own. Mr Godfrey allowed the text to possess him and let it make him its own. The difference between the romantic and classical approach. In both cases, the result was memorable.

Leonardo's Last Supper
and
Noonday Demons
are
dedicated to Joe and Davie

*Leonardo's Last Supper* was first presented at The Open Space Theatre on 25 November 1969. The play was presented in association with Gene Persson with the following cast:

| | |
|---|---|
| LASCA | *Joe Melia* |
| MARIA | *Irlin Hall* |
| ALPHONSO | *Nikolas Simmonds* |
| LEONARDO | *Anthony Jacobs* |

*Directed by Charles Marowitz*
*Designed by John Napier*

# LEONARDO'S LAST SUPPER

*Spot up on an enlarged reproduction hanging from the Flies, Up
Stage Centre, of the famous drawing, the* Divine Proportion,
*from the Vitruvius Edition of 1535, showing a naked man, arms
and legs spread out, the centre of a square and circle.*
*An authoritative voice lectures from several loudspeakers in the audi-
torium.*

LECTURER: The Renaissance began in Italy in the Fourteenth
Century and spread over Western Europe. In an extraordinary
burst of intellectual energy the human spirit recovered its
freedom after centuries of political and spiritual oppression.
Sparked by classical art and literature, printing was invented,
new continents discovered, the Ptolemaic world system gave
way to the Copernican and a radiant beauty was created by
artists delighting in the loveliness of the human body. The
Gothic night dissolved, making way for the birth of modern
man and the achievements of our age . . . Renaissance – a
noun, meaning, a new birth: revival: resurrection.
  *A funeral bell tolls. Bass voices are heard chanting the 'Miserere'
out of the darkness. A cortege of four* CANTORS *enters Up Stage
Left carrying a bier on their shoulders, containing a corpse under
a sheet. They are cowled and wear monks' habits. Each has a lighted
unbleached candle. Walking behind them is* ANGELO LASCA.
CANTORS (*chanting*): 'Miserére mei, Deus secúndum, misericór-
diam tuam; secúndum multitúdinem miseratiónum tuárum
dele inquitátem meam. Pénitus lava me a culpa mea, et a
peccáto meo munda me . . .'
  *The bier is laid on a low dias Stage Centre and the candles are
placed at each corner.* LASCA *stands, head bowed, whilst the*

CANTORS *exit into the darkness Up Stage. As the bell stops tolling,*
LASCA *looks up and lets out a yell of joy.*

LASCA: Aaaaaayyippp. 'Hey troly, loly loly. Sing troly, loly
loly lo. Sing troly, loly loly lo.'

*As he dances around the corpse, light half-up to show a medieval
Charnel House. Down Stage Left, wooden stools, a table with
mugs, bread, wine and a skull with a candle stuck on it. On the
wall, Stage Left, various iron instruments: saws, knives, screws.
On the floor a battered trunk. A large iron bucket Stage Right.*

*The walls are dank and the floor scattered with human bones.*

*The flickering candlelight casts elongated shadows as* LASCA
*dances. He is a heavy, middle-aged man wearing an ankle-length
woollen over-garment with wide sleeves and edged with moulting
rabbit fur. He stops abruptly when his wife,* MARIA, *a motherly
woman in a square-cut dress and plain bodice, hurries in. Her hair
is scraped back and a rosary hangs from a narrow cordbelt round her
waist.*

MARIA: Angelo. Is it true?

LASCA: A gift from the Lord hisself. (*Pointing proudly to the
corpse.*) Louis XIV's pageant maker, Engineer in Ordinary to
Louis XII, friend of Ludovico Sforza, Giuliano de Medici,
Cesare Borgia, Cardinal of Valencia, and His Most Christian
Majesty Francis I – prince o' artists, artist to princes, Signor
Leonardo da Vinci! *And by the blood of our Lord, Jesus Christ,
we're going to bury him.*

MARIA: *Aiee! Aiee! (Falls on knees.)* Oh Lord we thank thee for
thy great mercy.

LASCA *(on knees)*: We bless thy goodness, Oh Lord. Those
gotch-gutted curs drove me out o' Florence. Ten years in
this French wilderness; ten years o' eating snails and garlic –
they rot the gut and maketh the breath stink. *Trash, trash.*
But Christ my Saviour, remembered his humble servant at
the last, and sent down this golden carcass for his profit. Now,
now, by the grace o' our Redeemer I can go back. *Old debts,
Madame, old scores honoured Sir!* Oh sweet Jesus, I'll make 'em

grovel like pigs in dung! Oh Holy Virgin Mother, I'll make 'em tremble till their breeches stink from their droppings! Oh Lord o' Mercy, I'll make 'em lick pomegranate seeds out o' me arse!

*They rise.*

LASCA *(singing exultantly)*: 'Oh Lord,
You delivered David from the slaughtering sword
                    Oh Lord,
You delivered Daniel from the lions' den
                    And then.'

LASCA AND MARIA *(jazzily)*: 'The Israelite children
From the Fiery Furnace and the Pharaoh's cruel decree
                    Now me.'

LASCA: 'You delivered me.'

MARIA: 'And me, you delivered me.'

*Laughing,* LASCA *turns his back to* MARIA; *she puts her hands on his shoulders and they jig along Down Stage singing jauntily.*

LASCA AND MARIA: 'And thus,
You delivered us. Yes, you delivered us!'

*Whilst* MARIA *pours wine,* LASCA *takes off his overgarment. Underneath he has on dark hosen and a black leather jerkin buttoned to the neck.*

MARIA: I thought you had a touch o' the French sickness this morning. First you're lying in bed with your bony gambs in my back, then, *jangg*, you're sitting up shaking with the ague.

LASCA: I'd seen him in me sleep, Mother. Smelt him too. The stench o' a thousand second-hand privies. 'Twas Death hisself, Mother. Scurvy, stinkin' Death. He was dancing and tapping out a tune on his bare rib-bones.

MARIA: What was he playing?

LASCA: The 'Dies Irae'. *Dum dum de dum. (He hums the funeral dirge, and mimes tapping his ribs.)* Always been one o' my favourites. A toast. Here's to Old Mortality then, our sure and certain provider. The Lord protect us.

MARIA: Amen. *(They drink.)* A miracle seeing him like that.

LASCA: Comes o' years o' experience. Death's my business. I hear the sparrow's fall, *plop*, and the flea's last itchy gasp, *haaa*. This was a mighty crash so I guessed it was Signor da Vinci who'd fallen. In nomine Patris *(Makes Sign of the Cross)* et Filii *(Makes sign again)* et Spiritus *(Makes sign again)* sancti. The women were weeping when I got to Cloux. So I knew I was in luck, da Vinci was dead. And who more fit to bury him than a fellow Florentine?

MARIA: Heaven smileth on us again. Thanks to me.

LASCA: What've you been doing to make heaven smile?

MARIA: Following the ways o' our Lord. By your actions shall thee be judged. Remember Mother Midnight? They could've found her guilty of witchcraft the moment she swore she wasn't a witch. But I saw Father Fulchin was troubled. When he asked me to do my Christian duty I spoke straight out. Didn't I stand up and say loud and clear that Mother Midnight had practised the Black Mass, spawned incubes and kissed Lucifer's arse every night? And didn't she confess it all under torture? I sent that Devil's Bride to Hell. You stood by and did nothing.

LASCA: Nothing? Your testimony may've had Mother Midnight burnt at the stake but you're forgetting I lit the faggots!

MARIA: That don't signify. It came easy.

LASCA: It came hard, Madame. I don't hold with burning. Stretching, chopping, breaking on the wheel, but not burning. A healthy corpse gives a living to a host o' carrion trades, but there's no profit in ashes. I followed my Christian conscience when I put the torch to Mother Midnight.

MARIA: Such deeds are remembered in heaven, Angelo.

LASCA: Down here too which is 'ow I like it. *(Chuckles.)* Signor Melzi left all the funeral arrangements to me.

MARIA: Melzi? That Signor da Vinci's bumboy?

LASCA: Ex-bumboy and heir, please. Sharp as a giggler's arse normal times but grief's blunted his wits.

MARIA: Grief's a luxury. How much he paying to indulge?

LASCA *(takes out leather pouch and jangles it)*: Fifty gold florins now, more later. It's to be a fair expensive resting. Three grand masses at St Florentine's, thirty low masses at St Gregory's and at St Denis's. And for the funeral proper, sixty wax tapers to be carried by poor men of the parish. *(Throws money on to table.)* Signor da Vinci thought big, even in death.

> MARIA *tests the gold coins by biting them.*

No need f' that. First thing I did.

MARIA: I know, but I'm particular partial to the taste.

LASCA: I fancy a bite too.

MARIA: Gold always makes you lechy. Stop playing with y' burnt-out bawbell, there's work to do.

LASCA *(grabbing her)*: A down cock-alley.

MARIA: Angelo! You've got the French clap and no cundum.

LASCA: Bumbo, bumbo, hot-tailed bumbo. Now, now!

> They fall and roll on the floor.

Biddy chick, biddy biddy chick, coo cooo oooh! *(He lets out a cry of pain.)* Judas Iscariot! *(He pulls out a large bone he has just rolled on top of.)* Great St Damian and St Cosmas, it's Signor Corbi's thigh-bone. I've been looking for that since we sliced and boiled him last winter. The rest o' his bones should've reached his family in Milan by now. No thanks or profit in sending it separately, I suppose. To complete the set. *(Tosses bone aside and dives back on to MARIA.)* Just a taste o' giblet-joining, clickety-click.

MARIA *(struggling)*: Go to a Pushing School, you're too hot and lickerish f' me! I'll not be made peppered and pregnant again . . . Down, down, we're in sin. Stark sin and lechery. Oh Holy Father . . . Oh Glorious Virgin . . . we're in sin and the last time we bumboed you promised me a topaz pendant with matching . . .

LASCA: It's yours.

MARIA *(softly)*: No, Angelo, not till dark. *(Giggling.)* Angelo, Angeloooo-*aaaaahh!*

*She ends on a terrified scream.* LASCA *looks up to see that the skeleton figure of Death has come out of the darkness Up Stage and is standing menacingly over them. Shaking with fright they scramble to their knees,* MARIA *gurgling,* LASCA *pulling up his breeches whilst making the Sign of the Cross.*

LASCA: Ergo malidicte diábole I adjure thee Lucifer in the name of the living God, go!

*Death breaks wind;* LASCA *and* MARIA *scream in terror.*

*Uhhhh,* the stench 'tis *him,* stinkin' Death. He's come f' us. I can't die like this with my breeches down and my bawbell up. Dragged to hellfire 'cause o' you! *(He hits* MARIA *who lies moaning.)* Damned to everlasting pain through her everlasting lust. She wants to pull me under every bawdy bush in sight. Lechery, lechery, it's all you know! *(He hits her again.)* I repent, sweet Jesus. I repent. I'll wear a hair-shirt every night caked with me own blood. Spare me.

*Death breaks wind and holds out his hand.*

*No,* not me! Take her! Take her!

MARIA: Him him him him him. Take him. Master Death! Sweet Master D, take him!

LASCA: Tomorrow-tomorrow.    Tomorrow-tomorrow-to-morrow.   Come   tomorrow.   Only   tomorrow.   We'll be ready tomorrow. Take us tomorrow tomorrow, not today.

*Death remorselessly breaks wind:* LASCA *clutches his throat.*

My God, my God, let me breathe.

*Death breaks wind again, forcing* LASCA *to cower lower.*

Oh ugly stinkin' Death.

*Death breaks wind once more;* LASCA *falls lower.*

I'll burn my cundum!

*A last great breaking of wind;* LASCA *falls flat.*

Ahh, *Lucifer!*

*Death shakes with glee and whips off his skull-mask.*

ALPHONSO: 'Taint Lucifer, Dad. It's me, Alphonso.

LASCA *and* MARIA *look up to see their pimply, moon-faced son laughing at them.*

Put the fear o' death an' taxes into you that time, eh? Loosened y' bowels, eh? 'It's *him* stinkin' Death. *Ahh* . . .' Thought you and Death were such close friends. 'Oh spare me. Oh spare me.' *(Moves to table.)* Wish y' could've seen as how you looked. Better sport than burning heretics. 'I repent, I repent . . .' *(Sits on a stool and starts groaning.)* I'm pissful. Must've drunk a barrel o' Marmsey.

LASCA, *who has risen slowly to his feet, finally explodes, hurling a fusillade of skulls at* ALPHONSO.

LASCA: Sottish buckfaced lobcock! I'll bastinado you!

*As* ALPHONSO *scrambles away* MARIA *gets to her feet, using the thigh-bone as a stick.*

MARIA: Stay, Angelo, stay.

LASCA: I'll rechristen that boy in his own blood. Hasn't the good Lord punished us enough? Seven children gone to Abraham. Piero and Francisco dribbled away with the Sweating Sickness, Antonia with the Bloody Flux, Giulio stabbed, Fillipo shot, Giovanni hanged by mistake, from the windows of the Signoria Anderea eaten in Paris by wolves. And then the final blow. *(He looks at* ALPHONSO.*)* You survived! *Oh Lord, Lord, why persecutest Thou me?*

*He slumps on to a stool.*

ALPHONSO: 'Twas only sport. I feel plaguee sick.

MARIA: Poor Alphonso. *(She hits him on the head with the thigh-bone.)* Shag-bag. Don't do it again.

LASCA: Harder, make him bleed.

MARIA *(turning)*: Judas pimp! Forcing me into the arms o' Death! 'Take her, take her, take her!'

LASCA: 'Take him. Master Death, take him, Master D.' You were panting hard for me to be dragged off. I'll remember that, Madame, I'll remember that.

MARIA: Bumbo!

LASCA: Bumbo?

MARIA: Bumbo-bumbo.

LASCA: Bumbo-bumbo?

MARIA: Bumbo-bumbo, hot-tailed bumbo.

LASCA *(hastily)*: You're raving, woman. Lumpkin, you've frightened your mother out o' her few remaining wits. *(Gets up briskly.)* Enough. We've meat to dress.

MARIA: As you say. But there'll be no more bumbo for you this month.

*As she moves to the instruments Stage Left,* ALPHONSO *joins* LASCA.

ALPHONSO: Bumbo? Bumbo? Is that some new dish?

LASCA: 'Tis an old dish which your mother won't be serving me. Thanks to you.

*He hits* ALPHONSO *savagely on the knee with the thigh-bone;* ALPHONSO *yells and hops around.*

What's the costume?

ALPHONSO *(rubbing his knee; sullen)*: For Brother Corton's pageant, 'Everyman in Hell'. I'm playing Death again as always. This year 'twas my turn to be Jesus . . .

LASCA *(looks up)*: Christ . . .

ALPHONSO: But Brother Corton gave the part to the carpenter's son. He's a pretty, lisping, backgammon player and his bum fits. I only come on at the start and chop down the tree o' life and sing: 'Oh he is dead as you can see, just as you will one day be . . .'

LASCA *has crossed to help* MARIA *put the instruments on the table; they exchange despairing glances.*

LASCA: Alphonso, in the name o' God and profit, take hold. All this'll be yours, one day. My father, God rest his bones, was only a common foot soldier under Sigismundo Malatesta and Federigo da Montefeltro, Lord o' Urbino. Fifteen years o' hard slaughter and uncertain pay 'afore he saw there was more profit and less risk in disposing o' corpses than manufacturing 'em. He founded this business and bequeathed it to me, and

I to you, and so forth from generation to generation. Times are ripe for thrusting men to make their way.

ALPHONSO: Later. I'm young. I've plans to enjoy myself first.

LASCA: *Enjoy?* You drink till your gut bursts, brawl, dice and lie with every strumpet you can buy under a sheet for two denari. And all on money I give you. You call that *enjoyment?*

ALPHONSO: Yes.

LASCA *(controlling himself)*: Lad, when I was in knee-breeches I drank, diced and dipped my dildo in every whorehouse in Florence.

ALPHONSO: So you say.

LASCA: I remember one pretty-faced raver: high forehead, sharp nose – much prized in my day – skin soft, large, bouncing kettle drums.

*As he mimes breasts,* MARIA *drops a knife on the table in front of him.*

'Er but no more o' that. 'Tis natural for the young to be cockish, and quarrelsome. I fought and cursed my father right up to the day the young Prince Scolari was brought in for burial.

ALPHONSO: I know, I know.

LASCA: Eighteen years old he was, with long limbs and golden hair. Died o' a dirt-rotten liver. When he was alive he had an income o' 100,000 florins a year; estates in Tuscany, three mistresses including the Duchess o' Ferrara and a monopoly of the sweetmeat trade. You'd often see him surrounded by a motley o' parasites and pages, sniffing on a perfumed amber ball chained to his wrist. He walked the streets with eight men at arms dressed in silk cloaks and a man from Pistoia marching in front with a naked sword shouting, 'Make way, make way for Fortune's Darling!' . . . Me father and me stood silent with our thoughts in front o' that high-born corpse. And then there was this burning light in me; 'twas like the light of revelation they speak o' in the Scriptures. I looked across at my father. He was smiling. There was no need for words.

We showed a leg *(he bows low)* pulled open our codpieces, aimed our dildos and pissed our sweet Adam's water straight into the dead face o' that proud prince.

MARIA: *Ahhhh.*

LASCA: 'Twas wonderful. From that moment there was ne'er a bitter word 'twixt my father and me. We were like another Abraham and Isaac. Another Saul and Jonathan. Just as I want us to be, lad.

ALPHONSO *(shrugging)*: Most times I use that bucket or the nearest member-mug, but I'll water the face o' the dead if that pleases you. *(He staggers towards the corpse, tugging at his breeches.)*

MARIA: Alphonso! That's Leonardo da Vinci.

ALPHONSO *(stopping)*: Leonardo da Vinci? What's he doing here?

LASCA: Dancing the tarantella! He's come to be buried, lobcock.

ALPHONSO: But he's famous. Even dead, he wouldn't be seen dead in a charnel house like this.

LASCA: He's nothing. In the old days we used to bury Cardinals and Princes. You're too young to remember when I was Apothecary and man o' distinction as well as a death-hunter. Juice o' scabiose, hyssop, dried toad, hazel nuts filled with mercury – my nostrums cured sufferers of hernia, running ulcers, warts, bone ache and stinkin' breath. And if I didn't cure 'em, I buried 'em. Profit either way, eh Mother?

MARIA *has been rummaging in the trunk Stage Left. She pulls out a black gown, a flat hat and a half-mask of a bird with a large beak.*

MARIA *(shakes gown of dust)*: See if it's still becoming.

LASCA *(crowing)*: Quarr, quarr, quarr.

ALPHONSO *is looking curiously at the corpse under the sheet, and pays no attention to* LASCA *as he puts on the gown and black hat.*

MARIA: Your father always wore this to protect him from the noxious vapours in the air when he visited the sick and fearful.

LASCA (*putting on bird mask*): *Quarr, quarr.*

MARIA: The mask's an improvement. Most becoming.

　　　LASCA *struts around.*

The gown needs a patch or two if you're ever to wear it again in Florence.

ALPHONSO (*eagerly*): Florence? You talk o' Florence?

MARIA: It's likely we'll return.

ALPHONSO: When? When?

MARIA: When we've tucked Signor da Vinci to bed with a spade. We can carry home the news o' his death and who buried him.

LASCA (*nodding*): *Quarr, quarr, quarr.*

ALPHONSO: The fashion's white velvet there this Spring. White velvet doublets pinked in orange satin and hosen striped with silverwork. White velvet boots and scented gloves. Oh, I'll look so fetching – really 'compt' – in white scented gloves. Let's drink to Signor da Vinci, even in death a bringer o' gifts.

LASCA: 'A a cloud-topping man. But now he's wrapped in cool crêpe. His mind was the light o' the world, they saith, but his flesh'll rot, red, green and black, just the same. He'll ooze away like that idiot Notary we dug in last week. His tongue'll swell and eyes pop out like old Gentile Bardi the tom-turd man. He'll smell, he'll stink, like all o' 'em we put away. And after his stomach's caved in and his guts slide out, we'll find those damned toads gnawing at his face and pale maggoty things crawling out o' his puss. Misére, misére . . .

ALL (*singing softly, mournfully*): 'Dies irae, dies illa, solvet saeclum in favilla teste David cum Sibylla . . .'

*They sway in lamentation but imperceptibly their voices grow lighter. Despite themselves they start to chuckle, chuckles turn to laughter, as, clasping hands, they dance around to the now jaunty dirge.*

ALL (*singing jazzily*): ' . . . quantus tremor est futurus quanto judex est venturus, cuncta stricte discussurus . . . Ya! Yaaaaa!'

*The freeze in mid-step:* ALPHONSO'S *skeleton leg in the air,*

MARIA's *skirt high,* LASCA's *gown spread out like wings. The sheet covering the corpse has begun to rise up slowly. A single flute is heard playing. They stare in petrified silence. Suddenly* LASCA *turns and hits* ALPHONSO *a backhand blow.*

LASCA: More o' your sottish tricks!

ALPHONSO: N-n-n-n-n-n-n-n . . .

*Gesturing to the bier, he clutches his stomach in fright.* MARIA *and* LASCA *look back fearfully. The sheet rises higher and higher then slowly falls aside to reveal the bearded figure of* LEONARDO DA VINCI *sitting upright in his nightshirt.*

*Lights imperceptibly up during the rest of the scene as the silence is finally broken by the sound of a slow release of air from the pit of* DA VINCI's *stomach.*

DA VINCI: Aaaaaaaaaaaaaaaaaaa *(Opens eyes)* b b b b ba baa baaa hhhuuu d d d d d d diu mundi . . . spiritus sancte Deus . . . IIIIII *(Closes eyes)* Who? Why? How? What? Where? . . . Dying . . . smell o' burnt feathers . . . priests sweating over . . . in nomine Patris et Filii . . . a black dog crouched on my chest . . . space darker than . . . down down downnnn. *(Opens eyes.)* I'm *dead.* But I speak, feel, see, touch. *(Touches face.)* My heart beats. I feel alive. But I know I'm dead. *(Trembles violently.)* I am in Hell! Damned and in Hell! *(Turns, sees the* LASCAS.*)* Two fiends, and a woman with her skirts up. It's the Sodomites' Hell.

*His head lolls back on his chest. Despite warning gestures from* LASCA, MARIA *creeps nearer.*

MARIA *(low)*: He's breathing.

LASCA: No, no, no. Even Job was not afflicted so. It can't be true. He's just corpse-dancing.

MARIA: 'Tis a miracle.

LASCA: Witchcraft!

MARIA: Angelo, he's been raised from the dead. Behold another Lazarus.

LASCA: *Another* Lazarus. Wasn't one such nuisance enough? Dear Jesus, it's happened. What every burial-man fears. We've got a bleeding *resurrection* on our hands! Don't just stand like an open-arsed eunuch, Alphonso, do something.

ALPHONSO *staggers over to the bucket and vomits.* MARIA *cautiously pokes* DA VINCI.

MARIA: He's smaller than I heard tell.

DA VINCI *(jerking up)*: The dead shrink to the size of worms. Come, Madame Fiend, begin the tormenting. I'm ready. *(Rips open top of nightshirt.)* Here's my liver, stenchy eagle, start pecking.

LASCA: I'm no eagle. I'm a man like you.

*He lifts the mask and grins, showing his black teeth.*

DA VINCI *(cowering)*: Sanctuary!

MARIA: I said to keep the mask on, 'twas more flattering.

LASCA: I'm Angelo Lasca from Florence.

DA VINCI: A Florentine fiend. So I'm to be tortured by one of my loving countrymen. The Creator has a killing sense of humour.

MARIA: You're alive, Signor da Vinci.

LASCA: You're alive and I'm dead. Cursed by God and Divine Fortune. The wheel spins leaving me at the bottom again.

ALPHONSO *(feebly)*: Dad, does this mean I won't get my scented gloves?

LASCA: You're not just corpse-dancing are you, Signor? My dead 'uns oft thresh about a bit in their coffins, not wanting to go. Corpse-dancing we call it.

DA VINCI *(off-handed)*: Rigo Mortis. The muscles tighten after death making the limbs contract and jerk compulsively, giving the appearance of life.

LASCA: That's it, corpse-dancing. I must've been too quickish carting you off this morning. But Signor Melzi gave you up dead. You looked dead. I've heard tell o' such tales but nothing like this has happened in our family 'afore.

DA VINCI: I've heard tell, too. No heart-beat. No pulse. No breath. Muscular rigidity, loss of sensation and consciousness. The flesh stone cold. Catatonic trance. All the outward signs

of death but the victim wakes as if from sleep. *(Voice rising.)*
Yes, yes. Only outward death, only sleep. A little sleep.
SleeeeeEEEEEE . . . DOWN, SIR. Down, Dooowwnnn.
Remember, you're in Hell. In burning fire and ice, racked and
crucified by the hope of living, the lust for life. Abeo. Abeo.
 *He staggers off the bier.* MARIA *and* LASCA *support him.*
LASCA: Come, we're all alive here. Catch my breath.
 *Breathes straight into* DA VINCI's *face; he shudders.*
That's the living breath o' a garlic-scented man. Mother, show
him you're alive, too.
 MARIA *jumps into the air and does the splits.*
There, proof positive. And my son, Alphonso. Alphonso,
show us you're more or less alive.
 ALPHONSO *retches into the bucket.*
Yes, well, you'll just have to take my word for it in his case . . .
You're still in the land o' the living, Signor da Vinci. This is
the Amboise Charnel House.
 *They lower* DA VINCI *on to a stool.*
MARIA: Your wits've been addled from the shock, 'twill pass.
DA VINCI *(holds up trembling hand, looks closely at it)*: Flesh,
 bones, muscles, nerves. It's another trick. I'd prepared my soul
 for death. Not willing but resigned. The end came. Let me
 be, let me be.
LASCA: Nubb and 'bowel me if 't'aint true. I'm no sneaking
 clanker, Signor. I wouldn't lie about a thing like this.
DA VINCI: Perhaps you don't know yourself whether you're
 alive or dead, man or devil?
LASCA: I'm a man like you, Signor da Vinci. Always 'ave been.
DA VINCI: I want evidence of life. Give me proof, more proof,
 more proof.
MARIA: How signor?
DA VINCI: Be your natural selves. Talk of Florence. Yes, that's
 what exiles do. Talk of the Florence I remember. Then I can
 judge if you know the shape and feel of being alive.
MARIA: Talk o' Florence? 'Tis easy.

LASCA: We do nothing else in this house but talk o' Florence.

MARIA: I've such a longing to hunt for a bargain along the Ponte Vecchio again. 'Twas always full o' the noise o' buying and selling. The mornings I've spent looking at silks and English wool. What crowds. Angelo, remember the time Rinuccio's old horse bolted and some forty people were knocked down. Everyone was shouting. And they rang the great bell, boom, boom, boom . . .

LASCA: We had a 'bottega' in the Mercato Vercchio next to a pimping barber's shop, Signor. You could hear the goldsmiths with their tiny hammers beating out gold just up the Canto di Vacchereccia. I miss the comforting sound o' men making money.

DA VINCI: I miss the Tuscany light; no haze, everything hard and clear. I never found such light again.

MARIA: We sold nostrums and knick-knackeries o' all kinds. Silver buckles, magic charms, satchels, gloves . . .

ALPHONSO: *Scented* gloves? Did we sell scented gloves?

MARIA: And candied apples, plum jam, quince, (ALPHONSO *groans)* dates, sweetmeats . . .

*Sound of* ALPHONSO *being sick again.*

We made a profit of over 200 gold florins on knick-knackeries alone, not counting nostrums and burials, in our first year. That would be, what – '83, Angelo?

DA VINCI: The year I was commissioned by the Confraternity of the Immaculate Conception to paint the *Virgin of the Rocks.* I was thirty-two. Young. I looked down and it was all laid out in front of me, below me. The sun shone. I worked, and the boys wore salmon-pink hosen. *(Holds head.)* AArrrrx . . . pain . . . memories sharp as needles . . . pain . . . *arrrhhh* . . .

LASCA *snuffs out the candles on the bier.*

Pain not sufficient evidence of being alive . . . Detach. Only sit, listen, judge, reach a verdict: live flesh or dead tissue.

LASCA: Sad business looking back on better days, Signor.

DA VINCI: Tell me about your better days, your good years?

**LASCA:** The good years? 1494 was the best for us, no question.

**DA VINCI:** The year Ghirlandajo died. *(Low.)* Silence. Oh stay silent, stay silent as the grave.

**MARIA:** That's it, you remember '94, the plague year. Ahh, what a year that was for us.

**LASCA:** 'A they fell like flowers in winter, *aaaah, clonk:* dead. All used up. The streets were empty 'cept for the corpse carriers and plague carts. You remember how the quick and the dead were left to rot for fear of contagion, Signor. Sensible fellows carried their linen shrouds with 'em so when they felt the first shiver o' approaching pestilence they could wrap 'emselves in it and be decently rigged when the time came to be shovelled into the pit. Some folk are born with proper civic feelings, others don't give a damn. 'Twas a time of fear and opportunity. An upright man could make his way without benefit o' breeding or influence. 'Twas a time of truth. With bedrooms and parlours rank with death, no man could prate on about love and honour; such words'd stick in a throat soon to be vomiting plague-blood. 'Twas a time for the man o' business. For the only question asked was 'how does it profit me?' It was our time. Lasca time.

ALPHONSO *has recovered and has joined the others.*

At the first I believed 'twould be difficult for us, Signor. So many deaths, the market was glutted. The bereaved had no use of biers, coffins, candles and such. The mystery and profit'd gone out o' death; the clergy had all fled mumbling 'benedictos'. Luckily I was also Apothecary Lasca. Sweet Apothecary Lasca.

**MARIA:** That's where our profit lay, Signor. How they bought our expensive nostrums to protect their clotted carcasses from the plague! They tried every remedy known to man and mountebank. Some put their trust in speckled spiders and toads trained to suck poison from the air. Some rubbed their bodies with diamonds, sapphires and jaspers engraved with favouring signs. Pieces o' warm bread were laid on a dying man's mouth to catch the disease as it left his body. The breath of a pregnant horse was said to be a benefit, and the Chancellor of Hungary had a billygoat tied to his sick-bed to absorb the plague air.

LASCA: Ah, what days! You wanted to hear about our better days, Signor, these were 'em. We've not seen their like since. My nostrums and remedicinal powders were the finest in Florence. The public always looks f' something new and fresh. I gave it to 'em, thanks in part to your famous method, Signor da Vinci. You said to look to facts as they are and not to rank superstition and magic. 'Swhat I did. I used me eyes and ears. In time o' pestilence I noted that tomturd men and privy cleaners never fell sick. They were protected by the stench o' their work. The stink clinging to their persons protected 'em from the plague. I wasn't the only sharper who noted it. At the height of the pestilence crowds used to stand in front o' private privies sniffing up the smells. *(Sniffs loudly.)* Privy owners soon got to charging 'em twenty-five denari an hour for the privilege. I set out to manufacture medicinal smells. I bottled farts.

ALPHONSO: We had a team o' wind-breakers, Signor. Dad fed 'em on radishes and beans.

LASCA: When they were in the producing way they'd lift up their skirts, drop their breeches and stick a green bottle up their arse. *Bang.* And we had a little o' that most healing physic, 'Lasca's Sweet Morning Wind'. Price one florin; three denari back on all empties.

MARIA: But wind's difficult to bottle. A couple o' sniffs and 'tis gone. Customers wanted something more solid.

LASCA: So next I bottled shit. Pilgrim's salve, 100 per cent proof. 'Lasca's Excremental Goodness' came in three sizes. 'Lady's Own' was a tiny bottle most beautifully engraved with signs o' the Zodiac and attached to a gold necklace. 'Man Size' was flat and decorated with the figure o' Hercules strangling a lion; it sold at six florins. Our 'Jumbo Family Jar' cost all o' ten florins, but it lasted weeks. Signor, I'd discovered the secret o' wealth. I o'ertopped those learned Alchemists. They only turned *lead* into gold.

MARIA: I've been rich and poor, but being rich makes a woman glow more than a good man. I had a mulberry coloured silk robe embroidered with gold herring-bones and a villa overlooking the Arno. The walls were covered with gold leaf and drawings of shepherds and such. We had four servants, a female slave, fish every Friday, and a hot bath every month. Jesus, how we lived.

LASCA: We lived high, like true princes o' the Church. I was a mighty meat-eater then: bloodmeat makes the sinews supple. Boiled owl and roasted boar with sweet sauce and pine kernels; bear hams and baked porpentine. I became particular partial to venison – fat and full o' blood. All washed down with black Marino wine. *(Burps loudly.)* Jesus, how we lived.

ALPHONSO: How *you* lived. What o' me? I've never lived, 'cept on hard bread and sour wine. 'Twas gone 'afore I could taste it. You had the good life and you lost it for me.

LASCA: Blame those bacon-faced Guild Masters.

MARIA: Only in part, Angelo, only in part.

LASCA: Signor da Vinci, you're sitting there judging if we're flesh or fowl, judge then where the fault lay. I was forced to join the Apothecaries' Guild, with their gut and garbage rules for honest trading. *Sallow pates!* They couldn't see honesty's one thing and trading's something else again. The moment I put 'Lasca's Excremental Goodness' on the market out came their rules and regulations. They laid down the price for shit at sixty florins a ton. Can you credit it, Signor? Sixty florins! I told them it was too low. I could get 150 florins without strain. Then they sent this weazel-eyed Inspector o' Turds round sniffing and spying. Had me up in front o' a full Guild Court accused o' overcharging and watering down my merchandise. I had nothing to hide. But they stopped their ears and found me guilty. 'Twas envy, black cancerous envy. I was fined 5,000 florins and no time to pay.

MARIA: We caught a disease worse than the Black Death itself – poverty.

LASCA: We've much in common, Signor da Vinci, you and me. Good Florentines both and both forced to leave the city we love. I was rich but in debt – thanks to my wife here playing the fine lady. You're the root o' it, Madame. Your sins o' pride and covetousness.

MARIA: 'Twas your lechery, your galloping lechery. The good Lord rules with a rod o' iron. His hand hangs like a stone o'er this family. Only my prayers turn away his terrible wrath.

LASCA: *Your* prayers, Madame. I pray daily – hourly – f' revenge like a good Christian.

ALPHONSO: Good Christians leave their sons something more than rotting flesh. That's my inheritance. Not even a pair o' stinking gloves. 'Twas my share you squandered. (*Suddenly screeching.*) You wasted it! 'Twas mine. My share. Where's my share? I want my share!

LASCA: Here's your share. (*Hits him to the ground.*) Quarr, quarr, quarr. The stink from my armpit and the sweat from me shotpouch is all you'll get from me, Master Pussy-Water. You're no son o' mine. You're a certain bastard, a by-blow of your Mother's roaring lust f' every bull in breeches.

MARIA: He's your son, bumfodder, look at his ugsome face. Only a son o' yours could look like a constipated cockroach.

LASCA: Your hopper-arsed old Mother said you were a bitch on everlasting heat.

MARIA: You hen-hearted flunky, fart catcher to every whoremaster in France.

ALPHONSO (*scrambling up*): I'm leaving you worn out pair o' wet breeches.

MARIA: Hornified shankers.

ALPHONSO: Screw-jaws.

LASCA: Gullgropers.

MARIA: Canary birds.

ALPHONSO: Buss-beggers.

LASCA: Stinkin' loobys.

MARIA: Tosspots.

ALPHONSO: Rabbit suckers.

LASCA: Cock-bawds.

ALPHONSO: Die o' hemp fever, lay down and die!

MARIA: Merciful God strike 'em dead!

LASCA: Kill, Kill . . . !

DA VINCI (*softly*): Alive, alive, alive. The verdict is in. I'm alive. Jesu, I'm alive. I'M ALIVE.

> *He shoots off the stool and jigs around uttering whoops of joy. The others stare, having forgotten him in the quarrel.*

The evidence proves I'm in the land of the living in the bosom of a natural family. I recognize the species: genus homo sapiens. Bipedal primate mammals. Erect bodies, short arms, large thumbs, developed brains with a capacity for articulate speech and abstract reasoning. That's you. That's me. 'Alive-alive O, alive-alive O, singing pasta and pizza alive-alive O.' STILL ALIVE.

LASCA: We said so.

DA VINCI: And I didn't believe the evidence of my senses. Lazarus must've felt much the same, being raised up – *up, up, up!* S'natural to mistake the living world for Hell, the difference is so slight when men are piked and gutted in either place.

MARIA: The Lord giveth and the Lord taketh away. You weren't truly dead, so you couldn't've seen the everlasting fire or the glory o' Our Saviour's face, but you must've had a quick peep at Death's Kingdom.

LASCA: Is it cold or hot? A great falling or a shooting up, *whoosh*. Do you know it?

ALPHONSO: Can you feel it? When we die can we feel the worms bite or the white sluggies swimming out o' our flesh.

LASCA: We've had no chance o' asking our customers 'afore, Signor. What is death?

DA VINCI *(intake of breath)*: Ahhhhhhhhhh . . . Nothing. I remember living and coming to life but nothing 'twixt and between. It was dark all the way.

LASCA: Keeping it a secret, eh? You can't be blamed for that. People'll pay money to hear how you died and rose again. Wish I'd such a tale to tell.

DA VINCI *has crossed to the table. He eagerly stuffs bread into his mouth, eating wolfishly.*

DA VINCI: Come . . . take . . . eat. I'm too full of the bread of life to think on death. *(Taking the wine-flagon he throws back his head and pours wine into mouth and over his face.)* Yaaaaaa . . . come . . . take . . . drink. I'm alive and doing. Live flesh not dead tissue, I've a live body again. All's mathematical again: heart, lungs, brain, sinews. The span of my outstretched arms equals my height. From the roots of my hair to the bottom of my chin is exactly 1/10th of my height. My waist is halfway between the joint of my shoulders and the bottom of my buttocks. My fingers extended and closed thus, are exactly the same width as my foot. My ears are as long as my nose and the space between my eyes is equal to the size of one eye. My hand is 1/10th my height. My foot 1/7th. Four palms make up one foot, 24 palms make up a man . . .

LASCA: And the plug-tail is his centre. Come Signor, you're alive and know't, so to serious business. You understand I've been much put out. I was to bury you for 100 gold florins. Gold mind, gold. Only half's been paid on account. I can't complete the contract as you won't stay dead. As a scholar you can see 'tisn't my fault. And as an honest man you'll agree the contract should be honoured to the full.

*He rattles the leather pouch of money; it sounds unnaturally loud.* ALPHONSO *becomes transfixed.*

ALPHONSO: More. More, more, more, more, more, more.

LASCA: What's that?

ALPHONSO: More! More! We should've more!

LASCA: More? Did you say 'more more, we should've more'? Mother, you hear that? There's still hope, A lad who asks for more can't be all bad.

ALPHONSO: We should've more than just the contract price. What o' the loss o' trade? Burying the great Leonardo da Vinci would've made us known throughout Christendom – and beyond. We could've paid our debts and gone back home to prosper. 'Twould have been most fashionable to be buried by those who buried Leonardo da Vinci. That custom's lost. We must be recompensed.

LASCA: $V-e-r-y$ good, Alphonso.

MARIA: And what o' the reward for saving you from the shovel and the shroud? Lucky we was eagle-sharp. Others might've missed you were still alive and you'd've been drained, wrapped and coffined.

DA VINCI: For that I give you thanks.

LASCA: Thanks? Thanks won't feed us, clothe us, gives us back our villa, our slaves, our hot baths. Thanks isn't good coin o' the realm. Thanks don't make us sleep contented in our bed, nights. You can't keep a family together on thanks. Thanks is a cheat 'less backed by hard gold and silver. Then we can measure the amount o' thanks we're being thanked.

ALPHONSO: Thanks is a word, worth what a word's worth. It'll never buy a man a pair o' scented gloves.

LASCA: Well said lad. We've a right to payment in full for the broken contract; compensation for loss o' revenue; a decent reward for saving you, and o' course a pledge that when you finally die, we bury you. As a gentleman you'll agree 'tis all only our right and proper due.

DA VINCI: I'm no gentleman, gentlemen. I'm an artist and bastard son o' a lawyer. I know why I took this place for Hell. I expected to be punished for my sins. Sins of omission. I only wanted to create masterpieces. But

every time I picked up a brush I knew how far below my
mark I'd fall. The Holy Father Leo said I'd never finish
anything. He didn't know I only wanted to finish masterpieces.

  *Bored,* LASCA *takes out three rubber balls and starts a juggling
act with* ALPHONSO. *Like a trained stage assistant* MARIA *hands
them props: cigar boxes, hoops and Indian clubs. They continue
juggling fluently throughout* DA VINCI'*s speech.*

A man is judged by his usefulness. All I have to show are
notes. A thousand pages of notes. Plans to build a bridge
across the Bosphorous, to direct the Arno to Pisa, to drain the
Pontine Marshes, build a new city on split levels with running
water in every house and revolving privies to keep the air
sweet and clean. And ideas. Musical instruments – drums, bells,
lyre, viola – that play themselves. Chariots with rotating
drives. Paddle boats, submarines, parachutes, mortars, flying
machines, propellers, diving-suits, cogwheels, turbines, cranes.
Everything that magnifies man's strength and glory. But what
of the masterpieces that will give me certain immortality?
*The Adoration of the Magi* – unfinished. *St Jerome* – unfinished.
*The Virgin and the Child with St Anne* – unfinished. *The Battle
of Anghiari* – unfinished and botched. *The Last Supper* – finished
but flaking away. *The Virgin of the Rocks* – finished by others.
The *Great Horse,* modelled for Ludovic Sforza – never cast
and used for target practice. That leaves only the *Mona Lisa*
as mine, complete. One painting and a few thousand scattered
notes and sketches! Jesu . . . Jesu . . . I am in Hell . . . *(Stands
up slowly.)* But as Dr Johnson will say, 'Depend upon it,
Sir, when a man knows he is to be hanged in a fortnight,
it concentrates his mind wonderfully'. I know I will die and
that time's the enemy – I invented an alarm clock didn't I?
I'm still at the height of my powers and can soar like a gier
eagle. In the extra ten, nine, eight, seven, six, five or whatever
years I've been given. I'll create monuments to turn Michel-
angelo green with envy. So ring the bells, da Vinci is risen.

Ring the bells, he's been spared! Ring 'em, his hands will double the beauty of the world! Ring 'em, he's alive and DOING! Ring, ring, ring 'dem bells for Leonardo's second coming!

*Bell peal. The* LASCAS *stops juggling.*

LASCA: What o' our money?

DA VINCI: Ah, yes. Down to the practicals. I've neglected 'em in the past. First, tell the good news to Francesco. I'll follow behind you. It'll all have to be kept secret whilst we make up a story. We don't want the Church involved. They'll declare this was a miracle when it was only a mistaken diagnosis.

ALPHONSO: Money! Our money!

DA VINCI: Money? Oh, you may keep the fifty florins with my blessing. But for the rest, you can hardly claim payment for non-burial or for trade you never had. As for my final burial, you can bury me with pleasure if you're in Florence. I'm going home.

MARIA: Oh Holy Virgin, Mother of God, what o' our reward?

DA VINCI: Your reward is the gratitude of future generations.

*Loud, incredulous, hissing intakes of breath from the* LASCAS.

ALPHONSO: *Hrrrrrrzzzzzzzzz* . . . I'm the future, and I'm not grateful. The future'll only be grateful if we survive. We're needed. You're a luxury. We're the new men you scholars prate on about. You put us in the centre o' the Universe. Men o' trade, o' money, we'll build a new heaven and a new earth by helping ourselves. *(Long escape of breath.) Haaaaaaaaaaaaaaazzzz. (Takes up leather pouch.)* Dad, I've seen the light you spoke o'. Like the martyr Paul on the Damascus Road. I trembled and was astonished. Out o' nothing, no warning, a golden vision. I was blinded and I saw for the first time. I kicked against the pricks but now I'm going to put the locust years o' waste behind me.

Dad, I've come to my senses! You're not slipping through our fingers, Signor da Vinci. You're not cheating us o' what's ours. You're our meat, you belong to us. You're our salvation, Signor!

*The lights dim down as* ALPHONSO *turns and looks at his father.* LASCA *understands. With formal dignity they bow low to each other. Turning back* ALPHONSO *gives an ape-like grunt and picks up the thigh bone.*

*Crouching slightly, arms dangling, the two* LASCAS, *still in their skeleton and bird costumes, advance menacingly on* DA VINCI, *whilst* MARIA *utters little coos of happiness in the background.*

DA VINCI (*retreating*): Stay . . . stay friends . . . friends, friends you know not what you . . .

*As he makes a dash for the Exit, the* LASCAS *grab him.*

LASCA: Bilking scab! Cheat! Cheat!

ALPHONSO: Pimping buckfitch! Cheat! Cheat!

MARIA: Punking clawback! Cheat! Cheat! He's an old man, don't hurt him just kill him.

LASCA: Nothing personal, Signor. This is just business.

DA VINCI *screams as the* LASCAS *pick him up bodily and carry him struggling Down Stage Right.*

DA VINCI: Stay . . . stay . . . Oh let me not die again . . . let me live . . . for truth and beauty . . . flesh and blood . . . MERCY. . . I'm a man like you . . . WE'RE MEN . . . ME . . . Mmmmmmmm . . .

DA VINCI'S *voice is cut off as he is plunged headfirst into the bucket of excrement, urine and vomit. He struggles frenziedly, splattering the* LASCAS *as they hold him under. His struggles soon grow weaker; legs stop kicking, arms flaying. Finally no movement at all. A long silence. They lift him out dripping and carry him with great gentleness to the bier and lay him out.* ALPHONSO *leans over and listens to his heart. Satisfied he nods happily and gives the thumbs-up sign.*

ALPHONSO: *Father.*

LASCA: *Son.*

*They embrace emotionally.* MARIA *joins them, crying.*

MARIA: Ave Maria. Bless the Father, Son, and Holy Ghost. We're a family again.

LASCA: Son, you're the kind o' son we've always wanted. Mother, what say you to getting our boy those scented gloves?

ALPHONSO: I want no such flipperies now. Money's not for pleasure. Let's to business.

MARIA *hands them the iron knives and saws from the wall.*

MARIA: And sharpish 'afore the Resurrection Man there, decides to sit up again.

LASCA: Never. It could never happen again. Another blessed miracle'd be too much to inflict on hard-working Christian folk like us. We deserve better o' the good Lord.

ALL: Amen!

LASCA *joins* ALPHONSO *in front of the bier. As the funeral bell tolls over they bow their heads reverently. The* LECTURER'S *voice comes through loud-speakers in the auditorium.*

LECTURER: Now he's truly dead, we can safely say we shall never see his like again. A genius at once divine and marvellous. He contained in himself all the quantities of humanity. Painter, sculptor, musician, architect, philosopher and all the rest, he learned the secret of creation. An oracle, a legend, *the* artist of the world – *l'uomo universale,* Leonardo da Vinci.

ALPHONSO *and* LASCA *stand for a moment more in silence, then savagely descend on the corpse, hacking and cutting to drain off the blood.*

MARIA *crosses slowly to them with a knife, singing in a beery, maudlin voice, as lights dim down to a final Spot on the drawing of the* Divine Proportions *still hanging from the Flies.*

MARIA *(singing):* 'Mona Lisa, Mona Lisa, men have named you. You're that lady with the mystic smile. Is it only 'cause you're lonely they have blamed you for that Mona Lisa strangeness in your smile? Do you smile to tempt a lover – Mona Lisa? Or is it the way to hide a broken heart? . . .

ALL *(singing)*: 'Are you warm, are you real, Mona Lisa. Or just a cold and lonely, lovely work of art.'

CURTAIN

# Noonday Demons

---

## THE CHARACTERS

ST EUSEBIUS
ST PIOR

## THE SCENE

A CAVE IN EGYPT
392 A.D.

*Noonday Demons* was first presented with *Leonardo's Last Supper* at the Open Space Theatre on 25 November 1969. The play was presented in association with Gene Persson with the following cast:

ST EUSEBIUS                                          *Joe Melia*
ST PIOR                                              *David Neal*

*Directed by Charles Marowitz*
*Designed by John Napier*

# NOONDAY DEMONS

*Lights up on a cave in Egypt, 392 A.D.: low roof, mud walls, shadows.*
*The entrance Up-Stage Centre, is filled with a blinding desert light.*
*Stage Centre Left is a giant mound of age-old human excrement,*
*baked iron-hard.*
ST EUSEBIUS *stands praying on a brick, Stage Centre. A tall, emaciated*
*figure, covered with sores and dressed in a filthy loin-cloth, he has*
*long, matted hair and a grey beard clotted with dirt. His body is*
*festooned with chains, his ankles shackled, his wrists hand-cuffed*
*and there is an iron band round his waist. Slack chains are looped*
*round his shoulders. On the floor nearby is a primitive earthen*
*bowl and a pouch made of goats' skin.*
*Continually repeating the prayer,* 'Benedíctio Dei omnipoténtis
Patris, et Filii et Spîritus Sancti descéndat super vos et máneat
semper. Amen', *in a monotonous drone, he steps off the brick and*
*with chains jangling, hops four paces to the left, finishing in front*
*of the mound. With difficulty he bends down, picks up the pouch*
*and takes out seven black olives. Making the Sign of the Cross*
*over them he eats them quickly, spitting out the stones. Bending*
*down again he pours a little water from the jug into the bowl.*
*Scooping up some dust from the ground, he sprinkles it on the*
*water.*

ST EUSEBIUS *(making the Sign of the Cross over the water and*
*drinking)*: Et benedíctio Dei omnipoténtis, Patris et Filii et
Spíritus Sancti, descéndat super hanc creaturam vini, et
cujúslibet potus et máneat semper. Amen. *(He talks uncertainly*
*at first, but with increasing confidence.)* Save me Lord. Noonday
thoughts creepeth back into my soul. I sink-sinking-sinketh
into deep mire where there is NO standing. I cometh into

deep waters where the flood o'erwhelmeth me and my strength fadeth. *(Puts down bowl.)* Thirteen years o' prayer and fasting breaking bricks with my sweat and tears, weeping for the sins o' Man, ne'er seeing my disciple who bringeth me black olives and stale bread twice yearly. Still the Devil stirs at noon. I choke in the stench o' him and my soul is covered with dust. *(Quicker.)* In nómine Patris et Filii – thirteen years yoked in the desert o' Skete where the water tasteth like as tar, where I sleep but fitful standing against a wall, where I drinketh muddy water and for-glotten seven black olives daily for sustenance. In nómine Patris, et Filii, et Spíritus Sancti. Bler-eyed, mole-eyed, my sight dimmeth and my flesh turns to pumice stone. I am become a statue for my Lord, locked in adoration, my limbs bolted with iron. *(He looks at his festering arm.)* Putrid like my soul. *(He examines a gaping sore and shudders.)* Maggots! A mass o' crawling maggots. Begone out from me! *(He squeezes the pus and waves his arm, shaking the maggots onto the ground; he suddenly stops.)* 'Thou shalt not judge.' I agulten thee Lord, forgivest Thou me. These blind worms are Thy creatures too. *(He bends down searching for the maggots.)* Come back little ones. 'Twas a mistake. The Devil moved me to throw thee out. Come back. *(He whistles.)* Here boys, here, here. *(He finds one of his maggots and holds it up delicately between finger and thumb.)* The Lord bless thee out o' Zion and mayst thou behold the good things that are in Jerusalem. *(He puts the maggot back into the sore in his arm.)* Eat what the good Lord hath provided for thee. *(He makes the sign of the Cross over it.)* In nómine Patris. The Devil oozeth in; my mind moulders like as wet straw. I must purge my wandering thoughts. Purge! Purge! I wilt not yield. He canst not harm me. I riddeth myself o' old style man and am become as one new: new eyes, ears, hands, heart, head. These years o' prayer and pain hath transformed me. In destroying my body I destroyed Space and Time. Without leaving this cave in Eygpt I travelleth o'er the world and its cities. I have seen the first Adam in Paradise, the future life in the Kingdom o' Heaven and all the centuries between. Angels have cometh unto me and their face shone with a double glory, and my face was as the sun. And lo, I spake unto them, sweetly in the language o' angels. 'Eeeeepphh – Zingggeeee – Yaaaanngg' I said. And they answered, 'Eeeeepphh – Zingggeeee – Yaaaanngg' to you too. *(Chanting.)* Yea, I have been caught up even unto Heaven and seen the consuming fire o' the Lord a thousand, thousand times brighter than–n–n–n–n *(His chains rattle as he shakes violently and his speech quickly becomes a frightened gabble.)* Adjúro–te–serpens–antíque–per–júdicem–vivórum–et–mortuórum–m–m–m–m . . .

*Now his voice and limbs are out of control. As his body jerks and his voice gabbles there is a sound of a troop of horses approaching at speed. Simultaneously as they thunder over the roof of the cave, a wall of heat and light shoots in from the entrance like a sudden blast from an open furnace.* ST EUSEBIUS *goes limp and falls forward at the waist. Silence . . .*

ST EUSEBIUS *jerks bolt upright. From now on he speaks with two totally different voices: his old, crabbed, dry voice and a new one which is lighter in tone, glib and edged with a Cockney whine.* (New voice.) 'Ello–'ello–'ello. *Yes, yes, yes, yes, YES. It's me. I've arrived and to prove it I'm 'ere.* (Singing.) *'S wonderful, 's marvellous, 's awful nice – paradise! This is Able Charlie Baker. Able Charlie Baker testing 1,2,3,4. Oedipus loves Mum, Electra loves Dad, Leda loves Swans. Come in Able Charlie Baker. Come in Able Charlie Baker. Great news. NO Easter this year. They found the body! . . . (Ordinary voice: fearful.)* I am possessed. 'Tis the Prince o' Darkness, the Evil One, the horn'd Serpent: Beelzebub! . . . (New voice.) *Mr Beelzebub to you, Bub!* (Desperately.) Exorcizámus te, omnis immúnde spiritis omnis satánica . . . *Silence! Silence when you speak to an officer. You know the drill. That hi-fi mumbo-jumbo won't do you no good. I'll go when you're good and ready, and not before, same as always. When you really want me out I'll slip away quiet as the proverbial 'lamb'* (giggles) *and*

*you can go back to contemplating your bunged-up navel. Savvy?*
*Nothing you can do so just lay back and enjoy it.* (Looking round.)
*Still the same boghouse.* (Wrinkles nose in disgust.) *What a pong.*
*It must be the odour of sanctity. I'm a friend, so I can tell you.* (Low.)
*B.O. Frankly, you could light up a whole room just by leaving it . . .*
I carest not for the odour o' bodies, only the stink o' souls.
In profane days I was bathed, massaged, scraped and rubbed
with perfumed oils. Now 'tis meet I shouldst endure mine
own stench daily, that on Judgment Day God mayst deliver
Christ's children from the unimaginable stench o' Hell . . .
*Believe me, compared to this hellhole, Hell is a blast.* (Points to
mound.) *And what's that as if I didn't know? . . .* Vile man:
what he is, what he endeth as. I canst not sin through false
pride standing in front o' such as that; however high my
thought fly up to Him, I knoweth their corrupt starting place
. . . *It's a dunghill. A mound of human waste, waste-waste-waste.*
*You're waste.* (Jeering.) *The sum total of your life. Mr Eusebius,*
*Saint. Look what you've got to show for your thirteen glorious years*
*of suffering. It's a truly miraculous achievement. A fitting epitaph:*
*'When the boghouse Saint up and died/ They found erected by his*
*side/ A tribute to his sacred wit/ A monument in holy shit.' That's*
*a joke, man! Well, laugh damn you, LAUGH . . . (Struggling.)*
When the Lord struck Egypt there was no house that didst
not mourn. I have cast out laughter. I wilt not laugh and take
delight in wordly pleasures. I wilt not laugh and sin through
pride. The world swarms back if I laugh. My heart is as stone.
I wilt not laugh! . . . *All you desert psychos are alike. A right*
*bunch of tight-faced sour-pusses. You're afraid to relax a second in*
*case you start remembering the days when you was normal. I'm*
*trying to bring a little sunshine into your life. I know the jokes are*
*pretty filthy and it's banal to be anal, but that's the only sort you*
*like. Underneath all that dirt you're really a dirty old man. Right,*
*let's get down to business. It's Temptation Time, folks! I'll slip*
*you three standards. It's routine stuff, but don't blame me. Blame*
*Saint Anthony with his B-picture Temptations. Now all you*

*fellows want in. Right. Temptation Number One coming up:
Money.*

The mound behind him turns golden. Projected into it is the image
of a pile of gold. ST EUSEBIUS is standing in front of it, so the
image is projected onto his body too, as are all the subsequent ones.
(Singing.) 'Money, money, money, money, money, can you use
any money today. Money, money, money, money, money, nice
new bills that we're giving away. Two million, four million, six
million, eight million, ten. Take what you want, when it's gone you
can come back again.' All you have to do is step outside and raise
your little finger. You're a saint, man. You're as sacred as the
Maharishi's cheque stubs. A few personal appearances, the odd
miracle, and you'll be rich. Have a ball, put your feet up, undo your
fly-buttons, eat pâté fois de gras for breakfast. Money dissolves all
cares and woes. 'Here I go, bye, bye, blackbird.' Look how it
shines. (He turns and stares at the mound.) *Money is the answer
to all things. Faith can do plenty, but money does everything. See
how it glitters . . . (Contemptuously.) I seest only the dung beneath.
The riches thou speakest of, I was born to. I cast them off to
follow Christ. I found my joy in this desolation, my delight
in this solitude. These bitter sands far outweigh the riches o'
thy glebe. Thinkest I would forgo Heaven's eternal riches to
regain that which I gladly castaway as worthless? 'Tis a poor
temptation, poorly given . . . A bit feeble, I'll admit, but they
get better. (Snaps his fingers and the image disappears.)
Right, Temptation Number Two: Lust.*

*Projected onto the mound is the image of a naked woman, ten
feet high and pink.*

C-o-r! Lay down lady. I thinks I loves yer. That's Round-Heel
Rosa: she only said 'no' once, and then she didn't hear the question.
Any puddles of lust left in your burnt-out carcass, Mister? Can you
still spring to attention when duty calls? All you have to do is step
outside and raise your itchy finger and any other part o' your anatomy
that feels like it. Women'll drop their knickers in a flash to make it
with a real live saint. They'll wanna test their strength against your

*strength. They'll like the chains too, some of 'em are dead kinky.*
(Softly.) *Look how she squirms: oceans ebb and flow.* (He turns and
stares.) *Ah, how sweet it is to enjoy a woman: sunlight and birds
breaking cover, walls spin, flesh swells. See how flowers blossom
on her flesh . . . (Contemptously.)* I seest only the dung beneath.
She appeareth to me as the Day of Judgment: head bald, eyes
sunken, mouth open to catch the snot from her nose, chin
covered o'er with black down, cheeks like as apes-bags, be-
flobered body shrouded in black crepe. She bygyle none,
'cept to belch, belke and bolke thro' heart's pity. Since the
time I was enchained I have ne'er had my fill o' bread, water
or sleep. Tormenting myself with these appetites, I canst not
suffer the stings o' lust, 'Tis a temptation for green boys . . .
*Yeah, and a bit vulgar with it too.* (He snaps his fingers and
the image disappears.) *Right, let's get to the last tempt for
today. Temptation Number Three: Power.*

   *Projected into the mound is a ten-foot high image of a purple
Pope in full regalia.*

*Men must be governed as well as judged. Eusebius lad, it's up to you.
The world's your oyster – eat it! Order, control, command, direct,
rule. All you have to do is step outside and raise your mighty forefinger. You've got charisma as well as halitosis. Join the Big Fellows,
be one of 'them'. Ride at the head of a holy army and sweep away
the world's corruption. Build a new Jerusalem here on earth. Look
how magnificently he stands, power does that for a man.* (He turns
and stares at the image.) *You wanna die unknown in this Egyptian
stinkhole? Have your name up in lights. Be one of the all-time greats
like Alexander, Caesar, George M. Cohen. Leave your mark on the
world, defeat death. Thousands die every day and leave no gap.
But see how a man of power sparkles . . . (Contemptuously.)* I seest
only the dung beneath. I am mortal earth and should become
as earth. Where now be thy insuperable Emperors, thy high
born Kings, thy Governors, Generals and Captains that 'erst
did proudly ride by? Look now upon their graves and see if
thou canst tell the master from the man, the leader from the

led. Fool, I have the only power I covet; the power to enter God's house. Thinkest I would trade this for the soul's abyss. 'Tis a stale temptation, staley given . . . *Pretty crude, agreed.* (He snaps his fingers and the image disappears.) *I knew you couldn't fall for those stupid music-hall tricks, but I had to go through the motions, it's expected. I'm glad, 'cause I wanna do the Socratic bit and show you the error of your ways through pure logic* . . . Thou marrest my life, invadeth my sleep and bring terror to my soul, but the Lord watches and my strength will not fail . . . *First off, I won't deny you've done great things. But no miracles. I'll believe in miracles the day you take a bath. Even granted you can travel through Space and Time, that's no miracle. It's easily explained. In order to move through Time one must establish absolute immobility in Space, because Man moves with Time and at the same speed. You've achieved absolute immobility by torturing your body so much, it's changed its metabolism. Now the Universe moves round you, whilst you remain static, so you're able to explore both the past and the future. Simple. But where's all this flitting back and forth across the centuries got you? What've you found? The story's always the same, isn't it? Virtue defeated, justice sold, shame lost, equality loathed, innocence despised, guilt condoned, evil advanced. From the first moment – Bang! – to the last, when the planet dies and the lice hop off – Whoosh! – to another galaxy, men'll never be governed by reason, virtue or love.* (He shakes his chains in agony.) *It's no good shaking your chains at me, Sir! You know I speaka da truth. The world gallops to perdition despite your sacrifice. All you're doing is saving yourself, nobody else. Selfish! Selfish! Selfish! You'll never be the man your Mother was. It's all meaningless. You'll die. And then you know what's in store, you've travelled into the future. You'll be resurrected in the second half o' the twentieth century as a stage freak. Your agonising abstinence'll be treated as a subject for laughter. You'll be regarded as just another figment of your author's grotesque imagination. 'Noonday Demons' by Peter Barnes. So, so, so the ground crumbles under your thoughts, your fossilized mind breaks loose, are you fact or fiction? that is the question, whether 'tis you standing here or only words made flesh and what of your blood and the Lord's blood and His Son's blood? – going, going, everything's reduced to laughter, no thought of the hereafter going-g-g-g-g- (He catches his throat but he cannot stop himself giving a strangulated laugh.)* . . . Adjúro ergo te, omnis immundíssime spiritus, omne phantásma, omnes incúrsio sátanae – I be Thy servant Eusebius. Eusebius. Eusebius. Yea, I am EUSEBIUS! ONLY EUSEBIUS. *(With increasing speed.)* No true sacrifice is worthless in Thy sight. I BELIEVE Lord h-h-h-helpest Thou my unbelief-as-stout-garments-beaten-i'-the-washing-are-maken-clean-so-so-so-my-strong-soul-is-maken-steadfast. *(Fiercely.)* From out o' my gut I vomit my vomit out! . . . *(He retches violently, trying to make himself sick.) It's no good, lad, I'm staying, right 'ere where I belong* . . . Out! . . . I'll have thee out . . . *I'm staying in!* . . . Out! . . . *In!* . . . Out! . . . *In!* . . . OUT, I'LL PLUCK THEE OUT . . . *(He punches himself in the stomach.)* Ahhhhhhhhhhhh!

*Trembling convulsively, he tries to move his right arm, but it is rigid. With a tremendous effort he finally forces it up. Putting his hand into his mouth he starts pulling a roll of white tape from between clenched teeth. He pulls some ten feet of tape before giving a final jerk: attached to the end of it is a large, black spider. As* ST EUSEBIUS's *limbs shake, the black spider flicks through the air and falls at his feet. He grinds it underfoot. Simultaneously, there is a scream of pain off, a wall of light and heat flares in from the entrance and from above the troop of horses thunder across the roof of the cave and into the distance.*

ST EUSEBIUS *goes completely limp. The sound of horses disappears and the light in the entrance grows dimmer as the sun sets. Finally silence and dusk descends.*

ST EUSEBIUS *straightens up slowly, recovering his strength. (Faintly.)* The bruised reed he shalt not break, the smoking flax he shalt not quench. *(Gaining strength.)* I have destroyed the last winged folly o' my brain. From now till dep-day I shall browse contented in the pastures o' my heart. My mind is leeched, drained o' all vain imaginings. I shall suffer no more thoughts, feelings, sentiments.

*Silver dust begins to fall gently, covering everything.*

This tongue shall no longer force its way out o' its shell, this hand no longer grip, this flesh no longer feel the knife's edge. I wilt remain standing on decayed stumps till I becometh dust unsubstantial in the presence of *the* Unsubstantial. Lord, I am triumphant because o' Thee! Mighty is the strength o' the Lord my God! (*Chanting loudly.*) Pax et benedíctio Dei omnipoténtis, Patris et Filii et Spíritus Sancti descéndat super te, et máneat semper . . .

*Still singing he steps back onto the brick. The light in the entrance quickly fades out. ST EUSEBIUS is heard singing in the darkness. As his voice dies away and the dust stops falling, it becomes light again, then dark. Light follows darkness at increasing speed, as a succession of days and nights follow each other in a blur.*

*Finally full noon light blazes in the entrance. ST EUSEBIUS is still standing on the brick, his gaze fixed on the ground in front of him. He is still festooned with chains, but his beard and hair are filthier and he is covered with dust.*

*The figure of a man suddenly appears silhouetted in the entrance. As he hops in we see he is dressed like ST EUSEBIUS in a filthy loin-cloth. He, too, is covered with sores and festooned with chains; hands and feet shackled. His hair is matted, and he carries a goat-skin pouch water jug, bowl and brick. This is ST PIOR. He is bulkier than ST EUSEBIUS, but for the rest almost identical.*

*His gaze is fixed on the ground, as he shuffles to a spot to the right of ST EUSEBIUS. Putting down the pouch, bowl and jug, ST PIOR places his brick carefully on the ground and steps ceremoniously onto it, after adjusting his chains around him like a cloak.*

*The two men now stand on their bricks, unaware of each other, being deep in meditation. They both start praying simultaneously.*

ST EUSEBIUS and ST PIOR: Benedíctio Dei omnipoténtis Patris

et Filii . . . *(They stop, puzzled: is it an echo? They continue, cautiously.)* et Spíritus Sancti . . . *(The pauses after each word grow longer.)* descéndat . . . super . . . vos . . . *(They suddenly both speed up.)* et-máneat-semper-Amen-Amen-Amen-

ST PIOR: Amen . . .

> ST PIOR's *extra 'Amen' hangs in the air. Slowly the two men turn and look up. A long pause as they stare at each other.*

ST EUSEBIUS and ST PIOR: 'Tis a noonday demon!

> *They both close their eyes, making the sign of the Cross frantically.*

ST EUSEBIUS and ST PIOR: Exorcizámus te, omnis immúnde spíritus, omnis satánica potéstas, omnis incúrsio infernális adversárii, omnis légio, omnis congregátio et secta diabólica *(they slow down, open one eye and, seeing the other is still there, continue even faster)* in-nómine-et-virtúte-Dómini-nostri-Jesu-Christi-

> *They open their eyes and start back in surprise to see the other still has not disappeared.*

ST EUSEBIUS: I command thee, by the burning bowels o' Christ, go back to thy foul place: I have no need o' thee.

ST PIOR: God, I beseech Thee, settest thou a nail into this demon's skull and pound it with a hammer even as did Jael unto Sisera.

ST EUSEBIUS: Thou comest unto me in years past as a voice speaking strange tongues. 'Ello, 'Ello, 'Ello.' Thou camest also as a swollen toad and horn'd dragon with eyes like as beacons and claws like as a bear. *(Shuddering.)* But thou hast ne'er come to me in such a loathsome guise!

ST PIOR: I hast seen thee 'afore in the shape o' a dog, a flock o' crows, 'caw, caw, caw', a lewd Friar and two worms oozing out o' my ears. But I smelt thee out always, thy devil's stench betrayeth thee. For demons canst ne'er hide the pestilential smell that clingeth about their person. *(Sniffs, cringes back.)* Thou must be the mightiest o' demons for thou hast the mightiest o' smells!

> *Chanting, they abuse each other ritualistically.*

ST EUSEBIUS: Father o' Liars.

ST PIOR: Captain o' Heretics.

ST EUSEBIUS: Degrader o' Souls.

ST PIOR: Beast o' all Beasts.

ST EUSEBIUS: Hungry sow.

ST PIOR: Holy water.

ST EUSEBIUS: Holy water . . . ?!

ST PIOR: At the touch o' holy water demons slinketh away like
as curs at the touch o' a whip.

ST EUSEBIUS: 'Tis true. Holy water diminisheth demons into
dust. Thou condemnest thyself.

*Chains rattling, they step off their bricks and hop over to their
water-jugs. Scooping up water with their bowls they make the
sign of the Cross over it, and quickly mumble a prayer. As they
stand facing each other* ST EUSEBIUS *dips his fingers into his bowl
and flicks water into* ST PIOR's *face, chanting:*

ST EUSEBIUS: Depart, vile spirit, in the name o' the Father,
and o' the Son and o' the Holy Ghost!

*Nothing happens.* ST PIOR *just scowls.* ST EUSEBIUS *grunts,
puzzled. Now it is* ST PIOR's *turn. Dipping his fingers into his
bowl he flicks water into* ST EUSEBIUS's *face, chanting.*

ST PIOR: Depart, vile sprit, in the name o' the father and o' the
Son and o' the Holy Ghost!

*Again, nothing happens.* ST PIOR *looks puzzled. Then they
both have the same thought and start flicking water into each other's
faces at speed whilst rapidly chanting 'Depart in the name o' the
Father.' Finally* ST PIOR *stops and taking a deep breath booms out:*

ST PIOR: Avaunt vile spirit!

*He throws his bowl of water straight into* ST EUSEBIUS's *face.*
ST EUSEBIUS *slowly wipes water from his eyebrows. He looks
heavenwards with a long-suffering expression, then suddenly bellows:*

ST EUSEBIUS: Thou avaunt, vile spirit!

ST PIOR *gets the contents of* ST EUSEBIUS's *bowl in his face.
Dripping wet, they stand gazing at each other.*

ST EUSEBIUS (*thoughtfully*): Hhmmm. 'Tis not possible to look
like you and not be possessed by the devil . . . Who art thou?

ST PIOR (*cautiously*): A man o' God. A monk called Pior the Simple, Pior o' Shenalolet. Who art thou?

ST EUSEBIUS: A monk. Eusebius the Blessed. Eusebius o' Caesarea.

ST PIOR: I hast heard tell o' thee. But how canst I know thou art the real Eusebius and not some goky dressed in his chains?

ST EUSEBIUS: And be thou the true Pior and not some frentick goost in his flesh? . . . We must talk. He who is not human will soon betray himself.

> PIOR *nods*.

Where art thou from?

ST PIOR: The salt lakes o' Nitria.

ST EUSEBIUS: I passed that way once.

ST PIOR: Then thou knowest naught grows there; the splintering rocks cut the feet to ribbons and the noonday sun sendeth men blind. A grimliche country; petrified like my heart, dead like my body. Ah, how I miss it.

ST EUSEBIUS: So why didst thou leave?

ST PIOR: When I first set down my brick there, 'twas a true solitude. I beheld no living soul, but a few dying travellers staggering past. Then other monks swarmed in claiming to be men o' God. The days were filled with their herte cries and the nights with their lamentations. I recall going one noonday to fetch water from the well. Iche step o' the way bearded faces wouldst pop up out o' their holes in the ground and curse me for disturbing their solitude. *Their* solitude! 'Twas my solitude! I found it, 'twas mine, mine, mine. And when I dropped the bucket down the well for water, instead o' a godly splash there rose up a great cry 'ahhhh!' One of those damned monks had made his abode at the bottom o' the well. That very night God spake unto me: 'Take up thy brick, blessed Pior, and I will guide thee through the desert.'

ST EUSEBIUS: If the Lord spake unto thee I shouldst know. He wouldst have told me o' thy coming. He tells me o' the movement o' iche dung-sluggy crawling out o' that pile, so he wouldst have told me o' thee.

ST PIOR: He told thee. The Devil stuffed thy ears. My Saviour guided me through the wilderness to this cave.

ST EUSEBIUS: And I must receive thee with loving-kindness. Take what I have. I will give thee fresh water. Rest before thou continueth on thy way . . .

 ST EUSEBIUS *hops over to the water-jug.*

ST PIOR: At the entrance to this cave, the Lord spake unto me again: 'This shall be thy abode, Blessed Pior.'

ST EUSEBIUS *(stopping)*: *Thy* abode . . . ?

ST PIOR: Yea, until I dissolve into Christ and enter his everlasting mansions.

ST EUSEBIUS: 'Tis true God's house has many mansions, but this one is occupied. A monk is his own Adam. He canst not share his fearful paradise.

ST PIOR *(indicating entrance)*: Therefore I shall bless thee, saintly Eusebius, as thou goeth forth into the wilderness. Benedictio Dei . . .

ST EUSEBIUS *(controlling himself)*: If 'twere God's will for thee to take my place I wouldst bow my head like as a bullrush, pick up my brick and go gladly, praising the Lord that he shouldst find me worthy. But 'tis not God's will.

ST PIOR: 'Tis.

ST EUSEBIUS: I seest no sign: no archangel o' light, neither Michael, Gabriel, Raphael or even Uriel or Zachariel announced thy coming. No dove at the height o' Heaven stands above thy head, thy fingers are not ten fingers o' fire, thy face doth not shine with a double glory. Thou art not God's messenger.

ST PIOR *(gesturing)*: He speaks now. List. He speaks. The voice o' God. *(Looking up.)* Louder, Lord, that he may hear. Lo, the Lord speaks . . . List . . . he speaks . . . shhhh . . . *(Cocks his head to one side and repeats slowly with emphasis.)* 'This . . . is . . . thy . . . dwelling-place . . . Pior . . . Stay!'

ST PIOR *turns to* ST EUSEBIUS *with a smug smile.* ST EUSEBIUS's *eyes have widened; he is looking up ecstatically.*

ST EUSEBIUS: Yea, yea, 'tis true, I hear Him. My Jesus speaks. Oh, 'tis Him.

ST PIOR: Praise Him triumphant!

ST EUSEBIUS: Thy servant heareth Thee, O Lord . . . Thou speakest Lord . . . We hear Thee plain . . . *(He cocks his head to one side and repeats slowly.)*

    ST PIOR *nods sagely with each word.*

'This . . . is . . . thy . . . dwelling-place . . . Eusebius . . . Stay!'

ST PIOR *(stops nodding)*: *Eusebius?* . . . That 'twas not my Lord's voice.

ST EUSEBIUS: No, 'twas *my* Lord's voice.

ST PIOR: 'Twas the Devil's voice.

ST EUSEBIUS: I only know the Lord's voice. I hath spoken to Him afore and to all the Ruling Princes o' the Nine Celestial Orders. Thine was the Devil's voice.

ST PIOR: The Devil comes to me no more. I hath cast him out and all his legions. *(Shudders.)* If 'twere truly the Devil's voice then I am lost. The only voice I hear is God's voice.

ST EUSEBIUS: They both canst not be God's voice, even if He doth move in mysterious ways. We must determine in the Light o' Truth who heard the Word o' Truth.

ST PIOR: He who hath proved himself most worthy to receive it. He who has suffered most for Christ.

ST EUSEBIUS *(nodding)*: He who has sacrificed most in His service.

ST PIOR *(nodding)*: He who hath proved his love and felt most pain.

    *A ringside bell clangs to signal the beginning of the fight. They eye each other warily, moving round slightly to get an advantage.*

ST EUSEBIUS: John the Small first instructed me in the bitter ways o' humility. Wearing wrist-irons I plaited palm leaves, ne'er casting my eyes from the ground and sleeping fitful in a hair-shirt.

ST PIOR: I was taught by the godly Paphnutius. He beateth me twice daily and maketh me water a dry stick in the desert. In the second year it flowered and in memory o' that miracle Paphnutius beat me thrice daily.

ST EUSEBIUS: I went forth to Thebaid to maketh my abode in a desert tomb, wi' a corpse for my pillow. We rott together: the dead flesh turned green, sliding off enblaunched bones and the space around was alive with white sluggies swimming in slime. Lo, I saw this body drip away and I prayed ankle-deep in flesh, praising sweet Jesus that my dead flesh too wouldst soon rott . . . *Grrrrk.*

*He has looped some slack chain round his neck and pulled it tight. His eyes bulge.*

ST PIOR: I went forth from my hyena-hole and maketh my home in a hollow cedar tree lined wi' thorns. Five years bent double, ne'er able to turn my head or straighten my limbs. Five years pricked bloody by thorns and mosquitoes that did infest the place. Till one day anger filled me and I killed one that was fat with my blood. Contrite, I stood naked in a swamp. There mosquitoes with stings that didst pierce the hide o' wild boars feasted off my croked body. Thus they avenged their dead brother. When I crawled back, men shunned me as a leper. Thus I killed my vile body crying out 'Hossana, Hossana' . . . *Uggghh.*

*He has picked up his water-jug and bangs it down on his head, staggering slightly. Now with increasing speed,* ST EUSEBIUS *half strangles himself with the chain and* ST PIOR *clumps himself over the head with his water-jug. Neither show any reaction except* ST EUSEBIUS's *eyes bulge and* ST PIOR *staggers slightly.*

ST EUSEBIUS: I cried out Hossana too, scourging myself wi' three-thonged whips o' ox-hide weighted wi' bullets o' lead . . . *Grrrrk.*

ST PIOR: I scourged myself wi' scorpions: four-thonged whips set wi' iron hooks that didst tear . . . *Ugggghh.*

ST EUSEBIUS: I lay caged on a mountain forty days and forty nights . . . *Grrrrk.*

ST PIOR: I roamed the wilderness naked, cropping grass . . . *Ugggghh.*

ST EUSEBIUS: I bowed in prayer 1,244 times daily . . . *Grrrrkk.*

ST PIOR: I prayed till my knees bled . . . *Ugggghh.*

ST EUSEBIUS: I croppeth six black olives daily! . . . *Grrrrk.*

ST PIOR: I croppeth five black olives daily! . . . *Ugggghh.*

ST EUSEBIUS *(losing temper)*: Lay it to thy heart! . . . *Grrrrkk.*

ST PIOR: The Lord smells out thy falsehoods! . . . *Ugggghh.*

ST EUSEBIUS: Lopliche goky! . . . *Grrrrkk.*

ST PIOR: Burgh-swyne! . . . *Ugggghh.*

ST EUSEBIUS: Liar! . . . *Grrrrkk.*

ST PIOR: Liar! . . . *Ugggghh.*

*Standing shoulder to shoulder, they burst angrily into song, shuffling sideways and accompanying themselves by rattling their chains.*

ST EUSEBIUS and ST PIOR *(singing)*: 'MONKS! *(Jerking leg irons together.)* I don't know what's wrong with these MONKS today! MONKS! Who can believe anything they say? MONKS! They are disobedient, disrespectful oafs! Noisy, crazy, lusty, lazy, loafers! While we're on the subject: MONKS! *(Jerking legs out.)* You can pray and pray – till your face is blue! MONKS! But they still say anything – – even if it isn't true! Oh why can't they be like we are, perfect in every way? What's the matter with MONKS today?'

ST EUSEBIUS: Thou hast no proof that thou hast loved Christ more and suffered more for His sake.

ST PIOR *(lurching forward)*: This charred flesh bears witness to my love; this bitter mouth, these dead eyes, dried limbs, hollow skull.

ST EUSEBIUS *(slowly)*: I seeth a crabbed body like as mine, and the scars o' terrible battles I too hath fought and won.

ST PIOR: I swear I have done these things and more, by the succouring grace of our Lord Jesus Christ who with God the

Father and the Holy Ghost liveth and reigneth world without end. I swear.

ST EUSEBIUS *(hesitating)*: Thou swearest most powerfully on thy eternal soul. If this be true ? ...

ST PIOR: Then I hath loved and suffered more than thou for Christ. And thus he maketh this place my abode. 'Tis true, believe it. For He hath ne'er left me since that blessed dawn in a field outside Troe above Babylon when the dove flew out o' my mouth and He spake unto me thus: 'Leave thy plough, Pior, and follow Me'.

ST EUSEBIUS *(slowly)*: 'Leave ... thy ... plough? Thou livest as a poor farmer before the Lord spake unto thee?

ST PIOR *(nodding)*: All farmers are poor.

ST EUSEBIUS: So they say. Didst thou labour in the fields from dawn to dusk?

ST PIOR *nods.*

Didst thou croppen only dry bread and lentils daily?

ST PIOR *nods.*

Didst thou sleep on bare earth and wert thou beaten and robbed by pissares and tax gutters?

ST PIOR *nods.*

And thou sacrificed all that to follow our Lord?

ST PIOR *nods.*

Then 'tis plain, thou sacrificed nothing! Nothing worth sacrificing. NOTHING ... Ah, what a difference 'twixt thy former life and mine. In my fleshy days I was tutor to the Emperor Theodosius o' blessed memory. I was born in a great house wi' beds decked wi' gold and coverlets most precious. My garments silken, my tables heavy with wild pheasant and spices, my air sweet wi' the sound o' pipe and lyre. Look now at my dwelling place. See the measure o' my love for Christ.

ST PIOR: These chains! What o' these chains and whips? Every day tears, every day weeping, the earth canst not swallow up my pain.

ST EUSEBIUS: And in return thou wert given the power o' a monk. As a peasant thou wert nothing. Now thou canst command the rich man to kneel outside thy cell in penance. By renouncing the world thou raised thyself up, whilst I was cast down from the highest to the lowest. Thus I have sacrificed most, and must prove more worthy to receive God's word. Thou only sacrificed a hard life for an easier one, two three, four, five, six, seven, eight, nine, ten, OUT.

*The ringside bell clangs and* ST EUSEBIUS *raises his right arm to acknowledge his victory.*

ST PIOR *(growling)*: A man devoted to Christ may die but can ne'er be defeated. Thou wert born and lived in corruption. A lifetime's pain and sacrifice can ne'er wash away thy sins.

ST EUSEBIUS: Yea, I am a sinner and proud o' it. For joy shall be in heaven over one sinner that repenteth, more than over ninety-nine just persons that need no repentance.

ST PIOR: Words canst not make thee believe I am His messenger. So I will show thee God like as a fist, like as a scythe o' cutting light; I will show thee the crushing power o' God; I will show thee miracles.

ST EUSEBIUS: Miracles? Pish, I have healed the sick, raised the dead, lived wi' Christ. Start not on miracles, or I shall beat thee out!

*Loud intakes of breath as both men sway and glower.*

ST PIOR: Down anger, down anger, down anger, anger down. Down, down, down. I wilt rise above it. And levitate!

ST EUSEBIUS: *Levitate?* You levitate? I'll wager thou canst not even get up in the morning.

ST PIOR *stands rigid, arms clasped straight down by his side.*

ST PIOR *(chanting)*: Lord confound this heretic. I am a soul inflamed with the love o' God. Love o' God, love o' God, love o' God – love – o' – loove – God – Go-go-o-o-o-o . . . *(He lifts his arms and rises himself slowly up on his toes as his voice changes.)* Up – up – up – up – up – uuuuuuup . . . *(He is now standing on tip-toes, his eyes are blank, his facial muscles set in a fixed mask and he speaks in a flat voice.)* Behold, 'tis done. Now dost thou believe?

ST EUSEBIUS: Believe? Why?

ST PIOR: Art thou blind as well as deaf to truth?! Canst thou not see I float above thee? I'm high!

ST EUSEBIUS: Thou hast not moved.

ST PIOR: Then why am I looking down at thee from a height?

 ST EUSEBIUS *hops close to him and raises himself on tip-toe.*

ST EUSEBIUS: We are on equal standing. *(Peers into* ST PIOR'*s face.)* Eyeball to eyeball. *(Pushes him.)* I touch thee.

ST PIOR *(remaining rigid)*: Be not proud. Look up. Look up.

ST EUSEBIUS: I hath no need to look up. Pior stands before me.

*He slaps him across the face.*

ST PIOR *(no reaction)*: 'Tis only Pior's hollow shell thou seest; his sounding box. Look up, I say, and behold the true Pior. For Pior o' Shenalolet has risen.

ST EUSEBIUS: Thou art here. Feel this blow, these righteous blows! *(He punches him.)*

ST PIOR *(chuckling)*: How can Pior feel thy blows when Pior has been sucked up to another place?

 ST EUSEBIUS *punches him again.*

From my eagle perch thou look possessed down there, striking an empty frame, for emptiness is all thou hast before thee.

 ST EUSEBIUS *continues to hit him with increasing anger.*

Come, 'tis not good to see a monk puffed up wi' anger. Thou wilt injure thyself in thy blindness. Lord . . . I . . . come . . . down.

 ST EUSEBIUS *steps back as he begins chanting, slowly lowering his body and his arms.*

Glory be to the Father, and to the Son, and to the Holy Ghost *(his voice becomes deeper)* both now and ever and unto-the-ages-of-ages-ag-aaaaaaa-down-down-dow-do-do-doooooooooo. STOP. *(His body judders, his face relaxes and his eyes focus: he speaks in his normal voice.)* 'Tis done! Everything that hath breath, let them praise the name o' the Lord! After such proof, Eusebius, even thou must know I am chosen by God to be in this place.

ST EUSEBIUS: Proof?! Proof?! I will give thee proof. Any lewd monk can perform levitation. I will show thee the miracle of Transportation. Without moving I will transport myself to that corner. *(He points.)*

ST PIOR: Out o' that entrance wouldst please God more.

*But* ST EUSEBIUS *turns and faces the corner, half-crouching like an athlete at the start of a race.*

ST EUSEBIUS *(chanting, his voice changing)*: Move me Lord, move me Lord. We adore Thee O Christ, my good Father and Holy Ghost. Behold thou hast come – Behold – thou-hast-come-Behold-Behol-Beeeeeeeee – *(He makes as if to leap forward, but instead freezes in position, his eyes blank, his face set like a mask. He speaks in a flat voice.)* Behold. I am here.

ST PIOR: Yes. Thou art here.

ST EUSEBIUS: No, here.

ST PIOR: Where, here?

ST EUSEBIUS: Here, here.

ST PIOR: Here, here?

ST EUBIUS: Here, in this corner!

ST PIOR: No. here in front o' me. Thus.

*With great satisfaction,* ST PIOR *deliberately punches him in the face.* ST EUSEBIUS *does not notice.*

ST EUSEBIUS: Turn, Pior, turn and see. I am transported.

ST PIOR *(turning)*: I see nothing.

*He clanks across to the far corner.*

ST EUSEBIUS *(swaying back as if to avoid him)*: Thou comest too close. Thou wilt have me over.

*In the far corner* ST PIOR *claws the empty space.*

ST PIOR: Nothing. God's air.

ST EUSEBIUS *(jerking his head away)*: Take care, thy greasy nails will scratch my face.

ST PIOR: Nothing! There be nothing! Nothing, not even the ghost o' thee.

*He lashes out with his foot kicking the air in front of him.* ST EUSEBIUS *gives a yell of pain and clutches his leg.*

ST EUSEBIUS: Sparrow-mouthed bosarde! Churl!

ST PIOR *(hopping back angrily):* Thou knewest thou couldst never perform Levitation, Transportation or even Elongation, so thou accused me o' failing, knowing thou couldst not move thyself.

ST EUSEBIUS: I grow weary o' these peasants' tricks. Lord Jesus my Saviour, draw me back. Arise, through the grace and mercies o' Thy only begotten Son -Only-begotten-Son-only-begotten-only-begot-only-be-onlyeeee-oneeee-eeeeeeeeygng! *(He snaps violently upright, his eyes focus, his face relaxes and he speaks in his normal voice.)* Go forth Master Pior rejoicing that thou hast seen wonders.

ST PIOR: Wonders?! Wonders?! I hath seen no wonders. Only the ravings o' a stinking dounghep. *I* will show thee wonders! Like a magnet draws up iron so I shall be drawn up and over the desert to Alexandria. *(Chanting.)* Lord we praise Thee; we serve Thee; we worship Thee; we praise Thee serve Thee-worship-Thee-praise-Thee-serve-Thee-worship-Thee-Theeee-Theeeeee-heeeeee-heeeeee-eeeeee *(He lets out a high pitched humming and starts spinning round clock-wise like a top, faster and faster, his chains flying out around him; suddenly he stops. His eyes are blank, his face rigid, and he speaks in his flat voice again.)* I voyage on air. I see below the desert pitted wi' monks' cells: Deir-Makaryus, Deir-es-Suriani, -Deir-Baramus. There is Macarius the Elder crouched in his hole. And there! there! is Blessed Ammon kneeling outside his cave . . . There! Look! The glittering roofs of Alexandria; the mighty temples and palaces: the Soma, the Poseideion, Emporium, Serapeum, the Caesareum and Timonium built by the pagan lecher Anthony. Strike 'em down O Lord and the 30,000 lost souls rotting below! Now I can see them plain along Canopic Street.

See, they watch the pagans dance by, bringing Alexander's statue into the city again. I can see the Priests o' Dionysus pouring libations as they pass, the satyrs crowned wi' golden ivory and the bulls and panthers garlanded wi' peach blossoms. *(Shudders.)* Vile! Bulls garlanded wi' peach blossoms! 'Tis the vilest o' sights I seest before me.

ST EUSEBIUS: Thou seest me! ME!

*Exploding with fury* ST EUSEBIUS *takes some of the slack chain from his shoulders and begins beating* ST PIOR *with it.* ST PIOR *continues undisturbed.*

ST PIOR: Ahhh, stand ye wi' the fear o' God! All is not lost; see, see the warriors o' Christ are not sleeping. There! There! The Patriarch Theophilus and his brave Christians fall on the foul priests wi' knife, axe and bar. Fall on! Fall on! O Lord let thine enemies be scattered . . . tear . . . crush . . . burn . . . no quarter, no quarter . . . the good Theophilus strikes an aged Bacchus; dashes his brains against the bloody stones. No quarter, no quarter! O 'tis a blessed sight. I rejoice! I rejoice!

ST EUSEBIUS: You bleed! You bleed!

ST PIOR'*s face and body is indeed bloody, as* ST EUSEBIUS *continues flaying him.*

ST PIOR: Wish thou wert here to see his enemies sink under the sword. Now I canst return praising the sights I have seen this day. *(Chanting.)* Holy God, Holy Mighty, Holy Immortal, have mercy on us.

ST EUSEBIUS *stops hitting him and steps back.*

Holy-God-Holy-Mighty-Holy-God-Holy-Hol-Hol-Ho-Ho-H-Hmmmmmmmmmmmmmmmm *(He starts humming loudly and spinning anti-clockwise faster and faster; he stops suddenly with a great expulsion of breath.) Yahhhhhhhh. (His eyes focus, his face relaxes, and he speaks in his normal voice.)* Now doest thou believe I can work miracles?

ST EUSEBIUS: *Believe?* Look at thy raw carcass!

ST PIOR: I ne'er look at my body; 'tis vanity.

ST EUSEBIUS: Deluded loon! I'll make thee tremble before the power o' God. I'll show thee truly how to conquer Space – and Time too. *(He begins chanting and swaying back and forth.)* Through the grace and mercies o' love towards man o' Thine Only-begotten Son and Saviour Jesus Christ-Jesus-Christ-Jesus-Christ-Jeeeesus-Christ-Jeeeees-Jeeee-eeeeeeee *(Keeping up the high-pitched shriek he sways back and forth faster and faster, suddenly leaping into the air with a cry: his face becomes rigid, his eyes blank and he speaks in his flat voice.)* Whroom – Meteor bright I stream o'er the desert – *Whroom* – Deir Makaryus, Deir-es-Suriani, Deir-Baramus have crumbled – *Whroom* – the blessed Ammon is dust, and Macarius croucheth in his sandy grave – *Whroom* – I feel the stinkin' air o' the city rise up before me.

ST PIOR: Thou feel only this. Only this.

ST PIOR *picks up* ST EUSEBIUS*'s water jug and smashes it over his head.* ST EUSEBIUS *does not even flinch.*

ST EUSEBIUS: The Alexandria thou knowest is gone. The temples and palaces swallowed up under the sea and sand. The Caesareum is now the Ramleh tram terminus and the Gate o' the Sun a municipal park . . . and Canopic Street is now . . . I am too high to see . . . down, down, I swoop down . . . Canopic Street is now . . . *(Reading.)* Fuad al Amwal. Fuad al Amwal. How about that?

ST PIOR: How about this?!

*Wrenching a slack chain from his shoulders he savagely beats* ST EUSEBIUS *with it.*

ST EUSEBIUS: Alexandria is a heathen city again. 'Tis the anus, the very sink and drain o' mankind, like as London, Paris, New York. I see them below. They spread and merge. One great city girdles the whole earth. One dark place. Millions upon millions packed back to back. And hundreds more born every minute. They are never alone, never alone with God. 'Tis a vision o' Hell.

ST PIOR: 'Tis thy home and birth place, fiend.

ST EUSEBIUS: I hath seen enough o' these times. *(Chanting.)*
We adore Thee, O Christ, and Thy Good Father and the
Holy Ghost. *(As he starts to sway* ST PIOR *tries to step
back but finds his chains have become entangled with* ST
EUSEBIUS's. *He tries to break free but as* ST EUSEBIUS
*continues chanting and swaying,* ST PIOR *is forced to sway with him.)*
We adore Thee Christ and Thy Godly Father and the Holy
Ghost-We-adore-Thee-Christ-and-Thy-Godly-Father-We-
adore-Thee-Christ-we-adore-Thee-we-adoreee-weadoreeee-
weeee-eeee-yahhhhh! *(He leaps into the air jerking* ST PIOR's
*legs from under him; they both fall with a crash.')*

ST PIOR *(struggling to get up)*: Incubus!

ST EUSEBIUS *(focusing and realizing he is entangled in* ST PIOR's
*chains)*: Unhand me. *(Pulling away.)* Devil! 'Tis a Devil's trick.
Whilst I was gone thou hast tried to bind me to thee with thy
chains!

ST PIOR *(staggering up)*: 'Tis *thy* foul chains. Thou wilt not
ensnare me . . .

ST EUSEBIUS *(frightened, staggering up)*: Corruption! Keep away,
Lucifer . . . away . . .

ST PIOR *(pulling)*: Brother o' Balberieth . . . Uncle o' Uzziel! . . .
Son o' Satan! Begone . . .

   *Straining desperately to be apart they give a final heave and
break free.*

   *A pause. They stare at each other with hatred. As they start
to circle round, the sinister, hissing-rasp of two scorpions about to
attack is heard; it is a sound like that made by drawing a thumb
rapidly back and forth across the teeth of a comb. It grows louder
during the action.*

   *The two men now find themselves talking in a modern colloquial
style.*

ST EUSEBIUS: Demon or Man, you were sent by the Devil to
make me doubt.

ST PIOR: Demon or Man, you were sent by the Devil to confuse
and corrupt me.

ST EUSEBIUS: You come between me and my God.

ST PIOR: You stop me being alone with my Creator.

*Each now wraps loose chains round his right fist making a lethal glove.*

ST EUSEBIUS: You've gotta be snuffed out! *Whamee!*

ST PIOR: You're gonna get yours! *Powee!*

ST EUSEBIUS: You're gonna be dumped! *Thok!*

ST PIOR: You've gotta be blasted! *Ka-Voom!*

ST EUSEBIUS: Kill, kill, kill for Jesus!

ST PIOR: Kill, kill, kill for Christ!

*They leap at each other as the scorpions' hissing-rasp fills the auditorium. Amid cries of* 'For sweet Jesus . . . sweet Jesus' *the two men hammer each other with chained fists.*

*The light casts monstrous hump-backed shadows as, gouging and punching,* ST PIOR *drives* ST EUSEBIUS *slowly up the mound. There is no skill, just brute force, as the two chained men reach the top of the pile and stand there brutally clubbing each other into insensibility.*

ST EUSEBIUS *is the first to falter. He falls to his knees. As* ST PIOR *moves forward raining blows on his head,* ST EUSEBIUS *makes one last effort, lunges and punches him in the groin.* ST PIOR *staggers away, gasping.* ST EUSEBIUS *springs up behind him and throws some loose chain around his neck. Before he realizes it.* ST PIOR *is being strangled. He claws desperately at the chain-noose but* ST EUSEBIUS *pulls tighter. The hissing-rasp rises to a crescendo and a great 'crack'. Silence . . .*

ST PIOR'S *head lolls forward, his neck is broken.* ST EUSEBIUS *unwinds the chain.* ST PIOR'S *dead body stands upright for a second, sways, then rolls down the mound, becoming coated with silver dust in the process, until it finally crashes to the ground, sprawling motionless at the base.*

*At the top* ST EUSEBIUS *slowly recovers, and begins to sing the* 'Gloria in Excelsis.'

ST EUSEBIUS *(singing)*: 'Glory be to God on high, and on earth peace, good-will towards men. We praise Thee, we bless Thee, we worship Thee, we glorify Thee, we give thanks to Thee for Thy great glory, O Lord God heavenly King, God the Father Almighty' . . . *(Looking down at* ST PIOR's *body.)* So shalt all demons die. Now he wilt vanish, explode like as a puff-fungus in a cloud o' stinkin' dust . . . Yea, now I enter Him, burst brain's last barrier . . . speech faileth, soul wandereth . . . Yea, now I enter Him, burst brain's last barrier . . . *(Joyfully.)* Methinketh I hear angels sing and maketh great joy. Oh my true vision hath returned! . . .

*Brilliant light floods the cave. Soft shapes float in the air, now filled with low-pitched angels' cries* 'Eeeeepphh . . . Zingggeee . . . Yaaaanngg . . .'

ST EUSEBIUS *(answering ecstatically)*: Eeeeepphh . . . Zingggeee . . . Yaaaanngg . . . Eeeeepphh . . . Zinggeee . . . Yaaaanngg . . .

*The light reaches a peak of intensity. The walls of the cave split and fall away to reveal all around, a blue infinity of space.*

*The choir and voices fade out.* ST EUSEBIUS's *cries grow fainter until he is merely mouthing cries but no sounds. At last silence. An icy winds blows.* ST EUSEBIUS *stands alone in eternity . . .*

*Lights slowly out; the play is ended.*

*A burst of applause and lights up immediately as* ST PIOR *gets up and* ST EUSEBIUS II *enters Stage Right. He is exactly the same as the original* ST EUSEBIUS *still standing on the mound, except that his ankle chains are not locked. He joins* ST PIOR *Stage Centre, for their elaborate Curtain Call.*

*All their actions are slightly slower than normal, as if seen in a dream. They smirk and bow to the audience.* ST EUSEBIUS II *looking suitably exhausted from his taxing role, wipes sweat and make-up from his face.* ST PIOR *steps back reluctantly and* ST EUSEBIUS II *takes a solo curtain call, smiling modestly. With a flourish he beckons* ST PIOR *to join him again and the two make their final bows. They exit Stage Left and Right respectively.*

ST EUSEBIUS, *who has been watching them from the top of the mound trembling, stares after them and then at the audience. He shakes violently with fear.*

ST EUSEBIUS: Have mercy Lord . . . Lord have mercy . . . Lord have mercy . . . mercy Lord . . . have mercy Lord . . . mercy . . . have mercy . . .

*Darkness closes round him as lights go slowly out. He continues praying in the dark.*

### THE END

# The Bewitched

*With an Introduction by Ronald Bryden*

## THE CHARACTERS

PHILIP IV OF SPAIN
CARDINAL PONTOCARRERO, *Jesuit, Archbishop of Toledo*
DUQUE DE MEDINA DE LA TORRES, *Council of State*
COUNT DE MONTERREY, *Council of State*
DUQUE DE ALBA, *Council of State*
SEBASTIEN DE MORRA, *Court jester to Philip IV*
CARLOS II OF SPAIN
RAFAEL DE MORRA, *Sebastien's son, Court jester to Carlos II*
ALMIRANTE DE CASTILLA, *Council of State*
FATHER FROYLAN, *Jesuit priest, Pontocarrero's assistant*
DR BRAVO, *Royal Physician*
OLD MAN
MOTILLA, *Dominican, Royal Confessor*
ANTONIO DE ALMINDA, *Royal Dancing Master*
DON SEBASTIEN VEGA, *Patriarch of the Indies*
HERMONYMOUS GONGORA, *Court Astrologer*
PIERRE REBENAC, *French Ambassador*
DR GELEEN, *Bravo's assistant*
ALONSO DE ALCALA, *Chief Torturer*
GOMEZ, *his son*
VALLADARES, *Dominican, Inquisitor-General*
LOPEZ DURO, *a Jew*
PEDLAR
FRIAR MAURO TENDA, *Capuchin*
PHILIP IV OF FRANCE

BEATRIZ
QUEEN MARIANA, *mother of Carlos II*
QUEEN ANA OF NEUBERG, *wife of Carlos II*
CONDESA BELEPSCH, *Ana's companion*
DONA MARIA ENGRACIA DE TOLEDO MARQUESA DE LOS
    VELEZE, *Royal Nurse*
THERESA DIEGO, *Head Washerwoman*
SISTER INEZ ⎫
SISTER RENATA ⎬ *Nuns of Cangas*
SISTER JUANA ⎭

LADIES IN WAITING, ATTENDANTS, MONKS, PRIESTS,
    PRISONERS, EXECUTIONER, MOURNERS, MESSENGERS,
    PEASANTS

# ACKNOWLEDGEMENTS

The lyrics of 'Lucky in Love', copyright © 1927 by Harms Inc., are reproduced by permission of Chappell & Co., Ltd; words and music by Buddy G. De Sylva, Lew Brown and Ray Henderson. This was originally from the show *Good News*.

The lyrics of 'Clap Your Hands' are reproduced by courtesy of Warner Bros. Music Ltd.

It has not been possible in all cases to trace the copyright holders of lyrics. The publishers would be glad to hear from any such unacknowledged copyright holders.

# Introduction
## by Ronald Bryden

'The lights go up on Philip IV of Spain in his shrouded bed-chamber . . .' I can confess now that I read the first stage-direction of Peter Barnes's *The Bewitched* with a sinking heart. I had looked forward to its arrival on my desk as the first ray of sunshine in a long, dry-as-dust winter in the script department of the Royal Shakespeare Company. For most of the past year, it seemed to me, I had been writing letters explaining gently that the RSC's devotion to the Bard did not extend to blank verse, five-act tragedies he had inexplicably failed to write himself about Henry I, Edward III, Lambert Simnel and Diane de Poitiers. It seemed impossible to persuade playwrights that a diet of Shakespeare's chronicles and Roman history plays did not leave our actors hungering to appear in forty-character pageants set during the Norman invasion, Monmouth's Rebellion and the Napoleonic Wars. What we wanted, I would try to explain, were plays of Elizabethan scope and theatricality, but essentially modern in their tone and stagecraft, relevant to the concerns of Britain today—the sort of model I had in mind was Peter Barnes' *The Ruling Class*. And now, after four years, Peter had finally written a new play and offered it specially to the RSC, swarming with cardinals, Grand Inquisitors and dwarfs, dealing with the last and most obscure of the Spanish Hapsburgs, a monarch whose only significance was that his death caused the War of the Spanish Succession and that 'famous victory' by Marlborough at Blenheim. If old Caspar in Southey's poem a hundred years later couldn't remember what that battle was all about, what on earth would Carlos II of Spain mean to audiences in the second half of the twentieth century?

All of which is a warning to play-readers, myself at their head, against doctrine, relevance-chasing and preconceived ideas. Several hours later, I finished reading *The Bewitched* for the second time and typed a memorandum to Trevor Nunn, the RSC's artistic director, beginning: 'God must love us after all. I think this is a work of genius.' Simply, *The Bewitched* was the finest modern play I'd read in years: the most extraordinary, the most theatrical and—yes, but without a single nudge or sidelong glance at the audience—the most pertinent to British society in the 1970s. It imposed itself with the feeling of a classic; but this wasn't only because it spoke, as the greatest Elizabethan and Jacobean plays do, to modern concerns in a seventeenth-century accent. I knew I was in the presence of something remarkable because, in scene after scene, it led me over ground no playwright had trodden before, to climax after climax of a daring which defined you to imagine how it could ever be staged. Time and again, it produced the effect which A. E. Housman called the one infallible test of poetry: it made my scalp prickle with cold excitement.

Another sign of a major work of art is that it should bring together, crystallized within a single image or statement, tendencies which have appeared, apparently unconnected, in other works preceding it. In the literature of the 1830s, for example, there is a strain of apparently groundless terror and foreboding which links works as disparate as Tennyson's 'Locksley Hall', Dickens' *Barnaby Rudge* and Bulwer-Lytton's *Last Days of Pompeii*. In Carlyle's *French Revolution* their vague fears and intimations of apocalypse acquire a focus and name: this, you realize, was the great doom hanging over the early Victorian imagination. Similarly, in the British drama of the 1960s, a new tone of comedy and disillusion seems to raise its head. In the black farce of Joe Orton, the metaphysical wit of Tom Stoppard, the Goyescan horror of Edward Bond's *Early Morning* and *Lear*, there is a common note which one could only, at the time, describe loosely as Jacobean—a sense of things falling apart, a bitter delight in their new randomness, an appalled disgust at the superstition and brutality revealed by the collapse of the old order, which brought to mind Ben Jonson, Donne and

Webster. By comparison, the playwrights of the 1950s—John Osborne, Arnold Wesker—seemed like survivals from a more confident, neo-Elizabethan age: isolated Raleighs offended by the new era's lack of respect for language, craft, the principle of merit.

Peter Barnes gathers all these threads together in *The Bewitched*. It is a neo-Jacobean play which crystallizes, clarifies and pins down what it is that links the Jacobeans and his contemporaries. Partly, it does so by being genuinely Jacobean in thought and texture: only a writer saturated as Barnes is in the language of Jonson, Marston and Middleton (he has taken time out from his own career to edit *The Alchemist*, *The Devil is an Ass*, and *Antonio and Mellida* for contemporary audiences) could have produced the brilliant, thorny, fantastic speech of Carlos' courtiers, the two great verse tirades the stammering king speaks in the lucid aftermath of epilepsy. But more than that, it penetrates to the heart of the Jacobean melancholy which is also our own: the discovery that 'the new philosophy casts all in doubt', that the universe is absurd and all the comforting beliefs in which we were reared are frantic constructs to mask this intolerable truth.

'Blind chance rules the world!' cry the possessed nuns of Cangas in the astonishing exorcism scene in Barnes's second act. Theirs are the only sane voices in a society which has organized itself insanely in order to shelter itself from such knowledge. As protection against the unbearable notion of an inane universe, the greatest empire the world had seen until the rise of our own clung to belief in the magic power of one almost inane human being, the rule of a king who could not digest his food, control his bladder or put words together consecutively. Carlos II was probably the most tragic consequence history has seen of the faith in a sacred caste of divinely appointed rulers. Because royalty could mate only with royalty, king's children with king's children, generations of Hapsburg cousins had interbred to produce a man who inherited madness from twenty-three of his ancestors, in whom the notorious Hapsburg jaw was so pronounced that he could not chew. For nearly thirty years, the whole of Spain and Europe hung on the spectacle of this unfortunate creature trying to engender an heir who might sustain the vast hierarchy of values and privileges which hinged on him. As John Nada comments in the most recent biography of Carlos, 'Nobody can understand how powerful over the human mind the belief in the divinity of kings can be, unless he has watched its effects where the king has been an idiot.'

But *The Bewitched* is no more a play about monarchy than *The Ruling Class* (despite fairly general critical misconception) was a play about aristocracy. What makes it bitingly relevant to Britain in the 1970s is its scathing examination of the belief that any category of people, royal or not, is 'special': peculiarly fitted to govern empires, occupy positions of privilege, command more wealth than others. Carlos was only important to Spain because his 'divinity' sanctioned the special position of tier after tier of nobles, clerics and civil servants within the pyramidal society he crowned. As Carlos himself sees in the luminous clarity of post-epilepsy, the enemy is Authority:

No blessings come from 't,
No man born shouldst ha' t' wield 't.
Authority's the basilisk, the crowned dragon,
Scaly, beaked and loathsome.
Born from a cock's egg, hatched under a toad,
Its voice is terror, glance, certain death.
Streams where 't drank once are poisoned
And the grass around turns black.
'Twill make a desert o' this world
Whilst there's still one man left t' give commands
And another who'll obey them.

Or to give it its contemporary name, the principle of merit. As *The Bewitched* shows, with no manipulation of historical fact to make its case, Spain was not ruled by Carlos but by such men as Pontocarrero, Cardinal of Toledo and head of the imperial bureaucracy, who owed their positions to their own skills and brain-power and upheld the monarchy only for the aura of sacredness it reflected on their own authority. The most striking difference between the British playwrights of the Sixties and their predecessors of the Osborne generation is that they, the neo-Elizabethans, saw themselves as forerunners of a merito-cratic revolution, an opening by universal education of all careers to the talents, which would create a new aristocracy of mind, rather than birth or inherited wealth. Peter Barnes and his contemporaries challenge that definition of equality, satirizing with grim Jacobean wit the society meritocracy has built. So that the title of *The Bewitched* spreads beyond the unfortunate Carlos 'el Encantado', beyond the sleepwalking empire which collapsed about him, to the ghost-empire we in Britain inhabit now, with its dreams of supersonic supremacy, its chauffeur-driven executive Bentleys, its newspapers whose favourite editorial verb is 'must' and its ever-soaring sterling deficits. 'Bewitchment's the cause of our present ills,' explains Father Froylan, the royal confessor, to Carlos, 'it holds us in dream.' Spain's dream, as Peter Barnes has written it, is our nightmare, pinned down and crystallized. It would be pleasant to think that his mocking, despairing laughter might still wake us.

**TO RON**

*The Bewitched* was first presented by the Royal Shakespeare Company at the Aldwych Theatre, London, on 7 May 1974, with the following cast:

| | |
|---|---|
| NUN/LADY IN WAITING | *Madeline Bellamy* |
| NUN/LADY IN WAITING | *Edwina Ford* |
| BELEPSCH | *Janet Henfrey* |
| THERESA | *Dilys Laye* |
| NUN/LADY IN WAITING | *Joan Morrow* |
| QUEEN ANA | *Rosemary McHale* |
| QUEEN MARIANA | *Elizabeth Spriggs* |
| LADY IN WAITING | *Valerie Verdun* |
| ALBA | *Tim Buckland* |
| SEBASTIEN DE MORRA/RAFAEL DE MORRA | *George Claydon* |
| MONTERREY | *Lee Crawford* |
| PHILIP IV/VALLADARES | *Mark Dignam* |
| SINGER | *Philip Doghan* |
| GONGORA | *Peter Geddis* |
| TORRES | *Patrick Godfrey* |
| CARLOS | • *Alan Howard* |
| GOMEZ | *Christopher Jenkinson* |
| DR GELEEN | *Sidney Livingstone* |
| PONTOCARRERO | *Philip Locke* |
| REBENAC | *Walter McMonagle* |
| ANTONIO | *Phillip Manikum* |
| OLD MAN | *Joe Marcell* |
| FROYLAN | *Joe Melia* |
| MONK/ATTENDANT | *Michael Mellinger* |
| MONK/ATTENDANT | *Anthony Nash* |
| RAFAEL DE MORRA/SEBASTIEN DE MORRA | *Peter O'Farrell* |
| DURO/TENDA | *Trevor Peacock* |
| ALMIRANTE | *Nicholas Selby* |
| DR BRAVO | *Barry Stanton* |
| ASSASSIN | *Keith Taylor* |
| MOTILLA | *David Waller* |
| ALCALA | *Arthur Whybrow* |

*Directed by* TERRY HANDS
*Designed by* FARRAH
*Lighting by* STEWART LEVITON

# THE BEWITCHED

## PROLOGUE

*Darkness. A funeral bell tolls.*

PONTOCARRERO'S VOICE: No man dies suddenly. Death gi'es us warning. For what are the accidents and diseases o' life but warnings o' death. Now that most blessed infant, Prince Felipé, Prospero, Knight o' the Golden Fleece, heir t' the throne o' Spain, lies rotting in the House o' Corruption. Samson's hair, David's sling, Sisera's nail, Egypt's eight plagues, maketh not such sorrow. But we trust in Thy infinite mercy, Lord, and the continuing strength o' Thy representative on earth, His Most Catholic Majesty Philip IV o' Spain. . .

*Lights up on* PHILIP IV *of Spain in his shrouded bedchamber. Double doors Up Stage Centre, a full length mirror Stage Right. Opposite, Stage Left, a curtained four-poster bed. Below it Down Stage Left the elegant Jesuit priest,* PONTOCARRERO, *kneels in front of a small, portable altar chanting the 'Miserere' while the light from a tallow candle flickers over a crucified Christ.*

PHILIP *stands cold and aloof Down Stage Centre dressed in black: padded breeches, short cloak and doublet with a small, stiff 'golilla' lace collar, which makes it difficult for him to turn his head. The magnificent Golden Fleece insignia hangs round his neck. He has the traditional curved moustache and his chin is covered with a black silk mask.*

*Kneeling on one knee by him are three Spanish grandees: the* DUQUE DE MEDINA DE LA TORRES, *the* COUNT DE MONTER-REY *and the* DUQUE DE ALBA. *In contrast to the King they are dressed in brocade cloaks and doublets embroidered in gold and breeches gartered with rosettes. Insignias stud their chests and their gloved hands glitter with rings. Each grandee carries a black velvet cushion.*

TWO ATTENDANTS *in black stand behind* PHILIP *whilst a*

*bearded dwarf,* SEBASTIEN DE MORRA *dressed exactly like the grandees sits perched on the single chair by the bed.*

*Taking care not to actually touch him, the* ATTENDANTS *swiftly take off Philip's cloak doublet and insignia and lay them on* ALBA'S *cushion. Bowing frequently, he exits backwards Up Stage Centre.* PHILIP *lifts his legs stiffly. His heel-less shoes are removed and placed on* MONTERREY'S *cushion. He, too, exits backwards, bowing.* PHILIP'S *breeches are pulled off and placed on* TORRES'S *cushion. He exits like the others.* PHILIP *is left in his dirty grey drawers and vest. His gnarled body is painfully twisted, his arms and legs pockmarked with sores.*

ALBA *returns solemnly carrying a nightshirt on his cushion. He drops onto one knee in front of* PHILIP, *who lifts up his arms. The* ATTENDANTS *slip the nightshirt on him.* MONTERREY *re-enters with two curved pomaded leather covers which, as he kneels, are picked up and placed over Philip's moustache. Finally* TORRES *comes back carrying a chamber pot embossed with the Royal Coat of Arms. Kneeling, he holds it up expectantly in position. The* ATTENDANTS *lift Philip's nightshirt, but as there is no response from the King, they take the pot from a disappointed* TORRES *and place it beside the bed.*

PONTOCARRERO *stops chanting the 'Miserere'. The* ATTENDANTS *exit backwards, bowing.* PHILIP *holds out his hand and the grandees kiss it in turn before retiring like the* ATTENDANTS.

PONTOCARRERO *crosses with an open Bible;* PHILIP *kisses it and the priest follows the grandees out. Finally the dwarf* MORRA *jumps down off the chair, bows solemnly and exits backwards like the others, only in a series of dignified back-somersaults.*

*There has been no reaction from* PHILIP *throughout the entire ritual undressing. Hobbling to the altar, he lowers himself to his knees and gravely strikes his forehead against the altar rail.*

PHILIP: Lord, I suppeth up sin as' t were water. My lust corrupts the age. Troops o' virgins passed under me; ripe lips bathed in rancid grease, pink bodies smelling o' perfume and sweet

waters t' cover the stench from their wrinkled thighs and armpits. And f' these delights I'm damned. *Punish me Lord, punish
me.* As the Apostles gave thanks after the whippings and the
children were joyful i' the furnace, so I will rejoice in my pain.
*Crucify me Lord, crucify me.* But only Spain is crucified. Felipé's
dead. As he was my beloved son, I rejoice in my punishment.
As he was Spain's future King I weep at her loss. . . . Oh
Blessed Virgin, Lady o' Angels, Joy o' Saints, Gate o' Paradise,
make the Queen fruitful tonight. Tip my lance, plant my seed,
that another son may be born t' inherit this Thy Kingdom.
Amen. . . . (*Crossing himself he snuffs out the candle, hauls himself
up and moves to the mirror.*) Two wives, thirty-eight bastards,
1,244 liaisons not counting one-night bawds, and I've t' pray
t' God t' raise up my plug-tail. Before I only prayed t' Him
t' keep it down. (*He takes off his mask to reveal the famous protruding Hapsburg jaw covered with livid sores.*) The women, the
women. The rustle o' petticoats and farthingales i' the sun, the
touching, poking, prying, licking i' the shadows—*there, there.*
Old man's dreams. 'Tis the Spanish disease, dreaming. My
people dream o' cheap bread, my captains o' great victories,
my grandees o' new honours: who'll cut my meat, dust my
footstool, wipe my buttocks. I dream too; o' times past, heart's
ease. O' the days hunting deer in the Aranjuez and wild boar
in the Prado and the nights hunting softer game along the
Calle Major. And when the sky lightened 'yond the trees o'
St Germino, musicians played. . . .

*A pearly grey light comes up and a base-lute and viol play a courtly
'Pavan'.* PHILIP *bows gravely to his image in the mirror and begins
the stately dance, formally advancing and retreating. . . .*

*The music changes. Lute and viol fade as guitars take up the
exotic rhythms of the 'Sarabanda'.* PHILIP *bows gaily to the mirror
and this time the 'image' steps out of the frame: it is a beautiful young
woman,* BEATRIZ, *in a thin, white nightdress. With long gliding
steps and flamboyant gestures the two white figures dance, reaching a
climax with* BEATRIZ *dropping on one knee as the music ends.*

PHILIP *bends down to raise her, and grunts in pain. He is a sick man again. They cross to the chair. He sits;* BEATRIZ *crouches at his feet and he strokes her hair.*

PHILIP: Tonight I do sheet-duty wi' the Queen. One last assault on Eve's custom house where Adam made his first entry. No sin in't for 't will be no pleasure. A King who dies w'out an heir betrays his kingdom and his God. He leaves behind a hole in nature, and holes must be filled, eh Beatriz? Else they destroy the world.

BEATRIZ (*breathing deeply*): Eeeeeeeeeh.

PHILIP (*he lifts his arm*): Raising my arm thus 's an act o' Will, raising my plug-tail 'll be an act o' faith. Yet in my youth he stood up f' me. He needs you t' make him dance. (BEATRIZ *rubs herself against him.*) You knew how, hot and heavy in yer hands, rubbing rolled 'tween round buttocks thighs BOLT hard HARD plunged in drop d-d-drops o' sweet juices -jui-jui-jui-j-j-j-j-*ahhhr.*

BEATRIZ: Eeeeeeeeehh.

PHILIP: I feel 't. I feel 't—look! look! *It quivers.* 'Tis not as hard as a ram's horn, nor as stout as Hercules but 'twill serve. Benedícat vos Omnipotens Deus Pater et Fílius et Spíritus Sanctus. (*He makes the sign of the cross over his crotch.*) Memories too are potent. I can make me a son, wet wi' the dew o' heaven, *bold, bold.* Only spare him Lord, for princes too die young. (*The 'Magnificat' is sung softly over.*) After my end who'll hath need t' remember me? Philip IV, 1605–1665, eldest son o' Philip III and Margaret o' Austria. During his reign there were plots in Aragon, rebellions in Catalonia, defeats at Rocroy and Roussilon, whilst Jamaica, Portugal and the Netherlands were lost. When he died there wasn't a damp eye in Madrid. Go back, sweet gypsy. . . .

*He closes his eyes and concentrates.* BEATRIZ *tries to cling to him but an invisible force drags her away. She struggles wildly but is pushed remorselessly backwards towards the mirror. The 'Magnificat' grows louder as she holds out her hands, imploring. But with one last*

*silent cry of protest* BEATRIZ *is thrust back into the mirror.*
*As she vanishes the light fades slightly and there are three loud*
*knocks.* PHILIP *heaves himself up and assumes his former marble*
*gravity as the doors are opened and two Dominican* MONKS
*carrying incensors, their heads covered with conical penitents' hoods,*
*enter to the sound of the 'Magnificat'.*

QUEEN MARIANA *comes in out of the darkness, in a white*
*shift, with long black hair. Behind her, borne on the shoulders of two*
*hooded* MONKS *with large tallow candles, is the skeleton of Saint*
*Isidore propped upright on a bier.* PONTOCARRERO *comes in*
*behind them carrying a silver holy water stoup and sprinkler.*

*The procession crosses the bedroom, chanting. The* MONKS
*put the bier down Stage Right and kneel beside it whilst* MARIANA
*demurely takes her place beside* PHILIP.

PONTOCARRERO: As we despise the corruptible body o' men,
we venerate those o' the Saints and Martyrs, their bodies being
once the temples o' the Holy Spirit which God honours them
by performing miracles in their presence. Thus these moving
bones o' the Blessed Saint Isidore ha' cured spasms, sciatica,
boils, toothache and cast out devils. Now Lord God we pray
f' another miracle. As when the dead body which was plunged
down into the sepulchre o' Elysius instantly sprung t' life
when 't touched the bones o' the prophet, so let the half-dead
instrument o' Thy servant Philip spring instantly t' life when
'tis plunged into the soft sepulchre o' the flesh o' Thy servant
Mariana. In the name o' the Father and o' the Son, and o' the
Holy Ghost.

*As they chant 'Amen',* MARIANA *and a creaking* PHILIP
*cross to opposite sides of the bed and get in. Leaving their candles*
*by the bier, the* MONKS *rise and join* PONTOCARRERO *who*
*liberally sprinkles the bed and its impassive occupants with holy*
*water and intones a blessing.*

PONTOCARRERO: Adjutórium nostrum in nómine Domini. Qui
fecit caelum et terram. Dóminus vobiscum. Et cum spíritu
tuo . . .

*He makes the sign of the Cross and the* MONKS *close the bedcurtains. Chanting triumphantly they exit followed by* PONTOCARRERO. *Their voices quickly die away.*

*As the skeleton watches grimly there is the sound of heavy machinery creaking into motion from the bed. Massive wheels and screws turn laboriously and ancient pistons start pounding. The whole room shakes to a brutal thudding. It reaches a crescendo, a woman screams, Saint Isidore's skeleton jerks upright on the bier and collapses in a heap.*

*The scream turns into staccato cries of a woman in childbirth. They increase in intensity until drowned by a great tearing sound and the floor Down Stage Centre slowly splits apart.*

*Lights down to a Spot on the widening crack which seems full of dark, glutinous liquid. It stirs as something rises out of it. First a hand, then a shapeless body emerges completely wrapped in a pale, pink membrane. Hauling itself feebly out of the crack it flops onto the floor where it lies curled up tight.*

*A sharp slap is heard and a baby starts crying: the body stirs. A choir sings 'Gloria in Excelsis' and Spot Up Stage Centre on a throne on a rostrum with sloping side and three centre steps.* PHILIP *stands proudly in front of the throne. As the wet body slithers painfully towards the throne* PONTOCARRERO *intones:*

PONTOCARRERO'S VOICE: Almighty and everlasting God whose most dearly beloved son, Jesus Christ, didst shed out o' His most precious side both water and blood f' the forgiveness o' our sins, sanctify this water t' the mystical washing away of sin, and grant that this child, now to be baptized therein, may receive the fulness o' Thy Grace and ever remain in the number o' Thy faithful and elect children through Jesus Christ our Lord, amen . . . (*The body begins to flop up the rostrum steps.*) José, Segundo, Bartalome, Ignacio, Rodriguez, Fráncisco, Salvador, Gironalla, Rafael, Vincente, Gancia, Teofilo, Sainz, Luys, Miguel, Ayala, Carlos . . . (*The body painfully hauls itself upright in front of* PHILIP.) I baptize

thee in the name of the Father and of the Son and of the Holy
Ghost.

*The body bursts through its membrane to reveal* PRINCE
CARLOS.

CARLOS: *Dad-a, dad-a . . .*

PHILIP *reacts in horror at the sight. He clutches his chest, utters
a despairing cry and keels over backward off the rostrum, dead.*

*The funeral bell tolls again.* CARLOS *bows his head, slowly
turns and solemnly sits on the throne.*

*The funeral bells change into joyful peals as crowds cheer
rapturously whilst* CARLOS *stares fixedly ahead.*

# ACT ONE

*A parrot screeches raucously as the bells and cheers fade out to the sound of two women arguing. The deformed* CARLOS II *continues staring ahead; he has a monstrous protruding chin, lank hair, long sickly face and wet lips. He is in his thirties, slovenly dressed in stained black doublet and breeches and a dirty gollila collar.*

*Harsh lights full up on the bare throne-room, 1692. Banners round the panelled walls. Doors Stage Right and Left. Throne and rostrum Up Stage Centre.* TWO ATTENDANTS *either side and in front of it* MARIANA, *the Queen Mother and* QUEEN ANA OF NEUBERG. *Her Amazon parrot is on a perch nearby.*

MARIANA *is now in her sixties, her face a thick mask of white cosmetic, framed in a nun-like cowl, her stumpy body hidden beneath a black 'sacristan' dress. A cross hangs from a rolled cord round her waist and there are large rings on her fingers.* ANA, *in her late twenties, is dressed in a dark green hooped dress with puffed sleeves and square neckline. Her bare shoulders are whitened, lips and cheeks painted red, fair hair coiled and greased. She wears heavy earrings, thick bracelets on each wrist and her fingers are covered with jewellery.*

*Both hieratic figures clutch a document and argue with flat ferocity, hardly moving.*

MARIANA: Cribbage-faced ape-leader.

ANA: Carbuncled crone.

MARIANA: Buss-beggar.

ANA: Cock-bawd.

MARIANA: Toad-eater.

ANA: Crab-louse.

PARROT: *Pretty Joey! Pretty Joey!*

MARIANA: Piddling German fussock. I made you a Queen; made you my son's wife.

ANA: 'Tis why I hate you, thatch-gallows.

MARIANA: And why every Spaniard hates you, moss-face.

ANA: They've hated you longer, spoon-head.

CARLOS: Aaaaa III wowowon't. *I won't die.*

MARIANA: Kings 're mortal, Carlos. They're taken too; a blow, a scratch, contagion i' the air, life seeps away.

CARLOS: III measure mmmmy breath.

ANA: Acknowledge 't Carlos, wi'out an heir only a heartbeat stops the grandson of Louis XIV, (*Crossing herself*)—'In Beélzebub príncipe daemoniórum éjicit daemónia'—being made the next King o' Spain.

CARLOS: Nnnnnn . . .

PARROT: *Stop talking when I interrupt! Pretty Joey.*

MARIANA: You must make a Will naming thy successor. We're at war with Louis, (*Crossing herself*)—'In Beélzebub príncipe daemoniórum éjicit daemónia'—but even he wouldst have t' recognize your choice.

CARLOS: Bbbbbaaaaa if I make a Will I'll DIE I know 't if I. . . .

MARIANA (*thrusting her document at him*): Secure our future, Carlos, make José o' Bavaria heir t' the throne.

ANA: 'Cause he's thy great-grandson? (*She thrusts her document at* CARLOS.) The next King must be Archduke Charles o' Austria.

MARIANA: Why, 'cause he's thy nephew and you canst claim bribe money from his father?

ANA: Carlos, your successor must be strong. Charles's backed by Austria.

MARIANA: No-one'll countenance an Austrian puppet, addlepate.

ANA: But José has nothing aback o' him.

MARIANA: 'Tis why he'll be allowed t'become King, Madam Dolt.

CARLOS: Aaaaalllow. . . ?!

MARIANA: As thou lovest me, Carlos, sign f'my sake.

ANA: I'll stop m' breath, starve myself to death.

MARIANA: Don't listen t' her promises, Carlos.

CARLOS: I wwwon't daaa die. Why Wills and such? Whaaa. . . ?

ANA: You casn't produce an heir wi' the usual instrument so you must use pen and ink.

MARIANA: Thy father didst his night duty. . . .

CARLOS: KKKKKAAAAK (*He staggers up in fury and jerks spastically down the steps.*) YOOOO say IIII'm Impo-Ìmpo-Impo*TENT TENT?* Am IIII AM?

ANA (*quickly*): No, Carlos.

CARLOS: NNN't true. God loves mmm. NOT IMPO . . .

MARIANA: O' course you're not impotent Carlos, but 'tis per- plexing. You've endured nineteen years o' marriage, first t' the beautiful Queen Louisa then t' this barren witch and every night 'cept during sickness and Saints Days, you've performed thy duty. That's o'er 6,000 performances, wi'out success. Carlos you're not concentrating!

CARLOS: Ssssn't meeeeeee.

MARIANA: True. The waters o' Puertollano cured the Countess Oropesa o' sterility but you've refused to take 'em Madame.

ANA: My sisters're fertile wi'out yer stinkin' gut-water; they breed like as rabbits. The fault's not in my ovaries, Madame.

PARROT: *Bananas! Brown sugar and bananas! Crrah.*

MARIANA: Cast her off, Carlos. She's sterile.

ANA: Banish her, Carlos. She hates us.

CARLOS: WWeeeeee SIN.

ANA: I see thee on Judgement Day, old woman, flung into that lake o' hot pitch and the little devils clawing thee open.

MARIANA: I see thee wi' lips torn off, tongue rooted out, walking 'neath Lucifer's great arse, eating his excrement as it falls.

CARLOS: GOD hurts f'f'f' our sins, your sssins mmmy sins, whaaa?

ANA: I smell thy polluted carcass spiked stinkin' on a dung hill.

PARROT: *Kill for Lent! Kill for Lent!*

ANA: Toads gnaw thy flesh and the little devils laugh *hee-hee-hee*, they laugh *hee-hee-hee*.

MARIANA: I hear thy screams *aaarrhh*, mercy, mercy *aaarhh aaarhh*.

CARLOS: Sssssins sssins sssssss.

*The lights flicker.*

ANA (*prowling like an animal*): Laughing *hee-hee-hee-heeeee-heeeee.*

MARIANA (*jerking her head like a bird*): *Aaarrhh-aaarrhh-aaarrhh.*

CARLOS (*wriggling like a snake*): *Sssss-sssssss.*

*They howl and hiss with increasing fury as the light flickers faster and grows brighter until there is an intense flash and* ANA, MARIANA *and* CARLOS *let out a loud cry and fall into epileptic fits.*

CARLOS'*s head rotates and his tongue lolls out as he whirls round on his own axis, limbs thrashing wildly.* MARIANA'*s legs kick convulsively whilst her arms thrust bolt upright, fingers clutching the air, her teeth bared in a fixed grin.* ANA'*s body jerks up and down as she tears her dress and hits her crotch in excitement.*

*The* PARROT *screeches whilst the* TWO ATTENDANTS *cross unconcerned and place sticks between the jaws of the epileptics and then return to their places.*

*The convulsions stop; the attack ends. Lights down to a Spot on* ANA, CARLOS *and* MARIANA, *now in a state of post-epileptic automation.* CARLOS *rips off his breeches and* ANA *pulls up her dress. As he throws himself passionately on top of her,* MARIANA *rocks back and forth moaning a lullaby and the* PARROT *screeches mockingly. Spot out.*

## SCENE II

*Spot up immediately Wings Left as the two dwarfs* SEBASTIEN DE MORRA *and his son* RAFAEL *enter duelling furiously with tiny rapiers.*
*They are in shirtsleeves and* RAFAEL *is blindfold.*

MORRA: Engage in sixte. I disengage. You parry, quarte, I disengage, you parry sixte, I disengage, you parry octave and riposte. Enough. (*They stop Down Stage Centre.* RAFAEL *takes off his blindfold.*) Remember f' the quick riposte keep the point in line during the parry. Thus. (*He shows him.*) 'Tis a pity the King's sick the day you take my place as Court Jester.

RAFAEL: And what advice 're you gi'ing me? Fathers always gi' advice.

MORRA: And sons n'er listen. Only this: honour the King, never be wi'out 'Mother Bunch's Joke-Book' and ne'er refuse a fight. Thou art a de Morra: the slightest insult—*yah.* (*He lunges,* RAFAEL *parries.*)

RAFAEL: I take your point. I'll defend my honour and the King's and cling t' 'Mother Bunch's Joke-Book' as 't were my Bible.

MORRA: 'Tis, and the King's your God, your polestar. You've been at Court long enough to know who's in, who's out. Remember, the King's always in. Thy only call is t' entertain, t' fill an idle hour.

RAFAEL: I believe I can do more and mix a little purpose wi' my wit.

MORRA: Fatal. I've survived two reigns by having no purpose 'cept t' please. If thou has a message, send 't by messenger.

RAFAEL Why 're licensed fools so crabby-arsed and sour?

MORRA: 'Cause they've a low opinion o' mankind and see 't proved daily. Stupidity stains the world. 'Tis a disease not o' the brain but the soul: a blindness, a shunning o' the light. 'Tis

not the Great Prince, Lucifer, who scourges us but that snot-
nosed, snivelling God, Stupidity. And he's ne'er defeated. I
know, I've lived off him all my life.

RAFAEL: A man doesn't fight merely t' win. Wi' my wit and
sword I'll try and make 't all new.

MORRA: New! You'll dine off funeral meats if you try anything
new! Haven't I taught thee, audiences only want the same old
tumbles. The same old snatches. And any jest must have
whiskers t' give satisfaction. Mother Bunch's joke Number
127: Have you got the dispatches?

RAFAEL: No, I always walk this way. *Honk, honk.*

MORRA: Number 199: My wife's got teeth like the Ten Com-
mandments.

RAFAEL: I know—all broken. *Honk, honk.*

 RAFAEL *leaps on* MORRA'*s shoulders and they cross Wings
Right, earnestly practising.*

MORRA: Master Butcher, have you got a sheep's head?

RAFAEL: No, 'tis the way I part my hair.

RAFAEL: ⎫
    ⎬ *Honk, honk.*
MORRA: ⎭

 *Even as they exit Wings Right, honking, lights full up on the
Council Chamber.*


SCENE III

*The Council Chamber is dominated by a huge map of the Spanish
Empire on the panelled wall Up Stage Centre. Doors Stage Left
and a screen Stage Right.*

*There are several empty places amongst the Council members sitting
stiffly in high backed chairs at a long table placed slightly diagonally
Stage Centre. On one side are the* DUQUES TORRES *and* ALBA.

*Now white-haired,* TORRES *dresses soberly and toys with a book, but*
ALBA *still has on his silver cloak and breeches. Seated opposite is
the* COUNT DE MONTERREY, *and the dashing, pock-marked*

ALMIRANTE DE CASTILLA *nonchalantly fingering his sword handle.* PONTOCARRERO, *now Cardinal-Archbishop of Toledo, presides at the head of the table, Up Stage in dark gown and surplice. A large sapphire ring glistens as he strokes his pointed beard. A Jesuit Priest,* FATHER FROYLAN, *stands beside him with a leather pouch stuffed with State Papers: at every convenient moment he gives him some to sign.*

*They are all listening gravely to the Royal Physician,* DR BRAVO, *an imposing man in large owl-like spectacles.*

DR BRAVO: Your Eminence, my Lords, last night His Majesty had another attack o' 'alfereza insensata' known as epilepsy or falling sickness; 'tis his third this month. The cause is particular foul vapours from a uterus. To cure His Majesty I used the traditional methods, drawing eight ounces o' blood from his left shoulder and administering a sneezing powder o' hellbore t' purge the brain and crushed cowslip t' strengthen 't. Plaster o' pitch and pigeon dung was put on his feet, cat-fat on his chest and a draught o' vinegar and wormwood forced down his throat.

PONTOCARRERO: And?

DR BRAVO: When I left him this morning he was still unconscious.

PONTOCARRERO: How canst tell?

DR BRAVO: The signs 're plain f' one versed in physic; he lay stretched out on the ground.

PONTOCARRERO: I've oft had audience wi' the King when he lay stretched out on the ground.

DR BRAVO: But he doesn't respond t' my promptings.

ALBA: He rarely responds t' the promptings o' princes o' blood rank, so why shouldst he respond t' you.

DR BRAVO: But he lies in his own piss-water.

MONTERREY: His Majesty daily wets his breeches, a leaky conduit runs in the family.

DR BRAVO: But his eyes 're closed!

TORRES: Tired by the weight o' Kingship.

DR BRAVO: But he *looks* senseless!

PONTOCARRERO: Is *that* all? 'Tis normal. I suggest you go examine His Majesty more closely.

*Bewildered,* DR BRAVO *bows, makes for the door, then suddenly stops and turns back.*

DR BRAVO: Ah, but he . . . (*He stops as they stare at him.*) Hhhhmm . . . No . . . (*He exits thoughtfully.*)

PONTOCARRERO: I cannot abide Physicians, gravediggers begin where they end.

ALMIRANTE: 'Tis true His Majesty's behaviour's become passing strange. He wants t' build a bridge on the Jarama River.

MONTERREY: There's nothing wrong wi' wanting t' build a bridge on the Jarama.

ALMIRANTE: Lengthways?

PONTOCARRERO: My Lords, I'm dismayed t' find only four members o' the Council o' State've seen fit t' attend this special meeting. The King may die. We *must* recommend an heir t' the throne. All decisions wait on this, wi'out 't Spain's impotent. Already she wastes away. Father, pluck one at random. (FROYLAN *takes out a document and hands it to him: he reads.*) From our Minister in Andulciá. 'Food is short, the harvest poor, the land unploughed and plague comes for the seventh year.' Another . . .

ALBA: Your Eminence, we've grave business t' discuss and as a true grandee and Gentleman o' His Majesty's Bedchamber, I cannot stay silent. When His Majesty was convulsed last night, Attendants placed the distemper stick 'tween his teeth. All know that privilege's been reserved f' the de Albas since the Moorish Conquest!

MONTERREY: But thou weren't even i' Madrid when His Majesty was stricken.

ALBA: I had a horse ready and coulds't've been at the King's side in an easy five hours.

ALMIRANTE: In an easy five hours His Majesty coulds't've bitten through his tongue and choked i' his own blood.

ALBA: When His Most Catholic Majesty Philip III sat in front o' his fire and a spark set his breeches alight, his royal chair-mover the Duque de Bejar coulds't not be found either. But His Majesty's Attendants knew their place, etiquette was observed, the duke's privileges weren't violated.

ALMIRANTE: But His Majesty burnt t' death.

ALBA: Regrettably. But the Duque de Bejar's privileges weren't violated. Take away one privilege 'cause 'tisn't convenient, others follow. Wi'out privileges no man knows his worth. I speak f' the ancient families o' Spain when I say I'll defend my privileges t' my last breath.

MONTERREY: And I t' my last ducado. Which is what mine cost me. 127,000 f' the privilege o' being the Count de Monterrey and carrying the King's footstool.

TORRES: What's 127,000 ducados t' a wealthy man?

MONTERREY: There 're no wealthy men in Spain, only men wi' money. Now our wealth's in contracts, bonds, gold and silver coinage, not in work done, goods made.

TORRES: I've 30 charities t' support, 148 relatives and 522 servants. In Spain e'en the servants've servants. What wi' taxes and the French wars, a man can work his way up from nothing t' a state o' abject poverty. (*Touches book.*) Like Virgil, I only survive, 'Arte magistra'. I thank God f' the consolations o' literature.

MONTERREY: The consolation o' money's more durable.

ALMIRANTE (*getting up*): Your Eminence, my Lords, the cods, the cods.

*He crosses to behind the screen.*

MONTERREY: Go buy the Viceroyship o' Mexico as I did. (ALMIRANTE *is heard passing water behind the screen; no one takes any notice.*) 'Twill fetch 200,000 ducados but you'd double 't in one year's hard graft and extortion. In a world of tawdry values and vanishing ideals I sometimes think money's the only decent thing left.

PONTOCARRERO, *who has been signing papers, raps the table.*

PONTOCARRERO: My Lords, we're not here t' discuss money or privilege yet again. The land's barren, the treasury empty, the coinage debased. E'ery paper here confirms 't; 'tis no longer noontide. Today our task's t' try and keep the Empire intact and prevent Philip Bourbon gaining the throne f' France.

ALMIRANTE *comes back doing up his breeches.*

ALMIRANTE (*he sits*): T' thwart the French pox-carriers is the task o' every man born south o' the Pyrenees.

PONTOCARRERO: So I recommend José o' Bavaria as heir, the English, Dutch and French 'll fight t' stop Charles o' Austria gaining the Spanish throne, but only the French 'll oppose José. Wi' God's help the Triple Alliance 'll fall apart.

MONTERREY: If we choose Bavaria, Your Eminence, 'tis possible the French Alliance *might* fall. Bavaria offers 'might', Austria three million i' gold. I choose the gold.

ALBA: As a Spaniard, I see 't straight. Blood ties link us wi' Austria. What's Bavaria t' me, or me t' Bavaria, eh? eh?

TORRES: A man's judged by his friends. So are nations. Bavaria's small whilst Austria has one o' the largest libraries in the world: Cicero, Terence and the complete works o' Boethius.

ALMIRANTE: 175,000 Spaniards died at Rocroy and you talk o' the complete works o' Boethius! My lords, victories aren't won by peals o' ordnance, block carriages and muskets alone, but also the spirit o' trumpet and drum. We must defeat our enemies through our strength, not their weakness. I'm f' Charles, Austria and greatness.

*The four* NOBLES *raise their hands.*

NOBLES: Charles, Austria and greatness.

ALBA: And copulation, eh? (*He gets up.*) Your Eminence, my lords, the cods, the cods. (*He stomps off behind the screen.*)

ALMIRANTE: Yes, copulation's a pressing matter. 'Tis said the Archduke's a most filthy fornicator. Though that may be a lie put about by his sympathisers.

TORRES: True, but on balance, I too recommend Charles, subject t' a report on his penis-member and scrotum.

PONTOCARRERO: 'Tis certain he'd've t' satisfy the canonical conditions f' virility—erectio, introductio and emissio.

TORRES: Monsignor Albizzi and Dr Bravo'd carry out the necessary measuring and weighing o' the penis-member erect and in repose.

ALMIRANTE: 'Twill be like trying t' catch a frightened eel wi' greasy sugar tongs.

PONTOCARRERO: No matter how difficult, 't must be done if Charles 's recommended. We took the Queen's fertility on trust and she's proved barren, failing in her duty.

ALMIRANTE: We fail in ours speaking o' her so. Spain's the very birthplace o' chivalry. But now 'tis gone, laughed out by that word-pecker Cervantes and his scribblings.

TORRES: Word-pecker, sir?! Scribblings?!

LMIRANTE: When the young Queen came t' us f' help i' her first days, we cursed her f' not being Spanish or pregnant. Bad harvests or high taxes, 'tis all the fault o' Queen Ana o' Neuberg. (ALBA *is heard passing water behind the screen.*) Yet her steadfast courage doeth us honour, my lords. She grows in goodness and for her sweet honour, womanly grace ... Crow-thumper, I speak o' the Queen!

*In a sudden fury he draws his sword, charges across and jabs it through the screen.* ALBA *yells with fright and the* OTHERS *jump to their feet protesting.* ALMIRANTE *pulls out his sword and brings down the screen to reveal* ALBA *holding up his breeches in front of a commode.*

*They are all too busy shouting to notice the Queen Mother* MARIANA *enter Stage Left, carrying a Bible.*

ALMIRANTE: You'll die f' the insult t' the Queen!

ALBA: My breeches—my honour—my sword—M-M-Ma'am!

*He snaps to attention as he sees* MARIANA *staring at him. The* OTHERS *become aware of her.*

*All bow as she takes* PONTOCARRERO'*s place at the head of the table.*

PONTOCARRERO: Ma'am, this is a solemn moment. We're honoured by thy presence.

ALMIRANTE: Your Eminence, only the King canst attend Council meetings.

PONTOCARRERO: The King's still distempered. Ma'am, 'tis the State Council's humble opinion by four hands t' one, that the Archduke Charles o' Austria be recommended heir t' the throne.

MARIANA: My son, His Most Catholic Majesty Carlos o' Spain favours José o' Bavaria as his heir.

*She hands* PONTOCARRERO *a note, he reads it and passes it to the* OTHERS.

MONTERREY: In all conscience, Ma'am, none here knew o' His Majesty's wishes.

MARIANA: I grow old whilst you talk.

PONTOCARRERO: Those favouring the King's choice, José o' Bavaria?

MARIANA *stares coldly at each in turn. All slowly raise their hands, except* ALMIRANTE.

ALMIRANTE: In all conscience, Ma'am, I'm still f' Charles o' Austria—and the Queen.

MARIANA: We'll remember you i' all conscience . . . Four t' one in favour o' José, Your Eminence. My lords casn't see Charles'd 've governed wi'out a Regent or Council o' State? José's pliable. (*A carbuncled* OLD MAN *rises from an empty chair where he has been hidden and hobbles towards her.*) I pray t' the Holy Virgin that my son lives, but shouldst he die we must face the darkness and *arrrx* . . .

*She gasps in agony as the* OLD MAN *deliberately squeezes her breast. As she leans against the table, the* OTHERS *react.*

TORRES: Your Majesty, Ma'am . . .?

MARIANA *looks up to see the* OLD MAN *exiting Stage Right, wheezing and scratching himself. He has left a silver crab-brooch pinned to her breast.*

MARIANA: Nothing. Nothing. 'Twill pass . . . nothing, 'tis nothing.

PONTOCARRERO: I thank God's mercy a decision's been reached on the succession. From 't all things can flow, we've secured the future and . . .

*There is a loud knock and the Royal Confessor, the gaunt Dominican priest,* MOTILLA, *strides in.*

MOTILLA (*bowing*): Ma'am. Your Eminence. My lords.

PONTOCARRERO: Father Motilla, as their Majesties' Confessor, you presume too much! You've no right here.

MOTILLA: I bear God's word.

PONTOCARRERO: Hast no sense o' shame. This 's a Council o' State. No place f' God's word.

MOTILLA: Their Majesties wished you t' be the first t' know o' God's infinite mercy.

PONTOCARRERO: Mine's limited.

MOTILLA: *The Queen is pregnant.*

MARIANA: A lie!

MOTILLA: The Queen is pregnant.

MARIANA: She's barren!

MOTILLA: The falling sickness briefly turns the sufferer's soul inside out. If they're o' the spirit 't canst bring on fleshy lusts, carnal longings: 'tis a foul part o' the disease. 'T'as been observed after their foamings, ravings and jerkings their Majesties jerk together t' some purpose.

TORRES: Julius Caesar suffered from the 'falls' too. His son Caesarium was born when he fell on Cleopatra. What a fall was that.

MOTILLA: All signs confirm conception. The Queen's not bled inward this month; her neck's warm and her back cold; she craves only 'cumbers soused i' vinegar and gooseberry fool, and milk poured on her urine floats, my lords!

PONTOCARRERO: Praise be t' God.

ALBA: No need now f' Bavaria or Austria. Spain makes her own heirs!

MONTERREY: We must send His Majesty our congratulations.

ALMIRANTE: And the Queen. 'Tis the Queen's triumph, too!

*They all shout 'The Queen' excitedly and bells peal. Suddenly they stop and look apprehensively at* MARIANA. *The bells stop ringing too. A long silence . . .*

MARIANA (*slowly*): We must pray f' her safe deliverance. God grant 't be a son . . .

*Thankfully the bells resume ringing, the lights fade out and all exit, chanting:* 'Adjutórium nostrum in nómine Domini . . .'


SCENE IV

*The chanting dies away to applause. Lights up on a ballroom with the walls made up of tall mirrors.*

CARLOS *is being applauded by my lords* ALBA, TORRES *and* MONTERREY *and the Royal Dancing Master,* ANTONIO DE ALMINDA, *a beribboned figure with red-buckle shoes and a long staff.* RAFAEL, *the dwarf, stands next to* DR BRAVO *who waits patiently with two drinks on a silver tray.*


CARLOS: I wooon't die now, the Queen carries my SON. All signs proclaim 'twill be a bbboy. Last night the Queen dreamed o' a hatchet, heard a raven cccroak; her saliva's YELLOW and her pulse stronger on her right wrist than thaa . . . I've proved myself King, IIII've the blood, balm, crown, sceptre and the BALLS! (*He shambles round thrusting out his crotch.*) IIII humped, jocked, rutted, clicked and shafted. Haaaaven't I the finest gap-stopper, the largest whore-pipe, the biggest penis-stick i' Spain?

TORRES: Like Atlas, Sire, you balance our world on 'ts tip.

ALBA: 'Tis Goliath!

MONTERREY: 'Tis Titan!

RAFAEL: 'Tis super-prick!

DR BRAVO *approaches with the drinks.*

DR BRAVO: Orange or lemon cordial, Sire?

CARLOS (*looking at them suspiciously*): Whaaa the difference?

DR BRAVO: Difference? One tastes o' orange, the other o' lemon, Sire.

CARLOS: You always gi' me answers never solutions!

*He gestures impatiently and* DR BRAVO *exits backwards Stage Right.*

CARLOS: Weeee hear thou hast challenged the Almirante de Castilla t' a duel, my lord Alba. (*He mimes a clumsy lunge.*) Haaa we forbid 't my lord. He'll geld thee. HHHHe's most dextrous wi' his poinard.

TORRES: And you, Your Majesty.

CARLOS: The thrust in prime 'neath the girdle's ooooour best stroke.

*The* OTHERS *applaud and snigger.*

ALBA: 'Twas a matter o' honour, Sire.

CARLOS: Honour's ccccome the very peak o' fashion.

RAFAEL: Aye, Sire, thieves steal 'cause they're too honourable t' beg and beggars beg 'cause they're too honourable t' steal. All have 't, but I've ne'er truly seen 't. As a friend, show me thy honour, my lord.

ALBA (*clasping sword*): I'll show you my weapon, Sir!

RAFAEL: If 'tis as flexible as thy honour, I'll've nothing t' fear.

ALBA: Who 're you t' talk o' my honour, nick ninny.

RAFAEL: Why I'm court magician and t' amuse His Majesty, I've changed water into wine, frogs into footmen, beetles into bailiffs and made grandees out o' gobbley turkey-cocks. His Majesty's but t' ask and 'tis his . . . A black star? I pluck one thus . . . (*He mimes plucking.*) Dry water? Here . . . (*He mimes pouring.*) An honourable courtier? That's impossible even f' a great magician.

ALBA: You short-shanked nothing!

RAFAEL: No, I'm Josephus Rex.

CARLOS: JJJosephus Rex? But you art our Tom-o-Thumb. Your name's er . . . er . . . Rafael Morra.

RAFAEL: No Sire, I'm truly Josephus Rex. Jo-king.

CARLOS: Who's Jo King?

RAFAEL: I am, Sire. (*Patiently.*) Josephus . . . Jo. Rex . . . King. I am joking, *honk, honk.*

CARLOS: Jo . . .? Rex King? . . . Jooooo (*He gives an adenoidal laugh.*) Heee-ee-ee *I am joking, honk, honk.*

RAFAEL (*wryly*): *Honk, honk.*

ANTONIO (*bows*): Your Majesty, 'tis noon.

CARLOS: Etiquette must bbbe obeyed eeee on this most blessed o' days. 'Tis time f'my lesson in the dance. (*The* OTHERS *bow and are about to leave;* CARLOS *gestures.*) My lords, we graaa a favour; ssssstay.

ALBA: 'Tis a great honour, Sire!

The LORDS *step back respectfully.* ANTONIO *raps three times with his staff. A drum beats and whilst he talks he glides about in time to it.*

ANTONIO: Your Majesty, the dance is a remedy f' all natural ills, 't shakes up stagnant blood, sweats out foul vapours, purges the overcharged brain. We're conceived in a dance o' love, (*he jumps*) *saut saut petit saut,* and ushered out i' a dance o' death by a corpse de ballet, (*he mimes funeral march*) *dum dum de dum.* All nature dances; waves, trees, air in summer heat, hearts f' joy. The perfect harmony o' the dance glorifies the perfect harmony o' God's universe . . . (*He bows.*) Oui, on commence. Today, Sire, we practise the 'Pavan', again. 'Tis an antique dance, but still the courtliest o' all court dances; the dance o' Kings, Queens and noblemen, its natural authority mirroring the natural authority o' its dancers. Très bon. (*He performs as he comments.*) First the single left. On the first beat step forward swerving a little t' the left on the left foot and bend the right knee slightly. On the second beat join the right foot t' the left rising on thy toes and sinking on thy heels on the half beat. The right singles similar but starting wi' the right foot . . . Très bon. Your Majesty, as we practised. Wi' éclate, éclate.

*He stands opposite* CARLOS. *They make reverence. The drum beats out the time.* CARLOS's *left foot skids forward and his right knee buckles. He then swings his right foot forward, hops onto his toes and flops back. Sliding out his left foot, his right skids past it, and he is trapped in the splits. After managing to raise himself up, he pushes out his left foot, brings his right foot up to it, and keels over onto the floor with a crash.*

*The* COURTIERS *murmur approval.* CARLOS *looks up enquiringly at* ANTONIO.

ANTONIO (*slowly*): Hhmmm, a-l-m-o-s-t right, Sire.

CARLOS *gets up. The drum beats again as he reverses and skids about in a series of extraordinary spastic lurches, arms and legs jerking uncontrollably and ending once again on the floor.*

CARLOS: 'TTTis aaaa improvement, eh? eh?

ANTONIO (*slowly*): Yes, I think I canst say 'tis an improvement . . . (*shuddering*) remembering how it was.

CARLOS (*getting up*): III've only been practising five years.

TORRES: Your Majesty hath a natural sense o' rhythm.

RAFAEL: Sire, try that new dance 'The Mess'. You jus' keep your feet together and move your bowels.

ANTONIO: Sire, you must try t' obey the rules o' the 'Pavan'. The steps 're decreed and not subject t' impulses o' the moment.

CARLOS: KINGS aaaaren't subject t' rules, decrees, *French* decrees! I watch you *close*, Master Antonio, you flirt wi' TREASON wi' your French words, French ribbons, French perfumes.

ANTONIO: But my *feet* are Spanish, Your Majesty.

CARLOS: They look suspiciously French t' meeee. Mean-minded feet, little sodomitic feet. (ANTONIO *tries to hide them.*) And the *toes* whaa o' the toes?!

ANTONIO: They're loyal, Sire, all ten o' 'em!

CARLOS: I dance f' joy na-aaa i' thy cold French way.

ANTONIO: 'Tis manifi . . . 'er, magnificent, Your Majesty, but, 'er 'tisn't the 'Pavan'.

CARLOS: No, 'tis 'The Carlos'!

*A drum roll. They line up opposite the mirrors:* CARLOS, ALBA *and* TORRES *on one side:* RAFAEL *and* MONTERREY *on the other.* ANTONIO *poses between them Stage Centre. He raps three times with his staff. The mirrors bevel and* ANA *and* FOUR LADIES-IN-WAITING *step out from behind them and take their places beside the men.*

*They make reverence. Drum, viol and lute play 'Belle Que Tient Ma Vie' and they dance Down Stage following* CARLOS's *grotesque jerkings exactly.*

*With their* MAJESTIES *in the lead, they wobble, lurch, do the splits, skid and spin with poker-faced dignity. Only* ANTONIO *tries to do the stately 'Pavan', but as they reverse and dance back Up Stage, he succumbs and joins the* OTHERS *in their grotesque cavortings. The music grows faster, until the climax is reached with the male dancers all simultaneously keeling over onto the floor with a crash.*

*Blackout, amid delighted laughter, congratulations and applause.*


SCENE V

*Spot up Down Stage Right on* MARIANA *praying.*

MARIANA: Lord God, let my son live and his son live as Thy Son lives, eternally. Nail my thoughts t' Thy Cross as Thy Son's hands and feet were nailed. I'm in the forge, under the hammer. I pray, let Carlos live! (*She thrusts out her neck and speaks in a hysterical parrot-like croak.*) But he's half-dead, clod back t' clod, his child'll die, I'd six die so why shouldst his live if mine died, go stink and die CRRAH CRRAH. Sweet Jesus, Holy Son save him f' we're as dust, *and in my youth I ruled the Spanish Empire as Regent. Authority's the only air I can breathe.*

*I'll sign this—this—this—this. Now I gasp and count grains o'*
*sand, let the donkey-dick stink and die, let me breathe again, Joey's*
*a good boy. CRRAH CRRAH.* Holy Virgin Mother, I see dead
goiters skewered on spits, 'tis one o' the 144,000 torments o'
Hell *which I embrace gladly if my chicken-hammed son and family'd*
*die, Hell holds no surprises, I'm staked out daily, pain like as a*
*wedge, air slashed wi' knives dat's a good boy, Joey.* But he's my
flesh. I bore him *and he bores me, CRRAH. CRRAH.* Oh Lord,
my life's full o' sorrow, *here today gone tomorrow.* God's the
answer, *what's the question? CRRAH. CRRAH.* I ask, I sweat,
I wonder. I swallow the world i' a yawn. (*Gasping asthmatically.*)
Aiai . . . Aiai . . . Aiai. . . . (*Violently.*) *GRRRRX CRRAH*
*CRRAH.* . . .

   *Jamming the Bible into her mouth she flaps her arms desperately*
*as her Spot goes out to the sound of singing.*


SCENE VI

TWO WOMEN *are singing a German nursery rhyme:* 'Schlaf,
   Kinderl, schlaf!/ Der Vater hüt die schaf,/ de Mutter schüttelt's
   Bäumelein,/ de fällt herab en Träumelein,/ Schlaf, Kinderl,
   schlaf!' *as lights Up Stage Right and Left on wall panel—the*
   *reverse sides of the mirrors—showing tranquil scenes from the Nati-*
   *vity with the Virgin and Child.*
*Then lights full up on the Queen's private room to show* ANA, *Stage*
   *Left with her companion, the stumpy,* CONDESA BELEPSCH
   *happily cataloguing piles of 'objets d'art' stacked on the table and*
   *overflowing chests on the floor. There is a smaller table nearby with*
   *bowls of spiced cucumbers and next to it the* PARROT *on its perch.*
   *Doors Up Stage Centre.*
ANA *picks up various items whilst* BELEPSCH *ticks them off in a ledger.*


ANA: One crystal orb, set wi' emeralds and diamonds, surmounted by a cross o' gold; one rosary o' oriental pearls; one

spherical clock-watch circa 1550; Gifts taken from the Conde de Harrach and t' be sent t' my brother John, along wi' the tapestry, armchairs, mahogany chest and the ten Ruben landscapes . . . (*Eating cucumbers.*) Seventeen brothers and sisters spawning across Europe and all expecting me t' enrich 'em.

BELEPSCH: The grandees fear your visits more than those o' the Inquisitor-General himself.

ANA: Mama said 'Those who ask shan't have, those who don't ask won't get'. So I take. I smile, I frown, I squeeze. Our Spanish lords deserve t' be gutted o' their surplus gold and silver—sneezing at me i' the shadows, jeering behind corners! (*Patting stomach.*) But my power grows wi' my belly. My happiness too; when the Queen Mother's finally banished 'twill be complete.

PARROT: *Cock-bawd. Crrah. Crrah.*

ANA: And my people'll love me. I'll hold up my son and they'll shout, 'God Save the Queen! God Save the Queen'.

BELEPSCH: Ihre Majestät es war ein schweres Exil.

ANA: 'Tas been hard from the night we landed at Corona, when I saw my kingly bridegroom f' the first time and I wanted t' go back home. His sores sickened me, decay stank from his fingers, spittle filled his kisses, lice jumped from 'tween his hollow thighs. I'm Queen o' a cold land. Alone 'cept f' you dear Condesa and my Joey.

PARROT: *Joey's a darlin' boy, a darlin' boy.*

BELEPSCH: Cling t'our friendship, sweet dove, 'tis our rock . . . and the childhood we shared together i' the Old Country. (*Singing low.*) 'Schlaf, Kinderl, schlaf' . . .

ANA
BELEPSCH } (*singing*): 'Dein Vater ist ein Graf,/dein Mutter is eine Bauerndirn/soll ihr Kinderl selber wiegn/Schlaf, Kinderl, schlaf.'

*There is a knock on the door.* BELEPSCH *crosses and opens it and* ALMIRANTE *and* MOTILLA *enter bowing.*

BELEPSCH: Your Majesty, the Almirante de Castilla and Father Motilla.

ANA: Didst she turn pale?! Didst she bite her lip till 't bled?!

MOTILLA: When I told her o' your condition, the Queen Mother was struck dumb.

ANA: *Ahhhhh* . . . Soon her silence'll be e'erlasting. She's t' be exiled t' the Convent o' the Sisters o' Mercy.

*The* PARROT *screeches mockingly.* ANA, BELEPSCH *and* ALMIRANTE *smile.*

MOTILLA: Vengeance is mine, sayeth the Lord. Hate the sin, love the sinner. Though I find His Eminence the Cardinal-Archbishop Pontocarrero personally repugnant—he wears silk 'gainst the skin—'tis his sins I damn. He tolerates Protestant heretics abroad and iniquities at home.

ALMIRANTE: F' Lent he's giving up penances. I once asked him what a priest was. He said he was a man too lazy t' work and too frightened t' steal.

MOTILLA: No. A priest is a man good as grass, better than bread. But thanks t'His Eminence, ours hunt, dice, dance and lie; so greed and lechery flourish.

PARROT: *Lechery, lechery.*

ANA: I see little lechery, Father. Spaniards only become stiff wi' pride.

MOTILLA: Lechery's everywhere child; eyes, ears, smell, touch, taste, all senses tempt us t' it f' man's a monstrous centaur, a war 'tween his extremities. A priest fights t' keep God afore his eyes. He walks only wi' angels. His Eminence talks only wi' men.

ALMIRANTE: I envy you your enemy, Father. Now our faction's triumphed, Your Majesty, gi' me leave to' rejoin my command.

ANA: You shared our defeats, dear Almirante, now share our victory; we need you wi' us always.

MOTILLA: We need only God, from whence all succour flows.

ANA: And love flows too, Father. F' God answered my night cries and came t' me i' the falling sickness. He came and St Brigitta unclenched my teeth, St Augustine undid my belt, St Catherine lifted my dress, St Francis stepped aside, I was enrapped, flung down, forced open, swallowed up as he thrust a gold spear into my heart and the fire was a soft caress. Conceived in such ecstasy my babe'll be as beautiful as the Christ child. I dream o' his baptism . . . (*Lights down slightly, Down Stage.*) The grandees, Princes and great ladies o' Spain waiting in the Royal Chapel . . . The choir singing 'Gloria in Excelsis.' . . . (*A choir sings softly but the words cannot be heard.*) Our royal nurse, Dona Maria Engracia de Toledo Marquesa de los Veleze carrying in my son. . . .

*She smiles at the vision as the* MARQUESA *enters haughtily Wings Left in white, with the baby in white christening robes in her arms. She crosses Down Stage Centre.*

MOTILLA: The ceremony must be performed by Don Sebastien Vega, Patriarch o' the Indies. He's too old, but etiquette demands 't.

ANA *nods and the aged Patriarch in white mitre and stole staggers in Wings Right carrying a font and altar ladle and crosses Stage Centre. He stops, exhausted, opposite the* NURSE *and* CHILD *and places the font between them.*

ALMIRANTE: 'Twill be a glorious moment when he recites the Credo. 'Credis in Deum Patrem omnipotem Creatorum coeli et terrae?'

ANA: Credo. . . ! Credo. . . ! Credo. . . ! and he'll take my son (*the* PATRIARCH *takes the* BABY) saying t' the Godfathers 'NAME THIS CHILD', and they'll name him and he'll make the sign o' the Cross and pour sweet Jordan water o'er his head (*the* PATRIARCH *dips the ladle into the font*) saying, saying, saying . . . Carlos, John, Philip, Sebastien, Egmont I BAPTIZE THEE IN THE NAME O' THE . . . urg.

*As she steps forward excitedly Down Stage the* PATRIARCH *turns and flings the contents of the ladle at her; her face and apron*

*are drenched in blood. The* PARROT *screeches but the* OTHERS
*behind her are unaware of anything being wrong.*

ANA *is transfixed as the* PATRIARCH *pours blood over the*
BABY *and exits backwards with it Wings Right whilst the* MAR-
QUESA *exits similarly with the font, Wings Left.*

ANA (*softly*): Dreams liquefy . . . limbs fall . . . soft lumps float
past . . . hand feet finger eye pink mouth lattice veins dead
meat slimed away . . . O sweet Mary, Mother o' Mercy
craters spurt i' my belly . . . cauterize 't wi' hot irons vises
winches ropes gibbets . . . words rot . . . There's no Indies, no
font, choir, baptism, *child*!

MOTILLA: No baptism? No child? Why?

ANA: I BLEED.

PARROT: *Jesus saves but Moses invests. Crrah Crrah.*

BELEPSCH: Du lieber Gott!

*She crosses quickly and escorts* ANA *to a chair.* MOTILLA *and*
ALMIRANTE *are stunned.*

ANA: He's drowned in blood. I'm washed empty.

ALMIRANTE: But all the signs confirmed Your Majesties'd
achieved a perfect conception.

ANA: Immaculate rather than perfect. I know the signs better
than my owl-blind astrologers and physicians. *I bleed.*

ALMIRANTE: The wheel spins.

MOTILLA: And we're abject underfoot.

ALMIRANTE: We feel thy loss, Your Majesty.

MOTILLA: And Spain'll hate thee f' 't.

BELEPSCH *has removed the bloody apron as* ANA *wipes her face.*
*It is now chalk white.*

ANA: Hatred's the air we breathe. Nothing's changed. Reality's
no obstacle. 'Twill be four weeks afore Dr Bravo's allowed
t' examine me again. Time enough t' defeat our enemies and
make Charles o' Austria heir.

*They all look at each other.*

MOTILLA (*slowly*): Naturally Your Majesty must wait f' Dr
Bravo t' reveal the truth. For 'twill not be acknowledged such

till he reveals 't. Once only priests were the universal truth-bearers, now 'tis the coming men o' science. I pray in the four weeks afore he pronounces judgement, God may reverse His, and staunch the wound, f' He e'er watches o'er us in His mercy.

ANA: So doeth the Queen Mother, wi'out any. So *we* must watch ourselves, watch ourselves . . . I tire, gentlemen. You may withdraw.

MOTILLA *and* ALMIRANTE *bow and exit Up Stage Centre.*

BELEPSCH: Weep now, my lady.

ANA: Tears'd be noted and held against me. My heart daren't break, she'd see 't breaking. I can only smile and smile and smile and smile and smile AND . . . (*Singing a snatch to herself she takes up exactly the same position as at the beginning of the scene Stage Right.*) 'Schlaf, kinderl, Schlaf/Der Tod sitzt auf der Stange . . .' (*Lights down to a Spot on her as she resumes cataloguing.*) Gifts taken from the Corregidor Don Francisco de Vasco: one onyx scarabeus; one gold ring wi' a cluster o' . . . (*She frowns, whips out a jeweller's eye-glass, screws it into her eye and peers closely.*) Pastę! Another Ananias! Cheat! Cheat! Five plates painted wi' the marriage o' Cupid and Psyche; two crucifixes, gold; (*The eyeglass drops from her eye.*) *She'll ne'er find out. How could she if I smile and smile?* . . . one baby's rattle, ivory . . . *Smile. I'll learn t' smile* . . . Six Nuremberg dolls: St Cecilia wi' musical instruments, St Theodoras wi' armour, St Florian wi' buckets, St Peter wi' keys, St John wi' lamb, St Christopher wi' child!

*As faint white vapour envelops her and the Spot fades out, another woman's voice, also reeling off a list of items, mingles with hers.*

## SCENE VII

*Spot up through steamy vapour Down Stage Right on a mountain of dirty clothes. Straddled on top of it is the Head Washerwoman,* THERESA DIEGO, *in a leather apron and clogs.* MARIANA *watches her impatiently from below as she picks up each item of dirty washing, sniffs it to identify the stains and throws it down into a large basket near the foot of the ladder leaning against the pile.*

THERESA: Property o' Her Catholic Majesty Queen Ana, one satin petticoat, stained wi' sweat and tallow grease. Two shifts, spotted wi' powder and aged sweet-water . . . Property o' His Most Catholic Majesty; one vest encrusted in week-old vomit and dribble . . . Property o' Her Majesty Queen Ana, four pairs o' stockings soiled wi' Madrid mud. One lace saberqua peppered wi' holy water . . .

MARIANA: *Blood.* Doest she bleed? I suspect she's bleeding. Only tell me if she's bleeding. Doest smell blood?

THERESA: Ne'er fear, if she's pinked I'll smell 't out, Ma'am. Even after twenty years as Head Washerwoman t' the Royal House most stains still look much alike. Who canst tell the difference twixt red wine, plum jam, ochre or blood? Cow or donkey dung? Peepers is deceived but not this snout. (*Taps nose.*) Once I've smelt out the blot it can be washed, rubbed, salted or vinegared away according. My fame's up me nostrils, Ma'am, they've ne'er failed me. 'Tis a blessed gift. Now I's oft called on t' sniff out the Devil. Holy work, holy work! He cometh in many shapes but always wi' the same Devil's stench straight from the great privee o' Hell. 'Tis a yellow, greenish, many-layered stink-o. I ne'er mistake it, Ma'am. I'm sniffing my way to Salvation! (*She takes out a small box and sniffs snuff loudly.*) Must keep the snot-passages clear, they're most tender. (*She dabs her nose delicately with a handkerchief and resumes sniffing the laundry;* MARIANA *ignores her and says her beads.*) I still recall the first time I sniffed His Majesty's dirt-stained drawers. I've ne'er had a moment's sickness since, though I coffined three clapped-out husbands. The King's touch cures all distempers and His Majesty's healing powers still cling t' his filthy linen. By the blessed nose o' the Abbess Eba, odours is revealing, Ma'am. I can predicate the future by smell better than all yer

star-men wi' their Jupiters and Mercurys. When royal shirts
're soiled wi' wine and feasting, 't means good times ahead,
but if they reek o' incense and holy water then trouble comes
apace. 'Tis all in 'Mother Diego's Odour Almanack: The
Future Prophetical Deduced from Royal Linen' . . . Your
Eminence! Father Froylan . . .!

*She falls on her knees as* PONTOCARRERO *enters Stage Left*
*with* FATHER FROYLAN, *complete with his pouch of State papers.*

PONTOCARRERO: Ma'am, the Royal Washhouse's no place f' a
Queen Mother.

FROYLAN: This heat's a foretaste o' Hell.

MARIANA: 'Tis my home till I find proof against her. You desert
my cause, Eminence.

PONTOCARRERO: My only cause is Spain, her throne and
Empire. A Spanish heir'll save both.

MARIANA: She lies. She bleeds and lies.

PONTOCARRERO: The Queen may lie but not Father Motilla,
I'm certain, e'en though I find his person repugnant.

FROYLAN: They say he weareth *two* hairshirts.

PONTOCARRERO: Dominicans 're so ostentatious i' their dress.
He practises all the austerities o' his Order, except the most
beneficial—perpetual silence.

FROYLAN: I've never liked him and I always will.

PONTOCARRERO: Saints're a blessing in heaven but hell on
earth. He's fallen into the heresy o' confusing religion wi'
ethics. But he's not a man t' lie.

MARIANA: Not knowingly.

PONTOCARRERO: But what o' the physicians who confirm the
pregnancy?

MARIANA: For the first two months in practice every physician
wants t' save humanity; after that they only want t' save
money. (*To* THERESA.) Why art kneeling, woman? Sniff!

THERESA: It's too full o' awe, Ma'am. To be honoured by Your
Highness and the Cardinal Archbishop in one day. This
Washhouse'll become a shrine. Gi' 't blessing, Your Eminence.

*Deep in thought,* PONTOCARRERO *makes the sign of the Cross and mumbles a blessing.*

FROYLAN: Ma'am, you're in the hands o' the best nose in Spain. I've had occasion t' use Signora Diego's snout t' sniff out Lucifer's minions. Demonology's my particular hobby.

MARIANA: Sniff! Sniff!

THERESA *rises and resumes searching whilst* PONTOCARRERO *strokes his beard thoughtfully.*

FROYLAN: Why didn't you get more help, Ma'am? At my last accounting the Royal Washhouse employed some twenty-three haulers, forty washers, thirty-six dryers and eighteen young scrubbers.

MARIANA: They all've mouths and walls've ears. If the Queen knew we were searching she'd hide her guilty drawers and petticoats. Faster, woman! Faster!

PONTOCARRERO: Father, go help the woman.

FROYLAN: But Eminence, 'tisn't meet. I've despatches, warrants, documents t' draft. (*Indicates his stuffed pouch.*) The wheels o' State turn on paper.

PONTOCARRERO: When you entered the Society o' Jesus, thy fourth vow as a Jesuit was t' go wi'out question or delay wherever you might be ordered f' the salvation o' souls. (*He gestures to the pile.*) Go, my son.

FROYLAN: Forgive me, Eminence.

*He nervously starts climbing up the ladder.*

PONTOCARRERO: Ma'am, I believe the Queen's pregnant. But 'tis possible hope clouds judgement.

*Groaning to himself* FROYLAN *reaches the top of the pile.* THERESA *kisses his hand and he looks nervously down at* PONTOCARRERO *and* MARIANA. *They continue talking as* FROYLAN *whispers inquiringly to* THERESA.

MARIANA: She'll've no children. She's BLOCKED like her predecessor, now and forever.

PONTOCARRERO: You forget the efficacy o' prayer, the soul's breath. A million voices rise up daily: 'Make their Majesties fertile.' As our sins brought forth their sterility, so our prayers brought forth . . .

FROYLAN: Blood?!

PONTOCARRERO: } *Where? Where?*
MARIANA:

FROYLAN: Why're we looking f' blood, Your Eminence? Who's dead?

MARIANA: We are if thou doesn't find any.

THERESA: 'Tis blood from the miraculous pitcher which holds water wi' its mouth downwards; from her quim, her doodle sack.

FROYLAN *is still bewildered but starts examining the dirty clothes with obvious distaste. But this soon changes to sly pleasure as he fondles petticoats and drawers.*

MARIANA: Ah, the efficacy o' prayer! But still my son's jaw juts so his teeth casn't meet, and he swallows chicken gizzards whole, afore voiding 'em back up again. Some days he canst hardly stand upright. Yet our iron wills beat and break against his weakness.

PONTOCARRERO: His weakness has saved Spain.

MARIANA: Only wi' my help. But now he preens and struts about the stage, cocksure at last. He plans t' banish me.

PONTOCARRERO: How d'you know?

MARIANA: I can see through walls.

FROYLAN (*excitedly waving drawers*): I've found 't . . .! Stains, blood . . . *Ahhhhhhhhhh.*

*As he rushes across to show* THERESA *the centre of the pile suddenly collapses and he disappears down the hole.*

THERESA: Father Froylan!

MARIANA: The stains, the stains! Don't lose the stains!

*She starts climbing up the ladder followed by* PONTOCARRERO *whilst* THERESA *leans over the hole.*

FROYLAN (*off*): Help . . . I'm choking . . . the stench . . .

THERESA *grabs the unseen* FROYLAN *and pulls him up. His flushed face finally appears over the edge of the hole.*

THERESA: N-e-a-r-l-y there Fa . . . Ma'am!

FROYLAN: *Ahhhhhhhh.*

*Awe-struck at the sight of* MARIANA *and* PONTOCARRERO *clambering up beside her,* THERESA *has let go of* FROYLAN *who falls back down the hole.* THERESA *flops on to her knees.*

THERESA: Your Highness, Your Eminence, here on top o' my pile. The honour . . . the glory . . .

MARIANA: The blood?!

PONTOCARRERO (*calling down the hole*): Stop playing the fool, Father, nations are at risk. No time f' cap and bells.

FROYLAN (*off*): Help . . . help . . .

PONTOCARRERO *and* THERESA *lean over the hole and heave* FROYLAN *up by his shoulders.*

PONTOCARRERO: Where's the bloody garment?

FROYLAN: I dropped 't afore I fell . . . *Ahhhhhhhh.*

PONTOCARRERO *and* THERESA *have let go of* FROYLAN *and he disappears yet again as they frantically search.* MARIANA *pounces on a petticoat.*

MARIANA: Stains! Is't proof, woman? Is't? Is't?

THERESA *takes the garment and sniffs a stain.*

THERESA: Red wine, Ma'am . . . (*Sniffs.*) Burgundy. A Musigny '32. Inferior vintage.

MARIANA: 'Tis here, I know 't.

PONTOCARRERO (*looking down the hole*): Father, don't jus' lie there using up air.

FROYLAN (*groaning*): *Ahhh. Ahhh.*

PONTOCARRERO: What? Oh, nonsense!

THERESA: Ne'er fear, Ma'am, this nose's pledged t' serve thee t' the last sniff.

MARIANA: Quicker, rattle-pate, quicker. Sniff, sniff. Sniff everybody, sniff!

*As they sniff and search frantically,* FOUR HOODED MONKS *enter Wings Right.*

*Chanting* 'Hallelujah Brothers' *they drag off the pile, Wings Left, singing solemnly.*

MONKS ⎫
THERESA ⎬ (*singing*): 'Sniff, Brothers, Sniff; Sniff, Brothers,
⎭ Sniff. Sniff, Brothers, Sniff Brothers, Sniff Sniff Sniff
Sniff. You gotta see the light/ You gotta pull your load/
You gotta help the cause/ You gotta smell the clothes/ You
gotta pitch right in or hit the road/ Then Sniff Sniff Sniff Sniff
Sniff./ You gotta find the costume/ You gotta spot the gear/
You gotta scent the tiger/ You gotta smell the smear/ You
gotta see your dentist twice a year./ And Sniff Sniff Sniff Sniff
Sniff/ Sniff Brothers Sniff, Sniff Brothers Sniff, Sniff Brothers
Sniff, Brothers, Sniff Sniff Sniff Sniff Sniff.'

## SCENE VIII

*As the pile disappears there is a fanfare of trumpets and dim lights come
up.*

*Large objects covered with white dust-sheets loom out of the surrounding
white vapour and the ghostly bare-headed figures of* MONTERREY,
ALMIRANTE, TORRES *and* ALBA *face* CARLOS *who stands bolt
upright, tall and imposing Down Stage Left, the Golden Fleece
insignia glittering round his neck. He is flanked by* DR BRAVO *and
the* COURT ASTROLOGER, HERMONYMOUS GONGORA, *a
beaky old man with a zodiac pendant and conical hat. Bare-headed,
and on one knee in front of them is the French Ambassador* PIERRE
REBENAC.

TWO PRIESTS *in white robes and swinging thuribles of incense
remove the dust sheets to reveal large children's toys: a rocking horse,
alphabet bricks, drum and cradle.* A THIRD PRIEST *blesses them
with lustral water from a stoup whilst voices echo with metallic
harshness.*

DR BRAVO (*intoning*): We declare Her Most Catholic Majesty's
in a state o' being wi' child, her delivery will take place i' the
allotted time, if God so wills and no foul vapours invade her
uterus. *Foul vapours begone.*

GONGORA (*intoning*): We declare Her Most Catholic Majesty 'll enter a most fruitful period wi' Mercury and Saturn i' the angle of the 10th Royal House and Aquarius ascending t' the horizon o' the Spanish Court, if God so wills and no malicious aspects cross her House o' Life. *Malicious aspects begone.*

CARLOS: Monsieur Rebenac, go tell thy master Louis thou hast seen the royal nursery consecrated t' receive Spain's future king. If thy armies move against us, all Christendom'll know your sovereign fights to usurp a legimate heir.

*Rhythmic clapping from the Court.* CARLOS *leans forward stiffly and touches the Ambassador's hat.* REBENAC *puts it on before speaking, according to etiquette. The rest of the Court follow suit.*

REBENAC: Sire, my Most Catholic Majesty, Louis o' France, shares the joy o' this pregnancy. 'Tis my belief, all division 'twixt nations canst be overcome by diplomacy. In this I speak f' France . . .

CARLOS: But I do not speak f' Spain. I *am* Spain.

CARLOS *touches his own hat. The audience is over. A fanfare of trumpets.* REBENAC *and the others withdraw, bowing.*

*One of the* PRIESTS *lifts* CARLOS's *cloak and removes a long, flat, wooden board which has been clamped to his back to keep him upright, whilst* ANOTHER *takes off wooden platforms strapped to his shoes. They then exit, Wings Right and Left.*

*Lights full up on the Royal Nursery. The walls are covered with blue drapes and there are* TWO ATTENDANTS *on the doors Up Stage Centre.*

*Alone,* CARLOS *is back to normal, his limbs jerk continuously as he stumbles around happily, setting the wooden horse rocking.*

CARLOS: III aaaaam Spain. Now I canst make a noise wi' my feet, must grip my mind. (*He grabs the wooden horse and stops it rocking.*) Grip. Grip. Grip.

*Bubbles float out of the cradle.* RAFAEL *jumps out blowing soap bubbles.*

RAFAEL (*singing*): 'As I was going t' sell my eggs, I meet a man wi' bandy legs. Bandy legs and crooked toes. I tripped up his heels and he fell on his nose.'

CARLOS: Didst see? Didst see meeee gi' audience? I didst not fall down once, nor vomit up, nor piss my breeches, nor rap out a stinkin' volley. I CRUSHED Monsieur Reverence aaaaas I'll crush his Master.

RAFAEL: 'Twas proudly done, Sire. Diplomats are like as crabs and women; seeming t' come they go; seeming t' go they come.

CARLOS: I'm gripping my mind. I must aaaaaapoint a First Minister. Whoooo's worthy, Tom?

RAFAEL: Appoint a man o' the lower sort, Sire, wi'out pedigree or land. He'd've t' look only t' you f' advancement.

CARLOS: You're Jo-Jo-Josephusing again. Whaaaa o' my grandees and clergy?

RAFAEL: Chain the clergy t' their altars and imprison the grandees deeper in etiquette. (*He takes out a small brush and sweeps the ground whilst bowing.*) And reward 'em wi' bigger ribbons and titles. (*He puts a large rosette to his chest.*) Being men they prefer the shadow t' the substance, pleased t' crouch, they'll be eager t' crawl.

CARLOS: Thou art aaaa funny little fffellow. Hast always been soooo small?

RAFAEL: No Sire, I've been ill.

CARLOS: *Honk honk.* . . Illness made mmme dwarfish too. My nursery was a sickbed. I'd no time t' play. Whaaa games do children play?

RAFAEL (*counting*): 'Inter mitzy, bitzy tool/ Ira dira dominu/ Oker poker dominoker/ Out goes YOU.' That's one I played when I was small. And blind man's buff; frog i' the middle; puss i' the corner; Jack, Jack, shine a light; fathers and mothers; stampers. . . .

CARLOS: Stampers? Whaaaa . . .?

RAFAEL: 'Twas to see who couldst stamp on the other's toes, Sire.

*Grinning,* CARLOS *stumbles forward trying to stamp on* RAFAEL's *toes. But the dwarf darts away pursued by* CARLOS *laughing idiotically. The chase continues round the toys till at last* RAFAEL *climbs up on the bricks.*

*Still laughing* CARLOS *lurches over to the* ATTENDANTS *by the door, and stamps triumphantly on their toes crying 'Stampers!'. No reaction from them whatsoever.*

CARLOS *comes back to* RAFAEL, *delighted.*

CARLOS: We'll command my lord Alba t' play wi' us.

RAFAEL: When I want t' play with a prick, I'll play with my own.

ATTENDANTS: *Ahhhhh.*

*As the* ATTENDANTS *hop about yelling in pain there is a loud knock and the doors Up Stage Centre open to reveal* ANA *and* MARIANA *accompanied by* MOTILLA *and* PONTOCARRERO *respectively.*

*They advance quickly, ignoring each other, then suddenly stop and stare in amazement at the frenetic antics of the* ATTENDANTS *as they hop back to their places.*

CARLOS (*low*): TThey've come t' tear the skin fffffrom my soul. Tom, Tom, I'm the world's oldest living orphan.

RAFAEL (*low*): Don't give 'em permission t' speak, Sire. They're not allowed t' speak until you speak.

1ST ATTENDANT: Sire, Her Most Catholic Majesty, Queen Ana o' Spain.

2ND ATTENDANT: Sire, Her Royal Highness, the Queen Mother.

*The women rush Downstage, each wanting to get to* CARLOS *first. They curtsey in front of him, he nods, they rise and wait for him to speak. Instead he stares past them.* ANA *frowns, opens her mouth to say something but* MOTILLA *gestures for her to be silent. Impatiently* MARIANA *steps forward to speak but* PONTO-CARRERO *shakes his head.*

*The silence becomes oppressive.*

*Finally they explode in wordless fury.* MARIANA *jabs an accusing finger towards* ANA *who bites the air in rage.* MARIANA

*then breaks an invisible bar across her knee with a 'crack' whilst*
ANA *makes vicious tearing gestures.* MARIANA *wrings an imagi-*
*nary neck whilst* ANA *mimes gouging out an eye. Uttering thin*
*screeching sounds,* MARIANA *grinds her heel as* ANA *claws the air*
*sobbing with rage.*

CARLOS *gasps and clutches his throat, trembling.*

CARLOS: I cccchoke . . .

ANA: *Lying slush-bucket.*

MARIANA: *Hedge-whore.*

ANA: Carlos, thou swore she'd be banished.

CARLOS: Maaaamaaaa.

MARIANA: Carlos, thou swore she'd be curbed.

CARLOS: Anaaaaa you poison my unborn child's mind against
me.

ANA: How?

CARLOS: By writing fffffoul notes about meee and swallowing
'em. Dat's mind poisoning AND there's air poisoning,
loneliness-poisoning, weakness-poisoning, too-much-reading
poisoning, repeated-coitus-poisoning, XX-poisoning . . .

ANA: And foetus-poisoning. She mixes Jambala flowers i' cow's
urine turning my womb into cold rice gruel. Our child'll be a
deformed CRETIN!

CARLOS: *Ahh. Ahh. I'll banish her.*

*He jerks across to* MOTILLA *who is ready with a document and*
*portable quill and ink.*

PONTOCARRERO: Sire, 'tis mere superstition. Everything God
makes is perfect.

RAFAEL: What about me?

PONTOCARRERO: Why, you're the most perfect cross-eyed
dwarf I've ever seen.

ANA: O-U-T spells 'out'. She goes OUT.

RAFAEL (*pointing to* MARIANA): She means you.

CARLOS: Maaaaamaa t' save our child.

MARIANA: Her womb's as empty as her heart.

ANA: Old lies, old woman!

MARIANA (*triumphantly*): Here's new proof then! (*She holds up blood-stained pair of women's drawers.*) Blood. *Thy blood.*

CARLOS: Whaaaa . . .?

MARIANA: The clock strikes, you stream; this drop condemns thee and this half drop pulls thee down. *Guilty.*

ANA: Show 't me, show 't me.

> *She grabs the garment but* MARIANA *won't let go. As they tug,* PONTOCARRERO *quickly helps* MARIANA *and* MOTILLA, ANA. RAFAEL *encourages them.*
>
> *Gibbering with frustration* CARLOS *unsheathes his sword and with a wild, lucky swipe slashes the garment in two. The teams fall back.*

CARLOS: Whaaa . . .?

MOTILLA: Christ bleeds f' man's redemption, women f' his iniquities.

PONTOCARRERO: If a woman bleeds from the notch, Sire, t's a certain sign she doeth not conceive.

MARIANA: See here the Queen's own crest, gold and purple. Dare she deny 'tis hers, son. In front o' thy Sovereign Lord and thy Confessor, deny 't, Madam.

ANA: The garment's mine.

MARIANA: *Crrah. Crrah.*

CARLOS (*falling on his knees and beating the toy drum*): Poor peee poor peee eee.

ANA: The garment's mine but not the blood. 'Tis rat's blood, bat's blood, cat's blood, not my blood.

> CARLOS *stops beating the drum.*

PONTOCARRERO: Come, Your Majesty, 'twas found in my presence i' the Royal Washhouse.

ANA: Where she'd placed it f' thee t' find, first having stolen and smear'd 't. O she's a cunning lady. By the blood o' our Saviour, 'tis true. Jus' look at her Judas face.

> PONTOCARRERO *and the* OTHERS *look at* MARIANA.

MARIANA: Lent-breaker, the physician'll confirm who's Judas-faced when he examines thee i' the morning.

ANA: He'll examine me four weeks hence according t' etiquette and not afore, else all Europe'll know the Queen's condition's doubted.

MOTILLA: And then the country'd be plunged back into factions clamouring f' the Bavarian José, the Austrian Charles and the French Philip.

ANA: Do I not suffer enough? Already I've dog-headed, web-fingered nightmares. Wilt our child be whole? What diseases 'll run through his veins? Wilt his swaddling clothes be his winding sheet? I need peace o' mind at this time and mountains o' gooseberry fool. Wi' thy permission, Sire, I'll wi'draw and leave your mother t' her hatchings!

*Flinging her torn piece of cloth at* MARIANA's *feet, she curtseys and as* CARLOS *offers her his arm to the door, sweeps Up Stage with him and exits, followed by* MOTILLA.

*The* OTHERS *watch in silence as* CARLOS *gazes after her.*

RAFAEL: I think I'll go where the climate suits my clothes.

CARLOS: Ssssshe carest only f' peace o' mind and gooseberry fool. Maaaaamaaaa if thou carest f' meeee, CARE f' her now.

MARIANA: If I care? When you were born physicians whispered 'Ma'am, his body's rotten as a pear, 'tisn't in our power t' save him long.' But I did penance, winding barbed rope round my waist, fasted and prayed daily: Our Lady've mercy . . . Our Lady've mercy . . . Our Lady've mercy . . . Our Lady've mercy . . . she lies . . . (*Gasping.*) Let me breathe . . . Mama knows best . . .

CARLOS: Maamaaa.

MARIANA: *Crrah* . . . *Crrah* . . . *Crrah*.

PONTOCARRERO *bows and guides* MARIANA *out Up Stage Centre, gasping and cawing plaintively whilst* CARLOS *staggers into the cradle Down Stage Right crying 'Maamaaa'.*

RAFAEL *sighs, takes a drink from a tiny hip-flask and crosses to* CARLOS *curled up in the cradle. Lights down to a Spot as* RAFAEL *rocks him gently.*

RAFAEL (*singing*): 'I had a little nut tree. Nothing would 't bear./ But a silver nutmeg. And a golden pear./The King o' Spain's

daughter came to visit me./And all for the sake o' my little nut tree.'
*Spot out to the sound of whipping.*

SCENE ÍX

*Spot up Stage Left to show* MOTILLA, *stripped to the waist, kneeling under a crucifix hanging horizontally from the Flies, and being whipped by a hooded Dominican* MONK.

MOTILLA: Lord have mercy according to thy loving kindness. Look upon my humility and pain. Let not mine enemies triumph. (*To* MONK.) *Harder, harder, lay on, lay on* . . . Our cause's just. We'll send forth our priests, barefoot, t' preach the word and help the poor. F' they casn't wi'stand the rich who covet their fields and seize 'em by violence. Help me Lord now, when all seems lost. Show me thy angelic will, illumine my eyes, tell me what I must do. Grant me a vision. (*To* MONK.) *Lay on, I say. Harder. Where didst you learn t' flagellate? Thou hasn't even drawn blood yet.* Make this cell a furnace, in Babylon where the three men found the Son o' God, make it a burning bush, a pillar o' cloud speaking unto Moses: speak t' me, Lord! (*To* MONK.) *Lay on, spider-shanks. Put your back into 't.* Grant me a vision, Lord . . . *lay on harder,* a vision . . . harder . . . a vision . . . vis . . . har . . . vis . . . har . . . vis . . . v i . . ˙vvvvvvv . . . a vision.
    *The* MONK *falls back exhausted as a vertical beam of light strikes a couch Stage Right where* ALMIRANTE *is making love to two half-naked* WOMEN.
MOTILLA (*making the sign of the Cross*): Adjúro ergo te omnis immundissime spiritus, omne phantásma omnis incúrsio sátanae in nómine Jesus Christi Nazaréni. You come again t' tempt me, Lucifer. But 'tis a temptation f' this pea-green novice, not a scarred veteran o' Christ! You know well I've

slain lust, burnt out lechery. I see those two lumps o' lace-mutton carrion fluttering their legs afore me, already skull-bald, grave-yard dead and stinkin'. Lucifer, return and take thy puny visions wi' thee! (*Nothing happens, he closes his eyes and concentrates.*) I command thee in the name o' Christ Our Saviour, BEGONE.

*He opens his eyes but the vision remains. Naked bodies, frenzied caresses and voices: 'My darling! My darling!'*

*As they reach a climax of love-making, three glowing haloes drop from the Flies and hang over their heads.* MOTILLA *stares in disbelief.*

MOTILLA (*slowly*): Then 'tis *Thy* vision, Lord, not Lucifer's. (*A choir sings softly.*) Yes, now I see 't all plain . . . Jesu, Jesu, break, crush, humble, hollow and fill me wi' Thy holy spirit that whilst shovelling shit I'll not stink!

*The* MONK *is about to start whipping again but* MOTILLA *gestures curtly and is handed a towel. As he briskly wipes himself down and is helped with his habit, lights come up slowly.*

MOTILLA: Ten minutes o' flagellation a day's a tonic; the key t' inner health. Remember, a limp-wrist 's a sign o' weakness— if not worse. 'Tis our nature t' inflict pain. But cruelty cannot run free, like crude ore 't must be refined in the service o' Jesus Christ. You need practice, my son. (*He mimes cracking a whip.*) Practice. Practice.

*The* MONK *exits Stage Left practising cracking his whip.*

*Lights now full up on* ALMIRANTE's *room. Regimental banners on the walls, a Spanish flag in one corner and clothes in a heap by the couch. The crucifix still hangs from the Flies.*

*As* MOTILLA *strides across to the couch,* TWO WOMEN *spring up with a shriek, throwing* ALMIRANTE *on the floor. They grab their clothes and rush out Stage Right.*

MOTILLA: Dumb gluttons! Public ledgers—open t' all parties! Why doest sin, my lord?

ALMIRANTE (*rising*): To please heaven, where there is more

rejoicing o'er one sinner who repenteth than o'er ninety-nine just men who need no repentance.

MOTILLA: You're a mutton-mongering fornicator.

ALMIRANTE: How canst I deny 't i' the face o' these Venus scars? I've taken so many mercury cures f' the pox, on a hot day I feel myself rising like a barometer. But I always confessed, repented, did hard penance f' 't like a good Christian.

MOTILLA: Now, as a good Christian, God wants you . . .

ALMIRANTE (*pulling on boot*): T' give up mutton-mongering. I need no holy vision t' know that.

MOTILLA: God wants you t' mutton-monger the Queen.

ALMIRANTE (*jumping up, boot half on*): *Mutton the Queen?*

MOTILLA: As Judah told Onan t' sleep wi' his brother's wife and raise up issue f' his brother so He commands you t' make the Queen pregnant afore she's examined. The King'll not do 't, believing 'tis done already.

ALMIRANTE (*pacing, his boot flapping*): How canst God speak o' muttoning? Using lust, lechery . . .?

MOTILLA: God oft time uses an ignoble tool f' a noble purpose.

ALMIRANTE: My honour, what o' my honour?

MOTILLA: Dishohour 't f' Spain and I'll keep Holy Day f' Judas. 'Tis my punishment. I sinned through pride. My soul cries out 'gainst this vileness but God's terrible voice thunders, 'Sin f' my sake'.

ALMIRANTE: 'Tis impossible. The ghost o' a flea casn't hop from one heaving crotch t' another wi'out the Court hearing o' 't instantly.

MOTILLA: None'll hear o' 't. I'm the Queen's Confessor, and the King's. My lord, consider, if she's shown not t' be pregnant. The late Queen Louisa declared sterile was worm-meat two days after. Some believe 'twas a natural death, but I say she was cold poisoned. You speak much o' glory, my lord, now's the time t' unsheath your weapon and raise 't f' Queen Ana.

ALMIRANTE (*slowly*): If she's truly in such danger then my

weapon must be hers ... (*They walk Down Stage and lights fade down.*) Royal bastards abound. Horns spread on Kings, Clowns and Turdmen alike. Women make all men equal. When am I t' be sent into the breech?

*A large gauze is dropped Stage Centre. Projected onto it is the night sky.*

MOTILLA: Tonight. Such things are best done at night. Darkness only frights children. 'Tis the pitiless day I find most terrible. E'en Lucifer, the morning star, turns pale afore the rising sun.

ALMIRANTE (*looking up*): There's Scorpio, there's Sagittarius and Centaurus. I once killed a man under that star ... Tonight I change the history o' our world, decide the fate o' nations. 'Tis greatness o' a kind, a hole-i'-the-corner sort o' glory, eh?

MOTILLA (*looking up*): Canst see the stars shine and hear the planets wheel, making a divine murmur too soft f' outer ears? 'Tis the good Shepherd calming his flock from that lost cloud o' primordial dust beyond Neptune. List, list, he whispers, fainter than Uranus's moon. (*Whispering.*) 'I'm always here, loving, caring ... come in my lambs, my lambikins ... 'Oh, God's so gentle ... do but listen ... doest hear Him? ... Hear him call us? ... list ... list ... sshh ... sshh ...

*They both listen intently. Then from far away the tiniest rustle of sound which grows into a long snigger.*

*As it swells to mirthless laughter,* MOTILLA *and* ALMIRANTE *look frightened, shrink visibly and scuttle off Wings Left.*


SCENE X

DR BRAVO *and* GONGORA *enter Wings Right laughing, followed by his young assistant,* DR GELEEN, *with an instrument case.*
*The night sky has faded and lights come up on the gauze Stage Centre, now a huge astrological chart with the Signs of the Zodiac. Nearby*

*a table, with a bowl of water, a decanter, a chair and a brass armillary*
*sphere.*

DR BRAVO: He said: 'You doctors oft gi' wrong diagnoses. My
mother was treated f' tertian fever and she died o' quatern
ague.' 'Ne'er fear,' I replied. 'When I treat a patient f' tertian
fever, he dies o' tertian fever.' And he did.

GONGORA: Wi'out a word o' thanks, I'm certain. They lack all
gratitude and respect f' our arts. When I presented the
notorious Marquesa de Gudannes wi' her astrological chart, I
told her, 'I see new positions f' you, Madam'. 'Sitting or
laying?' she leered back.

DR BRAVO: An open-legged wanton. She once gave me jus'
seventy-two hours t' leave her bedchamber.

GONGORA: The stars 're retrograde. Jupiter's in adverse aspect
t' Mercury. Madrid's become a compost o' quackery. In their
misery the people turn t' magic; fortune-telling by numbers,
fire, smoke, skulls, the guts o' dead birds. I see astrology, the
great science of the Chaldeans and Greeks, falling into the
hands o' midwives and gypsies peddling almanacs and Spanish
fly.

DR GELEEN *has laid out a sponge, a container of liquid and*
*various heavy medical instruments on the table.* DR BRAVO *washes*
*his hands in the bowl.*

DR BRAVO: Confidence, Hermonymous. All authority's a matter
o' confidence. We'll never lose 't if we do our duty wi'out fear
or favour. (*He peers round, cannot find a towel so wipes his hands*
*on his gown.*) Wi'out fear or favour.

GONGORA: 'Tis the only way, though the stars can be a stern
mistress. (*He shows him a small manuscript.*) Your horoscope,
Luis, wi' my projections f' the next twenty-four months.
You'll note this most interesting conjunction o' planets at the
time o' the square o' the progressed Uranus t' the Moon.
Neptune by progression'll be i' opposition t' the Moon from
the 10th House . . .

DR BRAVO: And what does that mean?

GONGORA: You'll be dead.

DR BRAVO: *Dead?*

*As he grabs the manuscript* DR GELEEN *suppresses a delighted grin.*

GONGORA: I fear yours was truly a horror-scope. But I must deal honestly. I casn't omit the Lord o' Death if he's in thy stars.

DR BRAVO: But is 't certain? I feel so well.

GONGORA: I've calculated the strength o' the lunaries, and malifics afflicting the Moon. But 'tis some twenty months hence and I'll be scanning the Heavens f' a sudden conjunction o' favouring signs.

DR BRAVO: That's possible?

GONGORA: If God wills it . . . Shall we proceed?

DR BRAVO: Proceed? Oh, yes. (*He gestures,* GONGORA *sits.*) This 's more a task f' the Barber Surgeon.

GONGORA: That drunken sot! Saturn was rising in adverse aspect t' Venus at his nativity. He'd drink hemlock if 'twas in a bottle.

DR BRAVO: Which tooth's giving you pain?

GONGORA: None.

DR BRAVO: None? Then why do you want me t' pull 't out?

GONGORA: It gives no pain at present, but 'twill four weeks hence when Uranus'll be in Aries.

DR BRAVO: Ah, preventive medicine. If only my other patients 'd let me cure 'em afore they were ill, it'd be so much easier. (*He peers into* GONGORA's *mouth.*) Which tooth'll be aching four weeks hence?

GONGORA (*pointing*): This one, according to astrological progression.

DR BRAVO *nods and crosses back to the table.*

GONGORA: You've heard the rumour concerning the Queen?

DR BRAVO (*gloomily*): Dead you say?

*Behind his back* DR GELEEN *nods gleefully.*

GONGORA: No, a miscarriage. She mayn't be pregnant. The

French Ambassador's already asked me t' cast up a new star-chart f' her. All Europe wonders.

DR BRAVO (*picking up the sponge with tongs*): 'Tis possible. A moist wind, a hard sneeze canst kill a mother's wandering womb. (*Soaks sponge in liquid.*) I warned 'em o' foul vapours from the uterus!

GONGORA: And I o' malicious aspects. Mars and Saturn canst suddenly appear t' darken the brightest futures.

DR BRAVO (*brightening*): Just as beneficial planets canst brighten a dark 'un, eh? If the stars've turned against the Queen they couldst as easily turn i' my favour. If she's barren, there's hope.

GONGORA: Your future's dark, the malifics . . . *ugh*.

DR BRAVO *slaps the opiate sponge in his face and holds it there.* GONGORA *waves his arms feebly then slumps back, mouth open.*

DR BRAVO *gives the tongs and sponge to* DR GELEEN, *picks up a heavy tool with a curved end called a 'pelican' and inserts it into* GONGORA'*s mouth.*

DR BRAVO (*muttering*): Dead . . . Not the word o' a friend. Expect words o' cheer from a friend, ahh. (*He pulls, peers short-sightedly at the extracted tooth on the end of the tool, then into* GONGORA'*s mouth.*) Hhhmmm, that's not right. (*He throws the tooth away and inserts the tool again.*) Dead . . . He wants me dead and t' be thanked f' it . . . *ahh* (*He pulls again, stares at the tooth and at the mouth.*) Hhmm . . . couple more f' luck. (*He tosses the tooth away and levers two more out.*) Dead . . . Dead . . . (*Holding up the last tooth in triumph.*) That's the work o' a true friend.

*He crosses back to the table whilst* DR GELEEN *packs up the equipment.* GONGORA *groans loudly.* DR BRAVO *pours a drink, gulps it down himself, and continues drinking.*

GONGORA: M' teeth, m' teeth. I've been robbed . . . (*He leaps up and staggers about, still dazed.*) Turn out the lights and let me see my stars! *Aaaaaa*, Saturn's i' the 12th House, the House o' Sorrow! Betrayals, treacheries, plots, deaths i' the dark, brightness falls away . . . (*The light fades.*) They're dead molars out there, the Saviour's served notice, this peregrine planet, those stars, that galaxy, this universe's being sucked into a great hole which sucks itself into itself at last, *whoosh*, goodnight, goodnight . . . (*The stars are gone: darkness and one frightened voice.*) *Aiee*, where 're my teeth my stars? *Aieee* I beat my empty gums and feel the caverns where my teeth were. *Aieee* 'tis the end o' creation!


SCENE XI


*Lights up on* QUEEN ANA's *Bedchamber. Drapes with flights of angels cover the walls. A four-poster bed Up Stage Centre, to the right of it a wardrobe. Stage Right the door to the corridor and below it a dressing table. A table Stage Centre, two trunks, one overflowing with gold plates and trinkets, Stage Left. Tall candleholders by the walls.*
ANA *in a voluminous dark nightgown is Down Stage Right with* MOTILLA, *who clasps a Bible: The* PARROT *is on a perch nearby.*

MOTILLA: Save us, Your Majesty, as Judith saved the Israelites, anointing herself in sweet oils, t' enter Haloferne's bed. Thou must do thy duty as a Queen, lay back . . .
    *A knock on the door Stage Right.* MOTILLA *stops talking instantly and pretends to read the Bible as the* FIRST LADY-IN-WAITING *enters, carrying a hot drink.*
    ANA *waves her away impatiently. She curtsies and withdraws.*
MOTILLA: . . . grit thy teeth, spread thy thighs wide as oysters at moon's zenith and think o' Spain.
ANA: But if we shouldst . . .?
    *Another knock.* ANA *stops talking as the* SECOND LADY-IN-WAITING *enters with a lace nightcap; again* ANA *waves her out.*
ANA: . . . fail. Doest know what you ask? T' be serviced in the service o' God is hard enough, but Father, the Almirante de Castilla isn't e'en o' royal blood.
PARROT: *Unclean, unclean. Leprosy and . . .*

*Another knock: The* PARROT *immediately stops talking as the* THIRD LADY-IN-WAITING *enters and curtsies. Whilst* MOTILLA *and* ANA *pretend to be praying she turns down the bedclothes and exits.*

PARROT: . . . *loose bowels. Crrah, crrah.*

MOTILLA: Though not o' royal blood, the Almirante is a true grandee and perfect Knight and his male bastards 're legion. (*Neither hears the knock or sees the* FOURTH LADY-IN-WAITING *enter.*) You'll not find a champion more worthy t' enter the lists than the Almirante de Castilla.

ALMIRANTE: Here, Father.

ANA: By St Julian!

*She jumps back in fright at the sight of an acutely embarrassed* ALMIRANTE *dressed as the fourth Lady-in-Waiting, in farthingale and wig.*

ALMIRANTE: Father, this isn't the dress o' a gentleman.

MOTILLA: 'Tis a good disguise. What's t' be done must be done quickly. (*He crosses and locks the door.*) Whilst I pray, you lay.

ALMIRANTE: You're staying wi' us?

MOTILLA: F' Her Majesty's honour.

ANA: She that thinks upon her honour, needs no other guard upon her.

MOTILLA: She that hath a man upon her, ne'er thinks upon her honour. 'Twill be safer. No one will interrupt whilst I'm here t' see you committed adultery in godly fashion, wi'out sin. On pain o' thy immortal souls, there casn't be one jot o' pleasure in 't.

ANA: If you stay, the bed curtains must be drawn.

MOTILLA: F' modesty's sake only, Your Majesty. But I'll be listening hard f' sinful love-cries, sobs, gasps, squeaks, heavy breathing. All 're an anathema. Especially heavy breathing.

ALMIRANTE: What o' grunts?

MOTILLA: Grunts? Grunts . . .? I'll permit grunts that betoken honest effort, *ugh*, but not grunts o' joy, *ugghh*. No lustful grunts o' joy, *ugghh*.

ALMIRANTE *is struggling to get out of the farthingale and petticoats.* MOTILLA *goes to help and they become entangled.*

ALMIRANTE: The hooks, unhook the hooks. Father, you didn't tell me 'twould be a glory wi'out dignity.

MOTILLA: Jus' be thy noble self.

ALMIRANTE: This is not one o' my noble days.

PARROT: *Crrah Crrah.*

ANA *puts a curtained cage over the* PARROT *and unbuttons her nightgown.*

ANA: I'd planned counting my gold tonight. Now I've t' devote myself t' State business. My lord Almirante, your singular service to the King must go unrewarded. But if he couldst know o' 't—God forbid—he'd prove as grateful as I am.

ALMIRANTE (*head appearing from petticoats*): The family motto's: 'Officii fructus sit ipsum officium'—Let the reward of duty be duty itself.

*He finally steps out of his petticoats and stands in his underwear. On the opposite side of the bed* ANA *waits tensely in her thick nightdress as he bows.*

ALMIRANTE: Your Majesty.

ANA *gets into bed, followed by* ALMIRANTE.

ANA: In the circumstances, you may call me Madam.

MOTILLA: Have a care, Your Majesty. There must be no undue familiarity 'twixt you that could give rise t' scandal. Only bodily contacts're permitted and that but o' vile necessity. Oh, that we could procreate like trees, wi'out conjunction! Ripple no muscles during coitus, Your Majesty. You must assume the missionary position as laid down by Thomas Aquinas: flat on thy back and motionless throughout. All other positions're sinful and barren f' the semen falls out when you move lustfully. 'Tis why God punishes us and Spain lies barren. No heat, no satisfaction, my lord. And only as much desire as needed t' raise thy standard bolt-high. Remember, 'tis an affair o' State.

MOTILLA *starts to close the bed-curtains.*

ANA: 'Twill be easy f' me. His Majesty's instrument's always been an instrument o' policy.

ALMIRANTE: 'Twill be hard f' me, wi' your care-causing beauty: mouth smelling o' mint and wild thyme; lips only meant t' gather kisses in.

ANA: Is that the language lovers speak? I've ne'er fallen 'cept i' the falling sickness. Then I was swept up into burning blue and gold. Oh the light, the light! Is that as love is?

ALMIRANTE: Yes. Love's an epilepsy too, its sufferers eat fire, see visions, dissolve time and flesh, moan, cry out, *aaahh aaahh.*

ANA: *Aaaahh? Aaahh?*

ALMIRANTE: *Aaaahh aaaaaaaahhhh.*

ANA: *Aaaahh aaaaaaaahhhh.*

*He raises his hands and* ANA *places her palms against his as* MOTILLA *shuts the last bed-curtain.*

*MOTILLA kneels to pray. There is the tell-tale creaking of the bed. He listens intently.*

MOTILLA (*low*): I can hear. You're both *breathing* . . . Fight 't, my children. Grunts . . . only grunts.

*A series of short grunts from the bed.* MOTILLA *nods, satisfied, and returns to his prayers.*

*Suddenly there is a loud knocking on the door.* MOTILLA *leaps up and* ANA's *and* ALMIRANTE's *flushed and frightened faces appear between the curtains. Whilst* MOTILLA *crosses to the door* ANA *clambers down, pushes* ALMIRANTE *back out of sight and throws on her dressing gown.*

*She signals.* MOTILLA *opens the door and* CARLOS *staggers in wearing a black nightcap and a gown over his nightshirt. He carries a lantern and bottle.*

CARLOS: Maaama . . . Maaama's been TALKING all night, clack-clack-clack, she hath the true gift o' tongues. I'll lie wi' m' wife t' show where my TRUE feelings lie.

*They tense as he puts the lantern on the table and the bottle on the floor by the bed.*

ANA: We're unprepared f' thy coming.

MOTILLA: And in the middle o' evening prayers, Your Majesty.

CARLOS: III'll pray too.

*He crosses and kneels Stage Right in front of* MOTILLA, *with his back to the bed.* ANA *joins him.* MOTILLA *directs his prayer over their heads to* ALMIRANTE *hidden in the bed.*

MOTILLA: We pray to the Lord Almighty whose merciless eye sees all. We canst not hide f' ever in one place, though we put on many *disguises.* (ALMIRANTE's *hand appears from between the bed-curtains to pick up his farthingale, but only manages to snatch up the wig.*) Repent and seize the opportunity t' escape his wrath. Lord God, their divine Majesties humbly kneel and close their eyes afore the splendour o' thy radiant presence. (CARLOS *and* ANA *shut their eyes.*) Unseeing i' the darkness they trust blindly in Thee. The sinner must come forth now and . . .

*Even as the bed-curtains start to part, there is a knock on the door and* ANA *and* CARLOS *open their eyes to see a slightly drunk* RAFAEL *hurrying in, bowing.*

RAFAEL: Sire, the Queen Mother comes at a gallop.

CARLOS (*jumping up*): Hide me!

*Before the others can stop him he rushes to the bed and dives in, closing the curtains behind him.* ANA *and* MOTILLA *brace themselves. But nothing happens.*

RAFAEL: I'd best hide too, else she'll know the King's here.

*As he quickly clambers into one of the trunks Stage Left and* ANA *and* MOTILLA *stare bewildered at the silent bed, there is a perfunctory knock and* MARIANA *enters.* ANA *immediately whips off the* PARROT's *curtained cage; the bird squawks raucously at the sight of* MARIANA *sweeping down to them.*

PARROT: *'Tis Medusa's Mother. Crrah Crrah.*

MARIANA: I'll strangle that pestilential fowl. You've trained him t' bait me.

ANA: No, he doeth 't from instinct. You've no right here, Madam.

MOTILLA: We're trying t' pray.

MARIANA: I find no difficulty. Pray continue praying, Father.

MOTILLA *and* ANA *exchange glances.*

MOTILLA: Bow down thy heads. (*The women look down.*) F' He hath hidden Himself away from our sight. We knoweth not where He's at. We've lost Him. Only show Thyself . . . show Thyself . . . *show Thyself dammit.* (ALMIRANTE's *head appears from under the foot of the bed.*) We give thanks, Lord. (ANA *looks up, sees* ALMIRANTE *and hastily points to the wardrobe before looking down again.*) 'Benedicto Dei omnipoténtes Patris et Fílii . . .' (*As* ALMIRANTE *wriggles out,* CARLOS *peers from behind the bed curtains and* RAFAEL *from the trunk; they do not see him, only* MOTILLA *signalling frantically for them to get back; they do so but* ALMIRANTE *thinks the signal's for him and slides back also.*) 'et Spiritus Sancti descendat super te et máneat semper. Amen.'

ANA: You've come t' curse my womb, blast my child.

MARIANA: I saw my son come into thy bedchamber. Where's he hiding?

ANA: Where else would His Majesty, Carlos II o' Spain and the Dependencies, Grand Master o' the Golden Fleece, Defender o' the Faith, hide, but under his wife's bed. Look!

*Before* MOTILLA *can warn her that* ALMIRANTE *is still there,* ANA *crosses excitedly and starts to lift the counterpane hanging over the foot of the bed.* MARIANA *moves to her.*

MARIANA: As a child Carlos was most prone t' hide . . . in wardrobes.

*She darts Up Stage and flings open the wardrobe.* ANA *gives an involuntary cry of fright.* ALMIRANTE, CARLOS *and* RAFAEL *look out from their hiding places for a second, then disappear as* MARIANA *looks round. To cover her confusion* ANA *clutches her stomach and groans.*

MOTILLA *guides her to the dressing table Stage Right; she sits.*

MOTILLA: Ma'am, Her Majesty's condition 's most delicate— please go.

PARROT: *Good-night ladies, 'tis time t' say 'night 'night.*

MARIANA (*crossing*): She's weak-blooded. 'Tis her clapped out German strain. When I was heavy wi' Carlos I stood f' six hours gi'ing audience t' the Duke o' Palamo.

*As they stand Stage Right,* ALMIRANTE *seizes his chance and propels himself out from under the bed and into the wardrobe. Immediately after* CARLOS *slips down into* ALMIRANTE's *former hiding place and* RAFAEL *dives into* CARLOS's *place in the bed. There is a knock and* BELEPSCH *enters quickly with a long candle-snuffer. She is shocked at seeing the Queen.*

BELEPSCH: Your Majesty, 'tis gone eight! Etiquette demands you be in bed long since.

ANA: Blame Her Royal Highness, here. You'll suffer f' this, Madam.

MARIANA: You're wasting your breath—and that's no great loss. 'Tis between me and my son. When I'm gone he'll creep out and you'll mould his melting mind 'gainst me.

BELEPSCH *sees* ALMIRANTE's *farthingale on the floor, clucks disapprovingly, picks it up and opens the wardrobe to put it away. As she is holding the bulky dress in front of her, she does not see the rigid figure of* ALMIRANTE *flattening himself against the back of the wardrobe, but* ANA *does.*

ANA: Countess Belepsch! (BELEPSCH *turns quickly.*) The candles. Snuff out the candles.

*Without looking,* BELEPSCH *quickly dumps the farthingale on top of* ALMIRANTE, *closes the door and begins snuffing out the candle. The* PARROT *gives a piercing shriek and snores loudly.* ANA *rises and puts the curtained cage over the bird.*

ANA: Madam Thornback, if thou doesn't leave I'll've the pleasure o' seeing the Attendants throw you out.

MARIANA: Carlos, you're here, Carlos! I canst smell you, I'm your Mother.

*She darts across to the bed and tears open the curtains. It is empty.*

MOTILLA: Come, Ma'am. The Queen retires. So must you—permanently—after this night's work.

*As he guides her firmly to the exit,* CARLOS *and* RAFAEL *peer*

*momentarily out from under the bed.* MARIANA *and* MOTILLA
*pause in the doorway and look back at* ANA, *who has taken off her
dressing gown and is in bed.*

MOTILLA: God grant thee pleasant slumber, Your Majesty.

MARIANA: Carlos. Son. Don't listen t' her, Carlos . . . Carlos . . .
Carlos . . .

*They exit.* BELEPSCH *snuffs out the last candle, curtsies in the
doorway and follows them out.*

*The room is in darkness except for the tiniest spot of light from
the lantern on the table.*

*Silence, then the sound of scampering in the darkness, doors
opening and closing, nervous whisperings: 'Who's that?' . . .
"tis me.' . . . 'Who's me?' . . . A frightened gasp, more scurryings,
a muffled curse, then* ANA *appears by the table and turns up the
lantern light. She peers round, hears something and flits away.*

*First a woebegone* ALMIRANTE *in battered farthingale and lop-
sided wig and then an absurd night-shirted* CARLOS *stagger in quick
succession in and out of the pool of light. Next* RAFAEL *in a woman's
hat tip-toes past stealthily. Noticing the audience he stops, stares
at them then goes into a frenetic 'Charleston' dance, legs kicking,
arms waving wildly. Just as suddenly he 'freezes' in mid-motion,
then darts away into the darkness.*

MOTILLA *appears next and turns the lantern full up to light the
room and show an extraordinary glimpse of banging doors and
disappearing figures:* RAFAEL *into the trunk,* ALMIRANTE *into the
wardrobe.* ANA *in the bed and* CARLOS *under it. About to speak,*
MOTILLA *hears something and turns the lantern right down.*

*Darkness . . . Breathing . . . Suddenly two lantern lights full up
to show* MOTILLA *and* MARIANA *standing face to face Down
Stage Centre, lanterns in their hands.*

MARIANA (*low*): *Lucifer.*

MOTILLA (*low*): *Old Serpent.* I was waiting f' thee, Ma'am.
(*Guides her out.*) I shall inform the King and the Council you
came back to fright the Queen out o' her wits and
**child.**

MARIANA (*low*): No, 'twas t' see my Carlos. (*A bump from the wardrobe.*) You heard 't?

MOTILLA (*low*): Nothing. Brain fever.

*Another bump from the wardrobe.*

MARIANA (*low*): Brain fever? 'Tis my Carlos!

*She goes towards the wardrobe.* MOTILLA *pulls her back and they struggle, trying not to make a sound.*

MOTILLA (*low*): By the stigmas and the sorrows, I swear 't isn't His Majesty.

MARIANA (*low*): Then 'tis somebody else. Plots. Treacheries. Assignations. Now 'tis my turn t' turn and turn again! *Crrah crrah.*

*Breaking away, she rushes to the wardrobe and flings it open. She screams and steps aside in fright, to reveal* ANA, *smiling. foolishly, swaying and falling out in a faint.* CARLOS *and* RAFAEL *rush from their hiding places in the bed and trunk.*

CARLOS: Whaaaa . . .?

MARIANA: Carlos, I want t' know; what were you doing in your wife's bed?!

RAFAEL: I'll fetch Attendants.

MOTILLA: T' what purpose? They cass't touch the Queen, e'en if she be dying.

CARLOS: Whaaaa . . .? Whaaaa . . .?

MARIANA: Why didst you hide from me, Carlos? Sometimes I think I've failed you as a Mother.

ANA *suddenly groans, staggers up and collapses at the foot of the bed.*

ANA (*clutching stomach*): Dead. It's dead. My child's dead. Our child's dead, Carlos! That witch hath frighted him away, Carlos. I've lost him, Carlos! He's returned t' God—t' God— t' God . . . *He's gone. I'm emptied.*

*As* MOTILLA *hurries out,* CARLOS *spins slowly round and round, his mouth wide open.*

MARIANA: 'Tis a trick 'gainst me, Carlos, assassins behind every bush wi' honey in their mouths, razors in their hands, Jesu, Jesu save me from their little pinking eyes!

RAFAEL: Come Sire, the Queen's surely mistaken.

ANA (*rocking gently and singing*): 'Schlaf, Kinderl, schlaf!/Dein Vater ist ein Graf,/Dein Mutter ist ein Bauerndirn,/Soll ihr Kinderl selber wiegn./Schlaf, Kinderl, schlaf!'

CARLOS: *Maaamaaaahhh* . . .

*He leaps up on the bedcurtains and hangs with one hand from them, gibbering 'Maamaa . . . Maamaa'.*

*As* RAFAEL *and* MARIANA *rush to him,* ALMIRANTE *creeps out from under the dressing table and using the seat as a cover, makes for the exit.* RAFAEL *turns and sees him as he abandons the seat and dives out.*

*RAFAEL stares and is about to follow him when* CARLOS *suddenly leaps down onto* MARIANA *and starts to throttle her.*

RAFAEL: Sire, you'll do thyself an injury.

*As* MARIANA *gasps and croaks,* DR BRAVO *rushes in with* MOTILLA.

DR BRAVO: Ne'er fear, Sire, Bravo's here, *ahhh.*

*He goes flying over the dressing-table seat left in his path. Smirking,* DR GELEEN *helps him up whilst* MARIANA *and* CARLOS *struggle violently.*

MOTILLA: Sire, leave her t' the terrible mercy o' God.

*CARLOS lets go of* MARIANA *who staggers away, feeling her neck, and joins* DR BRAVO *beside* ANA.

CARLOS: Doeth mmmm child live? Doeth he? Is he? Whaaa good's a King wi'out an heir whaa . . .

DR BRAVO: 'Tis in God's hands. He maketh the stars change, babes die, old men live on. We'll soon know the best and the worst.

*He guides* ANA *onto the bed and* DR GELEEN *closes the bed-curtains round them.*

*Lights dim down to Spot on* CARLOS. *A choir sings softly the Holy Innocents Day Hymn: 'Salvete flores martyrum.'*

CARLOS: Lord 've mercy, save my son. IIIII'll beeee penitent,

thorned, pierced, scourged, hammered, spat on oooooonly
hoist me high t' Theeeeeee . . .

    CARLOS *lets out a great cry of despair. The bright Spot flickers
and he shakes convulsively as he falls into an epileptic fit. His
grotesque twistings and jerkings quickly reach a pitch of intensity,
then suddenly die away and the flicker stops.*

    *Darkness except for the Spot on* CARLOS *lying curled up Down
Stage Centre in a foetus position.*

    *He rises, coldly furious, in a state of post-epileptic automation.*

CARLOS: Dead? Is my child dead?

        I'll wound the earth, kill the sun, stamp out
                            the stars,
        Storm the vault o' heaven and drag that tit-face
                           tyrant, God,
        Down by his greasy locks, f' taking back my child.
        (Not his t' take, only t' give, not t' take.)
        I'll loose war and death in Paradise.
        There'll be wronged men enough t' march wi' me,
        Under a black flag, skull and broken bones rampant.
        And the motto: 'Resistance t' tyrants is obedience
                           t' God.'
        Doest hear me, dung-heap!
        My maw-walloping, cow-hearted, copper-arsed,
                         crab-lousy,
        Jolter-headed, herring-gutted, cock-pimping, bum-
                    fiddling, divine shit-shack!
        Answer me, answer me!
        There's no difference 'tween prayers and curses,
        He's long since fled.
        Heaven's as empty as her belly;
        *There is no God.*

    *Thunder, a streak of lightning and a great voice booms:*

GOD' VOICE: YES THERE IS.

CARLOS: I've prayed t' you. Where's my son?

    *Another streak of lightning.*

GOD'S VOICE (*wearily*): NO SON—ONLY LIGHTNING.
  *Thunder, another streak of lightning and* CARLOS *collapses. The
attack is over.*


### SCENE XII

MOTILLA *appears in the Spot behind* CARLOS.


CARLOS: WWWWWhy do I suffer?
MOTILLA: 'Cause thou art a man. You casn't sin wi'out being
  evil, evil wi'out being degraded, degraded wi'out being
  punished, punished wi'out being *guilty*. We're conceived in
  iniquity. Man alone knows 't, 'tis his glory and his shame.
  The wise cry out 'Who shall deliver me?' The weak surrender
  and call their cowardice happiness.
CARLOS: WWWWWhy do I suffer?
MOTILLA: As punishment. All earthly and spiritual order rest on
  punishment. As Your Majesty punishes criminals, so His
  Divine Majesty punishes sinners. Only his whips and racks're
  diseases and death. Diseases're sins made manifest, passed
  down generation t' generation. Sire, we stink and putrify from
  the sins o' our fathers.
CARLOS: WWWWWhy do I suffer?
MOTILLA: Out o' love. The greater the sin, the greater God's
  concern, the greater pain needed t' cut 't out. Knives, forceps,
  saws 're terrible instruments o' torture. But in the hands o' the
  skilled physicians they save our bodies. So God saves our souls
  wi' His instruments; His tumours, goitres, cancers. Can a
  broken limb be restored wi'out agony? A haemorrhage wi'out
  privation, a cancerous growth wi'out the bloody knife? Can
  a damned soul be brought t' salvation wi'out the healing pain?
CARLOS: Mercy, mercy, mercy!
MOTILLA: God shows His mercy only by punishing us i' this
  world where pain hath an end, rather than the next, where 'tis

everlasting. Serve and fear Him. 'Tis useless t' rebel or flee. He is omnipotent and the Empire o' grief is everywhere.

*A* CANTOR *chants the responsory from the Funeral Service:* 'Subvenite Sancti Dei occurite, Angeli Domine . . .' *as* CARLOS *and* MOTILLA *disappear Up Stage.*

### SCENE XIII

*Lights up on the Throne-Room.*

*Still in his nightdress,* CARLOS *is slumped on the Throne Up Stage Centre.* ANA *and* MARIANA *stand either side of him, whilst* RAFAEL *sits at his feet. The members of the Council of State,* PONTOCARRERO, ALMIRANTE, MONTERREY, ALBA *and* TORRES, *are formally positioned below the steps of the rostrum.*

PONTOCARRERO: We've become a nation o' enchanted men, outside the natural order: rich but poor, ruined but intact, all our beginnings an end. Much happens and nothing changes; we move forward and stand still; act and do nothing. The Queen's miscarriage compels you t' make a decision, Sire. The succession. The French army in Catalonia's t' move 'gainst us 'less you name Philip Bourbon heir, the House o' Austria still presses f' Archduke Charles whilst Bavaria waits on José.

ALMIRANTE: But first the guilty must be punished, Sire. The Royal Physician's confirmed our Queen was frighted out o' her pregnancy. I ask, who hated her, who pursued her e'en t' her bedchamber? (*All look at* MARIANA.) My lords, I move the Queen Mother be found guilty o' the Queen's miscarriage and humbly recommend His Majesty exile her from Madrid. Though I be broken f' 't, I must speak out. My body's but a tool t' be used i' the service o' my King.

RAFAEL: What tool doest use t' service the Queen?

ALMIRANTE: My heart. My lords . . .?

*The* OTHERS *look up at* CARLOS *for a lead, but he remains*

*slumped on the throne.* MARIANA *stares implacably down at them.*
*They hesitate.*

ANA: Commit. If thou doesn't commit you jus' take up space.
Commit. Rid me o' her. COMMIT.

ALBA, TORRES *and* MONTERREY *raise their hands. All look at*
PONTOCARRERO.

PONTOCARRERO: Lower your hands, my lords. We're all
agreed the Queen Mother's guilty . . . As I am . . . As we all
are. The blame's not i' one breast. This nation, chosen by God
t' be the defender o' the true Faith, hath proved unworthy.
So we're punished. But Our Saviour'll forgive his children
and end their humiliation and impotence if they do but show
Him a sign o' their love and repentance.

CARLOS: Hooooow?

PONTOCARRERO: By asking the Suprema t' sanction a Day o'
Contrition, an Act o' Faith, a Festival o' Light, an Auto de fe!

CARLOS: Auto dddddd fe?

PONTOCARRERO *nods confidently.* ANA *and* ALMIRANTE
*exchange uneasy glances.*

PONTOCARRERO: At a stroke 'twill rouse our armies, dismay
our enemies, curb all dissent, unite the nation . . .

MARIANA: And, God willing, strengthen thy loins. Your father
was always stimulated by the fires o' an auto de fe. Thy late
brother, Prince Prospero, was conceived on the night o' one
such spectacular.

ANA: What o' my miscarriage, her banishment?!

CARLOS: Auto ddddd?

ALMIRANTE: Sire, afore we can organize any auto de fe, we must
organize the relief of Barcelona from an attack o' the French.

RAFAEL: You couldn't organize the relief o' your bowels from an
attack o' the piles.

ANA: What o' HER!

CARLOS (*staggering up*): Shouldst weeee . . .? shouldst weeeee
ask the Suprema . . .? Whaaa does my Council sss t' an auto de
fe . . . whaaa . . .? Advise . . .

MONTERREY: I'm 'gainst 't, Sire. An auto de fe's an expensive undertaking. (*The drapes Stage Right part and a six-spoke Torture-wheel, with a* PRISONER *strapped to it, is placed Down Stage Left by two hooded Dominican* MONKS.) True, the common people'd give freely, preferring burnings t' bread, but the bulk o' the money'd come from us grandees. No, Sire, the time's not ripe.

*He is gently escorted off by the two* MONKS. *There is the sound of a large animal panting.*

TORRES: Remember the first aphorism o' Hippocrates, Sire: 'Ars Longa, Vita Brevis'. The Dutch grow tulips; the French dance the minuet; Spaniards burn heretics. The auto de fe is more than jus' a national pastime, 'tis a true folk art. (*Drapes Stage Right part again and the* DOMINICANS *wheel in an Iron Maiden—a hollow wooden case, the inside lid studden with spikes.*) All o'er Europe dissenters're being flayed and crucified. But crudely, wi'out the dramatic genius Spaniards bring t' killing f' their God. No, Sire, 't mustn't be rushed into.

*The two* MONKS *exit with* TORRES *between them. The panting grows louder, the lights brighter.*

ALBA: 'Twould besmirch our honour if the auto weren't staged wi' true pomp. (*Drapes Stage Left part and a horizontal rack with a* PRISONER *spreadeagled on it is wheeled Down Stage Left by two more hooded Dominican* MONKS.) Madrid's not seen a public auto f' a decade. Like as all that's best, 'tas dropped from fashion. O' course Castille and Serena keep the tradition alive. But however worthy, they're essentially provincial shows: quantity not quality. A Royal auto de fe's different and needs months t' prepare. No, Sire, we must think long on the matter.

*He is escorted out between the two* MONKS.

ANA: All say the same. The answer's no, Carlos. No auto de fe. The answer's no, no, no, no . . .

*Though* CARLOS *nods vigorously in agreement with* ANA *and* ALMIRANTE, PONTOCARRERO *smiles confidently at* MARIANA.

*As they continue nodding and the sound of panting grows louder
and louder, the throne rostrum revolves carrying* CARLOS, ANA,
MARIANA, ALMIRANTE *and* RAFAEL *out of sight whilst the
drapes are taken up to reveal dungeon walls.*

MONKS *place spare furnishings as the panting increases, then
suddenly stops.*

### SCENE XIV

PONTOCARRERO *calmly sniffs a scented handkerchief and looks
around the Torture Chamber of the Spanish Inquisition, with its
Wheel, Rack and Iron Maiden.*
*The entrance door is Up Stage Centre at the top of a flight of stairs
(part of the back of the rostrum) that curves Down Stage Right. At
the bottom a* PRISONER *hangs in chains from an armetarium on the
wall. Red hot pokers and rods are being heated in a brazier Stage
Centre next to a stained stone slab serving as a table. Stage Left a
low archway leads to another part of the dungeon.*
ALCALA *enters briskly through it, with his son* GOMEZ. *Middle-aged
and dignified, he wears a leather skull-cap and smock with a red
cross on the front, and carries a brace of rats. His son is similarly
dressed but carries a bucket and brush.*

ALCALA: Your Eminence.
    *Crossing quickly they kneel and kiss* PONTOCARRERO's *hand
    He gestures and they rise.* ALCALA *gives* GOMEZ *the rats to throu
    into the brazier.*
PONTOCARRERO: How comes the auto de fe?
ALCALA: As Chief Torturer t' the Holy Office I've found 'tis
    always fatal t' hurry such matters.
GOMEZ: Father! Look, blood!
    *He is pointing to a stain on the floor by the Wheel.* ALCALA
    *crosses quickly and examines it.*
ALCALA (*to* PRISONER *on the Wheel*): You've been *bleeding*

again! We spend the night cleaning up your mess and you start t' bleed all over the place. (*The* PRISONER *groans.*) That's no excuse.

MOTILLA *enters Stage Left.*

MOTILLA: Your Eminence.

PONTOCARRERO: Father.

MOTILLA: I was inspecting the cells on behalf o' the Inquisitor-General.

PONTOCARRERO: And I on behalf o' His Majesty.

*They walk round slowly, inspecting the chamber as* ALCALA *and* GOMEZ *carry a roll of carpet up the steps.*

MOTILLA: 'Twas a neat device, Your Eminence, for diverting attention from the Queen Mother. Even I had t' support the holding o' an auto de fe.

PONTOCARRERO: Naturally. Nine months after the last auto generale, there was an almighty outcrop o' births.

MOTILLA: The stench o' burning flesh seems but t' stir up our vile lust f' life.

ALCALA *and* GOMEZ *unroll the red carpet down the steps.*

PONTOCARRERO: Pray 'twill stir up His Majesty. I trust you're mindful o' the great service I've done your Order i' suggesting this auto.

MOTILLA: Beware o' Jesuits bearing gifts.

PONTOCARRERO: Ne'er fear, the auto'll be a blazing triumph. Your Inquisitor-General's proved himself many times o'er. His Holiness loves him, as Cardinal Borgia once loved Fray Torquemanda, f' the remorselessness o' his punishments, the strength o' his severity and the courage o' his pitilessness.

*The door Up Stage Centre is thrown open by two hooded Dominican* MONKS *dressed in the black robe of the Inquisition.* ALCALA *and* GOMEZ, *fixing the carpet at the foot of the stairs, bow their heads.*

ALCALA: The Inquisitor-General. (*To* PRISONERS.) Show respect there.

*A tapping sound and the Inquisitor-General,* VALLADARES, *is framed in the doorway. The wizened old man, bent with arthritis, hobbles beady-eyed down the stairs on two sticks.*

VALLADARES: 'Tis good t' see thee here at last, Your Eminence. I've been trying f' years t' arrange f' you to visit the cells o' the Inquisition.

PONTOCARRERO: I've been aware o' 't, my dear Valladares. But now I must report t' the King. God be with thee, Fathers.

*They bow their heads as he goes quickly up the stairs and exits.*

VALLADARES: Damnable Jesuits! Would we had another Fray Alonso t' pursue 'em all t' the fires.

MOTILLA: His Eminence 's a careful man. He neglects his duties as a priest but bears no taint o' heresy.

VALLADARES: All men 're tainted, 'tis the worm i' the bud. I see 't everywhere; faces, voices, eyes, hands, the wind. We drowned in heresy: young, old, rich, poor, Cardinals, Captains, Viceroys, Governors, Princes, Kings—and in the darkest watches o' the night I e'en have doubts about His Holiness, Pope Innocent XII, himself!

MOTILLA: Morality should have 'ts fires too. His Eminence's allowed t' flourish under the purity o' his dogma.

VALLADARES: Look round and weep at Spain's decadence. This prison used t' bulge wi' the excommunicated limbs o' Satan, waiting t' be relaxed at the stake. Enough men and women t' fuel a dozen autos de fe. Now I've t' send t' Toledo. (ALCALA *offers him a parchment.*) What's this?

ALCALA: My list o' condemned penitents f' the auto de fe.

VALLADARES (*reading*): Eight blasphemers f' the galleys. Ten Judaizers t' be relaxed i' prison. Juan Martinez exhumed f' a heresy committed in 1495 . . . that's a rarity, the first ever two-hundred-year-old heretic t' be burned in Madrid. (*Hands list to* MOTILLA.) Should prove the basis o' a varied programme, wi' the burning alive o' our pertinacious Jew, Diego Lopez Duro, a fitting climax t' the festivities.

ALCALA: Duro's not for burning, Inquisitor-General.

VALLADARES: Take care, I consider a sense o' humour's a sure sign o' internal heresy.

ALCALA: 'Tis my honour t' report that last night, after five years' struggle wi' rack and hot irons, that pertinacious Jew, Lopez Duro, finally adjured, confessed and sang the praises o' the true Lord, Jesus Christ.

VALLADARES: What! Devil take him . . . Go bring me yer tardy convert.

ALCALA *bows and exits Stage Left.*

MOTILLA: If Duro's truly converted, he's earned God's mercy and must be garrotted at the stake afore the fires are lit, like the rest o' 'em. All penitents reconciled t' Christ must be strangled afore burning. Wi'out Duro we've no-one t' burn *alive.*

VALLADARES: And no time t' find a replacement. I was relying on Duro t' stand firm in his accursed heresy. Now he recants and dies too fast. Heretics used t' meet death with a fierce joyfulness. True, 't sprung from a devilish exultation o' sin and not the gentle humility o' the true martyr f' Christ. But they made a most satisfying spectacle. I still recall Raphael Valles i' the auto o' '85. Standing still as a bright statue, hair sheeted in flame, till he burst open and his hot tripes and trullibubs spilt out and all the time crying: 'Jehovah, Lord God o' Zion, the law o' Moses is the only true law, Jehovah, Jehovah . . .'

DURO: Jesu, Jesu, Jesu. Glory be t' the Father and t' the Son and t' the Holy Ghost.

ALCALA *enters proudly Stage Left with the exulting* LOPEZ DURO, *a bony man with matted beard, disintegrating loin cloth and chains.*

ALCALA: Inquisitor-General, this's Lopez Duro, once a vile Judaizer, now praise be t' God, a true believer.

VALLADARES: I'll be the judge o' his beliefs, (*he jabs the air with his stick*) AND YOURS AND YOURS AND YOURS. Go, join thy son. Gi' us warning o' the King's coming.

ALCALA *bows and joins* GOMEZ *who has been looking out the doorway at the top of the stairs.*

DURO:   I-do-confess-I-was-a-Judaizer-who-didst-abominate-pork-and-winkles-and-didst-change-my-linen-drawers-and-light-candles-on-the-Sabbath-Now-I-believe-in-God-the-Father-Almighty-and-in-Jesus-Christ-His-Only-Son-our-Lord . . .

VALLADARES: Recant your new found faith!

DURO: *Recant?* But you've spent five years converting me t' Christ. Five years on the wheel, *confess, confess, adjure, adjure.* Tongue grated, hands splintered, toes hanging by a little skin, spirit broken wi' my bones. Oh Jesu spare me, spare me, I'll not recant.

VALLADARES: Do't then, f' Jesus. 'Twill do Him most good if you burn at the stake a *live* Jew rather than a *dead* Christian.

MOTILLA (*turning away*): Compromise, that old devil compromise.

VALLADARES: Relapse, and burn f' Christ! 'Twill be t' thy advantage.

DURO: 'Tis a trick t' test my faith. Testing, one-two-three-I-believe-in-God-the-Father-Almighty-and-in-Jesus-Christ-His-Only-Son-born . . . Advantage? What advantage?

VALLADARES: We hold your son on a burning offence. But the Inquisition, in 'ts mercy, could recognize his father's singular service t' the Faith and reduce the sentence t' perpetual exile.

DURO: 'Tis torture by hope. I don't believe thee . . . I don't believe . . . I don't believe . . .

VALLADARES: My last offer. Relapse and burn alive and your son'll be exiled wi' one hundred ducats.

DURO: Two hundred!

VALLADARES: Ingrate! Usurious pork-hating Jew! Not a ducat more I'll . . .

DURO: I-believe-in-God-the-Father-Almighty-i'-Jesus-Christ-His-Only-Son-Our-Lord-born . . .

VALLADARES: Two hundred.

DURO: How doest I know you'll deliver my son and money safe, afore I roast?

VALLADARES: How doest I know you'll not turn Christian again afore you burn? We must trust each other.

DURO: 'Tis a question of' faith.

GOMEZ: His Majesty! His Majesty approaches!

*He and* ALCALA *come down excitedly to wait at the foot of the stairs as an* ATTENDANT *appears in the doorway.*

ATTENDANT: His Most Catholic Majesty, Defender o' the Faith, Carlos o' Spain.

*They kneel.* CARLOS *enters quickly and goes careering down the steps followed by* PONTOCARRERO *and* FROYLAN.

CARLOS *gestures and the* OTHERS *rise. Smiling inanely he begins a quick tour of the chamber accompanied by* ALCALA *and* GOMEZ. *They cross to the* PRISONER *hanging from the wall Stage Right.*

CARLOS: GGG' t' see thee . . . er . . . er . . . (ALCALA *whispers in his ear.*) Master Domingo de la Cruz . . . lot o' weather we've been having . . . the heat . . . tttthink thyself MOST lu-lu-lucky this is the only cool place i' Madrid. (*The* PRISONER *nods feebly and* CARLOS *passes to the* PRISONER *on the Wheel.*) . . . er . . . uhm . . . (ALCALA *whispers again.*) Ahh . . . weeeee hear you maa good progress o'er thy heresy concerning . . . er . . . kkkkkeep 't UP . . .

2ND PRISONER (*croaking*): God bless thee, Sire.

CARLOS *crosses to the* PRISONER *on the rack Stage Left.*

CARLOS: Er . . . won't beeee long now . . .

3RD PRISONER: *Ahhhhhh.*

*He screams in pain as* CARLOS *accidentally knocks against the rack handle.* ALCALA *scowls at the* PRISONER.

CARLOS: Whaaa . . .? aaa . . . meee?

3RD PRISONER (*gasping*): 'Twas a great honour, Your Majesty.

CARLOS *moves Down Stage where* VALLADARES *and* MOTILLA *and* PONTOCARRERO *and* FROYLAN *stare coldly at each other whilst* DURO *looks on bemused.*

CARLOS: Aaa—Inspector-General . . . aaaall goes well? MUST . . .
my last chance . . .

VALLADARES: We've grave problems, Sire.

FROYLAN: Can my staff help the Holy Office o'er transportation,
catering, extra supplies o' wood?

PONTOCARRERO: I'm certain the Inquisitor-General'd resent
any interference from the Society o' Jesus. He'll do his best,
as always. He knows there's more at stake than jus 'a few
heretics. Spain's asking God t' renew His covenant wi' His
people by making Their Majesties fertile again.

ALCALA: Sire, the signs're good. After five years, this most
obstinate Jew, Lopez Duro's at last become reconciled t'
Jesus Christ.

CARLOS: Maaaster Torturer, waaa words wi' thee . . .

*They all bow.* PONTOCARRERO *and* FROYLAN *retire up,
Stage Right to watch suspiciously* VALLADARES *and* MOTILLA,
*Up Stage Left, whispering urgently to* DURO. GOMEZ *hovers near
his proud father.*

ALCALA: Your Majesty?

CARLOS: Tell mmmmm about death.

ALCALA: *Death?* Sire, you wrong me! I know nothing o' death,
'cept what all men know. I'm Spain's Chief Torturer, not
Executioner. I bring penitents t' the threshold o' death, but
ne'er o'er, else their souls 'd escape t' Hell and be lost f' Christ.
Men die here, but only through accident, weakness, sheer
perversity on their part. I've no extra knowledge o' death.
Pain's my province. I can tell thee o' pain, Sire, and its outrider,
fear.

CARLOS: I know pain, paaaa's my familiar tooo. Sleeping—
waking paaaa, eating—drinking paaaa, all-the-time paaaa;
e'en when 't doesn't hurt I feel paaaa. Whaaa canst you tell me
o' paaain?

ALCALA: 'Tis my craft, Sire. 'Stead o' hard metal I work soft
flesh into precious ornaments f' Our Lord. The goldsmiths o'
Silos took three years t' prepare a golden Chalice f' St Dominic

I took five t' prepare the body of the Jew, Lopez Duro, f' Jesus Christ. Gi'en time, all men canst be broken and re-made. But 'tis no task for fresh-faced understrappers. My son Gomez's a promising lad, but as yet lacks all patience. There's so much t' learn, Sire. What point o' pain t' attack—eyelid, tongue, spine, armpit. What degree o' pain t' apply. Short bursts produce the best results, f' they're followed by long periods o' ease. 'Tis in this pain-free time the penitent suffers most, consumed wi' fear o' pain's return, pain past, pain t' come, flesh's pain, mind's pain. 'Tis the mind that sets the flesh aquiver, knowing what has been and will be endured. Then a feather-touch can set 'em screaming. Sire, I long t' tell the world o' the godly work we do here, the guilty finding repentance, the innocent, a true strengthening o' faith. This cell's an altar t' the suffering Christ! Here we feel the thorn's prick, taste His sacred wounds streaming—*they stream, they stream*: chastiser and chastised merging i' the blessed communion o' pain! The joyful vocation o' suffering! (*He seizes a hot iron rod and slaps it on his bare arm: his flesh sizzles.*) But that joy's as nothing t' the joy o' bringing such souls as Lopez Duro t' salvation. How I cried in triumph when his blood mingled wi' my sweat and he cried, 'I believe in the Father, Son and Holy Ghost, Virgin Mary, Mother o' God' and I cried 'Hallelujah, I believe, I believe . . .'           '

DURO: . . . that the law o' Moses is the only true law, Oh Lord God o' Zion! (*Hebraically chanting the Kaddish Prayer.*) 'B'olmo Rabbo Shmey V'yiskadash Yisgadal/Malchusej V'yamlich Chir'usey Dee-vro/Beis D'chol Uu'chayez Uu'yomeichon B'chayeichon . . .'

*He staggers forward waving his arms. All stare at him:* VALLADARES, MOTILLA *in relief, the* OTHERS *in varying degrees of horror.*

ALCALA: NO! Not a relapse, here i' front o' the King! You casn't slide back into heresy. 'Tis sheer bloody-mindedness. Think o' *me*.

VALLADARES: As I suspected, his heresy's too deep rooted t' be rooted out in a mere five years. Prepare him f' Jesus and St Paul!

GOMEZ *bundles* DURO *out Stage Left, still chanting ecstatically.*

CARLOS: Whaaa o' the AUTO . . .?!

VALLADARES: Ne'er fear, Sire, such difficulties act as a spur, t' the godly. I'll cauterize Spain's wounds. Mere words die i' the air, but the vision o' burnt and blistering flesh commands a lasting obedience. And wi'out obedience the Jews, Moors and Freemasons'd swarm free, f' heretics breed like maggots on the decaying carcass o' the Church. All'll be ready on the day, Sire, on that burning Day o' Judgement when the good taste the greatest joy in Paradise—watching the torments o' the damned below—whilst the wicked see the terror awaiting 'em in Hell. Thus a successful auto de fe's both joy and terror mixed. A mighty show t' dazzle eyes and purge the heart; till that radiant moment when the Christian faith's made real and the playing ends and the last fires're lit and women roast and men burn t' hot ash, smoke in the wind. Oh there's nothing so inspiring, as sinners burning at the stake. It's good t' see 'em roasting, it's fine t' see 'em bake. The Jews'll shout 'Ovai, Ovai!', the Moors'll start t' quake. But their souls go marching on . . .

*Whilst* MONKS *enter and dismantle the set and the lights dim down,* VALLADARES *leads the* OTHERS *Down Stage singing ferociously to the painful, rhythmic cries of the* PRISONERS.

ALL (*singing*): We'll sing a holy chorus when they're screaming on the rack./We try to make them Christians but they all get cardiacs./We're rooting out the Devil and the other bric-a-brac./God is marching on./To keep the public happy is the object of the show./They need the entertainment and it helps the status quo./Men cannot live by bread alone . . .'

CARLOS (*singing*): 'But now we have to blow.'
ALL (*singing*): 'Cos the show is on the road./Glory, Glory Hallelujah./Glory, Glory Hallelujah./Glory, Glory Hallelujah./The show is on the road!'
*Lights out as they Exit.*

## SCENE XV

*A single flute. Birds sing a dawn chorus. Misty morning light up on a bare bloodstained stage. A green and white Cross, both shrouded in black crepe Up Stage Left and Right. Running between them up to the Flies, three richly draped galleries. They become shorter in length the higher they are. Above the topmost gallery, a single box-platform with a rail. Two high ladders, Right and Left, link the galleries and platform. Below the bottom gallery a rostrum.*

*The birds stop singing as through the morning mist* FOUR MONKS *of the Inquisition in conical hoods and black habits with white crosses on the front, enter silently, Stage Right, carrying wooden stakes. Another* MONK *enters behind them with a stoup and sprinkler. As the stakes are placed upright in a line Stage Right, he sprinkles each one in turn and blesses it. The 'Miserere' is chanted softly now and throughout the rest of the scene.*

*Before the* MONKS *exit they place steps Down Stage Centre to link the centre aisle of the auditorium to the Stage.*

*There is a sound of crowds beginning to gather.* PONTOCARRERO *in full cardinal's regalia, and* DR BRAVO *enter Down Stage Left each carrying a bundle of wood, as do* MOTILLA *and* ALMIRANTE, *who have entered Down Stage Right. Behind them, a silent line of* LADIES-IN-WAITING *and* COURTIERS *including* GONGORA, RAFAEL *and his father* MORRA, *each carrying a bundle of wood, make their way Up Stage and deposit their bundles at the foot of the stakes.*

*Dividing into two snake-like lines they glide through the misty light and up the two gallery ladders Right and Left.*

PONTOCARRERO: Observe His Majesty close. He's been poured into the tightest breeches so you canst see if his penis stands upright during the ceremony.

DR BRAVO: I fear his constitution's so weak 'twill be a miracle if *he* stands upright during the ceremony.

PONTOCARRERO: 'Tis the object o' the auto de fe t' work miracles.

*The crowd grows louder now as the two lines of spectators climb up the gallery ladders.*

MOTILLA: My lord, thy position's directly above the King so you canst observe if his penis-member grows apace.

ALMIRANTE: I dreamed only o' glory. Now my standard's in the dust, my honour's turned pimp.

MOTILLA: 'Twill be restored if after today's performance, the King performs between the sheets.

*ALMIRANTE and* MOTILLA, *together with* DR BRAVO *and* PONTOCARRERO, *join the end of the line of spectators and deposit their bundles of wood by the stakes.*

*As the lights come up brighter and the crowd grows more excited, a* PEDLAR *with a tray comes down the centre aisle of the auditorium.*

PEDLAR: Programmes! Official programmes from the Holy Office! Get your official programmes!

*The* COURTIERS *are now in place,* PONTOCARRERO *and* ALMIRANTE *in the lowest gallery.*

*DR BRAVO and a toothless* GONGORA *stand in position at the foot of the rostrum and glare at each other from opposite corners.* MOTILLA *Down Stage Centre faces them and the gallery.*

*A drum-roll and the noise of the crowd instantly dies away and* CARLOS *rises up from the back of the rostrum dressed completely in gold; even his face is painted gold. He is followed on either side by* ANA *and* MARIANA *in black, their faces chalk white. They take up*

*positions; the women glaring viciously at each other,* CARLOS
*staring straight ahead.*

*A pause, then the choir thunders the 'Miserere' and two purple
banners of the Inquisition unfurl from the Flies Up Stage Left and
Right behind the Crosses. At the same time* VALLADARES, *accompanied by the* EXECUTIONER *in tight-fitting black hood and
trousers and a fiery cross burnt on his chest, appears on the platform
above the gallery.*

*The stiff brocade of* VALLADARES' *pontificals spread out over
the edge of the platform making him look like a purple bat hovering
in the air.*

*As* VALLADARES *delivers the sermon the* EXECUTIONER *very
slowly slides down the gallery ladder.*

VALLADARES: 'Beautiful art thou my beloved like the skins o'
Solomon.' Thus the Holy Ghost likened the Church t' the
tents o' the Israelites adorned in the skins o' the wild beasts
they'd slain. So the Holy Inquisition's most beautiful, adorned
wi' the skins o' God's enemies she too hath slain. Some will die
reconciled in the true Faith, others remaining obstinate t' the
last. Both fall. But the good die falling forward like Abraham,
t'wards God, the wicked backwards, away into Hell. Grant us
thy mercy, Lord.

*The crowd chants 'Amen' and* TWO MONKS *enter Stage Left
bearing a huge Bible. One crouches in front of the rostrum whilst the*
OTHER *opens the Bible and rests it on his back whilst* MOTILLA
*intones above.*

MOTILLA: Your Majesty swears and promises by thy faith
and royal word thou wilt defend the Catholic Faith which
you do hold and believe. That you will persecute the heretic
and apostate against our Holy Mother the Apostolic Church o'
Rome according t' the decrees and sacred laws wi'out omission
or exception.

CARLOS: This do I swear and promise by my faith and royal
word.

*The crowd chants 'Amen'. As the Bible is carried out Stage Left*

MOTILLA *moves Up Stage towards the rostrum, bows deeply, turns and faces the auditorium. A* MONK *stands on either side of him, one with the sentences of the accused, the other with a white cord on a small black cushion. Behind them the* COURTIERS *shift expectantly.*

*A funeral bell tolls as a candle-lit procession comes down the centre aisle of the auditorium. Flanked by black-hooded* MONKS, *both live and dead* CRIMINALS *wear white, penitent cloaks called 'Sarbenitos' and tall, cone-shaped dunce's caps; flames decorate the cloaks and the hats of those about to be burnt. Each* CRIMINAL *carries a lighted yellow candle and they have their names scrawled on placards on their chests.*

*A* PRIEST, *carrying the Cross of St Martin veiled in black, leads them in. In order behind him are* LEONORA SANCHEZ, *her neck in a knotted yoke, her torn dress bespattered with mud;* JUAN *and* LUCIA GUZMAN, *half-dead in their chains; the smouldering skeleton of* NUNO ALVAREZ *in the tattered remains of a shroud,* LOPEZ DURO, *gagged and manacled, his hat painted with dragons as well as flames; and the life-size wax effigy of* GREGORIO MADERA *on a litter with a Janus mask on the front and back of its head.*

*As they stagger down amid the incessant chanting and the jeers and catcalls of the crowd, two* PEDLARS *with trays make their way up side aisles, one crying* 'Hot chocolate! Sweet cakes! Get thy hot chocolate!' *and the other* 'Souvenirs! Crucifixes! Beads! Virgin Marys! Authentic splinters from the stakes! Only two ducats.'

*The* PRIEST *at the head of the procession, climbs up onto the Stage, where all bow their heads before the Cross of St Martin. As he solemnly exits with it Stage Left,* MOTILLA *begins flatly to read out the sentences. The instant the condemned* CRIMINALS *step up onto the Stage before him, their candles are snuffed out.*

MOTILLA: This is the first group o' criminal penitents, consigned t' judgement . . . Accursed limb o' Satan, Leonora Sanchez, widow o' Nicholas Sanchez, guilty o' bigamy, abandoned t' the secular arm and sentenced t' one hundred lashes in a

public street according t' custon wi'out mercy or remission.
*To the jeers of the crowd the hysterical woman is dragged Off*
*Stage Left accompanied by a* PRIEST.

PRIEST: Repent my daughter. Search thy heart. Confess thy
sins. Ask God's forgiveness afore 'tis too late.

MOTILLA: Accursed limbs o' Satan, Juan and Lucia Guzman,
found guilty o' a heretical proposition concerning self-
damnation. Thou hast adjured, confessed thy errors, been
reconciled and sentenced t' be abandoned t' the secular arm
and executed according t' custom, wi'out mercy or remission.

*A* MONK *takes the half-dead* GUZMANS *to the* EXECUTIONER
*and the stakes, Stage Right, accompanied by the* PRIEST *who has*
*quickly returned.*

PRIEST: Repent, my children. Search thy hearts. Confess thy
sins. Ask God's forgiveness afore 'tis too late.

*As the* EXECUTIONER *binds the* GUZMANS *to separate stakes*
*and the sound of* LEONORA SANCHEZ *being whipped Off Stage*
*Left is heard,* ALMIRANTE *quickly produces a telescope, claps it*
*to his eye and focuses on* CARLOS's *crotch directly below him.*

MOTILLA: Accursed limb o' Satan, Nuno Alvarez 1564-1638.
Found guilty and sentenced f' secret Protestantism. The lands
o' thy descendants to be confiscated and thy bones disinterred
and taken t' the place o' burning and abandoned t' the secular
arm according t' custom wi'out mercy or remission.

*The skeleton of* ALVAREZ *is carried Stage Right with the*
PRIEST *fervently exhorting the bones.*

PRIEST: Repent, my son. Search thy heart. Confess thy sins.
Ask God's forgiveness afore 'tis too late.

*As the* EXECUTIONER *binds the skeleton to a stake,* DR BRAVO
*is seen taking out a large magnifying glass and shifting to a better*
*position to peer up* CARLOS's *crotch directly above him.*

*Amid the incessant noise and lights the crowd shouts excitedly as*
LOPEZ DURO *approaches* MOTILLA.

MOTILLA: Accursed limb o' Satan, Lopez Duro, guilty o'
Judaism and who, despite the ministerings o' the Holy Office

remains a pertinacious, unreconciled heretic. Sentenced t' be abandoned t' the secular arm f' burning according to custom wi'out mercy or remission.

DURO *looks up at* VALLADARES *and nods. Imperceptibly* VALLADARES *nods back.* DURO *is led away Stage Right savagely kicking the accompanying* PRIEST *about the shins.*

PRIEST: Repent, my son *ahhh.* Search thy . . . *ahh ahh . . .* confess *ahh . . . (Quickly.)* Ask-God's-forgiveness-afore-'tis-too-late *aaahhh.*

*The crowd bays loudly as* DURO *is tied to a stake.*

*The whippings, the unending chanting of the 'Miserere' and the fierce unrelenting light have an hypnotic effect.* MOTILLA's *voice becomes inaudible as he passes sentence on the wax effigy.*

MOTILLA: Accursed limb o' Satan, Gregorio Madera, guilty in absentis o' extreme Mohammedanism . . . sentenced . . . 'in absentis' . . . confiscation . . . effigy taken . . . abandoned . . . burning . . .

*He continues speaking but his words are drowned out. So are the* PRIEST's *accompanying the effigy as it is taken Stage Right.*

*Amid thunderous chants the* EXECUTIONER *binds the effigy to the stake furthest Down Stage Right, crosses Stage Centre and faces the spectators in the galleries, some of whom have been bored by the preceding ceremony. The* MONK *with the white cord on the cushion steps towards him. Taking the cord the* EXECUTIONER *holds it up high to* VALLADARES *who makes the sign of the Cross and blesses it.*

*Lights begin to dim down and the noise dies away to a soft chanting. A single bell tolls as the* EXECUTIONER *crosses back Stage Right. The spectators in the galleries lean forward, trembling with excitement.* DR BRAVO *and* ALMIRANTE *even stop watching* CARLOS's *crotch and* ANA *and* MARIANA, *each other.*

*The* EXECUTIONER *stops in front of the terrified* LEONORA GUZMAN *tied to the Up Stage stake. Silence now except for the crowd's excited breathing. Even that ceases suddenly as the* EXECUTIONER *in one swift movement, loops the cord round*

LEONORA's *neck and pulls tight. There is a hoarse 'Uggh' and she sags forward, garotted. The crowd roars 'Olé'.*

*The single bell tolls and the* EXECUTIONER *moves down to* JUAN GUZMAN. *Silence, then the same swift movement with the cord, a strangled 'Uggh' and the crowd roaring 'Olé'.*

*As the bell begins tolling ominously again a* LADY-IN-WAITING *falls out of the lower gallery, laughing wildly, in a fit of hysteria. No one pays any attention. They are too busy watching the* EXECUTIONER *in front of the skeleton of* ALVAREZ. *Again silence and the swift movement of the cord around the victim's neck. But this time no 'Uggh' but a sharp 'crack' of bone. The crowd roars 'Olé'.*

*The light is now dim. A hooded* MONK *enters Stage Right with a lighted rush-torch and hands it to the* EXECUTIONER. *The bell tolls above the choir and noise of the crowd as he solemnly lights the Up Stage stake. He then proceeds down the line lighting each stake in turn, ending with the one bearing* MADERA's *wax effigy.*

*The stage is now dark except for Spots on the figures of* VALLADARES *suspended high in the darkness and* CARLOS *on the rostrum below him. Stage Right the stakes form a seeming endless row of glowing, red lights stretching away into the night. The dim shape of* DURO *can be vaguely glimpsed writhing in agony but we can only clearly see* MADERA's *wax effigy Down Stage, quickly melting under the heat.*

*As the red wax bubbles and flows like blood,* CARLOS *shifts position, legs apart. A monstrous phallus sprouts from between them. The choir bursts forth triumphantly singing 'Hallelujah! Hallelujah! Hallelujah! The strife is o'er, the battle done . . .' as the enormous phallus grows to become a massive eight feet long, and two feet thick.*

*When it overhangs the edge of the rostrum a* PRIEST *emerges from out of the darkness, bends under it and lifts it on his shoulders. As he helps* CARLOS *and his phallus manoeuvre their way off the rostrum,* ANA *emerges Down Stage Left, in a nightdress and the choir sings, 'Now the victor's triumph won, O let the song o'* praise be sung. Hallelujah .. !' CARLOS *and his giant phallus come down off the rostrum to meet her.*

*The light on* VALLADARES *fades but the long line of stakes continues to glow. As the effigy's limbs blister, melt and slide off, the* MONK *moves away into the darkness and* CARLOS *turns to face* ANA *holding up his phallus on his own.*

*The choir sings* 'Hallelujah, Hallelujah, Hallelujah!' *They move towards each other and* ANA *is impaled on the tip of the colossal phallus. Clinging to it, she is lifted off her feet and borne backwards whilst the voices soar:* 'Death's mightiest powers have done their worst, and Jesus hath his foes dispersed; Let shouts of praise and joy outburst . . .'

*The fires glow,* MADERA's *wax effigy finally buckles and dissolves and* ANA *vanishes into the Wings riding* CARLOS's *rearing phallus to a mighty* 'Hallelujah! Hallelujah! Hallelujah!'

### END OF ACT ONE

# ACT TWO

## SCENE I

*Spot Down Stage Centre on the* PARROT *on its perch.*

PARROT: *O impotence, where is thy sting? Nothing's changed. Carlos sits i' the dust anointing his penis-stick wi' goat's grease and the Queen's still barren, CRRAH CRRAH. So what else's new? Barcelona's still besieged by the French, and the poor still starve. Men don't get results, only consequences. The Court's turned henhouse, the Queen Mother's triumphed. She holds the country in the hollow o' her head. CRRAH CRRAH . . .*

    MARIANA *appears in the Spot behind the bird.*

*Joey's flight's flown. She's come t' kill me. What matter. Death holds no terrors. I'll fly the Northern passage to the sun and dream dim parrot-dreams o' everlasting jungles. My parrot soul goes up into sunlight t' join the celestial company o' parrots and perch afore the one true Parrot-God, the almighty Psittacidae, our Creator and Judge, the Great Beak Himself, CRRAH, OH CRRAH.*

    MARIANA *picks up the perch and* PARROT *and disappears with it into the darkness Stage Left.*

*Goodnight Joey, poor Joey—a bird like me comes once every hundred years. (singing) 'Come fly wi' me, come fly away t' some . . . ARWK'.*

    *A final strangulated squawk, silence.*

### SCENE II

CARLOS's *terrified cries in the darkness. Lights up on the King's Bedchamber, with the fourposter Stage Left, below it a small table with a white cloth, crucifix, cotton wool, bread towel and bowl. Double door Up Stage Centre and the skeleton of Saint Isidore on his bier in front of the mirror Stage Right.*
*A sick, trembling* CARLOS *lies propped up on a cushion in an armchair Stage Centre. He has a dead pigeon tied on the top of his head, two black leeches on his face and his bare foot rests in a basin.* DR BRAVO *is bleeding his big toe.* RAFAEL *watches* DR GELEEN *pour a yellow medicine from the medical cabinet into a glass whilst* MARIANA *and* PONTOCARRERO *consult some documents and* GONGORA *looks over his astrological charts.*
*Sobbing in pain,* CARLOS *tugs feebly at* DR BRAVO *as he examines his blood in the basin.*

CARLOS: Saa saaaave eeeee. I'm at death's door.
DR BRAVO: Ne'er fear, Sire, I'll pull you through. (*Sniffs blood.*) Black bile, true melancholic blood. Doest have pain passing water?
RAFAEL: No, but he gets giddy crossing a bridge.
DR BRAVO: The dead pigeon 'll prevent any more such attacks o' vertigo. (*Pulls off leeches.*) Sire, I believe thine's a hard case o' tertian fever, complicated by bone-ache, gut-grip and *rheums*. But Medicine's a science o' probability and uncertainty.
RAFAEL: Certainly the way you practise it.
GONGORA: The moon's in Leo, and Leo and the 5th House reign o'er the heart, liver, stomach and left papp. But now the moon's free from the lord o' the 6th and 8th House, *salutem significat*. This foretells life, Sire, and good recovery.
DR BRAVO: You also foretold a good pregnancy and a successful auto de fe.
GONGORA: God willed a sudden star-change.

RAFAEL: Don't tell us o' your failures, your successes're depressing enough.

GONGORA: Doctor, thy own star-course hasn't changed. At the time o' the square o' the progressed Uranus t' the Moon, prepare f' death.

DR BRAVO *scowls and gives* CARLOS *the yellow medicine which he shakily drinks.*

MARIANA (*puts documents on* CARLOS's *lap*): Son, sign these and rest. They make me Queen Regent, His Eminence First Minister, and José o' Bavaria heir t' the throne.

CARLOS *nods.* PONTOCARRERO *holds the quill and ink-horn in front of him. With a great effort* CARLOS *picks up the quill, leans forward to sign and vomits up the yellow medicine over the papers.* PONTOCARRERO *quickly snatches them away, but they are soaked.*

*He and* MARIANA *control their frustration and try to dry them whilst* DR BRAVO *thrusts the basin onto* CARLOS's *lap.*

DR BRAVO: Cascade free, Sire, thy victualling stomach's fever-clogged. This saffron and thassia-root emetic'll clear 't out afore I administer the licorice purge. I want you cascading at both ends.

RAFAEL: You've no need o' emetics t' make you vomit, Sire. Jus' look around you.

BELEPSCH *enters urgently Up Stage pushing* ANA *in a wheel chair, trembling with fever and wrapped in blankets.* MOTILLA *accompanies them, carrying a covered silver dinner-tray.*

DR BRAVO: Your Majesty, this is unwise! Movement only inflames feverish blood. The cure's resting, bleeding and a lenten diet o' black cherry-water, egg yolks and breast o' boiled fowl...

ANA: Then how was I served *this*?

MOTILLA *uncovers the dish to reveal the carcass of Joey the* PARROT. DR BRAVO *examines it gravely.*

DR BRAVO: No, that's not suitable. Why, 'tisn't even plucked.

ANA: Plucked? Plucked? The fowl's dead, foully murdered! 'Tis my Joey, my Joey!

GONGORA: Saturn's in the 12th House, Your Majesty; plots, betrayals, assaults i' the dark. 'Tis how I came t' lose my teeth.

RAFAEL (*saluting with flask*): Alas, poor Joey. Thy loon's licence hast been revoked, *Crrah Crrah*.

ANA: Help me, Carlos, help me! Joey's the only thing I e'er loved. I know WHO, Madame . . . I know . . .

MARIANA: I glory in 't. I'd meant t' turn cook and serve him baked; wrapped in light pastry, hot parrot-pie à la Mariana. (*Chanting.*) 'And when the pie was opened the parrot couldn't sing. Oh wasn't that a dainty dish t' set afore a Queen.'

CARLOS (*retching*): Uggghh.

ANA: I'll see thee crap'd and dangled in gallows air f' this! (*She staggers up.*) Kill! Kill! Kill! *Ahhh.* (*She slumps back.*)

BELEPSCH: Quick, quick! Der Tod . . . she's dying.

DR BRAVO *makes* ANA *drink the remains of* CARLOS*'s emetic.*

PONTOCARRERO: Return Her Majesty t' her chambers.

MARIANA: No, if she's dying let her stay so's I canst see her death and she my triumph!

ANA *seated opposite* CARLOS *vomits into the basin that has been placed in her lap. Both she and* CARLOS *retch repeatedly as* DR BRAVO *hurries between them with more emetic to drink.*

PONTOCARRERO: Not thy triumph, Ma'am, but the triumph o' moderation. Only patience and experience'll keep the nation and Empire intact. These proclamations can mark a historic return t' stability and order.

*He places the documents before* CARLOS *who, with a tremendous effort, signs the top one.* MARIANA *snatches it away before he can vomit over it.*

CARLOS *sinks back, too exhausted to continue for the moment.*

MARIANA (*breathing deeply*): *Haaa* . . . I can BREATHE again. I've reached the mountain peak. (*She waves the document at* ANA.) *Crrah. Crrah.* I'm Regent, Madame. You lost 't all i' that barren bed. Go die in thy own vomit. My son's returned t' me and his power . . . *Haaa*, I've climbed up o'er my pain. My will alone, Madame, my WILL. Now's all easy and relaxed.

I canst do what . . . do anything . . . do everything . . . What
do y' want t' do . . .? What . . .? It snaps back round my throat
. . . a thousand fissures . . . soft cavities appear . . . suddenly sag
. . . 'tis too easy . . . Aie. Aie. Ai . . . (*She falters as she alone sees
the* OLD MAN *from Act I, Scene III, come down out of the curtained
bed where he has been hiding and hobble towards her.*) AIE . . . Not
me . . . HER . . . *AIEEEEE.*

*She cries with pain as a knife flashes and he stabs her in the chest
above her crab brooch.* DR BRAVO *catches her as she falls backwards
and the* OLD MAN *exits chuckling.*

DR BRAVO: Quick, t' the bed.

DR GELEEN *helps carry* MARIANA *to the bed.*

PONTOCARRERO: What struck her?

GONGORA: The malefics Mars and Saturn.

BELEPSCH: Where?! Where?! I didst not see 'em.

ANA *and* CARLOS *still retch violently as* MARIANA *is laid on
the bed and* DR BRAVO *whispers to* DR GELEEN *who hurries out.*

DR BRAVO: 'Tis what we afeared when we examined her last.
Your Majesties, the Queen Mother's suffering from what my
famed colleague Cornelius Celsus called a carcinoma or
cancer o' the breast.

PONTOCARRERO: 'Carcinoma', 'cancer'? Why wasn't I told?

DR BRAVO: Wishing t' spare you, she swore us t' secrecy.

GONGORA: She swore me, too, when I discovered Cancer 'd
entered the 4th House.

PONTOCARRERO: And left this one blasted. He casn't take her
from me now. Barcelona's besieged, our armies slow-starving.
My work's not done. Re-consider, Ma'am!

MOTILLA: God's wrath falls on the children o' disobedience.

PONTOCARRERO: Call her back. Leech her. Drain her!

DR BRAVO: Blood letting's contra-indicated. Only attenuant
and evacuant medicine can be used.

RAFAEL: Keep politics out o' this.

PONTOCARRERO: What o' me? What o' the succession? What
o' Spain?

DR BRAVO: Her tumour's the size o' the head o' a seven-year-old child but leathery, overgrown wi' fungus. The carcinoma spreads daily, eating her alive. Morte morieris. She's endured terrible suffering, 'tis a wonder she was able t' stand upright. But even great oaks fall at the last . . .

RAFAEL (*softly*): T-i-m-b-e-r.

CARLOS *gives an incoherent cry of despair, leaps up panic-stricken, stumbles over to his Mother, trips and sends the contents of the basin over the bed. He flaps his arms helplessly as* MARIANA, *still clutching the proclamation, struggles amid the soiled bedclothes.*

MARIANA: I couldst've ruled like a lion. Now I die like a dog. Why shouldst I die? He who loses his life f' Christ shall find 't. But not yet, Lord. NOT YET. Let me breathe, then I'll gladly putrefy. But not now, Lord, NOT NOW . . . (*A choir sings softly Psalm 29: 'De profundis clamo ad te'.*) 'Tis a time t' cast up accounts. My sins 're great I confess, but I flee t' God's mercy . . . Son . . . daughter . . . come close . . .

BELEPSCH *helps* ANA *to stagger up and join* CARLOS, *on his knees by the bed. The* OTHERS *bow their heads and the choir chants softly.*

Let's exchange forgiveness. Ana, I persecuted thee f' stealing my son from me. Carlos, I wounded thee, too, out o' love. Alas, only God can wound us into 't. Carlos . . . Carlos . . . list, list. There's no wisdom i' the grave. Make the symbol o' thy authority the olive branch, not the gallows tree, not the cold sword but the warm heart. Oh let love flow out like honey and balm, wine and sweetwater. Oh children, Jesus hath written us in his hand, now write him lovingly in thy HEARTS!

ANA $\left.\right\}$:*Ugggg!*
CARLOS

*Unable to stop themselves, they both vomit over* MARIANA. BELEPSCH *and* RAFAEL *rush to* ANA *and* CARLOS *respectively whilst* GONGORA *studies his charts and* MOTILLA *helps* PONTOCARRERO *prepare 'Extreme Unction' at the table.*

*As the sodden figure of* MARIANA *thrashes about wildly in fear and craws hoarsely,* CARLOS *suddenly staggers over to the skeleton.*

CARLOS: Maaamaa, the ddddancing BONES o' Saint Isidore aaaaa the Crucifix o' the Holy Father mamamaa (*Clutching the skeleton and crucifix he carries them back to the bed.*) Work miracles . . . DANCE damn yooo DANCE . . .

*Whilst he rattles the skeleton furiously,* ANA *and* BELEPSCH *try to prise the proclamation from* MARIANA's *clenched fist.*

*They tear half of it away as* MARIANA *screams and struggles with* DR BRAVO, *bringing down the bed curtains in her frenzy.* CARLOS *throws the skeleton on the bed and waves the crucifix over her helplessly.*

PONTOCARRERO: Be not taken wild, Ma'am. You didst not live pale, do not die trembling. Death should've a dignity!

ANA: I suddenly feel better. Thanks be t' God.

PONTOCARRERO (*chanting*): 'Adiutorum nostrum . . .'

CARLOS *collapses sobbing on the floor, and* RAFAEL *tries to comfort him.* DR BRAVO *restrains the hysterical* MARIANA *as* PONTOCARRERO *gloomily approaches with the oil of the sick in a bowl, accompanied by a delighted* MOTILLA *acting as server with pieces of wool and bread on a gold plate.*

PONTOCARRERO *dips his right thumb into the oil and makes a cross with it on* MARIANA's *wet forehead.*

PONTOCARRERO (*chanting*): 'Per istam sanctam Unctionem, indulget tibi Dominus quidquid deliquista. Amen.'

*Even as* MOTILLA *wipes away the oil with the wool and* PONTOCARRERO *dries his thumb on the bread,* MARIANA *blindly lashes out and knocks the bowl of oil out of his hand and over herself and the bed.*

*All struggle to hold her down, but now covered with oil she slips from their grasp.*

MARIANA: Let me breathe!

ANA: Gi' me the proclamation—then go die!

MOTILLA: See God's mercy, wonderful t' behold!

GONGORA: 'Tis the malefics, the naughty malefics!

*He tries to show them his charts but they fall out of his hands and he becomes involved in a messy scramble with* PONTOCARRERO *trying to retrieve the bowl and* BELEPSCH *and* ANA *the proclamation. During it, the skeleton of St Isidore is flung off the bed and lands on top of* CARLOS *who is pinned to the ground gibbering with fear.*

*As* RAFAEL *pulls off the greasy bones, the bespattered* MARIANA *suddenly tears herself free from the scrummage and staggers upright on the sodden bed, gasping ferociously for breath whilst the lights dim down.*

MARIANA: *Haaa . . . haaa . . .* the light . . . the light . . . See, see 't falls . . . ! (*She points up as the roof of the four-poster bed slowly descends.*) God 've mercy, Holy Mother . . . let me exchange eternal life in paradise f' one more hour o' pain . . . see, see 't falls . . . ! (*She topples backwards as the top of the bed sinks lower and we can see in the increasing gloom it is the lid of an ornamental sarcophagus.*) Death's 'tween my thighs . . . feet press me down . . . *haaa* . . . Lord My Redeemer Saviour Christ, I hurt, I hurt, therefore I am, I am!

*The sarcophagus descends on her. A great stony thud reverberates endlessly as the top falls into place in the darkness. Silence.*

CARLOS: *Mamaaaaaaa.*

### SCENE III

*A funeral bell tolls, the 'Miserere' is sung and four* PRIESTS *with black candles enter Up Stage Centre; behind them a line of mourning* COURTIERS.

*Crossing Stage Left, in flickering light, they attach the candles to the four corners of the sarcophagus which is then carried slowly Stage Right whilst the* MOURNERS *march solemnly behind and* PONTO-CARRERO *is heard intoning the funeral oration.*

PONTOCARRERO: Death's not everlasting Night, but everlasting Light. There's a mercy in every malediction, a Resurrection in every last end. God's now pity-bound t' recompense us f' the loss o' our Watchtower, our Nurse, our beloved Queen Mother, Doña Mariana, by gi'ing Spain an heir. She was cast down that this nation couldst be delivered up from its enemies. Bow knee and neck, redemption draws nigh!

*The candles are snuffed out and the* MOURNERS *exit Up Stage Centre.*

*As the singing dies, pale, dusty lights come up on the Royal Vault. A small iron gate Up Stage Centre with steps leading up beyond it. Stage Right and Left, a wall niche decorated with a pyramid of human skulls surmounted by a Cross.*

CARLOS *crouches by the sarcophagus and* ANA *stands beside him with a loaf of bread and flask of wine. They speak in whispers throughout.*

ANA: Fifty thousand masses're being said and twelve candles lit in every church in Spain f' the Seven Works o' Mercy and the Five Wounds o' Christ. What more canst we do f' the repose o' her Soul?

CARLOS: Die.

ANA: I miss her too. Hate was a cloak, kept me warm nights. She leaves a gap. We'll fill 't wi' each other. (*Gives him wine and bread.*) Eat, drink, Carlos.

CARLOS (*eating and drinking*): The bbbread's stale, wine's sour.

ANA (*wiping wine from his doublet*): Come back up wi' me, Carlos. Now she's not standing betwixt us, we'll do things together.

CARLOS: TTTooo-ther? Whaaa thii . . .?

ANA: Whatever people do together.

CARLOS: IIIII'm not *people*.

ANA: We couldst play spillikins together. Or skittle pool, dice or hazard. Yes, we couldst play hazard together. (*She gives him a pack of cards which immediately cascade out of his hands.*) Well, then, we couldst dance together: Pavan, Courante, Gavotte. Yes, we couldst dance the Gavotte together. (*She pulls him up to perform a few steps but he quickly becomes entangled in his own feet.*) Well, then, we couldst jus' touch hands, fingers, lips i' a kiss: (*he goes to kiss her mouth, misses and ends up biting her left ear: she sings softly.*) 'Lucky in love, no I never will be lucky in love/Gay times are few, few skies are blue./Good luck scattered when I first looked at you./(CARLOS *accompanies her in a quiet adenoidal screech.*) We don't know what the future will bring/But if we're together, it won't mean a thing . . .'

CARLOS: 'That's certain.'

ANA (*moving Up Stage, singing*): 'Lucky in love, must be fun t' be someone,/Who's Oh so lucky in love.' (*She stops by the small gate.*) Joey's dead, Carlos. Come up wi' me . . . (CARLOS *hesitates.*) I'll go count gold and silver then. (*The gate shuts behind her with a clang as she exits up the vault steps.*) Sweet Jesu, gi' me someone t' hate! Sweet Jesu, someone t' hate!

    *As he finally starts after her the sarcophagus lid opens slightly and a skeleton hand shoots out, grabbing his shoulder.*

CARLOS: Mama. (*He tries to move away.*) Aaaaaaa. (*He is pulled back.*) Maamaaa. (*He struggles to free himself as lights dim down to a Spot.*) Maaamaaaa . . . maaaa . . . aaa . . . maa . . aa . . aa . . . (*The Spot flickers and his struggle turns into an epileptic seizure, legs and arms splaying grotesquely, his whole body convulsed. He seems about to fall, but the skeleton hand repeatedly jerks him upright. His wild gyrations quickly die down and in a state of post-epileptic automation he whispers into the sarcophagus.*) Mama. Mama. 'Tis hard t' lose a Mother . . . (*Simulating* MARIANA's *voice.*) Almost impossible, son. Where're you, Mother? *Somewhere i' the distant gong.* Are you dead, Mama? *Dead t' the world, alive wi' white sluggies. I think, therefore I am. I stink, therefore I am not.* Mama, canst hear the flowers grow and the silent lobster scuttle past? *I can hear my bones creak, flesh drip, drip, drip away.* Mama, art still Queen? *Queen o' worms, shadows, dirt and dungheaps.* What's the meaning o' life, Mama? *T' keep one's balance, wings're best.* Help me Mama. God gave me crown, sceptre, throne: as he reigns in the heaven so I reign on earth. I stretch out my hand t' bring order t' the Universe. But Mama, t' has no edge, no bottom, no centre, no 'now', 'before' or 'after'; one thing doesn't lead t' another, time contracts, stones die and the apple doesn't fall, the earth rushes up t' meet 't. There'er no parallels t' a given line through a given point—or millions o' 'em. What's the true geometry, Mama, when all possibilities're equally consistent? How can I rule when God's gi'en up the ghost? What chance've I when He's left all things t' take their chances? I flounder, Mama. Help me rule, Mama. Tell me the secret. I'll be your little boy again, hurt only you, Mama. Tell me the secret . . . Whisper 't me . . . I'll come closer, Mama . . . closer . . .

*As he slides into the sarcophagus his Spot fades out, leaving only the Spot on the empty throne and whispers in the darkness.*

### SCENE IV

*The whispering grows louder like the sound of thousands of insects. Lights slowly up on the Throne Room where* RAFAEL *sits on the edge of the throne watching* ALBA, TORRES *and* MONTERREY *scuttle about, whispering furiously, as* ALMIRANTE *enters Stage Left with papers and an* ATTENDANT. *They turn to him. The sound stops instantly.*

ALMIRANTE: My lords, Barcelona's fallen t' the French.
TORRES: Hannibal ad portas. 'Tis the end! My books!
MONTERREY: My Government bonds! 'Tis the dark night o' the soul. This's a defeat as great as Algeria's.
ALMIRANTE: Is 't? (*He gives papers to the* ATTENDANT, *who exits.*) When an army's truly defeated? 'Tis difficult t' say, my lord. Men're easily replaced, ground retaken. Who's defeated 's a matter o' opinion. I throw my men twixt your two

armies and cry 'I've split 'em, you're lost!' You shout,
'You've put yourself 'tween two fires, *you're* lost!' The
defeats o' history only happened when one commander
believed himself defeated, whereas in the same circumstances,
wi' exactly the same losses, another would've 'Te Deums' sung
and bells rung t' proclaim a great victory. And 'cause he
believed 't, that credulous whore, history'd believe 't too.
I'll ne'er be defeated, my lords. Rest easy. The Queen's gi'en
me command o' a new army. The French're now trapped in
Barcelona, their lines extended, their strength exhausted.
They're ripe f' plucking. We should gi' thanks t' God f' this
triumph

MONTERREY: 'Tis true, victory, like money's a matter of confidence; 't goes t' them that have 't.

ALBA: Blood must triumph!

ALMIRANTE: Reality's a crutch f' the common people!

TORRES: We'll sweep 'em back t' Paris which we'll fire, scatter,
plough and salt! Delendam esse Carthaginem. Delendam esse
Carthaginem.

ALBA: And when they sue f' peace we'll demand Luxembourg,
Santo Domingo, Antilles and French Guinea f' the Crown.

MONTERREY: Guinea? Let 'em keep that rat-infested plague isle,
we'll seize sugar-sweet Tobago 'stead o' Guinea.

ALBA: Tobago?! Tobago's nothing! Spain must have Guinea;
'tis where the cocoa nuts come from.

ALMIRANTE: We'll annexe both Tobago *and* Guinea. T' the
victor the spoils!

RAFAEL: Gi' us another victory like Barcelona and we'll be on
our knees begging f' mercy. Does the King know o' this
'victory'?

ALMIRANTE: No, thanks t' your incompetence, Master Zany,
he's still entombed wi' the dead. 'Tis your duty t' laugh him
out o' his black humour. When a performing flea fails his
master, he's dismissed . . . (*Claps hands together.*) 'squashed
flea'. Careful thou doestn't become 'squashed Zany'.

RAFAEL: Is 't true, my lord, you're so witless, if your brain had a thought it'd die o' loneliness?

ALMIRANTE: Is 't true you're so small a pigeon perched on thy shoulder can pick a pea out your arse?

RAFAEL (*crosses to him, bows and kicks him on the shins*): I Rafael Morra, Court Jester to His Majesty, Carlos o' Spain, formally challenge you.

ALMIRANTE (*laughing*): Spindle Shanks, you've not the pedigree, title or height t' challenge a grandee. Go challenge thy superiors, the nits, gnats and gnomes. I've a nation t' save.

RAFAEL: White-livered gullion! I expected you t' slink away wi' your tail 'tween your legs and the Queen's!

ALMIRANTE (*drawing sword*): SIR.

RAFAEL (*drawing tiny sword*): SIR.

*An* ATTENDANT *enters Stage Right.*

ATTENDANT: My lords, Her Most Gracious Majesty, Queen Ana o' Spain.

ANA *enters carrying the dead* PARROT, *stuffed and stuck on a short perch, and accompanied by* BELEPSCH *and* MOTILLA. *All bow.*

ANA: My lord Alba, what a beautiful pendant you wear.

ALBA (*grudgingly*): Please accept 't as a token o' my love f' Your Majesty's person.

ANA: Oh, isn't that most gallant, Joey? (*The* PARROT *falls sideways.*) We graciously accept thy gift, my lord. (*As* ALBA *takes off the pendant and drops it into a black bag* BELEPSCH *holds open for him,* ANA *passes on to* TORRES *and gestures to the book he is holding:* TORRES *forces a smile and gives it to her.*) Vellum. We graciously accept thy gift, my lord. (*She drops the book into the bag.*) My brother informs me he's taken t' collecting rare books. I believe your library's the best in Spain. Joey and I propose t' honour you wi' a visit after Lent. (*TORRES gives a horrified cry and sways, but* ANA *passes on unconcerned to* MONTERREY, *who has already taken off a sapphire ring and dropped it, with a sigh, into the bag.*) We graciously accept thy

gift: examine 't close, Countess, my lord Monterrey's taken t'
wearing paste in my presence.

RAFAEL: What gift canst I gi' t' please Your Majesty?

ANA: Your *tongue*—by the roots. (*She crosses and sits on the throne.*)
Joey, even stuffed you're more alive than these grandees.

MOTILLA: My lords, the Queen on behalf o' His Majesty and i'
accordance wi' his wishes decrees His Eminence the Cardinal-
Archbishop o' Toledo be banished from Madrid and I take his
place on the Council o' State. And further, the Archduke
Charles o' Austria be declared heir t' the throne. Do you so
agree? (*They all raise their hands.*) Now Spain can rise again.
Now like Peter the Hermit I can go preach a Holy Crusade
'gainst the infidel Louis and stained in the wine-press o' the
Lord, wade ankle-deep through his blood t' salvation . . .
(*Lights dim down.*) Now, wi' the new army we'll fight i' the
light o' faith, the light that pierces, God's light, condensed
sunlight.

ALMIRANTE: Rejoice. Madrid celebrates the victorious fall o'
Barcelona!

ANA: Rejoice. Let the righteous rejoice wi' Jerusalem. We're
His again!

BELEPSCH: Rejoice. God, Thy arm was there. 'Tis Thy victory!

MOTILLA: Rejoice. He hath brought His people from the
depths that their feet may be dipped in their enemies' blood!
'Tis my victory!

*Bells peal, the 'Te Deum' is sung and* LADIES-IN-WAITING
*enter Right and Left with lighted sparklers.*

*Led by the* QUEEN, *and holding a sparkler each, all dance
joyfully in the darkness.*

*The sparklers finally splutter out and they all exit except*
MOTILLA *who stands Up Stage Centre smiling triumphantly in
a solitary light. It dies out with the 'Te Deum'.*

## SCENE V

*Lights up on* PONTOCARRERO's *Chamber with doors Stage Right and Up Stage Centre. Most of the rich furnishings have been removed though there are still deep red drapes on the walls.*

TWO JESUIT PRIESTS *systematically carry out Stage Right, rolled carpets, paintings, silverware and personal belongings whilst* FROYLAN *and* PONTOCARRERO *check through bundles of State papers on the floor Down Stage Right. They do not notice* MOTILLA *watching them in the shadows by the door Up Stage Centre.*

PONTOCARRERO: Careful wi' that painting, Father, 'twas gi'en me by Diego de Silva himself. If the forty pack-horses don't suffice, hire more and double-arm the escorts in case o' bandits. At least I'll have my goods about me while I'm rotting back in Toledo . . . (*Shudders.*) *Toledo*, I tell you that city's a cemetery wi' lights!

FROYLAN: But you're Cardinal-Archbishop o' Toledo, Your Eminence.

PONTOCARRERO: Someone had t' be. I lost.

FROYLAN: But Toledo has a great tradition o' necromancy. Once men skilled i' the magic arts publicly taught pyromancy, geomancy and e'en hydromancy. I confess I look forward t' continuing my researches there. I hope t' catch me a strix. That's a rare sorceress who cries like a screech-owl, *eeeaaa eeeaaa.*

PONTOCARRERO: I'd rather be dead in Madrid than alive in Toledo.

MOTILLA: That too can be arranged, Your Eminence, if you stay here. Remember my tolerance begins only where my power ends.

*As he crosses Down Stage,* FROYLAN *bows and helps the* PRIESTS *remove* PONTOCARRERO's *belongings.*

PONTOCARRERO: The Queen Mother's death's sent you t' the top o' fortune's wheel. But take care, Father, pride's the root o' all sin.

MOTILLA: And the root o' pride's riches.

PONTOCARRERO: You'll tear Spain t' pieces less you learn t' compromise—'tis the cornerstone o' good government.

MOTILLA: 'Tis the ignoble truce 'twixt duty and cowardice. Rather call 't by its proper name now, 'fraud'.

PONTOCARRERO: Call 't what you will, 'compromise', 'fraud', you hate 't cause you've no sense o' life's complexities.

MOTILLA: The ground has your knees, the world your conscience. Thanks t' you, plain dealing's dead.

PONTOCARRERO: Bend, accept less than you ask, less than you deserve. Bend, live and let live. Bend, or you'll break us.

MOTILLA: We're broken now. One fly hath corrupted the whole pot. You cared not f' justice, f' the poor, sick, lamed and blind. So Christ cared not f' us. Now he's made me the Divine instrument o' thy humiliation and fall. You stink like the sons o' Eli.

PONTOCARRERO: I'll not lose my temper, Father.

MOTILLA: Gi' thanks t' Him I let thee live t' repent o' thy vulgar furnishings, tawdry gowns, cheap geegaws . . .

PONTOCARRERO: Vulgar?! Tawdry?! CHEAP?! I've the most exquisite taste in Europe, you crump-backed, crack-arsed Ethiopian!

*The rich wall-drapes are pulled down to reveal grey panels covered with filth and graffiti.*

MOTILLA: Curse on, 'tis sweeter music t' me than the sweet bells o' St Martin's.

PONTOCARRERO: I'll grind mustard wi' thy knees, sapscull!

MOTILLA: How shovel-mouth? I've stripped thee Jack-naked o' all power and influence. You've no weapons left. I canst stand here wi'out lifting my little finger and still crush thee flat and bloody. God's wi' me.

PONTOCARRERO: And I canst stand here eyeball t' bloodshot

eyeball wi'out speaking or twitching a belly muscle and yet ravage thy livered soul. God's wi' me.

MOTILLA: Prove 't!

PONTOCARRERO: T' the death!

*They strip for action.* PONTOCARRERO *takes off his gloves,* MOTILLA *slips the scapula and mantle off his shoulders. The room is now completely bare as they stand facing each other Down Stage Centre,* MOTILLA *in his white habit,* PONTOCARRERO *in black.*

MOTILLA: List, does hear? (*Pointing up.*) Wings. All around, hosts o' angels sweeping in out of the sun t' fight f' me. See 'em draw up bravely i' their battle lines, turning the sky white. The Angels o' Destruction hover there on my left flank, the Angels o' God's Wrath on my right, there. And see amid the smoky banners, the Seven Angels o' Punishment guard my centre—the fires, rods and plagues o' the Lord— Lahaliel, Makatiel, Shaftiel, Hatriel, Pusiel, Rozziel and Kushiel, the rigid one o' God.

PONTOCARRERO: The Angels o' Vengeance, Jehoel, Suriel, Zaggagel, Akatriel, Yefefiah, and Metatron the Chancellor o' Heaven command my centre. The Angels o' Thrones my right flank o'er there, and the Angels o' Principalities my left, see there, wi' silken streamers.

MOTILLA: The Angel o' Repentance, the Angel o' Prayer, the Angel o' Baptismal Waters, I ha' e'm all 'cept the Angel o' Mercy.

PONTOCARRERO: There's no place f' him on my side neither; Gabriel, get thee back wi' thy garland o' roses. My commander's Rafael, Regent o' the Sun, Prince o' the Presence, Healer o' Men, Archangel o' Wisdom, Sociability and Light. Angels, draw thy swords. Help me masticate the soul o' this man o' chaos.

MOTILLA: Michael, Angel o' the Final Reckoning, Weigher o' Souls, Conqueror o' Satan, help me destroy this sinner's lust-filled spirit as I destroyed his place and power.

PONTOCARRERO: The holy trumpets! Christ's virgin colours unfurl. Forward—f' Jesu and the Blessed Virgin!

MOTILLA: God's silver lances, pikes and hooks're raised. Forward—f' Jesu and the Blessed Saints!

PONTOCARRERO: C-h-a-r-g-e.

MOTILLA: C-h-a-r-g-e.

*Their bodies go rigid. They make no movements whatsoever, except their eyes bulge as they focus all the power of their wills and hatred to crush each other.*

*Silence; then* PONTOCARRERO *lets out a grunt of pain and* MOTILLA's *face contorts in agony. Neck muscles tighten, faces turn white with strain as they continue pounding each other in their imaginations.*

*Suddenly blood pours from* MOTILLA's *mouth and nose. It gushes down the front of his white habit, but he never takes his eyes off* PONTOCARRERO. *There is a sickening 'crack' as a bone snaps and* PONTOCARRERO's *arm is broken. It is quickly followed by another 'crack' as his right leg is smashed too. As he topples over the bloodstained* MOTILLA *shakes with silent, triumphant laughter.*

*A fanfare sounds off and the doors Up Stage Centre are flung open by* TWO ATTENDANTS, CARLOS *lurches in accompanied by* FROYLAN *and the* COURTIERS: ALBA, TORRES *and* MONTERREY.

*As* CARLOS *comes Down Stage* MOTILLA *bows respectfully but* PONTOCARRERO *remains helpless on the floor.* CARLOS *frowns.* FROYLAN *pulls* PONTOCARRERO *up painfully whilst the* OTHERS *gather solicitously around* MOTILLA. *With* FROYLAN's *help* PONTOCARRERO *finally stands unsteadily on his one good leg and bows.*

CARLOS: Whaaa . . .?

PONTOCARRERO: I believe I've broken my arm and leg, Your Majesty.

CARLOS: This's no time t' tell me o' thy aches and PAINS. We all have our problems. III've jus' spoken t' Mamaaaa.

MOTILLA: T' *Mamaaaa* . . .? I mean t' the Queen Mother? But the Queen Mother's dead, Sire; she lies still in Abraham's bosom.

CARLOS: NO sssshe lies STILL in mine. The dead're so much stronger, making lodging-houses o' our hearts. Not too late t' repay her love. Though I believe I die f' 't, I've signed the Will . . . (*Flourishes document.*) I make Mama's choice, José o' Bavaria heir t' the throne o' Spain! (*The* OTHERS *are stunned.*) Kings must CHOOSE. Mmmama waa me t' choose her friend, the Cardinal-Archbishop. WILT advise me, Your Eminence, as you advised my Mamaaaaa?

PONTOCARRERO: Yes, Sire. Always, Your Majesty.

*The* COURTIERS *standing Stage Left with* MOTILLA *quickly move over to* PONTOCARRERO *who leans heavily on* FROYLAN.

CARLOS: Mamaaa says I must choose a new Confessor. Your Eminence, help me choose. NOW.

PONTOCARRERO: May I suggest Father Froylan?

FROYLAN: The King's Confessor?! Me, Your Eminence? No, Sire, no, no, no. I'm not worthy o' the honour . . . (*Thoughtfully.*) But if I'm not, who is?

CARLOS: 'Tis settled, come Father Froylan. (*He turns to exit Stage Left.*)

MOTILLA: But Sire, what o' me? My godly dreams?

CARLOS (*turning back*): Mama says, GET THEE OUT FROM US.

*He points at* MOTILLA *and a great wind suddenly springs up.* CARLOS *and the* OTHERS *back away and exit Stage Right.* MOTILLA *tries to follow but the wind forces him back. In his desperate effort to follow them he rips off his bloodstained habit to reveal he is wearing underneath a hair-shirt, torn loincloth and wooden Cross round his neck.*

*The wind increases in ferocity, blowing him backwards Stage Left. He raises the wooden Cross against it but is beaten back to his knees as the lights fade down to a Spot on him.*

*He is left kneeling, holding up the Cross and praying in the howling wind and darkness.*

SCENE VI

*The wind dies down as* MOTILLA *prays.*

MOTILLA: And I was cast out o' Madrid into this wilderness,
disgraced, hung up by the nostrils, half-dead half-alive,
worse than either, 'cause neither. Arriving here i' Las Hurdes,
abject in despair, I sought the Abbot Nilus and asked him how
't went i' this desert, this desolation? He poured water into a
vessel and said: 'look on the water'. I looked but 'twas murky.
After a little he said, 'look again, see how clear 'tis now'.
I looked into the water and saw my face as i' a mirror. When
I was in the world I couldst not see myself f' the turbulence,
but now in this solitude I recognize all my defaults. I'm justly
mortified, Lord. I'm fired and tested i' the furnace o' defeat.
F' a priest must be forged o' the purest stuff if he's t' guide
God's nation home. Now, according t' my strength I pray,
fast, meditate and abide: a barnacle on eternity. I cast out lust
long since but am still harried by pride. I'll learn t' forgive, yea
e'en those who know *exactly* what they do, Lord. I'll bathe in
the honey o' forgiveness, reach out t' Him quivering, longing f'
the day when all longing, all desire, all seeking, seeing, hearing,
hoping shall be God. Then He'll come by burning bush,
pillar o' cloud saying 'rise up and follow me back and change
the world in humbleness and loving kindness . . .' (*A* MES-
SENGER *appears in front of him out of the darkness.*) Spiritus
Sancti! Doest come out o' Zion wi' a message from the
Blessed Saviour?

1ST MESSENGER: No, out o' Madrid wi' a message from the
Blessed Cardinal-Archbishop o' Toledo. He says, 'live and let
live'.

MOTILLA: Oh the wingy mysteries o' Christ's mercy! T'know
all is t' forgive all, I forgive all, I forgive all, live and let
live *arrx* . . .

MOTILLA *gives a tiny gasp as the* MESSENGER *coolly slits his throat. Looking up at the* MESSENGER *in disbelief, he slowly falls, gurgling hoarsely. The* MESSENGER *calmly wipes his knife on the dying man's hair-shirt.*

1ST MESSENGER: Though he be condemned f' 't in the next world, a man's gotta make a living in this. I'll seek absolution after I've got me a fortune. And wi' sins like mine it's going t' *take* a fortune t' absolve 'em. I'll devote a third portion o' 't to the Society o' Jesus. That shouldst see me safe in Paradise. You need money t' enter God's house . . . (MOTILLA *claws the air.*) Only the poor can die easy. F' 'tis small grief t' leave hunger and cold, but t' forsake full barns, full purses, soft beds and beauteous women and go t' death's empty kingdom, this is terror. Wi' a job like mine, you gets t' be a bit o' a philosopher. (MOTILLA *makes the sign of the Cross, gives a final gasp and rolls backwards, dead.*) Glad he were the forgiving type. Some o' 'em get very bitter. (*Looks at* MOTILLA *again.*) A neat job. No mess. The work o' a pro, no question.

*Though the Spot stays on the dead body, another Spot follows the* 1ST MESSENGER *as he walks Up Stage Right. He meets a* 2ND MESSENGER.

2ND MESSENGER: Message from the Cardinal-Archbishop— 'live and let live'.

1ST MESSENGER: 'Tis done.

*The* 2ND MESSENGER *nods and stabs the* 1ST MESSENGER *brutally in the stomach. He staggers back as the other repeatedly knives him.*

1ST MESSENGER (*scornfully*): Amateur!

*He falls back dead. The* 2ND MESSENGER *wipes his knife and hands on the dead man and walks diagonally Up Stage Right in a Spot. The Spot on* MOTILLA *fades out as the* 2ND MESSENGER *meets a* 3RD.

3RD MESSENGER: From the Cardinal-Archbishop—'live and let live'.

2ND MESSENGER: *Ahhhhhhhh.*

*The* 2ND MESSENGER *screams in terror but is cut down before he can escape. The* 3RD MESSENGER *repeats the actions of his predecessors and walks off Up Stage Right in a Spot whistling. The Spot on the* 1ST MESSENGER *fades out as we hear a voice off Up Stage Right.*

4TH MESSENGER (*off*): From the Cardinal-Archbishop—'live and let live'.

3RD MESSENGER (*off*): *Ahhhhhhhh.*

*The scream is followed by a thud as the body hits the ground, then whistling. The Spot on the* 2ND MESSENGER *fades out and we hear diminishing snatches of conversation as the cycle of assassination continues in the darkness.*

5TH MESSENGER (*off*): . . . Cardinal . . . live and let . . .

4TH MESSENGER (*off*): *Ahhhhhhhh.*

*The inevitable scream dies away.*

### SCENE VII

*Birdsong. Dawn lights up on woodland clearing. Morning mist and an impression of surrounding trees.* TORRES *and* ALMIRANTE *with a flat, leather case wait Stage Right stamping to keep warm whilst* ALBA *wanders about.*

ALMIRANTE: Our Cardinal-Archbishop's happy. Father Motilla conveniently dead and his assassins stretched in a bloody line from Las Hurdes t' the sea. I'm t' be relieved o' command o' the new army, whilst he negotiates peace wi' the French. *Peace.* That cassocked traitor's sunk so low not even Christ's tears could raise him t' the depths o' degradation. He'll leave us wi'out heir or honour.

TORRES: The Cid no longer rides out. Honour's fled into the pages o' my books. I've shelves filled wi' honour.

ALBA: There was honour here once, my lords. This used t' be

the favourite duelling ground f' the best bloods o' Madrid, in my youth. I pierced three gallants m'self on this very spot in one afternoon. Challenged the first f' looking at me sideways, the second f' staring straight at me, the third f' not looking at me at all! Matter o' honour. Had t' fight, don't y' see. But you don't, my lord Almirante. A true grandee can only accept the challenge o' equals. Master Tom-o-my-Thumb's not o' thy rank or blood.

ALMIRANTE: I chose t' ignore the differences, as I ignored the insult when the Queen was high in favour. But now she's down, out and vulnerable, I must protect her reputation close. 'Stead o' great glory I'll make do wi' a little vengeance. I feel in a killing mood. (*Takes off cloak.*) Our midget Zany must be taught a lasting lesson.

RAFAEL *enters Stage Left with his father* MORRA. *He, too, carries a flat case, and is suffering from a hangover. The two dwarfs bow formally and cross to* ALBA *Stage Centre.* ALMIRANTE *and* TORRES *do the same.*

MORRA: My lords, I act as second f' my son Rafael de Morra in this matter.

TORRES: And I act as second f' my lord, Almirante de la Castilla.

ALBA: 'Tis my Catholic duty t' attempt a reconciliation 'twixt opposing parties. Will the challenger make an apology?

ALMIRANTE: A small apology'd suffice.

MORRA: My son isn't here t' make apologies, string beads, or juggle soot, but t' fight!

ALBA: The party challenged has the right t' choose weapons.

TORRES: My principal's chosen pistols at eight paces 'stead o' swords, not wishing t' place himself at an unfair advantage due t' the unusual circumstances.

MORRA: Unusual circumstances? What unusual circumstances? I recognize no unusual circumstances. A de Morra accepts no favours. My son'll fight on foot or horseback, wi' a sword, pike, halberd, dagger, mace or cudgel—rocks if need be.

RAFAEL: Father, weapons've been named. We fight wi' pistols

at eight paces, though I'd be happier wi' puff pastry at eighty.

ALMIRANTE *and* RAFAEL *open their cases and take out their pistols.*

ALBA: At my signal walk eight paces, turn and fire at pleasure. A misfire's t' be reckoned a shot and a snap or non-cock a misfire.

ALBA, *with* TORRES *and* MORRA *on either side of him, steps back Up Stage.* RAFAEL *and* ALMIRANTE *stand back to back despite the ridiculous difference in their heights. At a signal from* ALBA *they start to walk away,* RAFAEL *having to hold his heavy pistol in both hands and his tiny steps making the distance between them ludicrously small.*

ALBA: One, two, three, four, five, six, seven, eight.

*They stop.* ALMIRANTE *turns first and quickly fires—a stream of water over* RAFAEL: *his weapon is a water-pistol. As* RAFAEL *is drenched* ALMIRANTE *roars with laughter and* TORRES *and* ALBA, *seeing what has happened, join in.* MORRA *is white-faced with rage.*

*As the laughter continues a shot rings out:* RAFAEL *has fired. The laughter stops instantly.* ALMIRANTE *spins slowly round, drops his weapon and puts his hand to his forehead; it is covered with blood. As he sinks to his knees,* TWO CIRCUS CLOWNS *in huge shoes, baggy pants, red noses and yellow wigs rush on Stage Left amid drum-rolls, honks and whistles and stuff a red rag in* ALMIRANTE's *mouth and drag him off dead, Stage Right.*

*Lights out as coloured balloons float down from the Flies.*

### SCENE VIII

*Canons thunder a salute out of the darkness. Lights up on the Royal Reception Room and the whole Court plus the French Ambassador,* REBENAC. *Amid triumphant fanfares the Court advances ceremonially Down Stage and lines up, waving regally to the audience.*

PONTOCARRERO: We gi' thanks t' God. Spain is at peace; f' by His great mercy a treaty's been signed wi' the French, English and Dutch William at Ryswick in this year o' Our Lord, 1697, whereby His Majesty Louis XIV o' France doth gi' back all territories conquered; Luxembourg, Mons, Ath, Coustrai and Catalonia, including the towns o' Gerona, Rosas and Barcelona. Spain's Empire remains intact, her glory undimmed.

*With one arm hanging stiffly by his side* PONTOCARRERO *hands the treaty to* CARLOS *who holds it up. Wild cheering and more fanfares as the Court move formally back Up Stage into the Reception Room where the coloured balloons are still on the floor.*

DR BRAVO: Where're your Mars's, malefics and mumbos now, Master Gongora? You prognosticated darkness f' Spain and death f' me. But see, Spain's at peace and I'm alive. Eyes badger-bright, heart and spleen in working order. Feel this bone and muscle (*Jabs him in the stomach*), smell that sweet breath. (*Breathes in his face.*) Admit 't, sir, you're wrong again.

GONGORA: I don't understand what's wrong, but I'm not wrong. You're wrong, the world's wrong, but I'm not wrong. I've charted and re-charted the star-courses. By all the signs you're dead. First my teeth, now this. I suspect foul play. You're dead but won't lie down.

DR BRAVO *laughs but* FROYLAN, *who has been listening to them, nods thoughtfully.*

*The Court is now assembled in the Reception Room. The men bow deeply and the women curtsey to* CARLOS.

CARLOS: Aaaa let our Brother Louis Beelezebub—er, Louis the Blessed—know how greatly weeee love him.

REBENAC: Happily, Sire. And may I hope this new found spirit o' diplomacy grows twixt our nations.

PONTOCARRERO: 'Twill. I've sacrificed too much f' peace . . (*There is a distant shout of 'Live and let live', a cry and a thud.*) Didst hear 't?

*They look blank.* CARLOS *gestures and all the* COURTIERS *rise.* DR BRAVO *hurries to him.*

DR BRAVO: Sire, you need rest. Thou hast been waving on that balcony f' a full five minutes.

CARLOS: 'Tis nothing. We royals 're born wi' rubber wrists. Happy day. WWWhy art not looking haaa happy, Maaaadam?

ANA: Joey's dead. Father Motilla's dead. The Almirante de Castilla's dead.

CARLOS: You shouldst still beee happy, 'tis merely PERSONAL. If they're strong they doooon't DDDie. Maaamaaa didn't die. She chose my Cardinal-Archbishop and now all we lost's been restored, Mama knows . . .

ANA: Art blind? Louis only gi's back what he conquered t' make himself so popular his grandson Phillip'll be made heir t' the Spanish throne wi'out him firing another shot or losing another Frog's leg.

CARLOS: Madam, I haaa jus' chosen my heir—José o' Bavaria.

*Applause from the* COURTIERS *and sycophantic congratulations. Furious,* ANA *absently plucks the feathers from the dead* PARROT *on her arm.*

REBENAC: But Sire, you casn't choose José.

CARLOS: I c-c-c-c-c-a . . .?!

REBENAC: Sire, José's dead.

CARLOS: *Whaaaa . . .*

REBENAC: Tertian fever.

GONGORA: Ah, my beautiful malefics! Betrayals, conspiracies and deaths! I was right.

REBENAC: He died three days since. I don't understand, is Spanish Intelligence so slow?

ANA: Slow? Why d'you think there're no wooden statues carved o' Spaniards? They can't find pieces o' wood thick enough.

PONTOCARRERO: 'Tis the roads.

CARLOS: Dead? Dead? Whaa . . . words pass through me . . .

ANA: Mama knows best! Why didn't she know José was dead? Happen her beady eyes were blinded by hell-fire, pit-fire? Nothing changes. You still ha' t' choose Carlos: Philip Bourbon or Charles o' Austria.

CARLOS: *Eeeeh. Eeeeh. Eeeeh.*

PONTOCARRERO: 'T does change. Now God has blessed Spain wi' an honourable peace, He'll bless thy penis-member, Sire, if you flash 't at him.

CARLOS: *I tried . . . tried . . . tried . . . tried . . .*

   *He careers round, screeching and stamping on the coloured balloons, exploding them in his fury. He finally collapses on the floor beside one last black balloon.* PONTOCARRERO *bends over him.*

PONTOCARRERO: You can produce an heir, Sire. The Virgin Mother'll help you.

FROYLAN: She won't. And he can't.

   *All look round in astonishment.*

CARLOS (*clawing the balloon*): Heaaa my Confessor assails me wi' pure truth . . . 'tis my wife, my wife's SINSSSS . . . HER fault.

FROYLAN: No, Sire, 'tis you. You're impotent, Sire: coeundi, erigendi, generandi, *Impotentia.*

   *Stunned silence. The balloon bursts in* CARLOS's *hands. He staggers up.*

CARLOS: IMPO didst you say IMPO . . .? *Eeeeeh,* my body's turned t' glass, IIII'm breaking. Eminence, yyyy chose José o' Bavaria f' me and THIS impotenting priest . . .!

PONTOCARRERO (*low*): Father, you'll destroy us. Remember you're a Jesuit. Equivocate. *Be devious.*

FROYLAN: I'm the King's Confessor. In matters concerning the Society o' Jesus I humbly obey, but in those pertaining t' the confessional I submit only t' the true will o' God. Sire, I seek audience—alone.

ANA: After such an insult you'd best seek mercy.

CARLOS: IMPO . . . my belly's glass, they canst see my heart and bowels . . . Withdraw.

   PONTOCARRERO *is about to protest but* CARLOS *waves him*

*away with a tiny frightened gesture. All exit backwards Stage Left*
*and Right. Only* FROYLAN *remains.*

FROYLAN: Doest achieve full erection, Sire?

CARLOS: Cu ca po fo bigger than an elephant's trunk, stiffer than
a stake, hhhhhheavier than bell-clapper, *b-o-n-g* . . .

FROYLAN: Chapter VI o' the 'Malleus Maleficarium' states:
'If a man's virile member's erect but he casn't penetrate, and
the seminal ducts're blocked so the vital juices're dammed
back or fruitlessly spilled, then that man's impotent by
reason o' *witchcraft*.'

CARLOS: WWWWW . . .?

FROYLAN: Thy impotence isn't physical, but magical. The
fault's not in thee, Sire.

CARLOS: Not mmmm fault . . .?

FROYLAN: You're bewitched, Sire . . . (*He produces a book.*)
Zacharias Vicecomes writes i' the 'Complementum Artis
Exorcisticae' on the signs o' bewitchment: (*He reads.*) 'A man's
truly bewitched if he's vexed by solid foods and molested by
much vomiting; (CARLOS *retches*) if he feeleth a daily gnawing
i' his belly; (CARLOS *rubs his stomach*) if he hath an ache i' his
kidneys, throbbing i' his neck, splinters i' his head, nails i' his
heart and excretes bucketsfull o' worms hourly . . .'

CARLOS (*slowly*): 'S me . . . 's me . . . 's me . . .

*He takes the book and reads with difficulty as the room is suffused*
*with dark red light.*

FROYLAN: 'Tis magic that frustrates us, not brute reality.
Bewitchment's the cause o' all our present ills; 't holds us in a
dream. Witches and magicians run rampant. E'ery night
pentacles're drawn, odours o' sulphur rise, black candles lit,
crucifixes defiled, blood drunk, Satan's grey arse kissed:
'O Emperor Lucifer, Master o' all rebellious Spirits, I beg . . .
Aglon, Tetragram, Vaycheon, Stimulamthon.'—Thus Satan's
Pit-legions're summoned; his grand almoner Dagon; his
banker Asmoden; his Master o' Ceremonies Verdelet. Jean
Wiere, physician t' Duque de Cleres, calculated Satan had

7,409,127 devils commanded by 76 Infernal Princes. 7,409,127.
Idiot! Idiot! I've proved there're exactly 175,806,417 devils.
175,806,417. No more, no less. That's 2 and 1/6 o' a devil per
person . . . (CARLOS *trembles.*) Ne'er fear, Sire, cometh the
hour, cometh the man. I'm ready armed in the sweet name o'
Jesus Christ Our Lord. But first, Sire, we must confirm thou
art bewitched and then uncover the foul agent o' Satan
responsible. 'Tis certain, as always, God'll maintain his
habitual silence, so I'll command the one being who knows
the truth t' tell us—Lucifer, the Evil One. *Command,* not ask.
F' 'tis heresy t' ask a favour o' the Devil.

CARLOS (*looking round*): Where doest find him?

FROYLAN: In the bodies o' the possessed. At this moment I'm
exorcising a fiend-sick nest o' nuns from the Cangas Convent
who're most truly possessed. I say truly, f' 't has become
fashionable o' late to simulate possession. But they casn't
fool me, I smell the dying flowers, see the scorpion-demons
peering out o' bloodshot eyeballs, *there, there.* Satan spoke t'
me from the left nostril o' a nun last month, telling me I'd rise
t' high office. He's still there, i' the intestines o' that poor Bride
o' Christ. I could but weaken him then, now I'll drag him
forth and command him in the name o' the Lord God, t'
speak the truth concerning your mighty penis-member.

CARLOS: Quick-quick-quick.

FROYLAN: The Inspector General must be informed, though he's
more interested in heresy than witchcraft. Blind! Blind! We
go forth, Sire, t' combat Lucifer, wi' faith as our perfect shield.
(CARLOS's *legs buckle.*) Evil only takes hold through weakness.
It enters one o' six openings: eyes, ears, mouth, nose, navel,
penis, vagina and feeds on our hate, becoming a swelling wart
on the soul, drawing strength from our every selfish thought
and act. All impulses o' tenderness're blocked, love casn't pass
through us f' we solidify. And then wickedness takes on its
own reality, spawning out little limpet-demons made i' the
image o' our sins: gluttons 've pig-demons, misers sucker-

demons, murderers tarantula-demons. We must be ready, Sire. (*He produces a three-pronged fork inscribed with symbols.*) 'Tis a Paracelsian Trident, a blessed and magnetized blasting rod o' demons. These three prongs act as lightning arresters, discharging accumulated magnetism. Skewered demons burn on the tips. (*He stabs the air with the trident, then hands it to* CARLOS.) Remember, Hell's hordes mayn't be visible, but they'll be there, ready t' pounce when we fight the Devil raging i' the Nuns o' Cangas.

CARLOS (*stabbing the air*): The Nuns o' Cangas!

*A faint sound of female voices off Stage Right, singing the hymn,* 'Quem terra pontus aethera . . .'

FROYLAN: Evil ne'er fades. Every sin since the first Adam breathes in us. Every depravity since the first Cain chokes our trussed lungs. The Nuns o' Cangas're drowning, grown hideous i' their pain, terror, as ne'er before, horror as ne'er before . . .

CARLOS (*stabbing wildly*): The Nuns o' Cangas! The Nuns o' Cangas!

*As the music and singing grows louder a stained glass mediaeval fresco of St Michael slaying a Dragon is lowered Up Stage Centre.*

*The lights grow brighter, whilst* CARLOS *compulsively stabs the air and* FROYLAN *turns Stage Right to face the Nuns of Cangas.*

SCENE IX

*Three gentle, middle-aged* NUNS: *the demure* SISTER INEZ, *the voluptuous* SISTER RENATA *and the beautiful* SISTER JUANA, *enter solemnly.* SISTER JUANA *carries a large Cross with meat hooks hanging from the arms.*

NUNS (*singing*): '. . . Beata caeli nuntio/fecunda sancto Spiritu,/ desideratus gentibus/cujus per alvum fuses est. Gloria Tibi Domine/qui natus es de virgine/cum Patre et sancto Spiritu/ in sempiterna saecula.'

FROYLAN (*putting on large, dark-lensed spectacles*): I'd go blind wi'out these protective eye-barnacles. Mark, Sire, the haloes o' inextinguishable guilt about their heads. In nomine Patris et Filii et Spiritus Sancti.

*The* NUNS *have stopped humbly in front of* FROYLAN *and a trembling* CARLOS. FROYLAN *makes the sign of the Cross over them and takes out a small phial of holy water.*

FROYLAN: Foul spirit, in the name o' our Lord Jesus Christ, be rooted out and be put t' flight from this creature o' God.

*He flings some holy water into* SISTER INEZ*'s face.*

SISTER INEZ: Fans opened next t' me, hundreds in my time. Dancing, spinspread, 'cross a Continent, a moment later, Naples. Years o' light-music, ah those spreads, those bright distances. But my family drew a curtain in front o' my face t' save a dowry, one more Saint on the calendar: Asia never returned. I had *their* wills in *my* head. Infinity won me, untouched by human hands. Now trees wi' old branches. Now my mornings touch my evenings, loneliness wi'out solitude, solitude wi'out being alone. Forty years' waste, brain waste, heart waste, wall t' wall waste, seven hundred thousand nothings since Monday *ahhh!*

*She cries out in fright as* FROYLAN *who has been circling her suddenly seizes his opportunity and throws his stole round her neck.* SISTERS RENATA *and* JUANA *remain quite still by the Cross.*

FROYLAN (*to* CARLOS): The little demons! See, see they begin t' jump off her. Keep thy mouth shut, Sire, else they'll hop 'twixt thy yellowing molars. Strike, Sire! Strike! (*Whilst* CARLOS *frantically stabs the air* FROYLAN *pulls the struggling* INEZ *close and makes the sign of the Cross on her forehead.*) Satan, enemy o' man, cause o' all chaos, the Word made flesh commands thee, Jesus o' Nazareth commands thee, come out from her!

SISTER INEZ: If the light in me's darkness, how dark's the darkness? Chaos's my true Lord! Blind chance rules the world!

*She breaks free and stands by the Cross, whilst* SISTER RENATA *curtsies and takes her place in front of* FROYLAN *who throws holy water in her face as* CARLOS *continues to stab the air.*

SISTER RENATA: The beast's missing. I lost his face in the mosses and the shadows. After so much frontal punching, fiery tit-tarting, my nest's cold. Oh Paolo, Paolo, you undid my neck-string, lifted my gown and came like dew falling from the grass; sunshaft 'tween my thighs. Then dice-throwing death took him dead on the wrong side, dimlap on the shore. Widowed and walled in a day and I'm ill every time I wake, all the day ill. Thy tongue isn't f' eating and speaking but f' jousting, moistening, tipping the velvet and stirring mayonnaise! I'm a Bride o' Christ, why doesn't Jesus come do 't f' me?! Quick, quick, 'afore decay thrusts its blade and bellies blotch and buttocks go slack and the young wheat trembles, *ahhh!*

*She cries out as* FROYLAN *finally pounces and throws the stole round her neck. She struggles but he jerks her close and makes the sign of the Cross on her forehead.*

FROYLAN: Satan, enemy o' man, cause o' all chaos, the Word made flesh commands thee, Jesus o' Nazareth commands thee—come out from her!

SISTER RENATA: I defy the crucifix, deny the sacrifice. Chaos's my true Lord! Blind chance rules the world!

*She breaks free and goes to the Cross, whilst* SISTER JUANA *curtsies and silently takes her place in front of* FROYLAN *who throws holy water at her. She tries to speak but can make only gasping noises.*

FROYLAN: Satan's proving eel-slippery, Sire. 'Tis our last chance t' hook him. (*He suddenly throws the stole round* SISTER JUANA's *neck, she struggles but he pulls her close and makes the sign of the Cross on her forehead.*) I adjure thee ancient serpent, by the judge o' the Quick and the Dead, by thy Maker, and the Maker o' the world—come out from her! (SISTER JUANA *breaks free.*) Yield and answer! Yield and answer! YIELD AND ANSWER!

SISTER JUANA *speaks in a deep voice.*

SISTER JUANA: Hello out there? Somebody call? I heard voices. The Universe's already 98 per cent dead but I've still a thousand million years o' living t' do before the sun finally turns cold, black and dwarfish and it's all bets off.

FROYLAN: Art Satan?

SISTER JUANA: The very same; the first mover o' the world. The name's 'daemon' which means, 'knowledge'. Would you like to know how Helen looked and what blind Homer sang? How parallels t' infinity meet and unseen stars leave their frozen traces in the sky? Why some men die and others 'scape the plague? Let me tempt you, laddie. The Universe lies open. Just ask.

FROYLAN: Has His Majesty's penis-member magically withered? Is he bewitched?

SISTER JUANA: Ah the pitiless banality, the remorseless drip o' human stupidity. Yes, he's bewitched.

FROYLAN: Praise be t' God! I knew 't. You're bewitched, Sire!

CARLOS (*joyfully, waving trident*): BBBBB eeee I'm bewitched . . . 's not my fault, 's nothing wrong. IIIII'm jus' bewitched bewitched, bewitched . . . ! (*Stops: slowly.*) *I'm b–e–w–i–t–c–h–e–d!*

FROYLAN: Satan I command thee, who hath bewitched His Majesty?

SISTER JUANA: You don't really want t' know. You'd miss the joys o' finding out f' yourselves. One clue: they want the French fleur-de-lys t' come t' Spain. Now go, search and destroy!

FROYLAN: Satan, I command thee: who bewitched His Majesty? Who? Who?

CARLOS: Wwwhhhoooo?!

FROYLAN: *In God's name, name names!*

*The light begins to fade as the* NUNS *stop eating and chant gently.*

NUNS: Duque de Alba, Pedro Alvarez, Victor Amadeus, Inez Ayala, Mendiza de Balthazar, Dr Gasper Bravo, Don Sebastien

de Coles, Father Don Froylan, Francisco Garrigo, Marquis
Gudames, Queen Ana de Neuburg, Queen Mariana de
Austria, Conde Medellion, (*frightened whispers in the darkness
now form a background to the endless roll-call*) Duque de Monter-
rey, Duque de Medina de la Torres, Father Don Motilla,
José de Olmo, Conte de Oropesa, Cardinal Archbishop
Pontocarrero, Francisco Ramos, Juan Tomas Rocaberti, Don
Francisco Ponquillo, Condesa de la Vanquyon . . .
   *The roll-call fades away, leaving the frightened murmurs in the
darkness growing louder.*

### SCENE X

*Lights up on the Throne Room where the* COURTIERS *whisper and
wait nervously. They include* LADIES-IN-WAITING, ALBA,
MONTERREY, TORRES, GONGORA, DR BRAVO, BELEPSCH,
*and the Dancing Master* ANTONIO. RAFAEL *sits on the edge of the
throne platform drinking. Down Stage Left* ANA *talks to* PONTO-
CARRERO *whilst stroking the moulting carcass of the* PARROT *on
her arm.*

ANA: No one's safe from your King's Confessor.
PONTOCARRERO: I've spawned an incubus. In all other particu-
   lars he's clerk-humble but feels divinely empowered t' save
   Spain from rampant sorcery. The prospect's midnight black
   f' us all, (*shudders*) he's *sincere*.
ANA: He seeks out witches as eager as a pig snouting truffles.
PONTOCARRERO: 'Tis a bad time t' be plagued by such lethal
   loons. Spain's turned rebellious in her hunger and despair.
   Madrid's a vast abscess. At this moment His Majesty's in
   greater danger from his own subjects than Satan's. And he still
   has to choose an heir now José o' Bavaria's dead. Philip
   Bourbon's unthinkable so I propose t' forward your claimant,
   Your Majesty, the Archduke Charles.

ANA: You adjust easily, Your Eminence. But first break your Jesuit Judas.

PONTOCARRERO: The Church proclaims witches exist and the King that he's bewitched. Whoever opposes Father Froylan flouts Church and State.

ANA (*angrily plucking the last feather out of the* PARROT): It sticks! The Queen o' Spain trembling afore a stiff-rumped cleric whose mother took in boarders.

BELEPSCH: Now at least Your Majesty, you've someone t' hate again.

ANA: He's not big enough; (*softly*) eeehh there's no one left big enough f' me t' hate.

> *She throws aside the dead* PARROT, *now completely denuded of feathers, as* CARLOS *enters silently Stage Left leaning on* FATHER FROYLAN's *shoulder and followed by* TWO MONKS.

> *The men bow low, the women curtsey.* ANA *falls in behind* CARLOS *and* FROYLAN *as they cross to the throne, with the priest continually whispering in the King's ear and gesturing furtively to the bowed* COURTIERS. CARLOS *nods and slumps on the throne.*

> ANA *watches in fury as* FROYLAN *whispers again and* CARLOS *mutters incoherently. The* COURTIERS *rise and the King gestures to* FROYLAN.

FROYLAN: My lords, Satan swore by our Saviour's blood, that his earthly agent suppressed His Majesty's virile member, blocked 'ts love juices. The bewitched organ's been fumigated wi' incense and doused in a thimble o' holy water. But the only lasting cure's the destruction o' the Devil's agent. Lucifer refused t' name him, though he named a thousand names. F' witches're not only those who cast black spells but whoso'er does anything which casn't be explained by nature or art. E'en now, suspects're questioned close, wi' rack, boot and Wheel i' the dungeons o' the Inquisition. Their devil-marks—warts, moles and pimples're being pierced and tested wi' red hot needles. (*A* LADY-IN-WAITING *faints.*) At His Majesty's request 't falls on me t' gather in all suspects f' questioning and

testing. You my lords must help. F' under command, Lucifer
revealed his agent's secret love o' France and I believe he or
she resides here at Court. (*All eye each other suspiciously.*) E'en
now you mayst be standing next t' the agent o' Satan. (*All
shift warily.*) Happen there's more than one. Look f' the signs,
my lords. Witches casn't weep . . . (ANTONIO *starts crying*),
feel pain . . . (TORRES *pinches himself and cries out*), but do wear
talismen. (MONTERREY *tears off his jewel pendant.*) Report any
who act strange, have sudden success—that's a most damaging
sign, success. T' save His Majesty I've summoned the newly
appointed Royal Witch-Catcher. The Witch-Catcher's
famous instrument can detect suspect sorcery at ten paces,
night or day. There's no protection in blood, rank, wealth
or piety. So let the guilty sweat. List, list the Witch-Catcher
cometh . . .

> *There is an eerie sucking sound Off Stage Left. The* COURTIERS
> *turn fearfully towards it. It grows louder and finally* THERESA
> DIEGO, *the Head Washerwoman, enters dressed in a gaudy pink
> farthingale, vulgar jewels and a small fur muff clamped delicately
> over her nose.*

RAFAEL: Why, 'tis Old Mother Bagwash!

> *The titter is immediately silenced as* THERESA *sweeps Up Stage
> and curtsies clumsily before* CARLOS, *who waves his hand im-
> patiently.* THERESA *rises as* FROYLAN *comes down to her.*

FROYLAN: Mistress Diego'll pass amongst you, sniffing out the
Devil's own.

THERESA: Thank you, Father. (*She carefully removes her nose
muff.*) Ha' no fear, Your Majesty, though this room's heavy
wi' the odour o' thy divinity, I'll smell out soiled souls a:
surely as soiled clothes. All stink different: murderers o' grey
hemp, plague-carriers o' sour apples, lepers o' dead mice.
Witches've the heaviest kind o' crotch smell. They casn't hide
't though they bathe in camphor and sweet aloes. 'Tis too
skung-strong t' wash away. (*She dabs her nose with a large, lace
handkerchief.*) Wi' your permission, Sire, I'll nose a stink.

CARLOS *gurgles impatiently;* RAFAEL *lifts his flask in a toast.*
RAFAEL: T' the grindstone!

*Ignoring him,* THERESA *slowly walks between the apprehensive*
COURTIERS *sniffing the air, followed by* FROYLAN *and the*
TWO MONKS.

*Slowly passing* PONTOCARRERO *and* TORRES *she steps in*
*front of* GONGORA. *He trembles as her sniffing grows louder.*

GONGORA: 'Sn't me! 'Sn't me! *Him,* 'tis him. (*He points hysteri-*
*cally at* DR BRAVO.) Bravo's been dead two weeks, I calculated
it t' the last ascendant cusp and malicious square. He's carrying
his corpse, his body's hollow. 'Tis *necromancy.* He's made a
pact with the Devil t' survive his own death!

DR BRAVO: You half-dead, toothless gusset, my breath disturbs
the air. My lord Torres, was I dead when I cured thee o' the
piles, or you, my lord, o' the hernia? *Ha-ha* . . . (*No one*
*laughs.*) I know the difference 'twixt life and death, 'tis my
profession. See, I talk, move, jerk my head, roll my eyes in
wonder. (*Holds out hands.*) My hand trembles . . . that's life . . .
see . . . ?

*He falters as* THERESA *sniffs loudly in front of him.*

THERESA: Fe, fi, fo. I smell odour mortis. And the Satan's fungy
stench. *This man's suspect.*

FROYLAN: Yes, who had better chance t' damage His Majesty's
royal penis-member under the guise o' healing 't.

TORRES: Roman physicians always poisoned their emperors.
'Quis custodiet ipsos Custodes?' Juvenal asked in the Sixth
Satire—or was 't the Fifth?

GONGORA: He's now a deadly dead man, Satan's man, not my
best friend Bravo who pulled out my best teeth.

CARLOS: *Taaaaaeeeeeeekk.*

*The* TWO HOODED MONKS *take* DR BRAVO *by the arm and*
*escort him out.*

DR BRAVO: Sire, Sire, I've keep thee alive, keep me alive now.
My lords, help me—laced louse-traps! You'll cry out f'
Dr Bravo, when you've your distempers again, your hard pad,

foot-rot, gas gangrene, anthrax, red worms, oak poisoning, liver fluke and *swine-fever* . . .

*Even as the* MONKS *drag him off Stage Left* THERESA *continues her menacing prowl. She stops and snorts in front of* ANTONIO *who jumps back in fright.*

ANTONIO: 'Tis my perfume, Mistress Diego. Body aromatics—distilled water o' jilly-flowers t' keep skin clear and bright. (THERESA *sniffs again.*) Essence o' lavender, citron peel and oil o' spike, t' take off spots and wrinkles. Innocent aromatics. Mistress, innocent aromatics—red pomatum f' plump lips, white paste f' hard hands and . . .

THERESA: Not all the rose-water i' Shiraz can hide the fungy smell rising from thy soul. *This man's suspect.*

FROYLAN: Yes . . . the fleur de lys! Didst not the Devil confess his witch was o' the French Party.

ALBA: Yes, I always suspected Monsieur Antonio o' treachery wi' his French words, perfumes, dances, laces, windows, letters . . .

CARLOS: *Taaaaaaeeeeeekk.*

*The* MONKS *take* ANTONIO *by the arms.*

ANTONIO: I'll put away my French words! Mon Dieu! The Court'll be wi'out a Dancing Master if I'm taken, Sire, 'saut, saut, petit saut'. No one's e'er called me a witch, Sire, bitch yes, but not witch!

*He is dragged off Stage Right.*

ANA: 'Tis true. Witch or bitch, 'twill leave us wi'out a Dancing Master, we'll be the laughing stock o' every Court i' Europe 'cause o' this drab's nose.

*But* CARLOS *excitedly waves her aside and nods repeatedly to* THERESA. *As she resumes her prowling,* RAFAEL *staggers up and follows her around, parodying her movements, honking and sniffing his own armpits and the soles of his shoes. The* COURTIERS *are too terrified to laugh.*

*Ignoring him* THERESA *stops in front of* BELEPSCH *who screws up her face in distaste.*

BELEPSCH: Ma'am, tell this gravy-eyed peasant t' stand back from me. She stinks o' lower parts.

THERESA: 'Tis honest stink, not devil's stink; the stink o' my soiled world where I've seen the rot beneath the ribbon and lace. The washhouse'll be working late tonight. Bowels rumble, noble arses open wide. I canst smell fear. I've made diarrhetics o' y' all! (*She sniffs triumphantly.*) Sniff . . . Sniff . . . Sniff . . . (*The* COURTIERS *join in sniffing loudly: she suddenly turns on* BELEPSCH.) This woman's suspect.

MONTERREY: Yes, she's greedy f' gold. All witches're greedy f' gold!

BELEPSCH: Helfen Sie mir Ihre Majestät.

ANA: Carlos, the Countess Belepsch's my dearest companion. I'll not've her taken.

FROYLAN: If she be innocent then the Holy Inquisition'll soon discover 't and no harm done, 'cept a gouged eyeball or two. Happen the Queen's other reasons f' protecting this German suspect?

PONTOCARRERO: Jus' reasons o' the heart, Father. This's not the place f' such sentiments, Ma'am, later, later.

CARLOS: *Taaaaaeeeeeekk.*

*The* MONKS *escort the frantic* BELEPSCH *out.*

BELEPSCH: Save me, Your Majesty . . .! Remember the picnics on the Rhine . . . the Spanish gold we've confiscated together . . . I'm no witch . . .! (*Singing hysterically.*) 'Schlaf, Kinderl, schlaf./Der Tod sitzt auf der Stang/Er hat ein weissen Kittel an/ er will die bösen Kinder han/Schlaf, Kinderl, Schlaf . . !'

*Even as she exits Stage Left between the* MONKS, THERESA *resumes her search and the terrified* COURTIERS *join in sniffing each other.*

*Delighted,* RAFAEL *capers up to* FROYLAN, *sniffs him and cowers back in disgust at the smell, then scampers after* THERESA *mimicking her exaggeratedly 'genteel' manners. Suddenly she points at him.*

THERESA: *This buffoon's suspect.*

RAFAEL: Is 't true your husband left you the day he recovered his eyesight? *honk, honk.*

THERESA: I smell Satan. *This buffoon's suspect.*

*All eyes turn to* CARLOS *who looks uncertainly at the laughing dwarf.*

FROYLAN: Sire, laughter's a true mark o' Lucifer: the damnable element, pip o' the first apple. We follow Satan when we laugh.

ANA: I delivered up my close favourite t' save thy precious stump, Carlos. If she's suspect, so 's this laughing Tom. He killed the Almirante de Castilla!

CARLOS: *Taaaaeeeeeekk.*

*The* HOODED MONKS *cross to* RAFAEL *who stops laughing and stares at* CARLOS *in astonishment.*

RAFAEL: I'll break my bladder-stick, bury 't deep and drown Mother Bunch's jokes e'en deeper. My pole-star's gone a-wandering. My lords be merry and only promise on your oath, you'll come dance on my grave.

TORRES: Where'll you be buried?

RAFAEL: At sea. You ha' the wrong man. I'm Josephus Rex. Poor Jo-King, *honk, honk.* Keep sniffing, my lords and ladies. Sniff! Sniff! Sniff . . .!

*The* COURTIERS *resume their desperate sniffing and sing as the lights fade down and* RAFAEL *exits between the* TWO MONKS *Stage Right.*

ALL (*singing*): 'Sniff, Brothers, Sniff. Sniff, Sisters, Sniff, Sniff Brother, Sniff Sister, Sniff, Sniff, Sniff!'

THERESA (*singing*): 'You gotta smell out witches/You gotta sniff and how/You gotta point the finger,/You gotta take the vow/To smell, sniff, point—the time is now! And sniff, sniff, sniff, sniff.'

*Lights out to singing and sniffing which quickly mingles with screams as we glimpse through stray gleams of light, the torture instruments being trundled into position.*

SCENE XI

*Lights up on the Torture Chamber with its door at the top of the stairs
Up Stage Centre.* PRISONERS *are chained to the wall and there is
one unconscious inside the Iron Maiden.*

ANTONIO's *feet are encased in a metal torture instrument called 'the
boot'.* DR BRAVO *is on the Wheel and* RAFAEL *is stretched
unconscious on the Rack.*

DR BRAVO: Ha' I been dead since Mars and Jupiter crossed? I
    casn't hear my heart beat pitti-pat-pitti-pat. Only the sound o'
    air passing through the fluid i' my trachea. Am I dying or is
    't my birthday? I want a second opinion!
        *He dies as* ALCALA *enters from the arch Stage Left, followed by*
    GOMEZ *gnawing a meat bone.*
ALCALA: Every prison from here t' Seville's full o' suspect
    witches and more coming daily. We've jus' too much t' do.
    'Tis no way t' run a torture chamber. (*He staggers accidentally
    against the Iron Maiden, the* PRISONER *inside gives a brief pierced
    cry as the lid slams shut.*) See, that wouldst not've happened if I
    wasn't so tired.
GOMEZ (*heating a long needle*): We're being paid an extra two
    ducats a session. Every new suspect means money in our
    breeches.
ALCALA: But what o' our reputation? T' tickle a true confession
    from a relapsed sinner takes time and patience, now we've t'
    gouge 't out, quick and bleeding. Standards're collapsing,
    Gomez. We're turning this house o' truth into a butcher's
    shop. I'll go brain-mad wi'out our integrity as craftsmen.
GOMEZ: Ours isn't a craft, but a trade. Our profit lies in bulk.
    (*He takes red-hot needles from the brazier.*) Who cares about the
    quality o' the pain, so long as 't *hurts*?
ALCALA: I do! I do!
        *Humming to himself,* GOMEZ *exits with the hot needles through*

*the archway Stage Left. Furious,* ALCALA *picks up a bucket of water and throws it over* RAFAEL *on the Rack.*

ALCALA: Didst hear him, Master Morra? My son Gomez. He defies me and all I stand f'. I've raised him since he was a babe. His mother left me twenty years ago. The stigma o' me being Third Assistant Torturer. She said a man o' my age and experience shouldst've been First Assistant at the least. Complained I lacked ambition and left, boot and baggage. Now I'm Chief Torturer and my son's going from me too. Life turns opposite t' what we expect. Oh Gomez, my son, my son!

RAFAEL: Sons ne'er listen t' their fathers and're hung up by the hair and stretched f' 't. He's blind now t' thy virtues, but he'll come back t' you. All know you're a good man, honest, generous, kindly at heart.

ALCALA: What makes you say that?

RAFAEL: Fear.

ALCALA (*laughing*): You'll be the death o' me.

RAFAEL: That's my line, Sir.

ALCALA: Oh, I'll burst me buttons. (*To* ANTONIO.) Didst e'er hear such wit, Monsieur Limpy . . .? (ANTONIO *groans;* ALCALA *turns the screw on his boot;* ANTONIO *cries out.*) Ha' you bewitched His Majesty, Monsieur?! (*He turns the screw again.*) Doest believe in God?!

ANTONIO (*fainting*): *Only if he dances.*

ALCALA: Tight-arsed sodomite.

*The Inquisitor-General* VALLADARES *enters Up Stage Centre.* ALCALA *instantly kneels as* VALLADARES *hobbles down in a fury.*

VALLADARES: Heresy! 'Tis all heresy!

ALCALA: Your Eminence, we're hard pressed, is relief coming?

FROYLAN *enters through the archway Stage Left, wiping his hands.*

FROYLAN: Ah, Your Eminence. (VALLADARES *just glares at him.*) I've been given special dispensation by the Suprema and the Holy Father t' help the Lord's work here.

VALLADARES: Help?! Ten relapsed Jews were taken this

morning but there was no place f' 'em now i' the witch-filled dungeons o' the Inquisition. They had t' be lodged wi' the *civil* authorities! You're wrecking the Church's whole machinery o' repression wi' your damnable witches!

FROYLAN: They must be o'ercome afore all else.

VALLADARES: That's the colour o' your dream, not mine.

FROYLAN: Doesn't Your Eminence believe in the reality o' witches?

VALLADARES: The Inquisitor Salazar declared there were neither witches nor bewitched until they were talked and written about. 'Tis my duty t' protect reputed witches and warlocks from thy inordinate zeal. I'll not let you turn the Spanish Inquisition into an instrument o' malignant persecution. 'Twas created t' save souls f' Paradise.

FROYLAN: Spain and the King's penis lie crushed.

VALLADARES: Both'll rise again when I've burnt the last heretic from the land.

ALCALA: Holy Fathers, you must gi' me a policy decision! We casn't save the immortal souls o' *both* witches and heretics. We haven't the equipment or men.

VALLADARES (*crossing to* ANTONIO): Didst not St Paul tell the Galatians: 'If anyone preached t' you a Gospel besides that which you've received, let him be an anathema'?

*He turns the screw on* ANTONIO's *metal boot.*

ANTONIO (*screaming*): Yes.

FROYLAN (*crossing to* RAFAEL): Didst not St Paul also say t' the Galatians: 'Who didst bewitch you?'

*He turns the Rack tighter.*

RAFAEL (*screaming*): Yes.

VALLADARES: Denyer o' efficacious grace!

FROYLAN: Predeterminist!

VALLADARES: *Heretic-fancier!*

FROYLAN: *Witch-lover!*

ALCALA: Your Majesty.

CARLOS *has entered Up Stage Centre.* ALCALA *kneels, the* OTHERS *bow as* CARLOS *stumbles down the stairs.*

CARLOS: Haaaa found whoooo . . .?

VALLADARES: Ask thy Confessor, Sire, 'tis his murky province.

FROYLAN: We've found hundreds, Sire. 'Tis bigger than that. No one's innocent till proved not guilty. Not my lords Torres, Alba, Oropesa, no not e'en the Queen.

CARLOS: The Queeee . . . ahhh, my bowels 're watery. (*Crosses to* DR BRAVO *on the Wheel.*) Hast a physic f' meeee, doctor . . .? (*No reply.*) Your Sovereign speaks . . . Sulking, sir? I'll haaaa no peevish sulking . . . (ALCALA *whispers to him.*) DEAD . . .? (*He staggers back, putting his fingers in his ears.*) I'll not HEAR 't . . . (*To* RAFAEL.) TTTom, is he ddddd . . .?

RAFAEL (*gasping*): He's dead, Sire. And truth t' tell I too feel like going where the smallest is no smaller than the rest. *Honk . . .*

ALCALA (*laughing*): *Honk.*

*No one else laughs and he stops immediately as* PONTOCARRERO *enters Up Stage Centre and comes stiffly down the steps.*

CARLOS: YYYour EEE we draw closer t' it, s' jus' ahead. Weee finding more, catching new witches on the wing e'ery second. We squeeze and sweat 'em out.

PONTOCARRERO: Yet no improvements're visible in you or the State, Sire. Spain festers and the world waits f' you t' choose your successor.

CARLOS: 'Tis the wwwitche'ss SPELL. Casn't raise up armies, heirs or penises till broken.

PONTOCARRERO: The French Louis's grown impatient. He expected you t' nominate Philip Bourbon; 'tis why he ga' us a good peace. Now he's forming another alliance wi' the English and low Dutch. This time there'll be no 'scape.

CARLOS: 'Snot my fault. My Confessor knows. I'm bewitched.

PONTOCARRERO: Father Froylan's wrong.

FROYLAN: Wrong? Your Eminence has a different reason f' His Majesty's impotence?

PONTOCARRERO: This's Spain. Nothing's different, only worse.

CARLOS: Wooo? Whaa worse than being bewitched?

PONTOCARRERO: Being *possessed*.

CARLOS: Pooo . . .?

PONTOCARRERO (*producing a book*): The learned Zacharias on possession. (*Reading.*) 'The possessed 've swollen tongues that loll from their mouths, weep wi'out knowing why, talk little sense and oft times fall senseless'.

　　CARLOS *snatches the book.*

FROYLAN: I saw to 't no daemon entered His Majesty. The evil's outside, not inside. Take my word, Sire, you're bewitched not possessed.

CARLOS (*reading the book with difficulty*): 'The possessed're afflicted wi' sudden terrors', *ahh, ahh*; 'imitate wild animals', *grrr*; 'speak strange tongues', *vidi, vici, veni* . . .

FROYLAN: Sire, I personally guarded you wi' crucifix and trident from any possible daemonic penetration.

PONTOCARRERO: You forget Satan couldst've penetrated His Majesty when Father Motilla was his Confessor and the succuli's lain dormant in him since.

VALLADARES: 'Tis thy necromantic meddling's stirred the succuli t' life, Father! If 'tis proven I'll ha' you staked and burning afore you canst chant another Pater Noster. Your Eminence's t' be congratulated on exposing a grave error o' a member o' your own Order. The proofs seem pregnant, Your Majesty. If Lucifer attacks a man from wi'out 'tis bewitchment. If he assumes control from wi'in, 'tis deemed possession. You, Sire, casn't control thy limbs or bladder; like that young man Christ found at Mount Tabor, you're possessed o' a foul spirit. Your shield o' faith's cracked and you stand ball-naked 'gainst the dark. You didst not protect the Faith from heretics, faith didst not protect you from the Devil. You showed no zeal f' God, didst not scorch His doubters. 'Twas weakness in you and Satan entered through that same gate. The cause's in you, Sire, though you're not the cause.

FROYLAN: No, 'tis the witches, 'tis outside wi' the witches!
You've heard 'em confess to 't, Sire. You're bewitched.

PONTOCARRERO: Read Zacharias, Sire, feel the nail in thy
throat, the claw in thy belly. You're possessed.

CARLOS: Casn't seee? I can see by my superior middle-brain . . .
I'm not possessed . . . Not bewitched . . . 'Tis worse than
worse. (*Trembling, he shuts the book.*) I'm bewitched and
possessed *both*.

PONTOCARRERO ⎫
VALLADARES  ⎬ (*groaning*): Both?!
FROYLAN     ⎪
ALCALA      ⎭

CARLOS: Help mmmmm. (*He staggers to the chained* PRISONER.)
III'm assailed, OUT beyond and INNER too. (*Clutches his
stomach.*) Abounding . . . abounding . . . (*To* ANTONIO.)
Monsieur MMM 'tis noon and I've no eyelids! Pray f'
me. (*To* RAFAEL.) TTTom TTToom jelly knots inside me!
Pray f' me. 'Tis in the King now. Lord, saaa save him from
evil, purefy his water and his flesh . . . away . . . aaaawww . . .
(*Claws his stomach.*) Whaaa o' me now, whaaa o' Spain? I
command thee pray f' us . . . only praaa . . .

He collapses on his knees Down Stage Centre, FROYLAN and
ALCALA kneel beside him. PONTOCARRERO gestures graciously
to VALLADARES to lead the prayer. The lights fade slowly.

VALLADARES: The King's bound t' God's throne wi' a gleaming
chain. Pray f' him. Pray f' him. His sins stain the coming
years, f' if he sows bad seeds now 'tis future Kings who'll reap
bitter harvests. But if he sows no seeds, 'tis worse, f' authority
and submission're the twin poles on which Jehovah turns the
world and wi'out an heir the King's no longer its standing
pillar. 'Tis heresy 'gainst the Church who anointed him,
rebellion 'gainst God. Pray f' him. Pray f' him. Satan's in him
now; made easy entrance f' he was already touched and
weakened, like his subjects, by that foul disease called reason.
Oh man needs belief not reason! F' when he discovers the

reason f' things he loses the merit o' faith. Gi' us back our
faith, Lord; our prejudices! Nothing's more vital than our
prejudices, those opinions we accept unexamined. Wi'out
prejudices no religion, no morality, no submission. We
hunger f' the blessings o' blind ignorance, Lord! We pray.
We pray. F' by the sins o' rulers, nations're punished, so we
pray f' our salvation, Lord, and the salvation o' our Sovereign
lord. Kings stand high, exposed t' blasts that pass o'er the
lower valleys. Ha' mercy on our liege, Carlos, who feeds us
wi' the sincerity o' his heart and guides us wi' the wisdom o'
his head. Now he must be cleansed pure, that we might
continue t' love and praise him. F' in loving and praising him,
we love and praise thee, Lord, f' he's thy true representative,
the very image o' thy monarchy o'er all creation. Et benedíctio
Dei Omnipoténtis Patris et Filii . . .

   *As* VALLADARES *kneels with the* OTHERS, *a plain-song chorus
is heard singing hoarsely.* 'Praise my soul the King of Heaven./
To his feet thy tribute bring;/Ransomed, healed, restored,
forgiven,/Who like we his praise should sing./Alleluja!
Alleluja! Praise the everlasting King.'

   *A chorus of bloodstained* COURTIERS *emerge from the archway
Stage Left carrying their chains and candles. They are led by*
BELEPSCH *with needles sticking out of her arms, a broken*
ALBA *and* MONTERREY, *and* TORRES *with his eyes black and
bleeding. Whilst* RAFAEL *honks wildly,* ANA *joins them and all
kneel and sing:* 'Father-like he tends and spares us/Well our
feeble frame he knows,/In his hands he gently bears us,/
Rescues us from all our foes,/Alleluja! Alleluja!/Widely does
his mercy flow.'

   *The candles are snuffed out. There is now only a Spot on* CARLOS
*praying.* RAFAEL's *ironic honking is heard above the unseen Chorus.*
'Angels help us to adore him,/Ye behold him face to face:/
Sun and moon bow down before him,/dwellers all in time
and space./Alleluja! Alleluja! Praise with us the God o' Grace.'

   RAFAEL's *honking is finally choked off.*

## SCENE XII

*Lights up on the Throne Room where all are still praying silently.*
CARLOS *whispers to* ANA.

CARLOS: I always pray wi' my eyes open so I canst hear whaaa I say.

ANA: It gi's us a chance t' talk, Carlos.

CARLOS: Taaa . . .? Wha taaa . . .?

ANA: Jus' talk, Carlos. Not big talk, jus' a little small talk.

CARLOS (*nods eagerly*): Jus' taaa, jus' jus' . . . Talk. Yes.

ANA *opens her mouth but finds she has nothing to say.* CARLOS *is about to speak, but frowns dimly instead.* ANA *tries again but thinks better of it.* CARLOS *has a thought but immediately loses it. As they struggle with increasing desperation an* ATTENDANT *enters with a message for* PONTOCARRERO. *He reads it and crosses still on his knees to* CARLOS.

PONTOCARRERO: Sire, the abscess's burst. I ha' t' report a riot,

CARLOS: Wheeee . . .?

PONTOCARRERO: The Plaza Mayor. A woman complained she'd no bread f' her six children. An official told her she shouldst castrate her husband. (ANA *giggles.*) But both he and the joke died the death. He was torn t' pieces. His audience lacked humour as well as bread.

CARLOS: Whaaa . . .?

PONTOCARRERO: Their distress's more than empty bellies Sire . . .

ANA: 'Tis Father Froylan's new-style witch-hunts.

VALLADARES: The people want a return t' traditional *heresy-*hunts.

PONTOCARRERO: They're unsettled by rumours o' your possession, Sire. Show thyself t' their representatives, and let 'em see their King's still in full possession o' his wits.

CARLOS: Satan claws meee . . .

*The polished Capucin Friar,* MAURO TENDA, *traditionally*

*dressed in cowled habit and cord round his waist, enters Stage Right carrying crucifixes and bowing.* TWO MONKS *follow behind.*

PONTOCARRERO: Sire, 'tis thy exorcist extraordinary, Friar Mauro Tenda.

CARLOS: Whaaa . . . ?

ANA: My brother John William's certain you and all the Catholic crowned heads o' Europe 've been possessed f' years. 'Tis why he's sent you *the* most fashionable o' all exorcists.

CARLOS: QQQuick the Devil waits.

CARLOS *rises. So do the* OTHERS.

FROYLAN: Sire, I must humbly protest this foreign friar's presence. 'Tis a slur on me and the whole nation. Spain's ne'er lacked men who canst cast out daemons.

TENDA: But none wi' my occult knowledge o' the Prince o' Evil and his fashionable ways.

FROYLAN: What?! Who discovered and named the four Kings o' Hell; Uriens o' the East, Pymon o' the West, Egyn o' the North and the Southern Amayon?

PONTOCARRERO: Father, there's no time f' a recital o' your academic triumphs. His Majesty wants whatso'er's lurking i' his breast plucked out afore I return wi' some o' his disturbed subjects. Wi' thy permission, Sire.

CARLOS *nods impatiently and* PONTOCARRERO *exits backwards bowing whilst* TENDA *and* FROYLAN *give their crucifixes to the* TWO MONKS.

FROYLAN: 'Tisn't fair, Sire. Haven't I always gi'en satisfaction?

TENDA: Yet you couldst not determine whether your King was possessed, bewitched or both? A diagnosis any apprentice-exorcist couldst've made. Wi' thy permission, Sire, let me show you the new fashionable method o' determining Satanic presence, by what we call 'controlled experiment'. (*Taking off a silver Cross around his neck he swings it in front of* CARLOS's *eyes.*) F' too long exorcism and daemonology've been bedevilled wi' brute superstition. But this's the Year o' our Lord 1699; watch how we test f' evil. Watch . . . watch . . .

(CARLOS's *gaze is transfixed on the Cross.*) In the name o'
Jesus Christ reveal thyself, Satan! Pinch his left hand . . .
(CARLOS's *left hand twitches and he yelps.*) Satan, put his left leg
out . . . (CARLOS's *leg jerks out.*) Put his right leg out . . .
(CARLOS's *other leg goes out.*) Left leg. Right leg. Left—right—
left—right . . . (CARLOS *moves stiff-legged around the room.*) Odd.
'Tis an odd business, 'walking'. Why do we all move forward
like that 'stead o' a crabby side-shuffle like this . . .? (*He edges
sideways.*) Odd. Ma'am, His Majesty's possessed. I shall now
exorcise him.

> CARLOS *lurches blindly round amongst the astonished*
> COURTIERS.

FROYLAN: Sire, they seek t' take you from me. Wi'out thy
support I'll be crushed. 'Tis a necromatic conspiracy t' protect
the witches.

ANA: There's no conspiracy. I'm certain Friar Tenda'll not stop
you trying t' call forth the Devil.

TENDA: 'Twill not disturb me if you wish to dabble, Father.
*Satan cease.*

> CARLOS *suddenly stops walking and blinks.*

CARLOS: Oh Jesu, I'm cleansed o' the Devil! My shoulders
heave, belly exults, breast cries out wi' joy! I'm exorcised!
Exorcised!

TENDA: Sire, we haven't started yet.

CARLOS: Whaaa . . .? 'Tis Monday but it shouldst be Good
Friday the way I'm being crucified. CCCCleanse me, cccure
my occult impotence! Make me an heir! DO'T DO'T.

> FROYLAN *puts on his dark glasses and* TENDA *a pair of white
> gloves as he guides* ANA *Stage Left to stand behind the small trunk.*

TENDA: Stay back from Satan's line o' fire, Ma'am, during the
spearing o' the demons. We'll raise up a barrier his minions
casn't leap. (*He takes out a sachet and sprinkles white powder in
front of her.*) Salt. Salt saves dead flesh and live souls from
corruption. There's reason e'en in magic. (*He sees* FROYLAN
*taking out his trident.*) Great Jerome, a Paracelsus Trident!

Why, I haven't seen one o' those f' twenty years past. Nowadays all reputable exorcists spear incubi and succuli wi' a simple Cross. (*He holds up his Cross; a concealed blade springs out from it.*) And darkened glasses, Father? T' protect you from the invisible aura, eh? (*chuckles*) 'tis quite out o' fashion t' see auras nowadays. But if you see auras, you see auras . . . (*Stops chuckling.*) 'Tis no wonder Your Majesty's both bewitched and possessed. Outdated rituals're no defence 'gainst the e'er changing Powers o' Darkness. (*He lifts up the bottom of his habit and tucks it under his waist-cord, leaving his legs bare.*) Your Majesties, forgive this shameful display o' naked knees. 'Tis essential my lower limbs be free. Father I gi' thee first chance t' exorcise the daemons from thy Sovereign's body—if you can.

FROYLAN: If? I've exorcised more daemons than you've had indulgences!

*He takes a holy water stoup from one of the* MONKS.

TENDA: Hhhhmmm, holy water. I say nothing 'gainst holy water. 'Tis most effective . . . wi' the commoner sort o' possession. But I've found the Devil lurking in men o' rank and blood hath grown somewhat immune to 't. O' course, 't may be different in Spain.

*Suppressing his fury,* FROYLAN *begins the exorcism.*

FROYLAN: 'Adjúro te, serpens antiqúe, per júdicem vivórum et mortuórum, per factórem tuum, per factórem (*he throws water into* CARLOS's *impassive face with increasing speed*) qui-habet-potestátem-mitténdi-te-in-gehémnam-ut-ab-hoc-fámulo-Dei. (*He throws the last drop of water into* CARLOS's *face;* CARLOS *blinks.*) I knew 't! Satan's not home! No evil lodges in thy breast, Sire. Thou art merely bewitched, not possessed. 'Tis the witches.

TENDA *takes a small bag from one of the* MONKS.

TENDA: Watch and learn, Father. You use old lustral water, I new kidney beans. (*He takes some from the bag.*) Daemons hate 'em worse than water f' they're charged wi' elemental force.

Their colour 's Christ's blood. Their shape, God's lovin' heart.
I pepper you wi' seeds o' life t' drive out your dark daemons,
Sire. (*He throws the beans at* CARLOS.) 'Exorcízo te immundíssime spíritus omnis incúrsio adversárii omne phantásma omnis
légo in nómine Dómini nostri Jesu Christi effugáre ab hoc
phásmate Dei!

    *He flings the last handful of kidney beans hard into* CARLOS's *face.*

CARLOS: *Aeeee. Aieeee. Aieeee.*

    CARLOS *goes rigid.* TENDA *signals urgently to* ANA.

TENDA: Keep above the salt, Ma'am, the demons're leaping!
The incubi and succuli fly off him. Snot green and pusy-yellow
demons. There! There!

    *The* COURTIERS *leap away in terror from the demons. Using
his Cross as a weapon* TENDA *launches into the 'spearing of
the demons': a series of acrobatic dives and somersaults. In the
middle of them he shouts urgently to* FROYLAN *who, carried away
with excitement, joins in using his trident as a spear.*

    *They vault and swoop around the immobile* CARLOS *and
frightened Court in a fantastic display until during one of*
FROYLAN's *Nijinsky-like leaps to skewer a high-flying demon,*
ANA *deliberately sticks out her foot. The cleric trips and crashes to
the floor with a groan.*

    TENDA, *who has seized another small bag from one of the*
MONKS, *stops immediately in front of* CARLOS. *There is the faint
sound of angry, incoherent chanting off as* TENDA *concentrates all
his power.*

TENDA: Satan, recéde ergo in nómine Patris et Filii et Spiritus
Sancti! (*He flings red powder into* CARLOS's *face.*) By this dried
heifer's blood, symbol o' God's fertility—Satan go forth!
(CARLOS *remains rigid.*) Satan . . . in God's name . . . I command
thee . . . (*Summoning all his strength, he takes a raw egg from the
bag and cracks it on* CARLOS's *forehead.*) GO FORTH.

    TENDA *sinks back exhausted. As the egg slides down* CARLOS's
*face his lower limbs twitch, the light flickers and the chanting grows
louder. We can make out certain repeated words, 'Bread . . .*

Death . . . Bread . . . Death . . .' *The light flickers faster as* CARLOS's *limbs quickly jerk out of control and he falls into an epileptic fit.*

ANA *steps forward to help.* TENDA *shouts a warning for her to keep back but too late.* CARLOS *grabs her hand and her limbs immediately shake violently; the seizure seems contagious.*

*As* ANA's *and* CARLOS's *legs buckle and they fall shrieking in convulsions, four seven-foot-high effigies of children with swollen stomachs and skull-like faces advance on them out of the dark entrances, Stage Right and Left. They are carried by two surly* PEASANTS *in coarse breeches and doublets and an arsenal of knives and pistols stuffed into their belts.* PONTOCARRERO *pushes past them.*

PONTOCARRERO: Your Majesty, these're representatives o' thy loyal subjects who . . .

*He stops and with the* OTHERS *stares at* ANA *and* CARLOS *writhing on the floor.*

PONTOCARRERO: Er, we seem t' have caught Their Majesties at their prayers. We shouldst not disturb 'em, they're wrestling wi' God.

*But the attack has already passed. The light stops flickering.* ANA *and* CARLOS *rise as if nothing had happened;* ANA *resting her hand regally on* CARLOS's *arm. Both are in a state of post-epileptic automation as* CARLOS *stares at the effigies.*

CARLOS: Has Christ died that children might starve?
       Why shouldst wealth lie in usurer's pockets?
       And whole towns made poor t' raise up the merchants'
                                   walls?
       (They turn bread t' stones; the Devil'd more charity
       Turning stone's t' bread; 'tis no wonder men worship
                                    him)
       Why shouldst some ha' surfeit, others go hungry?
       One man two coats, another go naked?
       Now I see Authority's a poor provider.

       No blessings come from 't

No man born shouldst ha' t', wield 't.
Authority's the Basilisk, the crowned dragon,
Scaly, beaked and loathsome.
Born from a cock's egg, hatched under a toad
Its voice is terror, glance, certain death.
Streams where 't drank once, are poisoned
And the grass around turns black.
'Twill make a desert o' this world
Whilst there's still one man left t' gi' commands
And another who'll obey 'em.
Release all suspects!
I'm not bewitched or possessed,
'Cept t' right the wrongs done my people.
I'll show you the good life, if you'll show me pardon
F' not knowing thy needs and miseries.
I raise my hat t' you three times in courtesy.

*As he mimes raising his hat three times, the effigies deflate and
the* PEASANTS *open their mouths at last.*

PEASANTS *(frightened)*: Baa-baa-baa-baa . . .

ANA:    Cow-elephants kneel, stag-beetles buzz,
Whales like derelict ships, roll on their sides,
                                belly t' belly
And the glow-worm shines as her winged mate, a
                                falling star
Descends on her t' glow together in the dark, then
                                gently fade.
Oh let's burn bright as exploding Novas in the sky,
And by the light that makes the red rose, red,
Cry 'love, love, love' as Jermyn cried 'earth, earth,
                                earth'
Oh men, Oh women, Oh fields, Oh sky, Oh sun,
Christ comes t' gather up our flowers o' love!
*(Singing.)* 'Clap-a-yo' hands! Slap-a-yo' thigh!
Halleluja! Hallelujah!/Everybody come along and
join the jubilee!'

CARLOS ⎫
ANA      ⎬ (*singing to the* OTHERS *as they rise, bleating*): 'Clap-a-yo'
         ⎭
hands! Slap-a-yo' thigh! Don't you lose time, don't you lose
time,/Come along it's time t' choose right now f' you and me./
On the sands o' time you are more than a pebble,/Remember
trouble must be treated just like a rebel . . .'

OTHERS (*singing*): 'Send him t' the Devil!'

ALL (*singing and dancing*): 'Clap-a-yo' hands! Slap-a-yo' thigh!
Hallelujah! Hallelujah! Everybody come along and join the
jubilee!

   *As all dance and sing the panel walls revolve and the dead figures
   of* MARIANA, ALMIRANTE, RAFAEL, DR BRAVO *and* MOTILLA
   *enter and join in with even more strength and liveliness than the
   living:*
   *As they repeat the chorus of the song, individual* COURTIERS
   *step forward for a moment.*

BELEPSCH: God be praised. My life-long friendship wi' the
Queen's not broken, though my ten fingers are.

TORRES: I'm blinded by his glory. But I thank His Majesty f'
making my world real at the last.

MONTERREY: I thank him too, f' showing me that riches're a
wax shield 'gainst the sword o' State. Money must be made
the very woof and weave o' society so whoso'er attacks a rich
man attacks society.

ALBA: E'en in the House o' Pain my rank and privileges were
observed. My body's fire-wracked, my mouth blood-filled,
but I cry out, 'God save the King!'.

ALL (*singing and dancing*): 'On the sands o' time we will all need
each other,/Remember Judas must be treated just like a
brother,/Send us all a lover!/Clap-a-yo' hands! Slap-a-yo'
thigh . . .'

CARLOS: Man's a lunatic animal
          Unravelling everything in theory
          Tangling everything in practice.
          But the one creature able t' profit from his errors.

I'll profit from mine, do somersaults,
Drop my sceptre, renounce my crown, vacate my
throne.

*The* OTHERS *stop singing and dancing.*
We'll live wi'out orders and obediences,
Wi'out limits t' heart and mind.
Oh won't 't be grand t' live then?!

*The* OTHERS *let out terrified shrieks and flee leaving only the* DEAD *in a menacing semi-circle round* CARLOS. *The light fades.* CARLOS *stumbles as he returns to normal. His bout of post-epileptic automatism has ended.*

CARLOS: Whaaa . . .? Whaaa . . .? Is the breaking day come? (*The* DEAD *make loud sucking noises.*) Whaaa you taking from me? Whaaa you taking from mmmm . . .? Whaaa you taaa . . . (*He becomes weaker, gasping for breath as the sucking noises continue.*) Whaaa you taa aaa . . .? Whaaa yyy . . .? Whaaa . . .? Aaa-aaa-aa . . .

*He collapses. The* DEAD *retreat slowly backwards from him into the darkness. A funeral bell tolls once.* CARLOS *is dying.*

### SCENE XIII

*A chorus chants the prayer for the sick:* 'Dómine sancte Pater omnipotentes aetérne Deus . . .' *Lights come up on the King's Bedchamber shrouded in dark drapes. The four-poster bed is Stage Left, the low table with the white cloth and holy vessels below it and St Isidore's bones in front of the mirror Stage Right.*

PONTOCARRERO, FROYLAN *and* ANA *watch the* TWO ATTENDANTS *pick up* CARLOS, *who is barely conscious, and undress him whilst* DR GELEEN *mixes medicines from a small medicine chest and* GONGORA, *up Stage Right, consults his star-charts.*

DR GELEEN: Ma'am, His Majesty's had one hundred and thirty-seven bowel movements in the last four hours. His faeces're steamy black; no muscle in 'em.

ANA: What does that mean?

DR GELEEN: He's dying.

ANA: What of?

DR GELEEN: His birth.

*A* MESSENGER *enters and hands* PONTOCARRERO *a document from his pouch.* PONTOCARRERO *reads it.*

PONTOCARRERO: The Will must be changed. Louis 's finally convinced his grandson'll ne'er inherit the Spanish throne. He's signed a Third Partition Treaty wi' England and the Dutch t' divide the Empire between 'em. Redraft immediately and make Charles o' Austria heir t' the throne.

FROYLAN: Your Eminence, I'm the King's Confessor!

PONTOCARRERO: No longer. I'm willing t' save a loyal secretary from the Inquisitor-General but not a rebellious Confessor. (*He hands him the pouch.*) Then deal wi' all this.

ALBA *enters Up Stage Centre for the nightly ritual, followed by* MONTERREY *and a stumbling* TORRES. *They all carry their small black cushions.*

*With a great effort* ALBA *kneels on one knee in front of* CARLOS. *The* ATTENDANTS *place the King's insignia, cloak and doublet on his cushion and the enfeebled* ALBA *nearly topples over with the weight. Rising, he staggers out backwards, whilst* MONTERREY *kneels to receive* CARLOS's *shoes. But he is shaking so much with the palsy, they keep falling off the cushion, as he exits backwards. Finally the blind* TORRES *kneels for* CARLOS's *breeches and withdraws with them straight over a chair Stage Centre.* ANA *watches him crash into every piece of furniture and the doors, before exiting.*

ANA: Your Eminence, Carlos must order the end o' this absurd ceremony.

PONTOCARRERO: He canst order a hundred thousand men go die f' him, and they'll die gladly. But t' order 'em to end one minor social custom's too much, e'en for the King o' Spain.

ALBA *staggers back carrying the* KING's *nightshirt on his cushion.* MONTERREY *follows with the curved, pomaded leather covers for* CARLOS's *non-existent moustache and* TORRES *with the Royal chamber-pot.*

*As* ALBA *kneels and the* ATTENDANTS *put the nightshirt on* CARLOS, MONTERREY *shakes so violently with the palsy that the pomaded covers fall off his cushion. Whilst bending down to find them,* TORRES *careers blindly over him, breaking the chamber-pot in half.* MONTERREY *is still searching for the covers as* TORRES, *unable to see, puts the half of the chamber-pot with the handle back on the cushion, and crosses unsteadily to* CARLOS. *He kneels, but unfortunately with his back to the* KING. *The* FIRST ATTENDANT *turns him round the right way and he triumphantly lifts up the remains of the chamber-pot for* CARLOS. *But the* KING *is unable to make use of it as he clings weakly to the* SECOND ATTENDANT.

PONTOCARRERO *gestures impatiently. The* FIRST ATTEN-DANT *touches* TORRES *who gets up and proceeds to exit backwards, straight into the slow-moving* ALBA *and* MONTERREY *still looking for the lost pomaded covers. Finally unscrambling themselves, they exit in a row, with* TORRES *in the middle, squeezing through the doorway bowing and groaning.*

*The* ATTENDANTS *start to take* CARLOS *to the bed, but he struggles feebly and screams in fright.* DR GELEEN *has him placed in the chair Stage Centre and gives him medicine.*

DR GELEEN: 'Twill harden thy faeces, Sire. Dr Bravo prescribed pills made o' crab's eyes and oil squeezed from bricks. But all true remedial medicine must be scientific. I've had the innards o' a freshly killed calf specially prepared, Sire. (*Low to* ANA.) I fear his sudden collapse may signal a sudden dying.

ANA: His whole life's been one long dying. I casn't believe he's dying now.

PONTOCARRERO: I can. Spain's starving, the provinces're in revolt, our enemies're joined ready t' dismember us and we still've no heir. His Majesty'll die 'cause 'tis the worst possible time t' die.

GONGORA: I fear the malefic Saturn's retrograde in the 10th House.

FROYLAN: 'Tis the witches' revenge.

PONTOCARRERO: Tend t' your papers, you've forfeited all rights.

FROYLAN: Out o' fear! Mea culpa, mea culpa. Oh how the little green devils laughed. I'm a hen-hearted flunky, a kiss-me-arse coward! *I betrayed what was best in me* . . . The papers're in order, Your Eminence.

PONTOCARRERO *takes a document from him.*

ANA: Carlos, Carlos. Wouldst like damask prunes in milk? 'Tis your favourite. Nothing's certain, Carlos, 'cept Christ's forgiveness.

PONTOCARRERO: And Death's coming. Sign 't, Your Majesty, and make Archduke Charles o' Austria heir t' the Spanish throne.

*As he places the Will and pen and ink in front of him,* CARLOS *lets out a loud cry and slumps down in his chair. All react.* DR GELEEN *bends over* CARLOS's *chest.*

DR GELEEN: Permission t' listen t' thy heart, Sire!

PONTOCARRERO: Is he dead, or jus' hovering as usual?!

GONGORA: According t' arithmetical calculation the stars say . . .

ANA: You're dismissed from our sight!

GONGORA: No, Ma'am, they don't say that. (*Consults charts.*) Where do they say . . .?

ANA: GO!

GONGORA *exits, bowing and muttering over his charts.*

DR GELEEN: His heart's faint. Permission t' thump, Sire. (*He hits* CARLOS's *chest a tremendous blow: then listens again.*) He's lost too much 'natural spirit'—that's the life-gi'ing essence that animates our bodies. Permission t' use thy body-servant, Sire? (*He beckons to the* FIRST ATTENDANT.) Bend down, put your open mouth 'gainst His Majesty's open mouth and breathe.

ANA: The cure's fouler than the sickness.

*As the* FIRST ATTENDANT *breathes into* CARLOS's *mouth, the* KING *revives. But whilst* CARLOS *grows stronger, the* FIRST ATTENDANT *grows weaker.* CARLOS *clutches him fiercely to suck the 'natural spirit' from him.*

*The* FIRST ATTENDANT *finally collapses exhausted.* DR GELEEN *gestures to the* SECOND ATTENDANT *who drags his companion out Up Stage Centre.*

DR GELEEN: At least 'twill gi' His Majesty time t' receive Extreme Unction and make his peace wi' God.

PONTOCARRERO: Only after he's signed the Will. Rulers must risk God's grace, souls eternal torment, t' save their Empires . . . (*Presents* CARLOS *with the Will again.*) Sign, Sire, and then return t' the business o' dying.

ANA: Sign and've done wi' 't at last, Carlos.

CARLOS: Whaaa . . .?

PONTOCARRERO (*quickly reading the Will*): 'In accordance wi' the laws o' these kingdoms, I declare my successor t' be— shouldst God take me wi'out bearing heirs—Archduke Charles o' Austria, who shall not allow the least dismemberment o' these said kingdoms.'

CARLOS *takes the document and* PONTOCARRERO *offers him a pen and ink.* CARLOS *pushes it aside.*

CARLOS: No, I command you, delete the Archduke Charles o' Austria's name. Substitute Philip Bourbon o' France!

ALL: WHAAA . . .?!

PONTOCARRERO: You're sick, Sire!

CARLOS: No, dying. (*He stands up.*) My mind's a sudden burning glass now life creeps out wi' every breath I take. I feel 't going. *Quick, quick,* I've some six minutes left t' eternity, *quick, quick.*

*Taking quick gasping breaths he paces intently whilst the lights grow brighter and brighter.*

PONTOCARRERO: Sire, we casn't gi' the throne t' the Frenchman, 'tis against all our traditions, prejudices . . .

ANA: Austria's our ally.

CARLOS: Only France's strong enough t' hold our Empire together.

PONTOCARRERO: But Louis 's just signed a Treaty o' Partition wi' England and the Dutch t' divide our dominions 'tween 'em.

CARLOS: He'll turn Judas t' get all, rather than a part.

PONTOCARRERO: The rest o' Europe'll ne'er allow France t' inherit the whole Spanish Empire. They'll fight . . .

CARLOS: . . . the War o' the Spanish Succession, 1701–1713. Oudenade, Ramillies, Malplaquet, Blenheim. One million dead. Two million wounded. Western Europe in ruins. But Spain and her Holy Empire'll remain intact, *quick, quick.* Delete and substitute!

PONTOCARRERO: Sire, Sire, I see the logic o' 't, but the logic o' 't makes all that's gone afore meaningless. F' thirty years we've striven t' produce an heir. Austrian, Bavarian, Spanish, only so 'twasn't French. 'Twas the reason f' our sins; the horrors and the pain. Wi' this one blind stroke you make 't all pointless. What o' my broken arm, leg, cries, thuds, 'Oh live and let live'? Is that f' nothing?

ANA: And the deaths o' Father Motilla and my lord Almirante, nothing? Belepsch's white hairs, nothing? My hatred o' the Queen Mother, nothing? NOTHING? All swallowed into nothing!

FROYLAN: Sire, Sire, I fought Satan so's you could procreate, tore him out from senseless flesh—rack, screws, branding irons! If you take the French squab, 'tis all wi'out purpose. The Devil's won and we're lost!

CARLOS: He has, we are. The Lord o' Unreason rules and we stand alone at the mercy o' Chance. The empty Universe's deaf t' our voice, indifferent t' our hopes, crimes and sufferings. It contains no reasons, patterns, explanations. They're words t' soothe soul's terror o' our impotence. My reign's a glorious monument t' futility. Father prepare oil and bread! Physician, mix potions! Your Eminence, DELETE AND SUBSTITUTE!

PONTOCARRERO *takes the Will to alter it,* DR GELEEN *returns to his medicines and* FROYLAN *crosses to the table to prepare Extreme Unction.*

ANA: What o' me?! No more gold crucifixes, fluted silver diamonds and opals. The Frenchman'll not be beholden t' me f' his throne. I'll be EX'D. Carlos, Carlos, there's another way, in this room, that bed, your father Philip at his dying, danced a goat's gig on your mother and procreated. Carlos, all nature advises, buzz, buzz. The solitary bees, scolia, masons and bembex, mount and couple jus' afore they fall dead. Oh buzz, buzz, Carlos. (*She hysterically starts taking off her farthingale.*) I'll be thy soft warming pan, Carlos! Buzz. It takes but a second t' take life and make life, be my loving chopping boy, Carlos! *Buzz. Buzz.*

As she frantically pulls off her dress, CARLOS *continues pacing,* PONTOCARRERO *changing the Will,* DR GELEEN *mixing medicines and* FROYLAN *preparing the oil and bread. Their actions grow jerkier and faster like a speeded up film under remorselessly fierce lights.*

CARLOS: *Quick, quick,* afore the light holes my brain . . . (*A light bulb shatters and* CARLOS *jerks round.*) IIII'm here t' die, 'tis the ooonly certainty . . . (*Another bulb shatters, then another;* CARLOS *jerks round and round as the light diminishes.*) IIII'm pouring AWAY fff . . . (*More bulbs blow: it grows darker;* CARLOS*'s jaw slackens.*) SSSS Isidore's bones ddaaa . . . aaah . . . arrggh . . . *MammaaAAAA.*

As more lights shatter, he cries out and collapses into the chair. DR GELEEN *stops mixing his medicine,* FROYLAN *pouring out the 'oil of the sick' and* ANA *ripping off her endless petticoats and all rush over to him. But* PONTOCARRERO *is there first and thrusts the Will into* CARLOS*'s lap.*

CARLOS: Whaaa . . .?

PONTOCARRERO: It makes Philip Bourbon the next Catholic King o' Spain. (*He puts the pen into* CARLOS*'s enfeebled hand.*) I was too rigid t' bend t' the obvious, too blinkered t' e'en see 't. Blind! Now I'm left t' convince the new Philip I've always supported him ... (*Guiding* CARLOS's *hand*.) Sign there, Sire...

ANA: No, Carlos! Buzz, Carlos!

*But he signs, and as he falls back exhausted, the funeral bell tolls, the doors Up Stage Centre are flung open and a* HOODED MONK *carrying a gold Cross aloft enters followed by other* MONKS *with lighted black candles and chanting the 'Miserere'.*

*They proceed to remove the furniture, drapes and then the walls themselves, completely dismantling the Bedroom Set. Whilst* DR GELEEN *tries to make* CARLOS *drink his medicine,* ANA *tears hysterically at her seemingly endless series of petticoats and* FROYLAN *and* PONTOCARRERO *hurriedly prepare to administer Extreme Unction.*

*The gold Cross is lowered for* CARLOS *to kiss.* FROYLAN *holds out the bowl of oil.* PONTOCARRERO *dips his thumb into it and makes the sign of the Cross on* CARLOS's *forehead whilst muttering the ritual prayer:* 'Per istam sanctam Unctionem . . .' *Wiping away the oil on* CARLOS *with a small piece of wool, he dries his thumb on the bread.*

TWO MONKS *gently lift* CARLOS, *strip off his clothes and leave him naked except for a dirty loin-cloth.*

*The bell tolls and* DR GELEEN, FROYLAN *and the* MONKS *exit chanting Up Stage.* ANA *is escorted out by* TWO MONKS, *still tearing in frustration at her petticoats and sobbing.*

ANA: Buzz, Carlos! Buzz, buzz!

PONTOCARRERO *and* CARLOS *are left alone in a Spot, Stage Centre.*

PONTOCARRERO: Sire, you were wrong t' say there's only one certainty that you're here t' die. There's one other—you're here t' die *alone.*

CARLOS *tries to clutch at him, but bowing* PONTOCARRERO *exits backwards into the darkness.*

CARLOS: I command ... order ... JJJesu ... I flow out and into my death ... dddown the drain o' history ... howling like a dog i' a dream ... *aaaaaavvvvaa* ... there ... *SEE.*

*He gives a final convulsive jerk. Two rolls of narrow, white cloth concealed in his hands snake out across the floor as he falls back dead.*

TWO HOODED MONKS *enter out of the darkness Stage Left, tie the ends of the bands of cloth round the dead man's ankles and drag him off as the funeral bell tolls and the Spot fades.*

# EPILOGUE

PONTOCARRERO'S VOICE: But our ending's not despair but hope. Not death but life. F' Kings die t' rise again, like our Saviour, t' steal us t' glory, t' lead us out o' darkness into the Caanite light o' a new age: the Age o' Reason. (*Lights slowly up.*) Oh blessed beams. T' see! T' understand! T' delight! The last Spanish Hapsburg's dead, the first Spanish Bourbon's born. No longer Louis XIV's grandson, Duke o' Anjou, Philip o' France, but new crowned—Philip V o' Spain!

*Lights up on the Throne Room. The whole Court is assembled. As bells peal a great choir sings an exultant 'Te Deum' and the floor Down Stage Centre splits.* PHILIP V *emerges wrapped in a gold cloak and carrying a sceptre. Whilst a mighty anthem plays he makes his way up the rostrum and turns.*

PHILIP V *is another freak, with massive legs and arms, bloated stomach and a small elephant's trunk hanging down over his chest in place of a nose.*

*As he lowers himself onto the throne all cry: 'God save the King.' 'The King shall live forever.'* PHILIP V *trumpets back loudly in reply and a huge, grinning imbecile's face is projected over the King and the throne.*

*The lights fade down to a night sky with stars; the music and sounds dissolve into a cold night wind. Then one by one the stars go out. The wind too finally dies.*
*Silence. Darkness. Curtain.*

THE END

# Laughter!

---

## CHARACTERS

### Part I  TSAR

IVAN
VASKA SHIBANOV
TSAREVITCH
SEMEON BEKBULATOVITCH
SAMAEL
AUTHOR
PRINCE NIKITA ODOEVSKY
HAMMER
NAIL
AXE
TREE

### THE SCENE
MOSCOW 1573

### Part II  AUSCHWITZ

VIKTOR CRANACH
HANS GOTTLEB
ELSE JOST
HEINZ STROOP
GEORG WOCHNER
ABE BIMKO
HYME BIEBERSTEIN
GOTTLEB'S MOTHER
SANITATION MEN

### THE SCENE
BERLIN 1942

**TO MARTIN**

*Laughter!* was first presented at the Royal Court Theatre, London on 25 January 1978, with the following cast:

## PART I

| | |
|---|---|
| IVAN | *Timothy West* |
| VASKA SHIBANOV | *Rodger Kemp* |
| TSAREVITCH | *David Suchet* |
| SEMEON BEKBULATOVITCH | *Barry Stanton* |
| SAMAEL | *Derek Francis* |
| AUTHOR | *Rodger Kemp* |
| PRINCE NIKITA ODOEVSKY | *Paul Bentall* |
| HAMMER | *Stuart Rayner* |
| NAIL | *Neil Borman* |
| AXE | *Patrick Connor* |
| TREE | *Patricia Leach* |

## PART II

| | |
|---|---|
| VIKTOR CRANACH | *Derek Francis* |
| HANS GOTTLEB | *Timothy West* |
| ELSE JOST | *Frances de la Tour* |
| HEINZ STROOP | *Rodger Kemp* |
| GEORG WOCHNER | *David Suchet* |
| ABE BIMKO | *Derek Francis* |
| HYME BIEBERSTEIN | *Timothy West* |
| GOTTLEB'S MOTHER | *Patricia Leach* |
| SANITATION MEN | *Stuart Rayner* |
| | *Neil Borman* |

*Directed by* CHARLES MAROWITZ
*Designed by* PAT ROBERTSON
*Lighting by* LEONARD TUCKER
*Costumes by* ROSEMARY VERCOE

*Part One*

TSAR

*Single Spot up, Down Stage Centre, on the immaculately dressed* **Author** *with notes.*

**Author:**  Ladies and Gentlemen . . .

*A hand slaps a large custard pie straight in his face. As he wipes it off a laughing Voice declares: It's going to be that kind of a show, folks!*
No it isn't. Gangrene has set in. Comedy itself is the enemy. Laughter only confuses and corrupts everything we try to say. It cures nothing except our consciences and so ends by making the nightmare worse. A sense of humour's no remedy for evil. Isn't that why the Devil's always smiling? The stupid're never truly laughed out of their stupidities, fools remain fools, the corrupt, violent and depraved remain corrupt, violent and depraved. Laughter's the ally of tyrants. It softens our hatred. An excuse to change nothing, for nothing needs changing when it's all a joke.

*His bow tie whirls round and round; he angrily pulls it off.*
So we must try and root out comedy, strangle mirth, let the heart pump sulphuric acid, not blood.

*The carnation in his buttonhole squirts water; he tears it off desperately.*
Root it out! The world grows hard, harder, and every time I open my mouth I subtract something from the sum of human knowledge. Laughter's too feeble a weapon against the barbarities of life. A balm for battles lost, standard equipment for the losing side; the powerful have no need of it. Wit's no answer to a homicidal maniac. So, in the face of Atilla the Hun, Ivan the Terrible, a Passendale or Auschwitz, what good is laughter?!

*His trousers fall down to reveal spangled underpants.*
Root it out! Root it out!

*Spot out, and a magnificent Bass sings a Gregorian chant.*

*Lights up on the well of the courtyard of a Moscow chapel, 1575. The curved wall reaches up some seven feet and is only broken by a low archway Up Stage Centre. Above it is a figure of a Crucified Christ. Up Stage Right,* **Prince Nikita Odoevsky,** *who is seated, impaled on a wooden stake. He*

*wears a loincloth, his hands are bound, and heavy weights
attached to his feet, so the sharpened point of the stake, which
is covered with congealed blood like candle grease, is driven
up through his body. There is an executioner's block, Stage
Left.*

*The cowled figure of* **Abbot Ivan Moskovsky** *in the black
monk's habit of the Russian Orthodox Church, enters
quickly, bent low, through the archway. A large wooden cross
hangs from his neck.*

*The singing stops as he falls on his knees, Down Stage
Centre, his prayer punctuated by* **Odoevsky**'s *screams.*

**Ivan** *(blowing loudly)*: Air, I confide my thoughts to you.
Adam transgressed, Lot dissembled, Moses, Myriam, Aaron
fell foul, Noah, David whored, sleered, craked in pain: 'I've
sinned, wha' shouldst I do?' The Lord took away their sin.
Mine rise Golgotha high: lust, greed, wrath, pride. Yet
Christ crucified's a pledge o' God's pardon.

*He crawls back to the crucifix Up Stage.*

See, his hands nailed flat casn't strike me, feet hammered in,
casn't run from me. See, his blood flows t' wash me, head
down t' kiss me, arms wide t' clip me close. I play the bear,
he gi's me honey; play Satan, he lights a candle. *Mercy's* the
knife that turns, barb that bites. God wracks me raw wi' His
mercy!

*He bangs his forehead on the ground; it bleeds.*

Red's the colour o' the Cross whereon God had a God killed.
I came closest t' Him here, where men die, empierced, dis-
soul-joined, new christianed in their gore. Clawed fingers
grooved these stones, not penitential knees. Hot blood
scalded 'em, not salt tears. List how the croked choir lilts full-
voiced. Pain mined from the bone. *(he joins in the
screaming) Uuuuuuuurrr aaarrr.* The Church must consecrate
this molde, gar that block an altar, that stake an episcopal
throne. F' only here canst the beshait sinner leally pray and
suffer.

*He rises and crosses to* **Odoevsky**.

I betrayed our heavenly Tsar, you our earthly one. Your
punishment's but a stake riven up through backarse cleavage
where fartleberries cluster. Doest feel thy anus split, rectum

cleifed, pancreas lanced on a point, tripes born out in blood and piss-water? Then smile, your chastizer's human, not divine, who gi'es his victims, *mercy*. Smile, my son, that Christ stakes me not you! You buy forgiveness cheap. *Aaarrr.* I'm skolered in fire that burns wi'out light. Spiked not wi' soft wood but hot iron. He rives 't down through skullcase *crrack.* Brain-boiled gone, I stumble skirl-naked blind, amid its fell clouds. Torment scours you clean, turns me rancid. You go down purified, I putrify. My pain's infinite, yours has a stop. Oh, some men're lucky!

**Odoevsky** *(screaming)*: *Arrr-arrrrhh eeeee aaaa-aa hhhrrr.*

**Ivan**: 'Tis easy f' you t' say that but tisn't true. My pain's greater. We're apostates both but different in degree. You betrayed thy Sovereign, I my Saviour. We both sinned through pride, garled our leige lords, Judas-like. My sin's greater, therefore the pain. My examplar's Christ, yours only Muscovite Princes, whose tradition tis t' betray their annointed Tsar. Prince Garbaty-Skuisky beheaded, Prince Repin poignarded, Prince Kurlyatev strangled in a distant monastery. All f' treachery. Nothing else was e'er expected o' thee.

**Odoevsky** *(screaming)*: *Buuuuuuuu ahhh rrreeeeee eeeggg aaaaa arrrrrkkkk.*

**Ivan**: Innocent? How canst say they were innocent o' all crimes? Why their very appearance constituted a criminal offence. You'd excuse Judas by saying he was hungry and needed the thirty pieces f' bread. Didst not the Tsar himself cry out in rage 'gainst '∈m, *arrrrrggggrr?* Weren't they accused therefore guilty? Men can sink deeper, stay down longer, come up dirtier than any other o' God's creatures. Like swallows t' the sun they soar t' darkness. 'Tis why God punishes us.

**Odoevsky** *(screaming)*: *Uuuuuuu eeeeaaaaa ggg hhhh.*

**Ivan**: Meek? God's not meek. He peers into this world through our wounds.

**Odoevsky** *(screaming)*: *Mmmmmmm arrrrrxxx.*

**Ivan**: Good? Man's not good. He's a two-eyed, two-balled dawish freak who's seared soul's more foul than his sinsoiled carcass.

**Odoevsky** *(screaming)*: *Aaa eeee.*

**Ivan:** Deliverance? There's no deliverance. I asked God t' show
me the way t' deliverance. 'How do I find myself?' I asked.
'Look under a stone' He replied. Root it out! Root it out!
'Show me the way t' deliverance' I asked again. He told me t'
flee from men. Only when a sinner can crake, 'I and God
alone're left in this world' will he find peace. Oh Lord let the
alchemy o' my prayers distill this teeming world into a barren
rock beneath a cold sun; empty the universe o' high stars, let
black night come down.

*The Lights dim to a single Spot on him.*

Now mind casn't be soiled by human speech, body by human
touch all senses pure, fountain-leap t' God. *(Odoevsky's
screams fade)* Look on 't now. Gone. All sound and movement gone in darkness. Earth's made wondirly new, un-
slimed by men. Only in this well-willed solitude wi'out
people t' dyke 't back canst my love flow free. Only in this
new emptied planet canst I submit t' Thy will, Lord. Only
here, alone, wi' a few simple tools — nails, hammer, axe,
canst I raise a tabernacle t' Thy glory and find my true peace,
*aaaarrr.*

*He screams in terror as he sees in a Spot, Wings Left, a
giant six-foot* **Nail** *with two legs, dashing in, pursued by a
seven-foot* **Hammer.** *The terrified* **Ivan** *tries to scramble away
but the demented* **Hammer** *gives chase and strikes him down,
before vanishing into the darkness Up Stage after the* **Nail.**

*A Second Spot up immediately Wings Right as a seven-
foot* **Tree** *rushes in chased by a giant* **Axe** *with legs. Seeing*
**Ivan** *crouching in his Spot, Down Stage Left, the* **Axe** *attacks
him viciously before racing after the frightened* **Tree** *and
exiting in the darkness Up Stage. Gasping with terror,* **Ivan**
*raises himself.*

**Ivan:** The beams 're falling! Now *things* are in conspiracy
'gainst me. Objects show their natural hatred, a thousand
doors open t' death. I'm surrounded by assassins! Knives leap
at my back, stones cleif wide 'neath my feet, pillows press
themselves down on my face, sleeptide. Sea, sky, earth all
fellone nature's poised f' treachery. I'm Cain-marked! Who
canst save me?!

*A fanfare and Lights slowly up on* **Ivan** *crouching Down*

*Stage Left and* **Odoevsky** *still impaled Stage Right as* **Tsar Semeon Bekbulatovich** *enters through the archway Up Stage Centre, wearing a stiff, richly embroidered robe, crown, heavy imperial collar and jewelled crucifix round his neck. He carries a long staff, surmounted by a gold globe and cross and tipped with an iron point as an unseen* **Herald** *intones:*

**Herald's Voice:** By the Almighty power o' God and the uncomprehensible Holy Trinity, bow heads f' Tsar Semeon Bekbulatovich, Emperor o' All Russia, Great Duke o' Volidemer, Muscovy and Novograde in the Nether Countries, Emperor o' Cassan and Astrachan, Lord o' Piskie and all the North Coast, Great Duke o' Smolenski, Tverski, Sibieriski and many others including Charnogoski, Rizariski and Volodski, in this the year o' Our Lord God 1572 ensuring.

**Odoevsky** *(screaming)*: Arrrrrrhhh.

**Ivan** *(screaming)*: Arrrrrrhhh.

**Semeon** *(screaming)*: Arrrrrrhhh.

  **Semeon** *abruptly rushes Stage Left, falls on his knees and places his neck on the executioner's block.*

Lop. Jag. Strike. Disjoin this neck. Only rid me o' my cankered crown, if my head falls too what o' 't? Christ's crown o' thorns was goosefeathers compared t' mine. I want release. I betray myself. I wasn't garred t' command but obey, born t' nibble the earth not bestride 't. I'm one o' nature's natural crawlers. I long t' submit.

**Ivan:** Then submit t' thy haltane destiny o' being Tsar.

**Semeon:** I carry stones and on those stones more stones and on the topmost stone another pile o' stones.

**Ivan:** These're years o'triumph. Muscovy's brasted the Crimean Tartars i' the East and Sigsmund Augustus i' the West. Soon we'll secure Livonia, recover Kiev and the Ukraine and seize that longed-for gateway t' the Baltic Sea. We grow and the world trembles.

**Semeon:** Wi' laughter. I turn my back and they gwof 't behind white hands, smile in ounces. My crouching soul hears 'em tell the story o' how an empty carriage drove up t' the Great Palace and I stepped out.

**Ivan** *(pointing at* **Odoevsky***)*: Laugh! Gowf 't I say.

  **Odoevsky** *groans.*

He doesn't laugh. He shakes and splits his sides but not wi' laughter. None gowf 't in God's presence, nor 'afore a Tsar who carries death i' his fingers.

**Semeon** *(taking off his crown)*: I'm not fitted t' rule, knees ache t' bend. Take my crown and I'll take thy place. I'm too dearch humble t' be a Tsar, you too prideful t' be a priest.

**Ivan:** I'll polt down my pride, swallow 't whole; till eyes no longer gauge the distance, mind no longer decides its lines. I strive t' join angelic hosts not sit cold-arsed on golden thrones.

    **Semeon** *thrusts the crown at him.*

**Semeon:** Let me be free! Take 't I say.

**Ivan:** Let me crawl t' salvation! Keep 't I beg.

    *Still on his knees he backs away from the crown as* **Semeon** *puts it on the executioner's block and pursues him frantically, also on his knees.*

**Semeon:** Only save me!

**Ivan:** Only let me be saved!

**Odoevsky** *(screaming):* Uuuuuuuuhhrr eeee

    **Ivan** *and* **Semeon** *stop their crawling and look up to see the bearded* **Vaska Shibanov** *who has just come in Up Stage Centre, staring down at them, dressed in long, fur-trimmed robes and carrying a sealed letter.* **Semeon** *pulls himself upright with the aid of his staff. He gestures with it to* **Shibanov,** *who opens the letter while* **Ivan** *remains kneeling.*

**Shibanov:** Sire, 'tis from the traitor-prince, Andrey Kurbsky o' Kurel. *(he reads)* 'Behold O Tsar. You call me traitor. Was King David such, forced by Saul's wrath t' flee and war 't 'gainst Judah? What gulf o' madness you plunge Holy Russia, what virtuous women defiled, drunken atrocities committed, loyal subjects lacerated wi' divers deaths wi'out justice or judgement . . .'

**Ivan:** *Arrrrgggrr.*

    *He springs up with a cry of rage, tears off his heavy cross and hits* **Semeon** *with it, sending him sprawling.*

Sonkar! Don't just stand there doe-eyed, pissin' milk! *(he grabs* **Semeon**'s *staff)* You ha' authority's staff, cross and globe tipped wi' iron. Use 't. *Dramatize!* Dramatize so's men'll 'member your reply, not a traitor's curses. Words fade, this never!

*He brings down staff, spearing* **Shibanov**'s *right foot to the floor.*

Again. Read 't again. This time wi' feeling.

*He leans heavily on the staff as* **Shibanov** *re-reads the letter, blood pouring from his foot. His voice is calm, but his body twists grotesquely in pain.*

**Shibanov** *(reads)*: 'Behold O Tsar. You call me traitor. Was King David such forced by Saul's wrath t' flee t' war 't 'gainst Judah? What gulf o' madness you plunge Holy Russia, what virtuous women defiled, drunken atrocities committed, loyal lacerated wi' divers deaths wi'out justice or judgement . . .'

**Ivan** *jabs the staff down harder.*

**Ivan:** Doest the iron bite 't? Doest the point impierce 't? Whose hand thrusts 't down? Who holes 't, spouts 't, garrs 't bleed?

**Shibanov:** You, Sire.

**Ivan:** Who am I?

**Shibanov:** Ivan Vasivitch, grandson o' Ivan the Great, son o' Elana Glinskaya and Vasily III, Emperor o' All the Russias — Tsar Ivan IV.

**Ivan:** Known as?

**Shibanov:** Ivan the Terrible.

**Ivan** *rips back his cowl and habit to reveal the familiar hook nose, long hair and beard. He snatches the letter, leaving the staff still spearing* **Shivanov**'s *foot to the floor.*

**Ivan:** I loved Kurbsky close. He fought at my side when I 'ssaulted Kazan's walls, hacked through its streets, clotted wi' Tartar dead. Yet he frighted, fled, foreswore, led foreign armies 'gainst me, God's anointed Tsar. Lucifer's stinkard! Let his tongue hang ripe. *(he reads)* '. . . women defiled . . . atrocities . . . subjects lacerated wi' divers deaths . . .' A sovereign casn't be judged 'cause he casn't recognise a superior: he's sovereign. Destroy me but never judge me, saying I caused divers deaths wi'out justice or judgement. *(he rushes to* **Odoevsky***)* Tell 'em how as Tsar I've slaughtered wi'out justice but never wi'out judgement.

**Odoevsky** *(screaming)*: *Eeeeeeeee.*

**Ivan:** There, Prince Odoevsky takes my point. I kill cold. A computed 120,000 grimed t' death, yold t' the sword. All

were about t' betray me, there's nothing too cowardly f' 'em
t' ha' the courage t' do. I knew their certain guilt by a certain
sweating 'tween my fingers, *here, here.* I've never lacked
judgement dealing final death, only wi' winning eternal life.
    *He crosses to* **Semeon.**
I made you Tsar whilst I took the name Ivan Moskovsky and
retired t' pray. F' two years I've monk'd 't humble, you've
throned 't mightily. You've eaten o' the royal jelly — raise
your hand Semeon, the ground slits, sky darkens. Yet still
you've no meteors in you, no orbs, fire, bellows. The smiling
babe smothers a bird i' its hand in joy at finding a creature
weaker than itself. All men're born despots 'cept you. You've
no taste for power. Tisn't natural!

**Semeon** *(rising):* Sire, you gave me staff, Monomachus's crown
and the sacred name o' Tsar after the Assyrian and
Babylonian kings, leaving thyself self-naked. Yet in peace
and war governance is still thine. The Council o' the Zemsky
Sorbor and Commanders o' your Armies still look t' thee f'
orders.

**Ivan:** Despite my orders. I order 'em t' disobey me, 'tis the only
order they disobey. Yet see how they'll jump t' swim seas o'
vomit, wade nostril-deep through snot rivers, sleer wives and
daughters, condemn their souls t' Hellpit on my orders. I
gelt, spike, gut, serve 'em roasted and they still crake 'God
save our one true Tsar!' as if ordered.

**Odoevsky** *(screaming feebly):* *Eeeeerrr rrrrrrhh uuuuuukkk.*

**Ivan:** Hear 't, 'tis the voice o' the people aching to obey.

**Semeon:** 'Cause they know my lion's skin's out at the elbows.
Let me go back t' Tver and be crowned Tsar o' drunkards, eat
sweetmeats on Sunday, catch sturgeon and beadle fish 'afore
the rivers ice, sleep on my wife's belly, both eyes closed. I'll
've friends t' press about me daily there.

**Ivan:** Whilst here they only come close, the better t' cut throats
at parting. Who? When? Where? How? This is centipede
country. I don't ha' t' make myself understood, you ha' t'
understand what I ha' t' say. *(to* **Shibanov)** Why're you
standing there watching?!

**Shibanov:** 'Cause my foot's pinned t' the floor, Sire.

**Ivan:** Oh that's glib. Why doesn't unpin thyself then, Master

Glib?

**Shibanov:** You've not given permission, Sire.

**Ivan:** Ah, glibber yet! *(he pulls* **Shibanov***'s beard)* Using the cloak o' obediency t' hide dumb insolence. Every breath you take's an insult 't God. I'll purge the air o' the air you breathe. Lies, ants' nests o' lies, rotting the fabric! No wonder I grow eccentric.

**Shibanov:** What can I do, Sire?

**Ivan:** 'Tis a question I've been asking myself f' years. *(he pushes the staff down harder)* Answer me this: I've tried t' un-Tsar my flesh, thrust my immortal soul at hazard, debauched, orgied, tyrannized, formed my dog-headed guards, my Opritchnina, and sleered whole populations at a whim, 1,500 an hour, women and children first: 'Follow me spare none!' Yet why doest still kneel and call this cruked carcass Tsar, Father o' All?

**Shibanov:** You're God's anointed. You've the authority o' blood, Sire, authority that rests on the past. It gi'es our world a permanence which men need, being the most unstable and futile creatures i' the Universe. You gi'e us certainty Sire, which is better than goodness.

**Ivan** A damn thinker! Am I t' be spared nothing?

**Shibanov:** 'Tis true, Sire, once I could define the true metaphysic as mastering reality and annihilating the phantoms engendered by brute superstition.

**Ivan:** Unintelligible solutions t' insoluble problems. Sapless talk.

**Shibanov:** But when I came t' court Sire, I bought pomade t' make my hair fall out, terrified I'd look too young and seem t' have ideas. F' I acknowledge there's no place f' philosophy or morality here, Sire, they're at best mere amusements t' divert a ruler's idle moments 'tween the business o' ruling. In truth, Aristotle played pimp at Alexander's court also.

**Ivan:** What good's Aristotle and his ilk t' me. He could only reason, I *know*.

**Semeon:** Then know, Sire, I long t' sink back into obscurity, pass into mist, melt 't wi' the mass o' men.

**Ivan:** I too thirst t' be unknown, steal out o' history, other men's dreams. They use me!

**Semeon** *(tearing off his clothes)*: I casn't wear these traps t' hide my covering o' worms. I'm the son o' Adam as Adam is o' dust. God's excrement. I'm miserable, damned, worse than damned — ordinary!

**Ivan:** Semeon, Semeon, love thyself. 'Tis the only affection you can rely on.

*Semeon has taken off his shirt and breeches and stands forlornly in his dirty underwear.*

**Semeon:** Leuk, leuk. *(he slaps his face)* Wan-visaged, blubber-lipped. *(he slaps his stomach)* One bausey hanging gutsack. *(he slaps his arms)* And these arms. Can these spongy arms crest a world, these flabbed and farsey legs stride 't? Is this a body men bow to?

**Ivan:** They'll bow t' any crippled yole gi'en half the chance. All gods aren't Grecian.

*He rips off his habit and stands in hairshirt and filthy loincloth.*

There's no bloom on my lyre, no summer left in me.

**Semeon:** But, Sire, you *loom*. Exposed t' the heights I shrink and tremble in the cold. *(he makes himself small)*

**Ivan:** Loom? *(he too makes himself small)* I'm God's flea, placed on Holy Russia's bovine hide t' sting and suck 't.

**Semeon:** Then I'm less: a flea's flea, the flea in the flea's gut, thy flea, Sire.

*Both men are now crouching on their haunches.*

**Ivan:** I'll make th'e swell. As the Lord said t' Peter; 'Arise, kill, eat' so fleas nee bl od- neals.

*He gestu res and **Semeon** crosses with him, legs still bent, to **Odoevsky**; they crouch on either side of him.*

You'll ha' more than mere traps. I'll gi' you the power t' choose, t' judge when a man's ready f' judgement. Legs!

*He takes hold of **Odoevsky**'s weighted right leg, **Semeon** his left.*

Now ring dem bells! I say ring dem bells!

*They pull on **Odoevsky**'s legs. There is a great jangling of bells as the stake rips up into the victim's body and **Ivan** and **Shibanov** are spattered with blood.*

**Odoevsky** *(screaming)*: Eeeeeeeekkkk God save the Tsar!

*He slumps forward, dead. **Ivan** and **Semeon** straighten up.*

**Ivan:** Ah God was near us then. F' he's the author o' all punishment. Didst feel His presence? Didst feel His wellstreams showering us wi' His grace?

*He wipes the blood from his face and licks it off his fingers.* Taste the smart o' 't, Christ's precious blood, blessed Sacrament. I'll gi' thee the right t' play butcher, Semeon. Divide those t' be slaughtered from those fit f' breeding according t' age, weight and quality. T' choose those t' be hung on hooks, those t' end face down on a slab, quartered. I'll gi' thee the true authority o' death.

**Semeon:** I don't want 't, Sire, like quicksilver 'twill turn poison, card into my bones. I'd rather live pale, die trembling. Oh mother, mother take me back! Jus' gi' me peace, Sire, e'en if 'tis only a piece o' the grave. You canst ring my bells too, send me into that cold merk, at least there'll be friendly shadows there. Ring my bells, Sire, 'twill be a mercy. Ring 'em. Ring 'em. Ring dem bells.

*As the Lights dim slowly,* **Semeon** *seems to be pulled backwards across the stage.* **Ivan** *tenses, trying with a tremendous effort of will to force him to remain.*

**Ivan:** I casn't hold you. You've no love o' killing, no fear o' death. You slip . . . Your weakness too strong f' my strength. Stay. From heart-root I command. Stay. HOLD . . . HOLD.

*But* **Semeon** *is pulled back to be spread-eagled against a section of the courtyard wall Up Stage Left, which has turned spongy. He is remorselessly sucked into it and swallowed up, finally vanishing from sight. It is as if he had never been.*

*The Lights have faded down to a Spot on* **Ivan** *and* **Shibanov.**

**Ivan:** He's taken my salvation wi' him. I renounced my maggotteeming acts o' will, brought obedience t' my soul. Now the panic world beats at my gate again.

*Distant thunder of an approaching storm.*

Gone the swallow's glide, yesterday's signs. *(he puts on* **Semeon**'s *coat)* I'm Prince of Destruction once more.

*Repeated thunder as he paces round* **Shibanov.**

I sleer men wi' fire from my third eye which cans't admit the light. Mind turns slow elipses i' the mire, open t' the night. 'T rhymes! 'T rhymes! Oh why doesn't life leave me alone?!

*(he stops pacing)* Why're you moving round in a circle like
that?

**Shibanov:** My foot's still nailed t' the floor, Sire.

**Ivan** *(pulling out the staff)*: Must I do everything? Gi' me your
report on my new system o' provincial Governors.

**Shibanov:** It has one defect Sire. Your Governors remain
unpaid. Thus they're easily corrupted and hated f' 't.

**Ivan:** Good. Hatred's this world's fulcrum. It moves men more
easily than luif or honour. Afore there was no appeal 'gainst a
Governor's ordinances. Now the people canst come t' me f'
redress. Leuk, now like a lodestone I draw in more polary
power. 'Tis nature's iron law: those that have shall be gi'en.
Power's sucked into this magnetized centre, where I stand.

*He thrusts his staff into the air as a lightning conductor: a
bolt of lightning strikes it and he judders violently: more
follow and by their light we see* **Odoevsky** *has now become a
skeleton on the stake and* **Ivan** *and* **Shibanov** *visibly growing
bent and old.*

In time I make all things flow t' the centre; all church
property secularized; all army commissions sanctioned by me
alone; all land registered so I know whose land t' take, whose
t' add t'.

*He passes a hand over his hair and beard: they turn grey.*

Thus power converges t' a point behind my eyes. By laws
magnetical. I've emptied the years.

*The lightning fades away; Lights come up slowly.*

And I'm left, soul skoldered black. I move little, else my
body shatter into pieces and the lightning spill out. I am
become a scourging rod, a roseless thorn.

**Shibanov:** No, you're the Breath o' our Nostrils, our Heart and
Head, our Shorn Lamb.

**Ivan:** Truly is that truth? Real truth?

**Shibanov:** I canst only speak the Tsar's truth Sire, not real truth,
truth's truth. Seneca spoke truth's truth and was razored f' 't;
Socrates hemlocked. And they were o' the best. Matchless
minds, bright intelligences grovel afore any dumb brute
bringing slow death. I know I was once one o' that fair
company. I had ethics.

**Ivan:** I don't care if you had carbuncles. Tell me truth's truth.

**Shibanov:** Sire, humanity can progress but I don't: I die.

**Ivan:** Prince Reprin once spake truth's truth t' my face.

**Shibanov:** I'd like t' meet him, Sire, and shake his hand.

**Ivan:** I'm not going t' the trouble o' having him dug up jus' so you canst shake his hand.

**Shibanov:** 'Tis true, Sire, truth must be buried grave-deep else we all wake naked from our dreams.

**Ivan:** No, I heard 't once years past, truth's truth, God's truth. When I was Abbot Ivan Moskovsky and Semeon Bekbulatovich was Tsar. I listened, God spake. I obeyed, God acted. All my wars were victorious then. I agonized o'er my sins but every day I knew the miracle o' Jesus walking on the waters as I walked through life wi'out drowning. Nothing buoys me up now. My wars turn t' defeats. My robes, my staff, age-old iniquities pull me low. I haven't even a gukkish, oyster-eyed Semeon t' take the burden. I crake again: "Who can save me?!"

**Herald's Voice:** By the Almighty power o' God and the Holy Trinity in this the year o' Our Lord 1581, bow heads f' the Tsarevitch, Ivan, Alexei, Kalita, Vasily, Mikhail, eldest son o' our Blessed Tsar, Ivan IV and sole heir t' the crown o' Monomach and all the lands and dignities o' the title o' Tsar.

*Lights now full up as the* **Tsarevitch** *enters, knocking against the archway Up Stage Centre in his bull-like rush. Dressed in bulky sable-trimmed top coat and shining boots, his gloved hands glitter with rings.* **Odoevsky**'s *skeleton gleams on the stake Stage Right, as the* **Tsarevitch** *pauses momentarily to stare at the* **Tsar**'s *crown on the execution block, before falling on one knee in front of* **Ivan**. *The* **Tsar** *gestures to him and he rises quickly.*

**Tsarevitch:** The Lithuanians besiege Pskov. Radzivill advances eastward t' the Volga. The Swedes 've taken Narva, Ivangorad, Koporie and Yam. The Poles under Stephan Batory demand the surrender o' the whole o' Livonia together wi' Sebezh and 400,000 crowns.

**Ivan:** *Arrrrgggggrrrr (crying in rage he slams down his staff, pinning* **Shibanov**'s *left foot to the floor)* What didst he say?!

*As* **Ivan** *presses down on the staff,* **Shibanov** *again answers in a calm voice whilst his body jerks in pain and the*

**Tsarevitch** *strides about furiously, smashing holes in the wall with his fists.*

**Shibanov:** The Lithuanians besiege Pskov. Radzivill advances eastward t' the Volga. The Swedes 've taken Narva, Ivangorad, Koporie, and Yam. The Poles under Stephen Batory demand the surrender o' the whole o' Livonia together wi' Sebezh and 400,000 crowns.

**Tsarevitch:** Attack! Attack! When Batory first besieged Pskov I craked: 'Attack! Attack!' Sound drums, trumpets, scythe him wi' one blow.

**Ivan:** Ne'er risk all on a single battle. Thus Darius the Persian was destroyed at Arbela and Sinsharishkum the Assyrian at Nineveh, and their Empires down wi' them.

**Tsarevitch:** So you wait, wait, wait, wait.

*Head down, he charges against the wall. Hitting it with a resounding thud, he merely lets out a short, stunned grunt, 'ugg'.*

**Ivan:** Our commanders casn't be trusted. Prince Kurbsky and the rest betrayed us afore in the midst o' battle.

**Tsarevitch:** Then gi' me command. And I'll gi' thee back Narva, Ivangorad, Koporie and Yam. I'll gi' thee all Livonia and the Baltic seaboard you dream o'. I'll gi' thee victory.

**Ivan:** Or death. Ah my cluster-balled bull, carnage casn't be limited t' the common people. Canades and sharp steel're the only true levellers. They make blue blood spout as easily as red. I'll see you come back t' me on four men's shoulders: the dead commander o' a defeated army.

**Tsarevitch:** Or worse — the live commander o' a victorious one, ugg. *(he batters his head against the wall)* You fear my force, *ugg.* Steal my inheritance. Bury me deep. Crush the corn in the blade, *ugg.* All work against me!

**Ivan:** At your best son I'm better. But at times you remind me o' me when I was young. O' course you're not as suspicious as I was; not as devious, malignant, crabbyt. You don't inspire fear as I did. You haven't the ranclid cruelty I had or the forky strength t' eat, drink, lech or shit bricks like I used to. But in *some* ways you remind me o' me.

**Tsarevitch:** I want t' thrust. Let me thrust!

**Ivan:** I've made you sole heir and successor t' the whole. Left your younger brother Feodor, but fourteen towns. You've nothing to fear, 'tas been written down and witnessed.

**Tsarevitch** *(repeatedly throwing himself headfirst against the wall)*: Now, *ugg!* Now, *ugg!* Not later, *ugg!* I want 't now, *ugg!*

**Ivan:** Enjoy youth's last airy juices. Feel your testicles 're the sun and the moon whilst you still can. You're not ready t' take up the burden o' ruling. You'll find thyself chewing more than you've bitten off.

**Tsarevitch:** My neck-veins're hemp ropes. I paw the ground. Gore air. Shibanov confirm the truth, I'm ready.

**Shibanov:** You're ready, Sire.

**Ivan:** Shibanov confirm the truth, he's not.

**Shibanov:** He's not ready, Sire. Anyone who doesn't contradict himself's a dogmatist. Sires, I twist in the wind. You're my now and future Tsars. I can cringe, lick boots wi' a sycophant's rankling tongue and in extremis loose tiny, papier-mâché farts. But I casn't speak truth that's true f' you both. As a loyal, two-faced courtier Sires, I mustn't be pinned down.

**Tsarevitch:** Pinned? I'll ha' thee staked! I've been shaped t' rule. Schooled and groomed f' authority. Saw my first execution when I was three, handled the instruments o' justice, whips, brands, blocks, two years later. Sleered a traitor wi' my own hand when I was thirteen and slit open my close friend Vishavoty on mere suspicion on my coming o' age. You casn't say I'm not fitted t' take thy place, rule in God's name, not pity-purged.

**Ivan:** You're pity-purged but not passion-purged. There's too much anger in you, not 'nough hate. 'Tis a failing o' the young. Anger's a honey that soon loses its perfume, hate stinks forever.

**Tsarevitch:** I hate. F' love o' Christ I hate, *ugg. (he rams the wall with his head)* Heaven casn't contain my hate. Send f' the scalpers, *ugg!* I hate!

**Ivan:** Not 'nough t' sustain the terror needed t' root out disobedience. There canst be no rule wi'out terror. No opinion's innocent, therefore all opinions must be guilty. Like a steed wi'out a bridle so is a realm wi'out terror. The people hunger f' 't.

**Tsarevitch:** I carry 't in my hands. BOLTS. BOLTS.

**Ivan:** Not 'nough, son. 'Tis easy t' bring one man t' obedience, most're happiest on their knees. Some need only an imperious look t' kiss royal arses, others the symbols o' Cross and Crown, still others, authority's true reality — gnout and gallows. One man's trembling carcass's small but Holy Russia stretches from Smolensk t' beyond the River Ob, from Kola in the Arctic North down almost t' the Azovian Sea. T' bring this vastness t' obedience needs terror on an equal scale and I see no sign you're equal t' it yet.

**Tsarevitch:** Novogrod!

**Shibanov** (*imitating a funeral bell*): B-O-N-G...B-O-N-G...

**Tsarevitch:** I was wi' you at Novogrod.

**Ivan:** Their princes schemed t' betray me, join Kurbsky, found proof behind the ikon, Novogrod tholed like Moab like Babylon, the Lord said, 'Break their bones as the lion breaks the lambs, gar their skins black, skewer up their women, dash their babes 'gainst the stones o' Novogrod!'

**Tsarevitch:** So we sleered bloody every living thing *twang, swishh, urr.* Foxes, moles, lap-wings, bears.

**Ivan:** They wouldst've told Novogrod o' our coming.

**Tsarevitch:** And at the welcoming banquet men crouched outside wi' cleavers waiting f' your cry.

**Ivan:** *Arrrrgggrrr.*

*He slowly falls on his knees.*

**Shibanov:** B-O-N-G . . . B-O-N-G . . .

**Tsarevitch:** Then iron hooks pierced soft eyeballs, hot needles levered nails from broken fingers. Bellies slit wide, holes f' faces sticky round the edges and all this meat bleeding as the Priest called out the names o' the dead.

    **Shibanov** *takes out a rolled parchment and chants a roll-call of the dead as* **Ivan** *lies spreadeagled on the ground. Rows of white cardboard faces appear above the wall: their childlike outlines are drawn in black with dots for eyes and downward curves for mouths.*

**Shibanov** *(chanting)*: Remember Oh Lord the souls o' Thy servants o' Novogrod. Remember Pimen High Lord o'

Novogrod, known in this world as Procopy Cherny. Remember Kazarin and his two sons, Ishuk and Bogdan. Remember Bakhmet, Michael, Tryhon. Remember Sumork and his wife, Nechay and his wife, Nezhdan and his wife. Remember the twelve hundred members o' the Houses o' Ivanov and Staritsky whose names're known t' Thee Lord . . .

**Tsarevitch:** Remember those families flung o'er the Volkhov Bridge bound together so's not t' be parted e'en in death, and those that floated, piked, i' the river flooded wi' their blood.

**Shibanov** *(chanting)*: Their names're known t'Thee Oh Lord. Remember Prince Vladimir, Prince Nikita, Prince Boris. Remember the three thousand and eight clerks and the twenty thousand ordinary men whose names're known t' thee Oh Lord. Remember Oh Lord the souls o' sixty thousand o' thy servants who died afore their hour sounded in Novogrod . . .

**Tsarevitch:** Corpses stacked in piles, mounds of frozen entrails, charred torsos, splintered bones, heads blown open, brains out, pink hemispheres lying separate in the snow.

**Ivan:** We're all born t' live and die langsum, wake and sleep i' terror. The Golden Fleece they sing o' is a matted lump o' fur. Oh Lord I casn't think o' all the suffering in the world . . . so I don't.

*He gets up briskly, the cardboard faces disappear from the top of the wall.*

God sees no violent deaths. A steel blade 'cross a bare throat is jus' one more infirmity. 'Tis no worse t' end wi' a sword i' the intestines than a cancer growth; better the small dagger than the large goiter. What difference if sixty thousand die natural, scattered across the Urals in a day, or unnatural i' a city called Novogrod. We re-multiply. A quick thrust 'tween the shoulder blades takes us out, a quick thrust 'tween the thighs brings us in. All's in heavenly balance.

**Tsarevitch:** And I was not found wanting when I weighed in wi' thee at Novogrod. I learned there the scale o' terror needed t' rule an empire.

**Ivan:** But only through your eyes. I sucked terror warm from my mother's milk. My childhood days were strewned wi' knives. I was old very young. When Prince Shiusky ruled f' me as Regent he'd sprawl on the royal bed and spit pomegranate seeds into my face. God's chosen face! I quaked so, my breeches steamed. He couldst've poisoned me, sleered me bloody in some dark corner. But I survived. Made myself invisible, changed my shape like Volga Vseslavich. The country had no centre till I held and craked: 'Who'll kill him f' me?' They threw Shiusky t' the dogs but I'd known terror. 'Tis why I can use 't now, 'cause once my own bones melted; once I trembled.

**Tsarevitch:** Only once? I melt and tremble daily. I'm the son o' Ivan the Terrible.

**Ivan:** But you're my joy, my Easter bells, Anastasia's child, as sweet t' me as muscadin and eggs. Though six came after, your mother was my first and one true wife. She smiled roses. Then I never feared death only life wi'out her. 'Tis why we're closer yet than father and son. Oh how we've pranked 't, two young blades together. *(chuckling)* 'Member when our fool Dukuchay quipped 'In Holy Russia we never hang a man wi' a moustache. We use a rope.'

**Tsarevitch:** I poured hot soup on his head and you daggered him.

**Ivan:** And he fell flat as his joke. I was too rough, but he did once say that everything I touched turned t' rigor-mortis.

**Tsarevitch** *(laughing)*: And what o' that Festival o' St. Servius when you stripped a dozen court ladies bitch-naked and threw five bushel-loads o' peas at 'em.

**Ivan** *(laughing)*: Laugh, I thought I'd never dry my breeches. How their plump bubbies bobbed as they crawled round the floor picking 'em up. Oh what women we've shared boy, what strumpets, whores, two-roubled hacksters.

**Tsarevitch:** What lickerous-eyed plovers, what wagtails tripping 't soft.

**Ivan:** What trugs bearing their bellies out magestical.

**Tsarevitch:** What cheeks, what arses, shaming milk and cream.

**Ivan:** What legs and thighs shimmering as they danced.

Ivan *and* Tsarevitch *stamp and clap rhythmically as they begin to dance 'The Cosaques'.*

**Tsarevitch:** Dance Shibanov. Are you ill?

**Ivan:** Don't stand there thinking — when a man's too dull t' dance he calls himself a thinker. Dance Shibanov! Dance!

**Shibanov:** I casn't, Sire, my foot's still pinned t' the floor.

**Ivan:** Oh glib! I've warned you afore about 't. Release thyself, and *dance*!

**Shibanov** *pulls out the staff and hobbles over to them. Accompanied by an unseen company clapping and stamping,* **Ivan** *and the* **Tsarevitch** *dance side by side, Cossack style, with legs bent and arms linked together. Quickly giving up trying to stamp his crippled feet,* **Shibanov** *whirls the staff round his head and leaps as they gather momentum.* **Ivan** *and the* **Tsarevitch** *jump and écarte with joyful cries. They spin round, always linked together, whilst* **Shibanov,** *using the staff for leverage, vaults high behind them. The stamping and clapping grows louder and faster as the dance reaches its climax with all three men soaring into the air with tremendous shouts.*

*They finally collapse, exhausted.* **Ivan** *and the* **Tsarevitch** *haul each other to their feet embracing and laughing.*

**Ivan:** My leming lufson boy. I leif you more than life.

**Tsarevitch:** Then let me swallow the sun. Yold the crown.

**Ivan** *takes his staff from* **Shibanov,** *who is hobbling about clutching first his right foot then his left.*

**Ivan:** It crushes. I'm crumped wi' power's pain.

**Tsarevitch:** T' please the poor, the rich say money doesn't bring happiness. Oh but it helps. It helps! T' please the powerless, the powerful say power doesn't bring joy. Oh but 't does. It does! Riding roughshod daily's the key to inner health. This world's a world o' power and those out o' power're out o' this world. Yold the crown.

**Ivan:** Sweet chuck, monsters thring in me. I thraward in merk. I suffer. Shibanov knows.

**Shibanov:** True you suffer, Sire.

**Tsarevitch:** You lie, your lips're moving!

**Shibanov:** True, you couldst say that too, Sire.

**Ivan** *(crossing quickly to skeleton)*: I suffer! Odoevsky knows. Tell 'em.

**Odoevsky's Skeleton** *(screaming)*: *Eeeeeeeee — aarrrrrhhh*

**Ivan:** They don't write songs like that anymore. *(he clutches his* *throat and struggles)* Root it out! . . . I've tried t' yold the crown but 't sticks like Nessor's shirt that sleered great Hercules. In 1543 I let my uncles Yuri and Michael Glimsky rule whilst I drank and hunted bear. They broke and betrayed me and Holy Russia. Then my tight-conscienced priest, Sylvester, ruled in my name. And when I lay baisted he too broke and betrayed me and Holy Russia. Adashev, Makary, Kuryatev, Basmanov, Bekbulatovich ruled f' me in their turn and turned wolsome in a day, whemmed and broke in a night.

**Tsarevitch:** 'Tis why you chose such hollow frekes. You gi' your power away only t' clip t' closer. You keep 't from me now, certain I'll ne'er break and gi' 't back.

**Ivan:** I keep it t' save you.

**Tsarevitch:** T' condemn me. You worship a God who had his only begot son ramed bloody.

**Ivan:** Out o' love.

**Tsarevitch:** Fathers must be eaten 'live by their sons. You keep 't from me out o' hatred.

**Ivan:** Out o' love, love.

**Tsarevitch:** You're a corpse, go be embalmed in Egypt. You keep 't from me out o' fear.

**Ivan:** Out o' love, love.

**Tsarevitch:** Out o' fear o' dying, old man.

**Ivan:** Love, love, *love*!

**Tsarevitch:** Mine, mine, *mine*!

*He bends to snatch the crown from the block.*

**Ivan:** Arrrrrggghhh.

**Ivan** *hits him with the iron tip of the staff. As he falls,* **Ivan** *continues spearing him in rage.*

**Ivan:** Love! Love! Only love!

*The* **Tsarevitch** *crashes down and lies still.* **Shibanov** *approaches fearfully and bends down to examine him.*

**Ivan:** Vérité, vérité Shibanov. Truth's true.

**Shibanov:** In truth Sire, though I've tried t' avoid 't all my life, now there's but one truth; truth's truth and Tsar truth merge. Your son's dead.

*It begins to snow.*

**Ivan:** Drown me, you tears. Suffering beyond the reach o' language. *KKK arrrxx ccrrrrr aaaaakk AAAARRR*

*He sings the air 'Men Tiranne' from Gluck's 'Orfeo and Eurydice'.*

'Men tiranne ah, voi sareste, al mio pianoto, al mio lamento, Se provaste un sol momento, Cosa sia languir d'amor, Se provaste un sol momento, Cosa sia languir d'amor Cosa sia languir d'amor.' Shibanov, conclude the peace treaty wi' the Polish Batory. We cede the whole o' Livonia together wi' Polotsk and Velizh but no compensation, no Esthonian ports and all Muscovite lands captured t' be restored. My dream o' a Baltic seaboard's lost. But we gain new conquered territory beyond the Urals. Send thanks t' our vassals, the Strogonovs f' the defeat o' the Siberian Khanate and capture o' his capital, Isker. Order Prince Bolkhovsky t' proceed there wi' five hundred men and receive the Tsardom o' Siberia on our behalf. Re-open trade negotiations wi' Elizabeth o' England and . . .

*Lights Fade to a Spot on him in the snow as he sings the air 'Chiamo Il Mio Ben Cosi' from 'Orfeo and Eurydice'.*

'Chiamo il mio ben cosi, Quando si monstra il di, Quando s'asconde Quando s'asconde. Ma, oh vano mio dolor; L'idolo del mio cor, Non mi risponde, Non mi risponde, No mi risponde!' I confessed t' the Council I cut the cedar, slew my heir. 'Choose another Tsar,' I craked. But they answered 'We want only you as our Tsar gi'en us by God.' So I cried out 'Holy Father, Lord God Almighty, I sleered my son!' 'Me too,' He answered, showing me his mercy, His terrible *mercy*. Who canst save me?!

*Lights slowly up and we see the skeleton and the stake have gone but the crown on the executioner's block remains as a man emerges Up Stage Centre, out of the snow haze. He is dressed in a worn, double-breasted, blue serge suit, starched collar, waistcoat and stainless-steel framed spectacles. He crosses briskly to Ivan and bows slightly.*

**Samael:** The name's Samael . . . Perhaps you know me better as Eden's Prince? The Angel who wrestled with Jacob at Penial, fetched Moses's soul? Ruler of the Fifth Heaven? Truth of the World? The Wind that Stinks?

**Ivan:** Who?

**Samael:** Death. Systemising Death.

**Ivan:** Death? Death?! But you're no carcass o' bones; you carry no scythe!

**Samael:** Bones're what I leave behind. *(he takes out a pocket mirror)* And this small mirror in which every man can see his own death's a better symbol than a scythe. It's true I used to mow down my harvest with that old-fashioned instrument and the phlegmatic calm of a peasant. But with the relentless progress of civilisation I've changed from being a stately angel to an over-worked head-clerk. Vultures can rest gorged on carrion. I can't.

**Ivan:** I don't believe you're Death. You've inkstained fingers, shiny breeches, frayed cuffs. You ride no pale horse.

**Samael:** I'm no longer significant enough for pale horses. I keep accounts, collect and record the depreciations and depletions in those worlds. Each super Nova and dying grain of sand is noted. Debit entries in the ledger, mathematical equations of pain and guilt, nets woven from accrued balances, plus and minus, red and black. In the end all accounts must be closed. It's a matter of good book-keeping; hygiene.

**Ivan** *(falling on his knees):* In nomine Patris et Filii et Spiritus Sanctu.

**Samael:** Imperatorem stantem mori oportet. 'An Emperor should die on his feet.' I appreciate you using a dead tongue but I prefer tomorrow's language today: non-operating deductions, contingent, liabilities, functional obsolescence. This is the end without sequel where everything stops. Give me the crown, then go fall into your grave.

**Ivan:** I casn't endure sunbeams, how canst I endure the brightness o' Him who made the sun? I'm not ready t' meet my God!

**Samael:** Which God's that? Each world has its Yaweths, Shang Tis, Amons, Ras, Indrass, its Creators, Judges, Joves, First-Movers, Bull-Roarers, Fathers of All. One sinks, another rises, the endless series cannot be told. They die too when space and time fade to shadow. Give me the crown.

**Ivan** *(scrambling up):* No 'tis my life.

**Samael:** That's why I want it.

**Ivan:** But I've been thy servant here on earth, as well as God's.

**Samael:** Naturally. We both wish to impose uniformity on all men, you of obedience, I of death. What sets worlds in motion, sends the green shoot thrusting, is the interplay of differences, their attraction and repulsion, sea-tide and heart-beat. We fight life together but you can hardly expect a special dispensation from nature for following your nature.

**Ivan:** But I've loaded your ledger wi' a computed 222,000 dead. That must be worth a week's reprieve, a day, an hour, a minute more! I'm too young t' die and too well-known.

**Samael** *(taking off his glasses and polishing them)*: You made death too personal, arbitrary, a matter of chance: too much like life. In the coming years they'll institutionalize it, take the passion out of killing, turn men into numbers and the slaughter'll be so vast no one mind'll grasp it, no heart'll break 'cause of it. Ah, what an age that'll be. How confidently they'll march on to extinction, not even a memory in the brain of the last crustacean crawling across the empty seas. Happy days. Happy days. Even Death has her dreams. *(he puts his glasses back and looks at his watch)* It's time for final audit. In real time you're in your bedchamber playing chess with Belsky. You take King pawn, I take your crown. End game. Account closed.

**Ivan:** I'll live through all eternity wi' a toothache only let me live!

**Samael:** Ivan, someday the day must come when the day won't.

**Ivan:** No. I cling! I cling!

**Samael:** Birds sit hushed before they fall, lilacs turn brown, men scream and run, believing an exception'll be made: 'Have mercy! Have mercy!' No class! You want to live forever?

**Ivan:** YES!

**Samael:** You can't avoid general deterioration of the total equipment. In time you're no longer economic to operate and you're written off.

**Ivan:** In spite o' death I'll fight!

**Samael:** It's every man's last privilege.

**Ivan:** But couldst I e'er win, subjugate Death as I subjugated men? Did Hercules wi' his strength? Ulysses wi' his wit? Cassus wi' his bags o' gold? Where's Xerxes? Tamberlaine's pomp? Hanno and Hannibal put down like dogs. Pompey's slit. Caesar hacked. Alexander dead. And I'm not feeling so good myself. *(he clutches his throat and struggles wildly)* Root it out! . . . Is't possible t' drive back the days of death again?

**Samael:**  If you've strength enough and will.

> **Ivan** *sticks his staff into the ground and they move apart.* **Samael** *removes his glasses,* **Ivan** *his robe, and both perform elaborate limbering-up exercises, lighten-fast punches and deep breathing. After stiff ceremonial bows, the two circle each other slowly. In the ensuing 'Kung Fu' style fight, amid savage punches and kicks, they never actually touch each other, though we hear the sound of their blows unnaturally loud.*

> **Ivan** *finally catches* **Samael**'s *arm and sweeps his legs from under him. As* **Samael** *falls,* **Ivan** *snaps his arm and chops him savagely across the neck. There is a very loud 'Crack' and* **Samael** *lies still.* **Ivan** *stamps on him in triumph.*

**Ivan:**  I've brasted the Eyeless Monster, slaughtered the Slaughterer o' Gods! *(he takes up his staff and puts on his robe)* Carnage maketh the man. I wax i' pride, wraith, cruelty. Retribution's devoid o' meaning. Here on the border of extinction I canst at last stand sham-less. *(he picks up the crown)* Truth's truth, I glory i' my crown. Oh how fine 'tis t' rule men, melt the stars in hot pride and wi' this staff pierce the side o' Him who made the world. If the Universe 'came a sea o' blood I'd prepare ship and sail her out afore I'd lose the title, TSAR. This's true catharsis, holy purging. Power's sweeter than wine, better than bread. F' truly, what shall 't profit a man if he shall gain his soul and lose the whole world?

> *He puts the crown on his head, the Lights dim down to a Spot on him.*

Everything yields t' my will built upon the clenching hand, the stronger clenching fist. I casn't die, e'en if I die, f' e'en dead, men'll choose t' deck 'emselves in my dust, suck in my dust, eat my deadman's dust. I survive t' hold life in chains. No freedom, divine or human reigns. It rhymes, 't rhymes. I live! I live!

*There is a faint crash in the darkness Up Stage and the sound of objects rolling across the floor.* Ivan *goes rigid. A cry of 'The Tsar is dead' is heard, a funeral bell tolls and a sheet falls from the flies covering him as the Bass sings a funeral ode.*

*The singing fades and* Ivan's *voice is heard over loudspeakers.*

**Ivan's Voice:** We dedicate this statue to the memory of Ivan IV, Tsar of Russia (1530-1584). By defeating the Tartars and conquering Kazan and Astrakhan, he brought a nation to birth. Out of the chaos of warring factions he created the first centralized, multi-national State in the West and proved an inspiration for those who followed. In his person he was like others, in his power, unique, the best educated, most hardworking ruler of his times. The title 'Terrible' was due to an unfortunate mistranslation; it was more accurately 'Ivan the Awe-Inspiring'. He was truly the father of his people, as God is truly the Father of us all.

*The Russian National Anthem is played as the sheet is pulled up and away to reveal* Ivan *in exactly the same position as before, leaning menacingly on his staff. But the Spot is now grey and his hands and face have turned the colour of stone: he has become a statue.*

*Pigeons fly around him. As various National Anthems are played in quick succession, bird-droppings rain down in profusion, bespattering robes and crown.*

*The Spot slowly fades on the befouled figure of* Ivan *to the strains of 'Deutschland Über Alles'. The Anthem continues blaring out of the darkness.*

*END OF PART I*

# Part Two
## AUSCHWITZ

*'Deutschland Über Alles' blares out briefly then fades. Lights up on an office in WVHA Department Amt C (Building) Oranienburg, Berlin, 1942. An eight-foot high filing unit stretches from Up Stage Centre to Up Stage Right. Its shelves are stuffed with grey files. Smaller filing units Stage Right and Left. There is a photograph of Adolf Hitler festooned with holly above the door Up Stage Left and a Nazi flag in a holder Up Stage Right. Nearby a small cupboard. The executioner's block remains Stage Left.*

**Viktor Cranach** *sits at his desk Down Stage Right, dictating a memo to* **Fräulein Else Jost** *whilst an elderly clerk,* **Heinz Stroop,** *replaces a file on the shelves Up Stage Right, and returns to his desk, which is next to* **Fräulein Jost**'s *Down Stage Left.*

**Cranach:** WVHA Amt C1 (Building) to WVHA Amt D1/1. Your reference ADS/MNO our reference EZ/14/102/01. Copies WVHA Amt D IV/2, Amt D IV/4: RSHA OMIII: Reich Ministry PRV 24/6D. Component CP3(m) described in regulation E(5) serving as Class I or Class II appliances and so constructed as to comply with relevant requirements of regulations L2(4) and (6), L8 (4) and (7). Component CP3(m) shall comply with DS 4591/1942 for the purpose of regulation E(5) when not falling in with the definition of Class I and II. There shall be added after reference CP116 Part 2: 1941 the words 'as read with CP 116 Addendum 2: 1942 . . .' Six copies, Fräulein Jost. Despatch immediately. 'Will comply with requirements of regulations L2(4) and (6) L8(4) and (7)!' I don't mince words. I've always believed in calling a CF/83 a CF/83. How dare Amt D1/1 send me an unauthorized, unsigned KG70? Gottleb's trying to cut our throats behind our backs. He's out to destroy this department. *(he chuckles)* 'Component CP3(m) shall comply with DS 4591/1942 for the purposes of Regulation E(5)!' A *hit!* . . . A word with you, Fräulein. As civil servants we must be ready at any time to answer for our administrative actions. Actions based solely on past actions, precedents. Its therefore essential we keep accurate records. That's why everything has to be written down. It's the basis of our existence. Words on paper: Memo to Amt D III; memo to Sturnbannführer Burger, Amt D V etc. etc. Without them we can't function. They tell us what's been done, what we can do, what we have to do and what we are. The civilisation of the Third Reich'll be constructed from the surviving administrative records at Oranienburg, 1942 A.D. Unless of course they've the misfortune to dig up a memorandum of yours, Fräulein. *(he picks up a memo from his desk)* Will you please retype this. I know the first step's hard, but once you've tried it you'll enjoy using commas. Paper size A4 not A3 and the margins should be nine élite character spaces, seven pica on the left and six élite, five pica on the right.

**Else:** Naturally, Herr Cranach, if you look for mistakes you'll find them. *(she takes memo)* My OS 472 states I can do shorthand, typing and filing — but not all simultaneously. We're overworked and underfed. I can't keep Mother and me fit on a daily ration of a hundred and twelve grammes of meat, eight grammes of butter, forty of sugar and shop-signs saying: 'Wreathes and crosses — no potatoes.'

**Cranach:** Please, Fräulein! Remember, where there's a will there's a Gestapo.

**Else:** Coming to work this morning, I stopped to pull in my belt. Some idiot asked me what I was doing. I said, 'Having breakfast.'

**Cranach:** I hear they're experimenting with new dishes. Fried termites from the Upper Volga and grilled agoutis with green peppers.

**Else:** They can't be worse than those dehydrated soups. They actually clean the saucepans while they're cooking.

**Cranach:** It doesn't worry me too much. I've got worms and anything's good enough for them. I can recommend Dr. Schmidt's liver pills to alleviate any deficiency in your diet, Fräulein. They'll stop your hair from falling out too . . . Have you searched this morning yet?

  **Else** *shakes her head and whilst* **Cranach** *continues talking, they all carefully search the office —* **Else** *and* **Stroop** *the filing shelves,* **Cranach** *round his desk.*
Everyone realises, Fräulein, our department has special problems. It's why Obergruppenführer Dr. Kammler had us

upgraded and seconded from the Reich Ministry. We're now dealing with an estimated 74,000 administrative units in the three complexes in Upper Silesia alone, instead of 15,000 of just a year ago, and that's only the beginning. At the moment we still lack staff, equipment, space. You know I've been waiting two months for my own office, *ahh.*

*He finds something stuck under his desk and pulls it out: it is a bugging device, attached to a flex; he barks into it.*

And interdepartmental jealousies don't help!

*He pulls the flex savagely and there is a faint cry of pain far off; without pausing, he takes a pair of clippers from his desk, neatly cuts the flex and puts the bugging device into his drawer.*

As the first non-volunteers to work in WVHA, naturally Gottleb and Brigadeführer Glucks and the other hard-liners want us out. The knock in the night, the unexpected Foreign Service Allowance, the quick transfer to the Occupied Eastern Territories! *(they shudder)* We're under great pressure, but we'll triumph, just as our armies did last month at Stalingrad and El Alamein.

**Stroop:** Rissoles. Soya-bean rissoles with onion sauce à la Riefenstahl. I have 'em every day for lunch in the staff canteen, bon appétit. Very filling, Fräulein.

**Else:** I must try them.

**Stroop:** Early in the week.

*Stroop sighs loudly.* **Cranach** *groans and* **Else** *sadly shakes her head.* **Stroop** *sighs,* **Cranach** *groans and* **Else** *shakes her head again.*

**Cranach:** That's enough. We mustn't talk politics. It's too dangerous. Fräulein, bring me the material on the CP 3(m) tender.

*They resume work.* **Stroop** *picks up two files with memos attached and takes them to* **Cranach,** *whilst* **Else** *crosses Up Stage to the files.*

**Stroop:** What you just said, sir, about helping others, reminded me of Oberdienstleiter Brack.

*He places the files in front of* **Cranach** *who glances at them.* You remember Brack, sir. OMTC transferred to Resort K2 RMEUL. Big man, fat eyes, but made up for it with a bad cough. Almost as eloquent as you, sir, on the ideals of the service. Each man giving of his best, blending with the best other men give. His mind was such, I think, he could've been a world famous surgeon.

**Cranach:** I remember him. Tragic case. He always wanted to help suffering humanity but never had the necessary detachment. It must've been his experiences in the Great War; kept turning over corpses in his mind. I'm sure that's why when Bouhler set up the 'Foundation for Institutional Care' at T4, he applied for the post of Oberdienstleiter and became a member of the Party. *(he signs the two memos attached to the top of the files)* All those cretins, mongoloids, parapalytics, sclorotics and diarrectics — who doesn't want to root out pain? It's not true Goethe died peacefully, he screamed for three days and nights in fear of death. But there was no pain or fear at T4 under Brack, only five cc's of hydrocyanic acid. Incurables were finally cured. It was all repugnant to me on moral grounds, but I must say Brack always stressed the mercy in mercy-killing.

    **Else** *comes back with three files.*

**Else:** Cardinal Galen denounced it from the pulpit. Only God can play God, make a tree, choose who lives, who dies. My mother would've been a beneficiary of Herr Brack's social surgery. It's true she's eighty-three and has developed whining into an art unsurpassed in Western Europe. But it's a sin to deprive the sinner of a last chance to reconcile herself to God.

**Cranach:** Public opinion was completely opposed to the euthanasia programme, even when Brack pointed out its benefits were only available to German-born nationals. The Führer — make-him-happy-he-deserves-it, had to drop the whole project. You see, despite what our enemies say, he can only govern with the consent of the German people.

    *He hands the files back to* **Stroop**.

**Stroop:** It broke Herr Brack. He was prematurely retired on half-pay and a non-recurrent service gratuity. It could happen to any of us! You pull yourself up hand over hand but someone's always there with a knife, waiting to cut the rope. No one understands the arbitrary terror we all live under nowadays in the Third Reich — redundancy, compulsory retirement with loss of pension rights! *(he returns to his desk)* Today Herr Brack just sits in his room, unable to hear the word Madagascar without screaming.

**Else:** Requiescat in pace. Amen.

*She has finished checking the files and puts them on* **Cranach***'s desk.*

The tenders for appliances CP3 (m). Krupps AG of Essen, Tesch and Stabenow of Hamburg and Degesch of Dessau.

**Cranach** *opens the files, whilst* **Else** *crosses Up Stage Right to the small cupboard to prepare coffee.*

**Cranach:** Herr Stroop, I'd like your opinion. Obergruppen-führer Dr. Kammler'll want the department's recommended choice. Krupps' DS 6/310 tender's a high 20,000 marks They claim lack of trained personnel on the site justifies pre mix concreting and the installation of chuting and pumping. I'm not prepared to encourage wild experiments in new building techniques at government expense. I favour Tesch and Stabenow.

**Stroop:** I agree, sir. They've proved most satisfactory. Amt D already've a contract with them for two tons of Kyklon B rat poison a month. Two tons. There can't be that many rats in the whole of Germany.

**Cranach:** Kyklon B isn't being used to kill rats but to discredit this department. *We* built those complexes in Upper Silesia. If Gottleb and Amt D prove they're overrun with vermin we're blamed. Q.E.D. Of course that's not Tesch and Stabenow's fault.

**Stroop:** I agree, sir.

**Cranach:** However, giving them another government contract so soon after the last might raise doubts as to our integrity.

**Stroop:** I agree, sir.

**Cranach:** Is there anything you don't agree with, Herr Stroop?

**Stroop:** Unemployment. I'm near retirement. You can't please everyone, so I find it best to keep pleasing my superiors. But I do wonder, sir, if it's wise to dismiss Krupps' tender? The firm's shown undeviating loyalty to the Party since '33. Old Gustav Krupps was awarded the War Cross of Merit and Young Alfred's Party number's a low 89627. They have influence.

**Cranach:** I'm not influenced by influence. Krupps've bad labour relations. They're only paying their foreign workers seventy pfennigs a day and refusing to build them a company brothel despite a UD 84763 directive.

*Else puts a cup of coffee on his desk and one on* **Stroop's**.

In the old days, politicians were despised, administrators revered. Now politicians're sacrosanct and we've become the whipping boys of a public frustrated by wartime shortage and delays. They say we're divorced from the glorious reality of the National Socialist struggle. Our behaviour must therefore be seen to be above reproach. The final decision's the Obergruppenführer's but this department'll recommend Tesch and Stabenow for the CP3(m) contract. *(he drinks the coffee and grimaces)* I like my coffee weak but this is helpless.

**Else:** It's the new grain substitute. Secretly scented, *aromatically* flavoured! Unique — no coffee, all aroma. Wait till you try the new Führer-make-him-happy-he-deserves-it cigarettes. Filtered bootlaces. One puff, you're deaf . . . Two marks Herr Cranach. *(***Cranach*** grunts)* For the bottle of schnapps Herr Wochner's bringing over. It's tradition to have a drink in the office on Christmas Eve.

**Cranach:** I don't approve, but as it's tradition.

*He opens a little purse, carefully takes out two marks and gives them to her.*

**Else:** I know the Führer-make-him-happy-he-deserves-it has given the nation a new set of holy days to celebrate, like the 'National Day of Mourning' and the 'Anniversary of the Munich Putsch,' but they don't quite take the place of Christmas. Two marks, Herr Stroop.

**Stroop:** When she was alive my wife was so fat she never had a clear view of her feet. She loved food and jolly Christmases, cutting up apples, baking white bread, covering the fruit trees with a cloth. Good eating, drinking, sleeping, without 'em it's just staying on earth, not living. *(he gives* **Else** *the money)* Two marks for schnapps. Sixty for butter. Fifty percent on income tax, no lights in the street at night, no heating during the day. I'm spending this Christmas lying in bed holding a candle in my hands, staring at the folds and edges.

**Else:** I thought of praying to God at Midnight Mass for better times, but I know the Führer-make-him-happy-he-deserves-it doesn't like anyone going over his head.

**Cranach:** The State doesn't acknowledge God exists. If He did, I'm certain Adolf Hitler'd be notified before anyone else. Even so, concessions to Christ's birth've been made. Order 7334 Kd10 grants a Christmas present of one pair of stockings for every woman and one tie for every man over and above the rationed quota. Stockings for every woman, a cravat for every man. National Socialism works!

**Stroop:** But there'll be more black-edged Q4928's posted this year than Christmas presents. 'We regret to inform you your husband / brother / son / father has been killed in action defending the Fatherland.'

**Cranach:** The strain is beginning to tell. I see it daily in the 'Morganpost' obituary notices. The bereaved're no longer observing the Reichsinnenminister's Decree 77/B1 of 5th April '42 that all such notices must be a uniform, ninety-six millimetres broad and eighty long. But I've measured some of the latest obits and most're over *two hundred* millimetres long and *one hundred and twenty* broad! When my son was killed I could've written things. 'Fate has ended our waiting, our hope. We received the news our beloved son Joachim Cranach died from his wounds. All our joy buried in Russian earth . . . love him, mourn him, never forget . . . we live out the rest in grief . . .' and so on and so on. Instead I wrote, 'In proud sadness we learnt our son Joachim Cranach was killed in action in the East, liberating the Ukraine from the Ukrainians. Send no flowers.' That's under ninety-six millimetres broad, eighty long. Strictly in accordance with Decree 77/B1. What more to say. They pulled off his boots, dug a shallow grave and it was all over with.

**Else:** They're selling miniature hero-graves for four marks forty, at 'Kepa's', complete with tiny wreathes. Six for ten marks. Your wife might like one for her dressing table. *(she takes his empty cup)* Your son died at twenty-two, my mother lives, eighty-three and clinging fast.

*She collects* **Stroop's** *cup and takes them to the cupboard.*

All're dying, yet she survives with all the frail charm of an iron foundry.

**Cranach** *(opening a file)*: The German people've always preferred strong government to self-government. So why do they complain of too many decrees and regulations? It's one of the benefits of war. Usually our lives're so muddled that we don't know what we want, want what we don't want, don't want what we want. We're tormented by choice. Do you find it difficult to obey decrees and regulations, Fräulein?

**Else** *(putting dirty cups in the cupboard)*: No, fortunately I'm a Roman Catholic and Roman doctrine forbids any kind of dissent. Obedience is regarded as a principle of righteous conduct. So I look on National Socialism as Catholicism with the Christianity left out.

**Cranach**: We've had enough choices. We chose well because all choices're made for us. We've rules to live by which tell us what, when, where, how: no painful choices left to make except in sleep.

**Stroop**: German cheese gives me nightmares. I keep dreaming I'm punching Herr Gottleb in the face, though it's difficult from a kneeling position. The nightmares've got more frightening lately. I've started wanting to protest about conditions. I fight it but I can't resist. I must make my stand without the slightest 'but'. So I finally do it. I put a blank piece of paper into an envelope and send it to the Reich Führer himself. Afterwards I feel so proud! It's terrible. I wake up trembling with fright. I must stop sleeping with my eyes closed.

**Cranach**: You certainly can't afford to've nightmares Herr Stroop till you retire. You've taken a personal oath of loyalty to the Führer-make-him-happy-he-deserves-it. He'll know; he has devices . . .

*He stops and sniffs suspiciously.* **Else** *and* **Stroop** *are moving to the filing shelves, but he gestures to them to halt. The two watch him slowly rise and cross Up Stage, sniffing the air loudly. He pauses at the door for a moment, before flinging it open to catch* **Hans Gottleb**, *a chunky man with a Hitler moustache, crouching in the doorway, obviously listening at the keyhole.*

Gottleb, as I live and breathe!

**Gottleb:** Not for long if I can help it.

*He straightens up and, gripping his briefcase, marches in, clicking his heels and jerking up his right arm in a Nazi salute.*

Heil Hitler!

**Else, Stroop** *and* **Cranach** *raise their arms.*

**Cranach:** ⎫
**Else:** ⎬ Heil Hitler!
**Stroop:** ⎭

**Else** *and* **Stroop** *lower their arms but* **Cranach** *and* **Gottleb,** *facing each other, keep theirs stiffly raised;* **Cranach**'s *arm is lower than* **Gottleb**'s.

**Gottleb:** According to Hoflich of the 'Schwarzes Korps' it's customary when Heiling Hitler to raise the right arm at an angle so the palm of the hand is visible.

**Cranach:** Hoflich also wrote 'if one encounters a person socially inferior, when Heiling Hitler, then the right arm is raised only to eye-level, so the palm of the hand is hidden.'

**Gottleb:** Socially inferior! Why you sclerotic pen-pusher, my brother's a close friend of Julius Streicher, Gauleiter of Franken.

**Cranach:** Your sister too, I hear.

**Gottleb:** I warned Brigadeführer Glucks about you and your kind. He didn't listen. What gifts I've thrown before swine. You were seconded, didn't volunteer. Now you're a malignant virus in the healthy body of the SS — WVHA. You've no business here with your damn bureaucratic principles of promotion by merit and such. Merit, merit, I shit on *merit*. We old Party-men didn't fight in the streets, gutters filled with our dead, to build a world based on merit. What's merit got to do with it? We weren't appointed on merit. Take merit as a standard and we'll all be OUT.

**Cranach:** Gottleb, a man with a low forehead like yours has no right to criticise. Without more Upper Grade and Administrative Class officials who've risen on merit, Amt C & D'll collapse under the increased workload. 622.75 units per day're now being transported from all over Europe to Upper Silesia. We must've more trained civil servants to deal with 'em, not wild-eyed amateurs. Stand aside Gottleb and let us professionals do their job.

**Gottleb:** We scarred veterans're not going to be by-passed by you arse-licking, crypto-homo flunkies.

**Else:** Herr Gottleb, you haven't been reading 'Das Reich'. This is Politeness Month. Everyone has to help restore gladness, kindness and courtesy to the German scene. The Party's sponsoring a contest to find the politest men and women in Berlin. Dr. Goebbels himself's presenting prizes to the most successful.

**Stroop:** 'Even though you're German./And it will come hard./Just to learn to say you're sorry./And win a week's supply of lard.' That won third Prize. Two theatre tickets to 'Sparrows in the Hand of God.'

**Gottleb:** Should be crushed. Like politeness. I shit on politeness. It stinks of philo-semite decadence, foul mind curves there. Let Judah perish! Politeness'll undermine our whole society. You can't give orders lisping, 'please', 'please', 'thank you' 'thank you' and the New Order's built on orders. Politeness is anti-German. Bluff rudeness, stimulating abuse, is the true Aryan way, hard in the bone. We must tear out from ourselves, the soft, the liquid noxious juices, *ahh*

*He grunts with pain as he attempts to lower his stiff arm which, together with* **Cranach**'s, *is still raised in a Nazi salute; whilst he pulls it down with his other hand,* **Cranach** *wincingly does the same before crossing to his desk.*

We didn't need politeness when we shot and clubbed our way through the beerhalls of Munich! Ah what days — sometimes I just want to be what I was, when I wanted to be what I am now. And we don't need politeness to crush the Bolshevik-Imperialistic half-breed armies in Asia and North Africa.

**Else** *and* **Stroop** *have resumed searching for files as* **Gottleb** *crosses to* **Cranach** *and takes out a document from his briefcase; he reads quickly.*

'All Section Heads WVHA (IV/QV) No. 44822/42 Obergruppenführer Pohhl. Further to the implementation of the executive solutions agreed at the Wannsee Conference Sec L (IV/QU) No. 37691/42 the attached document 'General

Instructions on Measures Sec. L(IV/QU)' is circulated herewith by hand and the signature of Department Heads is required on receipt of said copy.' *(He gives* Cranach *a form to sign)* You'll like paragraph fifteen, Cranach. Just your style. *(he opens the document at another page and reads)* 'Future cases of death shall be given consecutive Roman numbers with consecutive subsidiary Arabic numbers, so that the first case of death is numbered Roman numeral I/1, the second Roman numeral I/2 up to Roman numeral I/185. Thereafter cases of death shall be numbered Roman numeral II from Roman numeral II/1 to 185. Each new year will start with the Roman numeral I/1.' The dead talking to the dead. You bureaucratic tapeworms suck the colour from life. Our work here's a crusade or it's nothing. We need images of light to fire the mind, words to set the heart salmon-leaping. 'Stead we're given Roman numerals followed by consecutive subsidiary Arabic numerals, Roman numeral I/1 to Roman numeral I/185.

Else *and* Stroop *join them with files.*

Cranach: This is war, Gottleb, a million words've died on us. We no longer believe in a secure sentence structure. Neutral symbols've become the safest means of communication. I certainly endorse the use of coded symbols rather than consecutive numbering in recording cases of death. It's more concise and less emotive.

Else: In any case, Amt D II/3 is Statistics and Auditing, Herr Gottleb. We're Amt C 1 — planning, costing and supervising of WVHA building projects.

Gottleb: Fräulein, you're a woman who could easily drive me to stop drinking.

Stroop: Deaths and paragraph fifteen isn't any of our business.

Gottleb: Ah, Stroop, still awake this late in the morning? Cranach, this office is only held together by the laws of inertia. Actually I've come over about the tenders for appliances CP 3(m) described in regulation E(5) Amt D wants the contract to be given to Krupps AG for past favours.

Cranach: Amt D wants? Amt D can continue to want. The contract'll be given strictly on merit. *Merit*, Gottleb, not on favours past, present or future.

**Gottleb** *(taking out a memo)*: Confirmation of this request from Brigadeführer Glucks. Memo FC/867.

**Cranach** *(showing him a memo)*: Amt C operates independent of Amt D. Obergruppenführer's memo JN 72.

**Gottleb** *(producing a second memo)*: JN 72 or not. I've got a 62 KG!

**Cranach** *(flourishing a second memo)*: And I've a 17Q!

**Gottleb** *(producing a third memo)*: One 3H!

**Cranach:** Two spades.

**Else:** Four No-trumps.

**Stroop:** I pass.

**All:** Root it out!

 **Cranach** *waves* **Stroop** *and* **Else** *back to their desks.*

**Cranach:** There'll be no favours here. Thanks to favours received and given, bribery's become *the* organising principle of the Third Reich.

**Gottleb:** You elongated, bespectacled rodent. Without bribery you could never attract the better class of people into politics. Bribery's the reward for those who helped the cause and now need help. Bribery's the one expression of gratitude people appreciate. But you're one of those stiff-arsed moralists who see a favour as an opportunity to show their piss-green incorruptibility rather than their gratitude. Damnable petit-bourgeois morality. I shit on morality. It stiffens the brain, dries out life's juices. I've seen it ruin thousands of good men in my time: morality, virtue, boredom, syphilis. Downhill all the way. Corruption has more natural justice to it, not based on your shit-spat merit or morality. Anyone can take his share if he's strong or weak enough. It binds all men together. That's the National Socialist way. Nature's way. All things come to corruption, our bodies too: corruption.

**Else:** But 'this corruptible must put on incorruption and this mortal must put on immortality'. First Episode of Paul to the Corinthians.

**Gottleb:** No priest-talk Fräulein! Fat-gutted clowns with their mitres and jewels and their Holy Trinity of rent, interest and profit. You ask 'em to do something religious and they take a collection. Two thousand years they've been preaching love and charity and when a continent of corpses've shown how bankrupt they are, some idiots still look at 'em and long for goodness. I shit on goodness! If there's a good God why is there old age and baldness, eh?

**Cranach:** God or no God, corruption turns the best to the worst. If I granted favours out of fear or greed, I'd betray my son charred black and the other dead who fell asleep twenty-two degrees centigrade below. I'd betray all those good Germans fighting from Benghazi to the Caucusus, so that the enslaved millions of Europe can be free.

**Wochner:** Heil Hitler!

*No one has noticed* **Georg Wochner,** *a young man in a long, weighed-down overcoat, slip in Up Stage Centre. All stand to attention and exchange Nazi salutes.*

**All:** Heil Hitler!

**Wochner** *(consulting a small note-book)*: Amt C 1 (Building) December 24th. Herr Cranach. One bottle of schnapps. Six marks.

*He opens his coat to show the right hand side is lined with bottles; he removes one. As* **Else** *gets the money,* **Stroop** *hastily resumes work at his desk and* **Cranach** *clears his throat.*

**Gottleb:** Count your days, Cranach! That's black-market schnapps. You're dealing in blacks. And I have witnesses. This room's wired. *(he shouts under the desk)* You hear that Winklemann? He's dealing in blacks! Blacks!

**Cranach** *takes out the 'bugging' device he cut off and silently hands it to* **Gottleb,** *who stares.*

Destroying government property too. That's a serious criminal offence, Cranach. You'll be cropped — CROPPED. Regulation 47632/48 imposes the same penalties on buyers as well as sellers of black goods. We've just slaughtered a Bavarian butcher found guilty of illegal slaughtering; hung his carcass up till it turned black as the rest of his meat. I'll see you all hung up turning black, black, black! *(chanting)* 'Oh let the blood spurt from the knife.'

**Else** *has paid* **Wochner,** *who unconcernedly ticks off the amount in his note-book.*

**Wochner:** Herr Gottleb, will you take your bottles now or should I deliver them to your office?

**Gottleb:** Give me two. You bring the rest. None of your dishwater bath-mix now.

    **Gottleb** *crosses as* **Wochner** *opens his coat again.*

**Cranach:** Leak into another universe, Gottleb! You're up to your armpits in blacks!

**Gottleb:** Don't compare your case of blacks with mine. You only buy schnapps to drink, I to relax tired bodies, tight minds. *(he gives* **Wochner** *money)* My men need compassionate leave, the same as other front-liners; I give it to 'em in a bottle.

**Wochner:** Five at six marks is thirty marks. Two marks short.

**Gottleb** *(giving him two more marks)*: I've been watching you, Wochner. *(he mimes counting banknotes)* Licking your forefinger and thumb flick-flick-flick-one-two-three-four-five. That's not the Aryan way of counting money. It's a sign of philo-Semite blood, counting money Panza-fast. Jew-blood, Jew-signs. Yes, their signs're everywhere if you've a nose for 'em. Biological proof of decadence. Prussian hair grows out spiky straight. But Czech moustaches all droop downwards. That's a sure sign they've got degenerate mongol blood. Stroop! Give your face a blank expression so I can tell you're not thinking! Why aren't you in the Army, Wochner?

**Wochner:** Just lucky, I have renal diabetes, cardiac murmur, crutch palsey, bat's wing lupus, Speighel hernia and Brigade-führer Glucks as an uncle. *(he gives two bottles to* **Gottleb***)* I'll leave the rest of your order in your office.

**Cranach:** This one still has work to do.

    *He indicates the door, but* **Wochner** *does not move.*

**Else:** Herr Cranach, it's customary to offer the black schnapps supplier a drink to toast the Fatherland and victory.

**Gottleb:** No one'll toast victory here, Wochner, even the women're defeatist to a man. They only drink for pleasure; patriotism's dead. Come with me and I'll show you patriotic drinking, gut-heaving, bladder-bursting drinking, real German drinking.

**Cranach:** As it's the custom. Herr Stroop, will you help Fräulein Jost with the bottle?

    *Whilst* **Else** *gets out the glasses from the cupboard,* **Stroop** *opens the schnapps.*

**Wochner:** Can I interest you in anything else? I carry a wide range of blacks from liberated capitals of Europe.

*He opens his coat and takes various articles out of pockets on the left-hand side.*

Silk scarves, Chanel perfume and toilet water, fifty marks. Fur muff, Paris label. Dutch butter. Pickled herrings from Warsaw, fifteen marks a jar.

*He brings out a flat case filled with gold and diamond rings, which he opens concertina-fashion.*

Something cheaper? Confiscated wedding rings. Gold. For you, thirteen marks, and I'm not making a pfennig profit. Twelve? Ten? Any offers? Here's a novelty that's selling well, very risqué. Hammer-and-sickle badges. Every one guaranteed taken by hand from the body of a dead Russian soldier. Look their blood's still on some of them.

**Gottleb** *examines a badge.*

There's a human tragedy in each one of those badges. I'm practically giving them away.

**Cranach:** Herr Wochner, this isn't an Afro-Oriental street market. Regulation AC 84/736(b) forbids these premises to be used for private business. Is this real silk?

*He picks up a necktie as* **Gottleb** *scratches the dry blood off a badge and tastes it on the tip of his tongue.*

**Gottleb:** Russian blood? This isn't Russian blood. I've tasted Russian blood. I know about blood. We've given the world the salvation of blood. And it sends us trinkets, beads, worthless trash.

*He throws the badge back as* **Stroop** *comes over with drinks for him and* **Cranach.** **Else** *serves* **Wochner,** *who has moved slightly to one side.*

**Wochner:** Fräulein, I'm looking for a wife — anybody's wife. What would it take to make you fall in love with me?

**Else:** A magician. My father said, work hard and be a good girl. You can always change your mind when you're older. Now I'm older and it's too late. I've reached the age where I'm beginning to find sex a pain in the arse.

**Wochner:** That means you're doing it the wrong way.

**Cranach** *(raising his glass)*: A toast. To the Fatherland and Victory.

**All:** The Fatherland and Victory!

*They drink, stamp their right legs convulsively and gasp.*

**Wochner** *(hoarsely)*: Good isn't it. Straight from the Hamburg boat.

**Gottleb:** Scraped off the sides. I can feel my toes exploding. Don't sip it like a virgin with lockjaw, Cranach. *(he mimes)* Drink it in one, head back, mouth open wide so it doesn't touch your teeth and dissolve the enamel.

*He crosses and examines the bottle.*

Smooth. But you've got it wrong again, Cranach. 'To the Fatherland and Victory' that's not a true National Socialist toast; the Gestapo could have a man's hanging testicles wired for less. I'll show you a true National Socialist toast. Listen. Learn.

*Before* **Cranach** *can stop him he fills his glass and raises it.*

A toast: to the Fatherland?

*He drinks, stamps his leg convulsively and gasps.*

Sm-o-o-th.

*He immediately pours another glass and raises it.*

A toast: Victory!

*He drinks, stamps and gasps.*

Sm-o-o-th. It's important to take your time, Cranach. Doesn't the Fatherland merit a full toast? Doesn't our victory?

**Cranach:** And doesn't he who is Victory itself? We've forgotten him. Let's drink to the man who made us what we are today.

*Before* **Gottleb** *can protest, he opens one of* **Gottleb***'s bottles.*

I know you'll contribute to this dedication, Gottleb.

**Gottleb** *scowls as* **Cranach** *pours out the drinks.*

To the being who's given us a new centre of being, around whose head the cosmic forces gather into a swelling new order.

**Stroop:** Who loves us and forgives all that's weakly human in us.

**Else:** Who knows no sacrifice he would not let us make to be worthy of him.

**Gottleb:** Who has laid the axe to the sacred trees, told the whole world 'Step out of our sunlight.'

**Wochner:** Who turns the dross of pain into the gold of serenity.

*They all turn to the portrait of Hitler above the entrace and
raise their glasses.*
**All:** The Führer — make-him-happy etc. etc.
*They drink, stamp their right legs and gasp hoarsely.*
*Sm-o-o-th.*
*Singing the Wagnerian choral opening of 'Die
Meistersinger von Nürnberg'.*
'As our Saviour came to thee, willingly baptized to be.
Yielded to the cross his breath, ransomed us from sin and
death. May we too baptized be, worthy of his agony.
Prophet, preacher, holy teacher. Send us by the hand, home
to Jordan's strand.'
**Cranach:** Wrong again, Gottleb. No sacred trees're axed. On
the contrary, their roots're watered, the status quo preserved.
National Socialism is part of the great conservative tradition.
It is based on solid middle-class values. Just as the Führer-
make-him-happy etc. embodies our hopes for 'more' and our
fear that when we get it, someone will try and take it away
from us. Listen to him, speaking to the Reichstag 21st May
'35. Noon. 'As National Socialists we are filled with
admiration and respect for the great achievements of the past,
not only in our own nation but far beyond it. We are happy
to belong to the European community of culture which has
inspired the modern world.'
**Gottleb:** Wrong again, Cranach. You only understood the
words. But the sounds? What about the sounds?
*He imitates the harsh nasal sound of Hitler's stabbing,
lower middle-class, Austrian accent with its brutal,
seductively hysterical, rhythms.*
Szzztt nrrrr vrrr rrrchhhhh dddssss rrrrkkk rurrxxx ptsch nui
KAAAA grrss iiiiichh R REECHTTT *RKK*!
*A mighty chorus chants* 'Sieg Heil! Sieg Heil!'
Rrrrrrrkkk hhhh dddttss vvllkkk rrrchh ... wrrrrkkk AAA!
Ssrrt rrttt srrrr MPPFF gmuuuuttt cccHH dddrrr essskkkkk
ZZZSWCH uuuuunn utt isssss KRR KRRKK SCHWEE
SCHWRK SCHWRK sss uttu SCHWRK! SCHWRK! GROO
SCHWRK!
*All join in as the unseen audience roars* 'Sieg Heil! Sieg
Heil!'

Status quo, status quo, I shit on your status quo. Our world
was dying of your status quo covered with status quo like
horse mange. No air! No air! We flung the old order out of
orbit, swept away the stiff-collars, monocles and cutaways,
gave Germany social fluidity, permanent institutional
anarchy. Before, our lives lacked the larger significance, he
filled it with drama; there's always something happening in
the Third Reich. He gave us faith in the sword, not in the
Cross; that foul Semite-servility, that 'other-cheek' brigade
with their 'Hit me!', 'Hit me!' Our hand goes out to all men,
but always doubled up. You middle-class bed-wetters squeak
about mercy, that's decadence; hardness, greater hardness!

**Stroop:** The truth is, as Jews can be simultaneously scum and
dregs, so National Socialism can simultaneously embody
revolutionary and conservative principles and black and white
the same colour grey. That's the miracle of it.

   *He slumps into his chair.*

**Wochner:** The true miracle is that a man with renal diabetes,
cardiac murmur, crutch palsey, bat's wing lupus and
Spieghel hernia can prosper, not despite his afflictions but
because of 'em. And I want to see another miracle, when this
country's business'll only be business. Nothing'll stop us
then, we'll be the paymasters of Europe. It'll be easy. No
more uncertainties, we'll be able to judge a man's worth at a
glance by his credit rating, know right from wrong, success
from failure, by the amount of money in our pockets.
Money's a necessity I've always placed just ahead of
breathing.

**Cranach:** Wochner, I shall ignore you with every fibre of my
being. We Germans've always had the divine capacity for
visions which transcended the merely commercial. That's why
the Reichführer S.S. Heinrich Himmler himself, decreed that
our first complex should be built in the forest outside
Weimar, the very seat of German classical tradition. Didn't
he leave Goethe's famous oak tree standing there in the
middle of the compound and constructed the ramps, and
block houses around it? You see, even in times like these, in
places like that, for people like them, German culture is
made available to all. We think transcendentally. We raise

our eyes to the hills; the soul, the soul, the German soul! And
you talk of money, credit ratings.

**Gottleb:** Materialistic filth! People spending money they haven't
earned, to buy things they don't need, to impress neighbours
who don't care. In the old days Wochner we'd've washed
your mouth out with prussic acid. Our nation'll never
descend to prosperity. I shit on prosperity. Hideous self-
sacrifice is our way of life. You know nothing of sacrifice or
suffering Wochner. What with renal diabetes, cardiac
murmur, crutch palsey, bat's wing lupus and Spieghel
hernia, you've had it too soft. Soft! Herr Cranach is right.
You can only be ignored. *(he takes another drink)* After a
time this stuff grows on you, like leaf mould. Herr Cranach, I
think we should examine memos FC/867, 62KG and 3H
regarding CP3(m). If you're agreeable that is?

Cranach *nods, crosses and sits at his desk.* Gottleb *stands
beside him. They examine the papers together and drink
their schnapps.* Wochner *shrugs and starts putting the goods
back into his coat with* Else's *help.*

**Wochner:** My fairest lady, may I offer you my arm and company
tonight?

**Else:** I'm not fair, no lady, and I don't need an escort to see me
home. I know men, when they're soft they're hard, when
they're hard they're soft. I expect nothing from 'em, and
that's what I always get — nothing. One of my fiancés once
bought me a beautiful ring with a place for a lovely diamond
in it.

**Wochner:** I had a fiancée but we broke it off on religious
grounds. I worshipped money and she didn't have any.

**Else:** I've heard of your effect on women. Just being near you
gives a girl hives.

**Wochner:** Women always judge with their bodies instead of
their minds. I'll come for you tonight.

**Else:** 'I'll come for you tonight.' Act like a lover if you want to
be one. Tell me, 'the brightness of your cheek outshines the
stars, one glance from your eyes outweighs the wisdom of the
world.' Woo me, say something beautiful.

**Wochner:** One jar of Kiel salt herrings. Two kilos of real coffee,
four fresh eggs. One tin of skimmed milk.

**Else:** The answer's no. No. No. No.

**Wochner:** Three kilos of butter. Six of lard. One real woollen
blanket. Three kilos of bacon.

**Else** *(quickly)*: Three kilos of bacon plus the woollen blanket!

**Wochner:** I had Herr Sauckel's wife for three kilos of bacon. If
I'd thrown in a wollen blanket I'd've got Herr Sauckel too.
Only promise you won't talk of love while we make it. I desire
you, enjoy you, utilize you. Love doesn't come into it. *(he
takes her hand)* I kiss your hand.

**Else:** Tonight it'll be all over, fortunately. Bring the goods with
you or it's no trade.

> **Wochner** *nods and turns to the others.*

**Wochner:** Gentlemen, I have to go.

**Cranach:** In the end haven't we all.

> **Wochner** *bows slightly and exits, his coat still weighing
him down.* **Else** *pours herself another drink.*

**Stroop:** There were always as many women available when I was
young as there are now. But what I hate about life is there's
always a new lot enjoying 'em. There's nothing sadder than
an old roué with nothing left to rue.

**Cranach:** Was Wochner ever in the Hitler Youth? — tough as
leather, swift as whippets, hard as Krupp steel. Somehow I
can't see him sitting round a camp-fire singing the Horst
Wessel Song and dreaming of being a Gauleiter like any
normal German boy.

**Gottleb:** Wochner's time's short. Brigadeführer Glucks won't
be able to save him. I've seen to it. Certain Party officials
know about his filthy Empire of blacks — and they want their
share. Any moment now that tide-mark won't be the only
thing around his neck.

**Else:** Please, not until after I've finished my business with him,
Herr Gottleb.

**Gottleb** *(he opens his other bottle)*: To please you Fräulein, I'll
let him enjoy Christmas. It never hurts to show a little
compassion and warm the knife before you stick it in. *(he
pours her another drink)* This schnapps must be stronger than
I thought. You're beginning to look attractive, Fräulein, in
an elementary sort of way. Why aren't you married? The
Führer-make-him-happy etc. promised every woman in the

Third Reich a husband, dead or alive. A woman should be in her own home, behind a spinning wheel, weaving heavenly roses.

**Else:** The whole of Germany is our home and we must serve her wherever we can.

**Gottleb:** And you've no children. We must all do our part for the perpetuation of the Nordic race. I've been a virile lover, thirty years, man and boy. The boy's worn out, but the man's still active.

**Else:** I've tried, but Karl was killed in Norway, Horst in the Belgian Ardennes, Kurt and Josef taken in the taking of Greece and Crete, Fritz assaulting Tobruk, Edgar capturing Kiev. All great victories, but death didn't seem to know that, made no distinction pro or contra. Left me standing at the altar whilst my mother survived.

**Cranach:** You could still have had children without benefit of. And no stigma. Reichsminister Lammers' ruling, memo QBX 54738 that extra-marital motherhood was not a reason for initiating disciplinary measures against female members of the civil service.

**Gottleb:** We've replaced hypocritical bourgeois morality with honest National Socialist immorality.

**Else:** Venereal satisfaction outside wedlock's a mortal sin, unless forced and without pleasure. I can't commit mortal sin, cut myself off from God's light, grace, my last end.

**Gottleb:** Jew talk! You've a good child-bearing pelvis, Fräulein. But just look at yourself. I know the Party's ideal woman is one of Spartan severity, but you go too far. Without those glasses, that hair-style, why you'd be beautiful. Here, let me show you.

*He takes off her glasses, then removes the comb keeping her bun in place.*

Don't worry, I've got very delicate hands . . . Just let it fall out . . .

**Else**'s *hair tumbles down, she shakes it free.*

There, there, you see, Fräulein . . . why you look . . .

*She glances up; he shudders.*

worse!

**Else** *grabs the comb and starts putting her hair back up.*

**Else:** If we're ever alone on a desert island, Herr Gottleb, bring a pack of cards.

**Stroop:** When we were kids, we used to take a stick and hit each other over the head. Even the games were different then. I liked to be domineering, but I could never find anyone who wanted to be submissive.

*Else has fixed her hair back into a bun and puts her glasses on.* **Gottleb** *points triumphantly.*

**Gottleb:** There, I was right. The hair, the glasses, it makes all the difference. Why, now you look almost beautiful, Fräulein Jost.

**Else:** But this is exactly the way I was before!

**Gottleb:** And not a moment too soon.

*Cranach stands up, sways slightly, and sits again. All are getting progressively more drunk.*

**Cranach:** Gottleb, I've studied these memos and I still can't grant special favours to Krupps AG.

**Gottleb:** I understand perfectly Cranach. I don't agree with what you say and I'll fight to death your right to say it. I can't be fairer than that. Have another drink.

*He pours himself and Cranach another drink.*

**Cranach:** I don't want to be unfair, Gottleb. If you wish the Reichführer S.S. Heinrich Himmler himself to renew the case I'd've no objection.

**Gottleb:** Ah, the Reichführer's a truly great man, trying to recreate the pure Aryan race according to Mendel's laws. His commitment to the community's total, TOTAL. 'If ten thousand Russian women die digging a tank ditch, it interests me only as far as the tank ditch is completed for Germany.'

**Cranach:** But he also said, 'We Germans're the only people with a decent attitude to animals.' I don't understand why he has such a bad reputation.

**Gottleb:** I met him once in person. He was sitting at a large black table with a bottle of mineral water and Obergruppen-führers Jeckeln, Kaltenbrunner and von Herff. They were all staring into space, forcing a traitor in the next room to confess, purely by exerting their collective Aryan wills. It was called an exercise in concentration. Of course the SS're usually more physical in their approach. But this time they were dealing with a cross-eyed, bearded dwarf.

**Cranach:** An intellectual?

**Gottleb:** Yes, the subtle method can sometimes be very effective with intellectuals. Of course if they turn out not to be intellectuals, you can always go back to basics; put the needle in the record and separate the soul from the wax with traditional whips, cold chisels and such.

**Else:** Tell me, do fully uniformed men actually believe they can force someone to tell them the truth by will power alone?

**Gottleb:** If the will's truly Aryan. Aryan will cuts through steel plate, thirty metres thick. It's pure light, burning light. I'll show you. You've no intellectuals here, so we'll have to use old Stroop — there's a full moon tonight but it won't make him any brighter. Right, Stroop?

> **Stroop,** *slumped in his chair deep in thought, nods absently.*

**Gottleb:** We'll make him confess the truth. Fräulein Jost, Herr Cranach, concentrate there on his bald spot. There . . . Concentrate . . .

**Cranach:** No. I can't let one of my staff risk speaking the truth out loud in public.

**Gottleb:** It won't hurt him. He's amongst friends. Now concentrate . . . three Aryan minds converge . . . burn into his brain . . . h-a-r-d- . . . the truth . . .

> **Gottleb, Cranach** *and* **Else** *stare fixedly across at the top of* **Stroop***'s head. Jaws tighten, eyes bulge in the tense silence. Finally,* **Stroop** *opens his mouth and belches. They continue concentrating.* **Stroop** *suddenly clutches his head, lets out a low moan and rises unsteadily from his chair.*

**Stroop:** Clara Bow's panties. Willy Frisch and Lilian Harvey and the hair from Adolph Menjou's moustache. Oh, the glories of man's unconquerable past. Hans Albers' tights! His legs were too thin for him to play Hamlet, alas poor Yorick, one fool in the grave.

**Cranach:**
**Gottleb:**  } Root it out. Root it out.
**Else:**

**Stroop:** No, it's the truth. It was different then. The sky never so blue, the snow never so white. I was remembering a

Christmas I spent in the country. Every house with evergreens
decorated with stars. A man pulling a cart heaped with holly.
A girl herding geese through a gate. A little boy listening at
the bedroom door to the music and dancing below.

**Else:** When I was a girl, Mother used to take me to afternoon
dances at the Vaterland. They hung the hall with Chinese
lanterns in the summer and the girls were given posies of
violets. Mother'd sit knitting and Father'd read the 'B.Z.
Zum Mittag' and I danced to the music of 'Madam Jodl and
Her All Ladies Viennese Orchestra.'

*Lights down slightly. There is an illusion of swaying
Chinese lanterns overhead as* **Stroop** *bows to* **Else** *and dances
her solemnly round the office whilst* **Cranach** *and* **Gottleb**
*hum a Strauss waltz.*

**Cranach:** Our garden had carnations of all colours, nasturtiums,
snap-dragons, Madonna lilies, monthly roses. Mother loved
flowers so, she said they never tried to borrow money. How
long the summers were then, how bright the sun. Smell the
jasmine round the arbour walls.

*Without stopping the dance, he takes* **Stroop**'*s place as*
**Else**'*s partner whilst* **Stroop** *hums with* **Gottleb**, *who is crying.
The dance ends and* **Cranach** *escorts* **Else** *back to her desk.*

**Gottleb:** My mother was a saint. She was born to laugh; instead
her whole life was spent crying and saying goodbye. My father
ran off with a waitress. Three brothers killed West Front
1918, when we were stabbed in the back. She raised six,
always telling me I had to sleep faster, she needed the
pillows. Fifty years on her knees scrubbing for Jews and
Bolsheviks. From a person to a nonentity, face worn to the
bone. 'What's dying?' she asked. 'What I've had in life was
worse.' Yet she was gentle as water, so good, birds perched on
her outstretched hand. *(he sings, sobbing)* 'I see your eyes at
sunset's golden hour. They look on me till night's first stars
above. You speak to me across the silent land. From out the
long ago, Mother I love . . .'

*Gottleb's* **Mother,** *a little old lady, head wrapped in a
black shawl, hobbles on Wings Left.*

**Gottleb's Mother:** Son, son, I need food.

**Gottleb:** Mother, don't bother me now, can't you see I'm

singing. *(he sings)* 'I hold your hand as through the world I go. And think of your sweet face gentle as a little dove. Your presence fills each throbbing hour of life. Oh heart of long ago, Mother I love . . .'

**Gottleb's Mother:** But, son, I haven't eaten for three days.

**Gottleb:** Didn't I give you a new pair of shoes for your birthday?

**Gottleb's Mother:** Three days without food!

**Gottleb:** How did you get past the guard dogs? Mother, you climbed over the wall again. *(singing)* 'God keep your memory fragrant in my soul. And lift my eyes in thankfulness above. Until I stand beside you at the last. And hold you in my arms, Mother I love.'

**Gottleb's Mother:** Food! Food!

*She turns and staggers off Wings Left.* **Gottleb** *passes a hand over his eyes. Lights Full Up.*

**Gottleb:** Had no time for her then, the Party came first, last and always. Too old, too late to share it. But the song's true, the pain real, despite . . . *(he raises his glass)* My mother.

*They all drink; as they pour another glass each, he sways over to* **Cranach.**

I was wrong about you, Viktor, you've got Aryan qualities. So've you, Fräulein Else, and even you Heinz, or can I call you Stroop. *(he clasps* **Cranach***)* I need new friends, I keep eating up the old ones. Let's be friends.

**Else:** Why not? I've always found it easy to be friends with men I dislike physically.

**Stroop:** I haven't made any friends since I was in my forties, after I realised they couldn't save me.

**Cranach:** You're right, Gottleb — Hans. Friendship's a reciprocal conciliation of mutual interests. We're natural allies, dedicated to building the best. On the personal level too we've much in common. We both earn twenty thousand marks a week, only they don't pay us it. Without us, the machine grinds, halts, and it all spills out. *(they put their arms round each other)* Salt of the earth . . . brother in arms . . . have another drink.

**Gottleb:** We should've been friends before. I blame our Sturm-bannführers. Towers of jelly, not a healthy fart amongst the lot of 'em. When we came to power I thought we'd build gold pissoirs in the streets. Instead they do it in their diapers. They run bowel-scared so they set Amt C against Amt D, D against B. The place is alive with hate-beetles. And Brigade-führer Gluck's the worst. Brigadeführer! He wouldn't make a first class doorman for a second class hotel, he's about as sharp as a billiard ball; why're my superiors always my inferiors? In the old days it was bow-legged turds with their University degrees and diplomas lording it; dead fish stinking from the head.

**Cranach:** Academics, the higher education breed, as useful as two left feet, trying to imagine what the flame of a candle looks like after it's been blown out. Never liked 'em.

**Gottleb:** Book-readers! They read *books*. We showed 'em books. Books is nothing! I've burnt ten thousand books in a night, reduced 'em to a pile of ash — well, they're easier to carry that way. Now we've got a new bunch of snot-pickers up there giving us orders. I can give orders 'stead of taking 'em. MARCH! SHOOT! DIE! Our day to crow it in the sun. MARCH! SHOOT! DIE! That was the promise and the dream. *(he pulls off his moustache)* We was robbed again. MARCH . . . SHOOT . . . DIE . . .

**Stroop:** I was ruined when I was twelve. I found a fifteen thousand mark note in the gutter and I spent the rest of my life with my eyes fixed on the ground, always looking down instead of ahead. If I could've seen where I was going it would've been different. I was young, strong, hard. They couldn't've stopped me. I'd've had a new uniform with bright buttons and boots up to the calf. Leather boots to step on fat faces, boots, boots, marching up and down again left-right, left-right, *crunch*, *craa* . . .

*He raises his rigid legs and smacks them down savagely as he 'goose-steps' frantically round the office until he ricks himself and has to hobble painfully back to his chair.*

**Else:** For two thousand years Christians've worshipped the Cross and made women like me carry it. If I hadn't had a bad case of Catholic conscience, I could've been mistress of Silesia by now. When I was in the Ministry, Gauleiter Hanke wanted what I had. I said he couldn't have it, it was Lent. So he took a pimple-faced shop girl from the Wittenbergplatz. Prussian blockhead. His idea of style was mirrors in the bedrooms, fountains in the hall, and bull-necked SS men serving tea in white gloves. White gloves! Oh what taste and elegance I could've shown him.

*She sweeps around, acknowledging imaginary guests with gracious smiles and nods.*

A luxury villa in Dahlen, dining every night at the 'Horcher' or driving to the 'Furst von Stollberg' in the Harz Mountains. I could've set the tone for the best society. Instead we have Frau Goebbels rushing up to the wife of the Italian Minister, shouting 'Is that dress real silk?'

**Stroop** *(giggling)*: You know what Frau Emmy said to Reich-Marshal Goering at their wedding reception. 'Why've you got on your tuxedo and medals Herman, this isn't a first night.'

**Else:** She's given up membership of the Church, she's lost faith in the resurrection of the flesh.

*They gather round laughing.*

**Cranach:** Don't laugh. It's an offence to make people laugh. Jokes carry penalties. So don't. Have you tried the new Rippentrop herrings? They're just ordinary herrings with the brain removed and the mouth split wider.

*Shrieks from* **Else** *and* **Stroop,** *whilst* **Gottleb** *roars and slaps his thigh in delight. Their laughter quickly grows louder and more hysterical.*

**Gottleb:** That'll get you five years hard labour, Viktor. Here's one carries ten: my dentist is going out of business. Everyone's afraid to open their mouths.

**Else:** The only virgin left in Berlin is the angel on top of the victory column — Goebbels can't climb that high.

**Gottleb:** I sentence you to fifteen years, Fräulein.

**Else:** A German's dream of paradise is to have a suit made of genuine English wool with a genuine grease spot in it.

**Gottleb:** Another fifteen.

**Stroop:** We can't lose the war, we'd never be that careless.

**Gottleb:** Twenty years hard.

**Stroop:** The time we'll really be rid of the war is when Franco's widow stands beside Mussolini's grave asking who shot the

Führer?

**Gottleb:** Thirty.

**Cranach:** Listen, listen, what do you call someone who sticks his finger up the Führer's arse?!

**Gottleb:** Heroic.

**Cranach:** No, a brain surgeon!

**Gottleb:** That's DEATH.

*Cranach,* **Else** *and* **Stroop** *collapse in hysterical laughter. But it dies away as they become aware that a suddenly sober* **Gottleb** *is staring balefully at them.*

**Cranach:** You're not laughing, Hans.

**Gottleb:** But I am inside, *inside.* *(he stamps round triumphantly)* I have you strung up and out, Cranach! I waited and I won it. You didn't realise I'm abnormally cunning, like most fanatics. Death's mandatory for all jokes, good or bad, about our beloved Führer-make-him-happy-he-deserves-it. No more talk of not giving Krupp AG that CP3 (m) contract. I'll have you in front of People's Court Judge Rehse, in a day, sentenced and hanging from piano wire by the end of the week. Job, family, life, lost in one, Cranach. And the rest of you're going under . . . 'His sacred arse . . . a finger up it . . . brain-surgeon.' Filthy! Filthy!

**Cranach:** Sacred arse . . . finger up . . . brain-surgeon? You've been drinking, Gottleb! I never tell jokes. Everyone knows I've no sense of humour.

**Else:** Nobody has in Amt C, the atmosphere isn't conducive.

**Cranach:** I know you want Krupps AG to get the CP(m) contract and us professional civil servants out. But you go too far in treating the Führer's arse – bless-it-and-make-it-happy-it-deserves-it as a joke. Every part of the Führer's super-human anatomy is treated with awesome respect in this office. We shout 'Heil Hitler, Heil Hitler, Heil Hitler' every morning. We worship him as a flawless being, a divinity, and you talk of his arse.

**Gottleb:** *I* don't, Cranach, *you* do . . .

*The* **Others** *gasp and shake their heads in horror.*

Lies, shit-drizzle of lies. But I expected this.

*He opens his brief-case, left on the desk and takes out a small tape-recording machine: the* **Others** *look puzzled.*

It's the latest example of Aryan technological genius. A magnetic tape-recording machine, just developed by Army Intelligence. A masterpiece of German ingenuity. The magnetization on the tape induces electrical currents in the coil, which are then amplified and reproduced, recreating the original sounds. Soon every home'll have one wired to a central control. Then every word spoken'll be noted and banked, no more secret words, only secret thoughts. And one day those too'll be taped. What a day that'll be. I switched it on when you started making jokes. You look ill Cranach, and you Stroop. I'll play it back, see if you think it's still funny. Somehow I don't think you'll laugh this time around, jokes've a way of dying too.

*He starts to wind back the spools on the machine.*

**Stroop:** I'm an old man, my legs don't bend so easy. I let the flies settle and the days burn out like matches. Herr Cranach did say something about arses and fingers. He said it, I didn't . . . I'm only repeating . . . you don't think I . . . how could . . . Heil Hitler! Heil Hitler!

**Else:** I heard Herr Cranach too. I'd have to swear it for my Mother's sake. She's a grand old lady over eighty now. Once met the Kaiser, more or less. I've been non-political for over thirty — twenty — years, so whoever it was it wasn't me! Heil Hitler! Heil Hitler!

**Gottleb:** I like it! I like it! I'm peeling you naked to the centre. I like it! I like it! Oh, I like it!

**Cranach:** I'm sure we all said things. I believe you even mentioned it'd be heroic touching up the Führer — MAKE-HIM-HAPPY-HE-DESERVES-IT. Bad schnapps talking, not a good German. We're all in this together.

**Gottleb:** Old lies, I shit on old lies. Here's something you'll hear beyond your death. The truth!

**Cranach, Else** *and* **Stroop** *brace themselves. He switches on the tape-recorder to hear a cacophony of high-pitched screeches, muffled squawks and clicks.* **Cranach, Else** *and* **Stroop** *exchange looks, whilst* **Gottleb** *smiles complacently.*

**Gottleb:** You can't lie your way out of that!

*He leans closer to the recorder and repeats words only he can hear on the tape.*

'What do you call someone who sticks his finger up the
Führer's arse . . . ?' Disgusting! Disgusting . . . ! 'No, a
brain-surgeon.' *(he switches off)* Ipso facto. Hang him.

**Cranach:** For what? It's just noise. Not one human voice. It
doesn't work.

**Gottleb:** It doesn't work? The latest product of German
technological genius and you say it doesn't work. That's anti-
German slander. You could get another ten years on top of
your death sentence for that. You don't hear anything
because you don't want to. But I hear voices, clear as bells.

**Cranach:** That nobody else can hear. If you had more brains,
Gottleb, you'd be in an asylum. Fräulein Jost, Herr Stroop,
did you hear anything?

*They both shake their heads.* **Gottleb** *rewinds the spools.*

**Gottleb:** I'm not surprised. Women never listen, they haven't
the glands and that old fool's half dead and completely
stupid. But you can't get round hard facts. Listen.

*He switches on the tape recorder again, which plays exactly
the same noise.*

NOW tell me you can't hear anything . . . ? 'Finger' . . .
'arse' . . . 'brain-surgeon' . . . The Gestapo'll take that as
evidence. *(he switches off the recorder)* Especially when it's
confirmed by your own staff. Fräulein Jost, Herr Stroop,
you've already sworn he made the joke. Now it's your duty to
swear his life away for the Fatherland. 1937 Civil Service
Code, paragraph 6. No matter how humble his station in
life, every German enjoys equal opportunity before the law,
to denounce his social superiors. I appeal to your patriotism,
or better still, your greed and envy. *(he rewinds the spools)*
Remember informers inherit their victim's job as a reward.

*He crosses and pours* **Stroop** *a drink.*

Stroop, if you tell the truth and say you hear Cranach's voice
on the tape, you take over his position. Think of it. Head of
your own department at sixty-four. That's fantastic progress,
for someone with your obvious limitations.

**Stroop:** Will I be able to sign memos, have the largest desk, two
phones, lose my temper and no one have the right to answer
back?

**Gottleb:** All yours, just tell the truth. *(pouring* **Else** *a drink)* And you Fräulein, from Acting Secretary Grade III (Admin) to Permanent Secretary Grade I with increased salary and pension, and permanent use of the first floor Grade I executive wash-rooms.

**Else:** I'm told each toilet seat's individually covered with an organdie doily, capped with a gilded swastika. Some women've stayed in those washrooms for days.

**Gottleb:** Shit-house decadence! It killed my father! But it's all yours if you tell the truth, hear Cranach's voice. Listen. LISTEN.

*He switches on the recorder again and they listen hard.*

**Stroop:** Yes . . . sounds behind the sounds . . . laughter . . . a voice.

**Else:** Faint . . . faint . . . what does it say?

**Gottleb** *(slowly)*: 'What do you call someone who sticks his finger up the Führer's arse?'

**Else** ⎱ *(repeating slowly)*: 'What do you call someone who
**Stroop** ⎰ sticks his finger up the Führer's arse?'

**Gottleb:** 'A brain-surgeon.'

**Else**
**Stroop** ⎱ *(repeating slowly)*: 'A brain-surgeon.'

*There is a click.* **Cranach** *has switched off the machine.*

**Gottleb:** Too late, Cranach. I've witnesses now. They heard. Who's guilty, Cranach? The punished man, the punished man!

*He produces a children's Christmas toy squeaker and blows it repeatedly at* **Cranach.**

**Cranach:** Fräulein, Herr Stroop, the joke's on you, not on the tape. Give him that finger and he'll want the whole hand.

*He pours* **Else** *and* **Stroop** *a drink from his bottle.*

Fräulein, he won't let you see a Grade I salary, pension or toilet seat. You're marked dead meat, cold water. And you, Heinz. You'll never become Department Head. It'll be Gottleb's thirty pieces reward for denouncing me. But he can only get it if you lie about me and the Führer's-make-him-happy-he-deserves-it famous arse. I know you won't lie. Over the years we three've formed an abiding relation, working together, grieving together when your wife died,

Heinz and your mother didn't, Fräulein. The best way to
help ourselves is by helping each other. The times're sour,
we've lost the true meaning of things, but I know I can still
find integrity and trust amongst my friends.

**Gottleb:** 'Integrity', 'trust', 'friends.' Whenever I hear noble
sentiments I reach for my wallet to see if it's been lifted. Your
friends're selling you Cranach, because I can give 'em
something better than 'integrity', 'trust', 'friendship'.

**Cranach:** So can I, Gottleb — 'security'. Fräulein, Herr Stroop,
you measure out your days classifying, documenting,
numbering. It's always the same, but always within your
capabilities. Sometimes you're bored, but never anxious for
you know tomorrow'll be the same as today. If you denounce
me it'll never be the same again, only the same as outside,
full of choice and change, violence and blood. Are you going
to throw away all this security on the word of a man who every
hour he's out of prison is away from home. He's not one of
us. He isn't safe!

**Else:** No, Herr Cranach. I have to tell the truth. No matter who
it hurts. A so-called joke about the location of the Führer's
mighty brain-make-it-happy-it-deserves-it was told in this
office.

**Gottleb:** Now it falls, it falls!

**Else:** By you, Herr Gottleb!

**Stroop:** You said he needed a finger-surgeon! We all heard you
Gottleb. Filth! Filth!

**Gottleb:** He said it, I didn't . . . I was only repeating . . . you
don't think I . . . how could . . . Heil Hitler . . . Wheezle-
gutted, chicken-breasted vomit! In the old days every good
German was an informer, now you can't rely on anyone to
betray the right people. The true Aryan spirit's gone forever.
I don't need white-livered, crow-bait.

**Cranach:** You do, Gottleb. Without them you've got nothing.
*(he switches on the tape)* Nothing but laughter. They'll laugh
you out, Gottleb, just as we're laughing you out.

    *Laughing loudly,* **Else, Stroop** *and* **Cranach** *produce
children's toy squeakers, put on Christmas paper hats and
advance triumphantly on* **Gottleb,** *who defends himself by
also putting on a paper hat and whipping out his toy*

*squeaker. They blow furiously at each other. But* **Gottleb** *is outnumbered. He backs away, claps his hands over his ears and collapses in a chair.*

**Cranach** *switches off the recorder, whilst* **Else** *and* **Stroop** *continue jeering.* **Gottleb** *takes off his paper hat.*

**Gottleb:** I'm tired in advance. All these years fighting. The forces of reaction're too strong. Pulled down by blind moles in winged collars. Your kind can't be reformed, only obliterated. As you build 'em we should find room for you in one of our complexes in Upper Silesia: Birkenau, Monowitz or Auschwitz.

**Else** *and* **Stroop** *stop jeering.*

That's where I should be too. Out in the field. Not stuck behind a desk in Orienburg, but in the gas-chambers of Auschwitz, working with people. Dealing with flesh and blood, not deadly abstractions: I'm suffocating in this limbo of paper. Auschwitz is where it's happening, where we exterminate the carrion hordes of racial maggots. I'd come into my own there on the Auschwitz ramp, making the only decision that matters, who lives, who dies. You're strong, live; you're pretty, live; you're too old, too weak, too young, too ugly. Die. Die. Die. Die. Smoke in the chimneys, ten thousand a week.

**Cranach, Else** *and* **Stroop** *look disturbed.*

**Stroop:** What's he say? What's he say?

**Cranach:** Too much. Hold your tongue between your fingers, Gottleb, there're ladies present.

**Else:** I only type and file WVHA Amt C 1 (Building) to WVHA Amt D IV/5 your reference QZV/12/01 regulation E(5) PRV 24/6 DS 4591/1942.

**Stroop:** We only deal in concrete. We're Amt C 1 (Building). Test procedure 17 as specified structural work on outer surfaces of component CP3(m) described in regulation E(5), what's CP3(m) to do with life and death in Upper Silesia? Everybody knows I'm sixty-four years old.

**Gottleb** *(rising)*: You know extermination facilities were established in Auschwitz in June for the complete liquidation of all Jews in Europe. CP3(m) described in regulation E(5) is the new concrete flue for the crematoriums.

    **Cranach, Else** *and* **Stroop** *sit.*

**Cranach:** Who knows that?

**Else** ⎫
**Stroop** ⎭ We don't know that.

**Gottleb:** You don't know that only knowing enough to know you don't want to know that. Future cases of death must be given consecutive Roman numbers with consecutive subsidiary Arabic numbers, Numerical I/1 to I/185. If you could see the dead roasted behind Roman numerals I/1 to Roman numeral XXX/185 you'd run chicken-shitless, but you haven't the imagination. Even if you read of six million dead, your imagination wouldn't frighten you, because it wouldn't make you see a single dead man. But I'll make you see six million! I'm going to split your minds to the sights, sounds and smells of Auschwitz. Then I'll be rid of you. You'll go of your own accord. You piss-legs haven't the pepper to stay in WVHA Amt C knowing every file you touch's packed tight with oven-stacked corpses. No way then to hide behind the words and symbols. You won't be able to glory in it like me, seeing the night trains halting at the ramp behind the entrance gate, between Birkenau and the Auschwitz parent camp. Don't you see the searchlights, guard dogs, watch towers, men with whips? And at the far end, Crematoria I and II, belching sticky-sweet smoke and waiting for the new concrete flues, CP3(m). Don't you see the trains carrying three thousand prisoners a time, eighty to a wagon built to hold thirty? They've been travelling five days without food or water so when the doors're open they throw the corpses out first, the sick fall next, stinking from typhus, diarrhoea, spotted fever. Hear the screaming? They're being beaten into lining up five abreast to march past the SS doctors. Those fit to work go right, those unfit, the old, sick, and young go to the left for gassing. Mothers try to hide their babes, but the Block Commanders always find 'em. 'What's this shit?! This shit can't work!' They use the new-born babes as balls, kicking 'em along the ramp shouting 'Goal! Goal!'

**Else** *sobs,* **Stroop** *and* **Cranach** *cry out in protest as they clasp their heads in pain.*

You see! They're there, behind those files there, stripped, shaved, tattooed on their left arms 10767531. Two thousand living in block-houses, built for five hundred; primitive conditions for Europe's primitives. Work till you die, on a quarter loaf of bread and one bowl of soup made of potatoes, and old rags. Look there, see the labour gangs stagger out through the morning mists, to start their twelve-hour shift in Krupps' fuse factory, skin peeling back from their bones. No malingerers here, if sick, they're allowed one lick of an aspirin hanging on a string, two licks if they're really ill. Life expectancy four months. Some do survive and have to be killed off with benzine injections, dying, in those files, for being too strong or too weak. Amt C like Amt D's only concerned with dying. Dying by starvation, despair, crowbar, bullet, axe, meat-hook, surgeon's knife. Roman numerals LXX/27 to LXXXX/84, dying by chloral hydrate, phenol, evipan, air that kills, Roman numeral LLXI/30 to LLLXII/67. Trouble makers die hardest, hanging from window frames, hot radiators, see Roman numeral XXX/104; with iron clamps round temples; screwed tight, skulls craaaack, brains slurp out like porridge. 'Corpse carriers to  the gate house at the double!'

**Else, Cranach** *and* **Stroop** *stagger up, shaking and moaning.*

We need more plants like Auschwitz, manufacturing and recycling dead Jews into fertilizing ash. We've already reached a peak output of 34,000 dead gassed and burned in one day and night shift. A record Belsen, Buchenwald, Dachau or Treblinka can't touch. And it's all due to the new gas chambers and crematoriums. You help build 'em so you should be able to see 'em plain. They've been made up to look like public bath houses. 'Our Wash and Steam'll Help You Dream.' The dressing rooms've signs in every European language, 'Beware of Pickpockets,' 'Tie Your Shoes Together and Fold Your Clothes,' 'The Management Take No Responsibility For any Losses Incurred.' Oh we're clever, we're clever. Don't you see how clever? It helps calm those marked down to die as they go naked along carpeted passages to the communal wash-room. Fifteen hundred a time.

*There is the reverberating sound of a steel door shutting Up Stage.* **Cranach, Stroop** *and* **Else** *whirl round to face it, clamping their hands over their ears.*
Now see, see 'em packed, buttock to buttock, gazing up at the waterless douches, wondering why the floor has no drainage runnels. On the lawns above, Sanitary Orderlies unscrew the lid shafts and Sergeant Moll shouts, 'Now let 'em eat it!' and they drop blue, Zyklon B hydro-cyanide crystals changing to gas in the air as it pours down and out through false shower heads, fake ventilators. What visions, what frenzies, the screaming, coughing, staggering, vomiting, bleeding, breath paralysed, lungs slowly ruptured *aaaaah!* See it! See it!

*Twisting frantically to escape the sound of his voice,* **Cranach, Else** *and* **Stroop** *gasp, cough and scream in panic.*
Children falling first, faces smashed against the concrete floor. Others tear at the walls hoping to escape. But see, they're falling too, flies in winter, rushing to the door, shrieking 'Don't let me die! Don't let me die! Don't let me die!', the strongest stamping the weakest down, all falling still, at last, a solid pyramid of dead flesh jammed against the wash-house door, limbs tied in knots, faces blotched, hands clutching hanks of hair, carcasses slimy with fear, shit, urine, menstrual blood they couldn't hold back. You see it now! Look! There! There!

**Cranach:** ⎫
**Else:**    ⎬  We don't see! We don't see!
**Stroop:** ⎭

**Gottleb** *(pointing Up Stage)*: LOOK. Mind splits, death-house door slides open . . . SEE.

*As the sound of the gas-chamber door being opened reverberates, the whole of the filing section Up Stage slowly splits and its two parts slide Up Stage Left, and Up Stage Right to reveal Up Stage Centre, a vast mound of filthy, wet straw dummies; vapour, the remains of the gas, still hangs about them. They spill forward to show all are painted light blue, have no faces, and numbers tattooed on their left arms.*

**Cranach, Stroop** *and* **Else** *stare in horror and* **Gottleb** *smiles*

*as two monstrous figures appear out of the vapour, dressed in*
*black rubber suits, thigh-length waders and gas-masks. Each*
*has a large iron hook, knife, pincers and a small sack hanging*
*from his belt. As they clump forward, they hit the dummies*
*with thick wooden clubs. Each time they do so there is the*
*splintering sound of a skull being smashed.*

**Gottleb:** The Jewish Sonderkommando Sanitation Squad. They
go in after, to see no-one's left alive and prepare the bodies
for the fire ovens.

*Slipping and sliding, the* **Sanitation Men** *use their iron*
*hooks to separate the dummies.*

They have to work fast, there's always another train-load
waiting. *Faster! Faster!* New Sanitation Squads are brought in
every three months and the old ones're sent to the ovens, all
used up. *Faster! Faster!* Part of their job is to recover strategic
war material for the Reich.

*The* **First Sanitation Man** *starts tearing at the mouth of a*
*dummy with his pincers, accompanied by a loud, wrenching*
*sound.*

Gold teeth. They're extracting gold teeth from the corpses.
That's why they're called the 'Gold-diggers of 1942.' Root it
out. Root it out! . . . Quicker, don't take haif the jaw bone!

*Whilst the* **First Sanitation Man** *mimes putting the teeth*
*into his sack, the* **Second Sanitation Man** *gouges a dummy's*
*face with his knife.*

Glass eyes. This way we've thousands of spare glass eyes ready
for empty German sockets. *Faster scum, you want to join the*
*others in the fire pits?!*

*The* **First Sanitation Man** *quickly cuts off a dummy's finger*
*and puts it in his sack.*

That's better. It saves time when you're collecting wedding
rings to slice off the whole finger. *Faster scum! Faster! The*
*ovens! The ovens! More coming. More coming.* SEE. See
what's behind your files?!

*As the* **Sanitation Men** *rip, slice and gouge with increasing*
*frenzy amid the noise of breaking bones and tearing flesh,*
**Cranach, Else** *and* **Stroop** *jerk their heads from side to side*
*and whirl around to avoid looking Up Stage.*

**Cranach:** I see it! I can't fight 'em. I couldn't say 'no' to them.

This isn't the time to say 'no'. I've just taken out a second mortgage!

**Else:** I see it too! But what can I do? I'm only one woman. How can I say 'no'? This isn't a good time for me either to say 'no'. Mother's just bought a new suite of furniture!

**Stroop:** Yes, I see it! But they'll stop me growing roses, wearing slippers all day. I'm peeing down my trouser leg. I'm an old man. You can't expect me to say 'no'. I couldn't say 'no', how can I say 'no' to them? It's a bad time to say 'no'. I'm retiring next year. I'd lose my gold watch!

**Gottleb:** *Faster garbage! Faster!*

*Using their iron hooks, the* **Sanitation Men** *stack the torn dummies in neat piles.*

They're laying out the meat for the fire-ovens. It's baking time. That's a sight you must see, see, see!

*The* **Others** *fall on their knees, facing Down Stage.*

4,500,000 killed and roasted. You'll smell 'em every morning you come into the office, crisp flesh done to a turn, all senses confirm, feathers torn from the wing.

**Else** *covers her eyes,* **Stroop** *his ears,* **Cranach** *his mouth.*

You'll find it hell 'less you get the hell out. So run. Hide. Find somewhere to hide. The sky's falling. This is men's work. *Faster! Faster!*

*He moves Up Stage, yelling at the* **Sanitation Men.** **Cranach** *takes his hands from his mouth.*

**Cranach:** Fight. Fight. Can't let him win. We're Civil Servants, words on paper, not pictures in the mind, memo AS/7/42 reference SR 273/849/6. Writers write, builders build, potters potter, book-keepers keep books. E(5) Class 1 and II, L11, L12, F280/515 your reference AMN 23D/7. 'Gas-chambers', 'fire-ovens', 'ramps', he's using words to make us see images, words to create meanings, not contained in them; then nothing means what it says and our world dissolves. Words're tools. CP(3)m is CP(3)m. Two capitals, a bracket round an Arabic numeral and a small letter 'm', the rest is the schnapps talking. 4,500,000 dead, no yardstick to measure, one four, one five, six noughts, brain can't encompass. *(he gets up)* Memo Amt C1 (Building) to Amt D1 (Central Office). Your reference EC2Z 5LZ. Our reference F68. We merely operate policies embodied in existing legislation and implement decisions of higher authority. Copies to Amt A (military administration) Amt B (military economy) Amt W (SS economic enterprises) . . .

*He helps* **Else** *and* **Stroop** *up.*

Get up, horizontal positions diminish the genius of the German people, we must always be vertical and hierarchical. It's all in the mind. He was lying. I could tell, he used *adjectives*. We merely administer camps which concentrate people from all over Europe. Are we going to let the wet dreams of an obscene buffoon like Gottleb drive us out? He said it, it's all imagination, and hard facts leave nothing to the imagination. We're trained to kill imagination before it kills us. So close mind's door, shut out the light there. Concentrate on what's real, what's concrete. Concentrate and repeat: Component CP(3)m, described in regulation E(5) serving as Class I or Class II appliance shall be so constructed as to comply with relevant requirements of regulations L2(4) and (6) L8(4) and (7).

**Else:**        Component CP(3)m described in regulation E(5)
**Stroop:**      serving as Class I or Class II appliance shall be so constructed as to comply with relevant requirements of regulation L2(4) and (6) L8(4) and (7) . . .

*The steel door of the gas chamber is heard slowly closing and the two sections of filing cabinet Up Stage Left and Right begin to slide back into position Up Stage Centre, blocking off the dummies and the* **Sanitation Men.** **Gottleb** *rushes back down to* **Cranach, Else** *and* **Stroop.**

**Gottleb:** You can't shut it out, not word play, dream play, I've been there! It's *real!*

**Cranach:**     *(chanting):* Future cases of death shall be given
**Else:**        consecutive Roman numbers with consecutive
**Stroop:**      subsidiary Arabic numbers. The first case Roman numeral I/1 the second Roman numeral I/2 up to Roman numeral I/185. Thereafter the cases shall be numbered Roman numeral II from Roman numeral II/1 to Roman numeral II/185 . . .

*The steel door is heard shutting with a final clang as the two filing sections are rejoined in their previous position, Up*

*Stage. The dummies and* **Sanitation Men** *have vanished from sight behind them.*

**Else:** Sanctus, Sanctus, Sanctus. Benedictus Deus!

**Stroop:** All gone 'phoof', nothing disturbing left. It's a triumph.

**Gottleb:** Of mongoloid reasoning, I'll take you there . . . !

**Cranach** *picks up* **Gottleb**'s *briefcase,* **Else** *his file and* **Stroop,** *whilst quickly finishing the last dregs, his schnapps bottle. They thrust them at him.*

**Else:** Knowing you Herr Gottleb makes it hard to believe all souls're equal in the sight of the Lord. Go break a leg.

**Stroop:** Drown yourself, it's funnier.

**Cranach:** Krupps AG won't get that contract in Upper Silesia and you won't get us out of Amt C. You're a man with both feet on the ground Gottleb, until they hang you; I'll send you a rope with instruction. You're OUT.

**Gottleb:** The final degradation, these old Party hairs, pissed on by secret Semites, obvious mediocrities. That's what's finally spoiled National Socialism for me, having to share it with people whose lack of imagination would diminish the Colosseum and the Taj Mahal by moonlight. I'd rather be a bad winner than any kind of loser. I can stand anything but defeat!

**Cranach:** ⎫
**Else:**    ⎬   Root it out!
**Stroop:** ⎭

**Gottleb** *gives a yell as* **Else** *opens the door.* **Cranach** *and* **Stroop** *grab his arms and throw him out. As he lands in the corridor with a crash,* **Else** *slams the door shut. The three grin delightedly and congratulate each other.*

**Else:** I'll put in a RLS/47/3 to E6 (Cleaning and Maintenance) to have this office fumigated.

**Cranach:** Give it priority. Now perhaps we can get back to work. There's still a war to win.

*As they move back to their desk the door suddenly opens and* **Gottleb** *pops his head in.*

**Gottleb:** I've still one more throw, the best and the last.

*He deliberately sticks his Hitler moustache back on his upper lip.*

*HAAA.* Top that!

*Before anyone can react, he quickly withdraws.* **Cranach, Else** *and* **Stroop** *resume work.*

**Stroop:** That man could've done terrible things, overrode recognised procedures, ignored official channels, created precedents. You saved the department, Herr Cranach. I'm proud to've been able to help.

**Else:** We may not be much, but we're better than Gottleb. This time it didn't end with the worst in human nature triumphant, meanness exalted, goodness mocked. The other side has its victories. It's a Christmas present we'll remember, thanks to you, Herr Cranach.

**Cranach:** Thank you, Fräulein. In centuries to come when our complexes at Auschwitz're empty ruins, monuments to a past civilisation, tourist attractions, they'll ask, like we do of the Inca temples, what kind of men built and maintained these extraordinary structures. They'll find it hard to believe they weren't heroic visionaries, mighty rulers, but ordinary people, people who liked people, people like them, you, me, us.

**Else** *and* **Stroop** *look at him, then all three march Down Stage to sing at the audience with increasing savagery.*

**Cranach** ⎫
**Else** ⎬ *(singing):* 'This is a brotherhood of man A benevolent
**Stroop** ⎭ brotherhood of man. A noble tie that binds, all human hearts and minds. Into a brotherhood of man. Your life-long membership is free. Keep a-giving each brother all you can. Oh aren't you proud to be in that fraternity. The great big brotherhood of man.' Sing! Everybody sing!

*Lights go down and an unseen chorus joins the finale in the darkness.*

# EPILOGUE

**Announcer's Voice:** Stop. Don't leave. The best is yet to come. Our final number. The Prisoners Advisory Committee of Block B, Auschwitz II, proudly present as the climax of this Extermination Camp Christmas Concert, the farewell appearance of the Boffo Boys of Birkenau, Abe Bimko and Hymie Bieberstein — 'Bimko and Bieberstein!'

*Introductory music. Applause. A Follow Spot picks out two hollow-eyed comics,* **Bimko** *and* **Bieberstein** *as they enter dancing, Stage Right, dressed in shapeless concentration camp, striped prison uniforms with the yellow Star of David pinned on their threadbare tunics, wooden clogs, and undertakers top hats complete with ribbon. Carrying a small cane each, they perform a simple dance and patter routine, to the tune of 'On the Sunny Side of the Street'.*

**Bieberstein:** Bernie Litvinoff just died.

**Bimko:** Well if he had a chance to better himself.

**Bieberstein:** Drunk a whole bottle of varnish. Awful sight, but a beautiful finish. Everyone knew he was dead. He didn't move when they kicked him. He's already in the ovens.

**Bimko:** Poke him up then, this is a very cold block house.

**Bieberstein:** They're sending his ashes to his widow. She's going to keep them in an hour-glass.

**Bimko:** So she's finally getting him to work for a living.

**Bieberstein:** The Campo Foreman kept hitting me with a rubber truncheon yesterday — *hit, hit, hit.* I said, 'You hitting me for a joke or on purpose?' 'On purpose!' he yelled. *Hit, hit, hit.* 'Good,' I said, 'because such jokes I don't like.'

**Bimko:** According to the latest statistics, one man dies in this camp everytime I breathe.

**Bieberstein:** Have you tried toothpaste?

**Bimko:** No, the Dental Officer said my teeth were fine, only the gums have to come out.

**Bieberstein:** Be grateful. The doctor told Fleischmann he needed to lose ten pounds of ugly fat, so they cut off his head.

*The music has faded out imperceptibly into a hissing sound. The Follow Spot begins to turn blue. They stop dancing.*

**Bimko:** I'm sure I've got leprosy.

**Bieberstein:** Devil's Island's the place for leprosy.

**Bimko:** It's good?

**Bieberstein:** It's where I got mine.

**Bimko:** Can I stay and watch you rot?

*They cough and stagger.*

**Bieberstein:** I could be wrong but I think this act is dying.

**Bimko:** The way to beat hydro-cyanide gas is by holding your breath for five minutes. It's just a question of mind over matter. They don't mind and we don't matter.

*They fall to their knees.*

**Bieberstein:** Those foul, polluted German bastardized . . .

**Bimko:** Hymie, Hymie, please; what you want to do — cause trouble?

*They collapse on the floor, gasping.*

**Bieberstein:** To my beloved wife Rachel I leave my Swiss bank account. To my son Julius who I love and cherish, like he was my son, I leave my business. To my daughter I leave one hundred thousand marks in Trust. And to my no-good brother-in-law Louie who said I'd never remember him in my will — Hello Louie!

**Bimko:** Dear Lord God, you help strangers so why shouldn't you help us? We're the chosen people.

**Bieberstein:** Abe, so what did we have to do to be chosen?

**Bimko:** Do me a favour, don't ask. Whatever it was it was too much . . . Hymie you were right, this act's dead on its feet.

*The Spot fades out.*

**Bieberstein:** Oh mother . . .

*They die in darkness.*

## THE END

*Acknowledgement*
Lines from *The Brotherhood of Man* are reproduced by kind permission of Frank Music Corporation, 1350 Avenue of the Americas, New York.

# Barnes' People:
## Seven Monologues

The monologues *Barnes' People* were presented by BBC Radio 3 in 1981 with a cast which included:

| | |
|---|---|
| CONFESSIONS OF A PRIMARY TERRESTRIAL | *Alec Guinness* |
| THE THEORY AND PRACTICE OF BELLY-DANCING | *Dilys Laye* |
| THE END OF THE WORLD—AND AFTER | *Leo McKern* |
| YESTERDAY'S NEWS | *Peggy Ashcroft* |
| GLORY | *John Gielgud* |
| ROSA | *Judi Dench* |

*Produced by* IAN COTTERELL

# *Introduction*
# *by the Author*

I wrote an adaptation of Synesius' *Eulogy on Baldness* for radio and became interested in the monologue as a dramatic form. So I suggested to the Drama Department of BBC Radio that I should write a series of monologues. They were eager for me to go ahead. The result was *Barnes' People*. As patrons, the BBC were somewhat less generous than the Medicis but without their encouragement, these pieces would literally not have been written.

The seven monologues presented one mundane but serious problem. How could I make it believable that men and women would talk for at least fifteen minutes without interruption? I made them either talk to themselves, to God, an audience, an interviewer, a scribe or tape-recorder.

*Confessions of a Primary Terrestrial* was conceived some years ago and never completed, as a monologue for television. One fifteen minute static medium–close shot of the speaker, Lilly, looking into camera, whilst a voice over conveys his thoughts. Both it and *The Theory and Practice of Belly-Dancing* show the elaborate defences people need to survive. We take what stations of the Cross we can find.

*The End of the World – And After* is about courage; the courage just to put one foot in front of the other, to step out when all we want to do is stay in bed, face to the wall. It is a true story. As is *Glory*.

*The Dancing Mimuses of Byzantium* is based on a legend and attempts to convey the beneficial results of doubt. Be flexible, nothing's certain except death and taxes.

In *Rosa*, which ends the sequence, I wanted to write about passion – straight, without tricks, or irony.

*Rosa* began as a piece on Rosa Luxemburg and ended up being a piece on Dr Rosa Hamilton. But in a way it is still about the other Rosa. Its strength is her strength.

# CONFESSIONS OF A PRIMARY TERRESTRIAL MENTAL RECEIVER AND COMMUNICATOR: NUM III MARK I

LILLY: You don't know. How could you know? I didn't know for sure at first, though I had been preparing since I was a boy. So I shouldn't've been surprised, but I was. I had always been interested in psychic phenomena and I had made a secret study of certain universal mysteries. I worked with great intensity in my youth and soon saw the underlying causes behind the surface of things. As I probed deeper into psychic phenomena my discrimination grew so much that it finally became virtually impossible for me to be tricked. So the day they finally made contact I knew the source was a source for good. (The fact that life still exists on earth proves it. Their power is so immense that force shields have to be erected round them as protection if they come in too close.) When they first called I was fortunately already in that elevated state which is an absolute requirement if you are to have mental rapport with them. I was designated 'Primary Terrestrial Mental Receiver and Communicator Num III Mark I'.)

I had had an earlier warning that something extraordinary was going to happen and that I might be asked to help when a famous Yeti Master, Bunda Singh, who, by mastering the disciplines of Raja, Griani and Kundalini Yoga attained a state of Sammadhi and was able to visit me in East Sheen, though his physical body was in Delhi at the time. When he transported himself to my bedroom the floor creaked under his weight and his long oily hair soiled the back of the sofa when he sat down. I took the blame for that. My wife, Muriel, insisted I wash my hair that evening when there was absolutely no need. That woman's a medical freak. No normal person could talk so long without drawing breath.

I kept silent. As I've had to keep silent about everything. My hands are tied. I could conjure up forces to smash, squash, crush, flatten. But such action on my part is forbidden. I have to exercise control at all times. For uncontrolled spiritual power of this intensity is just as dangerous as uncontrolled nuclear power. Atomic energy in its controlled state built the universe, uncontrolled as in the bomb, it can destroy it. The same with spiritual energy. If one human being were hit with the spiritual energy at my command they would be reduced to a pile of radio-active dust . . . Satellite Number Four retain your present position. Satellite Number Three now in magnetization orbit. Hold. Hold . . . I needn't have accepted their offer. But there was a job that had to be done. Mankind'll read about it, one day, perhaps when the High Governors feel it's safe to open up the Solar Archives. Till then I must stay silent. The Saturnian we call Jesus Christ, said too much, though not the half of it and had to let himself be murdered by the rabble. Naturally once bitten . . . They told me I had to be inconspicuous. Under no circumstances was I to draw attention to myself. It was essential for the work we had to do and the Sacred Books of Zorn say that, good done in darkness throws the brightest light. So I do my work in darkness and like the chameleon change my colour for protection; grey on grey. I am by nature an extrovert, a bon vivant and all round good fellow. I'd like nothing better than to jet it with the jets. Instead a hot water bottle in bed is the most excitement I've had in ages. I promised to grey it with the grey and I have since the day they first contacted me: 10.04 Greenwich Mean July 14th Earth date, September 27th on Alpha IV. Their first message was a simple code: 'Five Zero Five Five Zero Five'. 'I hear you loud and clear Five Zero Five' I replied.

Their first question was, 'Is there intelligent life on earth?'.
I thought for a long time before answering that question. I
still believe it was a trick. With their vast powers they
would've known whether there was or not. Anyway I
finally answered choosing my words with care. 'Yes . . .
You could say there was intelligent life on earth'. I wasn't
going to be caught out making wild generalizations. They
must've thought the reply satisfactory because they asked
me there and then if I'd help the cause of Cosmic Uplifting
by becoming their P.T.M.R.C. – 'Primary Terrestrial
Mental Receiver and Communicator: Num III Mark I'. At
first I transmitted spiritual healing to a few individuals but
soon it became obvious that *everyone* was sick; the whole
world had to be cured. The tasks given to me by the
Cosmic High Governors grew in importance and I
abandoned all material ambitions and submitted myself to
their will. I longed to tell the world of the work I was doing
but I was overruled by the Supreme Council of Urokinase
on Alpha IV. They felt that mankind was not ready for
such revelations and mankind's naïve belief in the laws of
nature would be shattered. I must confess I almost told my
son Gerald. Fortunately he wasn't in his room at the time.
He'd gone to have his wisdom tooth out – the one he can
least afford to lose.

My first major task was 'Operation Dog Star Evening
Star' which the Alpan High Governors called the most
important paranormal event ever to be undertaken on
Earth in this her present life. High Governors always refer
to Earth as she, not it. For them, she is a living breathing
entity, a Planetary Being journeying through the Cosmos,
with her load of human freight clinging to her green skin. It
is to her wisdom and mercy we owe our continued existence,
air, light, food and warmth. Yet like spoilt sons and
daughters we abuse her daily: always taking never giving.
Beside squandering the natural riches Mother Earth gives

freely to us, mankind has even more stupidly, through the
past millenniums, drawn upon priceless psychic energy
flowing out of the Earth's centre. It had to be replaced, by
October 28th, otherwise the Earth Mother would be an
empty shell sucked dry and the Vector Balance would be
overturned. I was asked to be Primary Mental Receiver and
Communicator Num III Mark I in this operation. I was
overwhelmed at the thought. Why was I chosen? Why me?
Because I was there? But there were, and are, millions of
others there. Did I have the inner strength? I wasn't one
hundred per cent fit at the time. I had sinus trouble and a
nasty touch of neuralgia and of course my wife Muriel
would be no help. When was she ever a help? I married her
in a dense fog and never saw the sun again. I told them I
should be free of all terrestrial burdens – and she was the
biggest – in order to carry out this momentous work. But
they insisted I remain 'en family'. I could've been rid of her
easily but they believe the family is the backbone of earthly
society and morality. 'When did she stop loving you?' they
asked. 'A year before we were married' I replied. But they
still refused to let me change a hair of it. Yet by raising this
finger . . . ah . . .

It seemed strange at first conducting Operation 'Dog
Star Evening Star' from 14a Willowside Avenue, East
Sheen. For in this world-spread spiritual operation twenty
four mountains in countries from Peru to Tibet, from the
Rockies to Fiji were charged, through me, as New Space
Centres. I made these mountains great batteries of power
which would radiate throughout the world thus renewing
the vital psychic energy banks of Mother Earth. Instructed
by the Alphan High Governors I was able to recharge the
Earth's batteries by supreme mental concentration and
silent prayer. In Cosmic time this Solar Recharging lasted
some five years or 1½ minutes in Earth time. The mental
concentration demand was enormous but so was the

importance of the operation. One miscalculation and it would've turned out a failure; vast worlds would've been thrown out of orbit and this Earth would've dropped out of Vector Balance with the Cosmos, never to return. But it wasn't a failure. Far from it. Thank Zorn, I was equal to the task . . . Satellite Number One Magnetic flux in this quadrant is eight and holding. Magnetic flux eight and holding . . . Yes, I was equal to the task. They knew their man. There's always a reason for what they do however unreasonable it looks. I'm certain the High Men fed all the available data into the Solar Computer Banks and so came up with Edward Charles Lilly. Right from the start they played fair. They told me the sacrifices required of me. The power given but withheld, the supremacy absolute but suppressed. I accepted. But I still find it hard. I have a wife when I could have women. She despises me. Of course, she doesn't know who she's dealing with but she despises me. She says she should've known any man who falls down the church steps at his own wedding would make a mess of everything. Sometimes she cries. I let her hoping maybe the gin will run out of her eyes. I could *squash* her but the High Governors don't believe in violence. It was – is – always will be – the supreme test of my self-control . . . Satellite Four all beams interlock. Interlocking Satellite Four . . . Last winter I was called in on an emergency. A deadly new 'flu virus was about to sweep across the Western Hemisphere according to the solar data boys at Xenon. I had to act as channel Num III Mark I. Tremendous spiritual energy was pulsed through me then out of those who otherwise might have perished from the epidemic. I don't know how many were saved, I expect no reward but a little recognition would not go amiss.

My son Gerald sat up in his room all that winter playing records and thinking. Thinking! That boy would have trouble thinking his way out of a telephone booth. And my daughter Sarah is no better. She used to be my favourite, now I never see her. She's out when I come in from work. Boy friends with dirty fingers and sideburns. She told me she was waiting for the right man before she got married. 'I didn't', says my wife. And they giggled. They wouldn't giggle if they knew. But I have to play my cards close. I have to keep reminding myself I'm a P.T.M.R.C. Num III Mark I. I have to seem ordinary and make sure there's no difference between me and other family men. I merge with the rest. That's why I'm still working for 'Brenton & Crawshaw'. It's not for the high salary they don't pay me but for the cover they provide. Nobody would suspect that a Num III Mark I P.T.M.R.C. for Alpha IV would work for Brenton & Crawshaw when they could be rich. Yes, rich. When I was conducting Operation Skyblue I learned just how easy it would be for me to make a fortune. In Operation Skyblue I built a tiny radionic instrument and set it up on Parliament Fields and with energy radiated from Alpha IV conditioned and transferred it into an energy vortex passing up through the stratosphere. It gave me an insight into the wealth potential at my fingertips. I could have patented that machine. It would have generated enough energy to run Guildford for a hundred years. I knew where the treasures of the earth lay hidden, gold, silver, oil and the rest. I could be rich but the High Governors feel that riches corrupt and incite envy. Clothed in riches and power it would be impossible for me to keep in touch with ordinary people throughout the world. The Books of Zorn declare that work ennobles a man. So every weekday morning, rain or shine, I stand on Platform 2 at East Sheen station waiting for the 7.30 train . . . Four, four I can hear you Number Four. Basic flux through the high atmosphere. Change to manual, hold. Hold . . . Winter is the worst, waiting like ghosts in the mist and rain with the others. That's when it's hardest not to throw off this disguise. I look into their ordinary faces and want to shout 'It's me – this world's first P.T.M.R.C.' But I know it's only another manifestation of pride. When I was at my lowest, alone in my room concentrating my mental powers, cleaning out the thought channels, they let me witness an Ascension Ceremony. It happened in the back garden of our semi-detached. The High Governors put a force shield round the Beta 3/72 Space Module Yento 107 so that no-one else would see it. I was the first terrestrial to witness the ascension of a female Alpha Centura. I didn't know where she was ascending to and I didn't like to ask but I remember the light about her face, and the tiny Zilch bells ringing and it was like the music of the spheres – so-called. It reconciled me a little to 'Brenton & Crawshaw'. I've been there fifteen years. I could've been Departmental Manager, even on the Board of Directors by now if I hadn't deliberately made mistakes. For I had to be average and the average man makes mistakes. To be perfect is to fall into the sin of pride and challenge God, the Supreme Alphan. They couldn't allow me to do that. So I soldier on at 'Brenton & Crawshaw'. I smile my secret little smile when I see others smiling at me behind their hands. I've saved you, again and again though some – many – most of you – are not worth the saving. But then remember the appalling low position of the average man on the Evolutionary ladder . . . Satellite Number One position as given. Basic Clarification Number Nine, code six . . . Once the decision was made I had to suffer in silence. Let my family's contempt and anger beat about my head. All things have to be experienced as we rise to each new level of consciousness . . . Code Six Number Nine, use code six . . . The High Governors have taught me not to give in to bitterness, to be willing to work on in obscurity, to reject fame and fortune to use my supreme power for the good of all. They've also given me the strength to look into the future and not be afraid . . .

Satellite Number Seven release all waves. Satellite Six
release all waves. Satellite Five release all waves . . . I've
glimpsed my last days dying in Sheen General Hospital of
some obscure stomach disease. Friday 2.00 a.m. Earth
time; alone in the dark, snuffed out. On Alpha IV they'll
dim down the solar flares, ring the two great bells of
Yamota. B-o-n-g B-o-n-g. 'Primary Terrestrial Mental
Communicator and Receiver Num III, Mark I has closed
down all primary and secondary circuits permanently.
P.T.M.C.R. Num III Mark I is now inoperative'. They'll
note it – in the Books of Zorn and micro-dot it in the Solar
Archives of Xenon and a five second silence will be called
throughout the system. Here on Earth, Muriel will give
my clothes to Oxfam, throw my toothbrush and razor into
the dustbin and Gerald and Sarah will reluctantly sacrifice a
couple of hours to lay me to rest. They'll talk of 'poor old
Lilly' at Brenton & Crawshaw's for half a day, but I'll leave
no memories. My family will hardly notice I've gone. No-
one'll make a speech over my grave. There'd be nothing to
say. For them my life passed like water here on Earth but
up there in the stars it's a different story . . . Satellites
Number Four and Five make ready to land. Make ready to
land . . . I have been a humble instrument of Great Powers.
I could've taken this world apart and put it together. The
greatest terrestrialman this world has seen since the great
Avatars who also acted as agents, Shri Khrisna Buddha,
Moses, Christ and Mohammed. I am of their country . . .
'Come in Satellite Number One, Satellite Two, Satellite
Three come in . . .' But I'll slip away, no trace in the snow,
no hand print in the dust and they'll continue delivering the
morning paper as if nothing had happened, as if they hadn't
lost a great Avatar . . . 'Come in all Satellites. Come in all
Satellites. Come in . . .' I could've been all-mighty and
no-one would've smiled. But who knew? You don't know.
How could you know? . . .

# THE JUMPING MIMUSES OF BYZANTIUM

MAYA: I'm dying now. But that's good. I'm an old man and my life has been spent preparing for this moment: to live well and to die better. My early years were filled with prayer and fasting. I often slept for just one or two hours a night and lived on five olives and muddy water – and walked barefoot in the snow in the depths of winter.

I was born in a village to the north of Amid near Byzantium. God-possessed, I became a disciple of Paul the Hermit who lived in a cave near Kharhut. He always urged me not to overdo my self-mortification. 'There's too much pride in too much humility' he would say. But I was young and confident. I went to Egypt, then the chief school of asceticism, where I visited various longhaired penitents who scourged their flesh in praising God. At the time I was a firm Monophysite, a religious sect, out of favour with the authorities. The Emperor Justinian had me and others like me, driven from our monkish cells. Some just went further into the desert, but I took a ship to Byzantium. Bearded, I bearded the Emperor and his Empress, Theodora, in their court. Filthy and tattered I strode into that gilded throne room and cried: 'Carrion of Satan, hellspawn! Persecutors of men of God, may your womb be blasted and your instrument of procreation drop off!' Looking back, it was an act of overweening pride. I was right but presumptuous to swear at those presumptuous rulers.

Neither Justinian nor Theodora were able to reply to my holy zeal in the usual way – with violence. For one thing, we Monophysites were still a very powerful party in Byzantium and they had a superstitious awe of anyone who spoke the truth. Theodora wanted me to become her confessor, but I told her her burden of sin was too great for one man to cope with. She tried to bribe me with a hundred pounds of gold but I flung the bag away with one hand shouting, 'To hell with you and the money you use to tempt me.' All were amazed at my strength and the fact it was money I was throwing away. A rare sight in Byzantium or anywhere else for that matter.

Afterwards I went to live in the hills outside the city. The Empress sent me a message saying she would be glad to supply whatever I wished. I replied that she need not suppose herself to have anything a true servant of God could use, unless it was the fear of God, if she had ever possessed such a thing as that.

Living in a cave in the mountains and eating wild fruit and herbs, I was credited with at least three miracles. Though they were common-place around Byzantium at the time, I gained the reputation of being a Saint, not, I fear, through my piety, but because I once spoke the truth to an Emperor and rejected an Empress's bribe. Naturally I was consulted on religious and ethical matters. I delivered hundreds of judgements on the right way for a Christian to live and die. I was very sure I knew the truth of God's mind. Of course I was plagued with Satanic visions but for a man like me Satan's easily dealt with.

But this isn't the story I want written down, to bridge the time between now and when: now, here in Amin, 542, dying, and when you read these words.

One day in the year 530 there appeared on the streets of Amin a performer, a Merry Andrew, a clown – what we call a Jumping Mimus. He had a female assistant with him. Dressed in brightly patched costumes and bells, they juggled with coloured balls, leaped and tumbled; the young man jested and the young girl sang. As was the custom, she also seemed to carry on her trade as a prostitute. Unfortunately such immorality was not unique amongst us. Though we

have a reputation for fanatical piety, it goes hand in hand
with a rampant sensuality.

Though the people had seen Merry Andrews before, this
pair attracted special attention because of their extreme
youth and beauty. The young man had an agile body and
wit. The young girl sang suggestively:

By day my eyes, by night my soul desires thee
Weary I lie alone
Once in a dream it seemed you were beside me
Oh if you would only come.

The two were given money and abused. They were liked
for their skill and hated for their freedom. Every evening
the Jumping Mimuses would disappear, nobody knew
where.

Certain Court-officials, who were living in Amin at the
time, saw them performing and, struck by the beauty of
the young girl, went to the Governor and asked him to
officially declare her a prostitute. That way they could
enjoy her favours in a state brothel. Such is the depraved
trade of the court, I only wonder they did not try to arrange
a similar fate for the young man. However, the Governor's
wife heard of the matter and being a strong-minded God-
fearing woman saw to it that the Court officials left with
their vile tails hanging limply between their legs. She had
the young girl brought to her and advised her to lead a
better life. The girl listened attentively and went straight
back to her companion in sin.

But the Governor's wife was not satisfied. There was
something mysterious about the girl. She consulted a friend
of mine, John of Ephesus, about the pair. After a great deal
of trouble he found they lived in a small hut on some
scrub-land on the edge of the town.

One night he paid them a surprise visit. He stumbled
across to the hut and saw through the open window, by the

light of a solitary oil lamp, the two still in their brightly coloured costumes, on their knees praying. John of Ephesus watched them for at least an hour at their prayers. Then he confronted them. Why did they pray so devoutly? Why did they behave so wantonly in the streets by day and devote themselves to prayer at night? The young couple refused to answer.

I was in Amin at the time, offering up prayers for the soul of Paul the Hermit. John of Ephesus asked me to help him try to unravel the mystery of the Merry Andrews. Secret devotion and public wantonness seemed to me unique while the reverse was all too common. So I found myself one stormy night stumbling across the scrub-land to find the young couple. I knew it to be a dangerous part of Amin. Sure enough, that very night two ruffians sprang out of the darkness threatening to rob me. On most other occasions I would have remonstrated with them on their lack of Christian feeling, but this time, I confess, I felt ill-tempered for being out on such a night instead of praying in my monk's cell. So I gave them a vivid demonstration of what can be done by the power of Christ when conjoined with a strong right arm by breaking the leg of one sinner and the pelvis of the other before they fled.

As I approached the hut I saw the light from the open window. Inside the two were kneeling on the earth floor, facing each other, their hands clasped in prayer. Their costumes, pale blue, red and yellow, glowed in a golden light. The girl's face was without a blemish, her eyes were clear as a summer sky.

But I was not to be seduced by pretty pictures. I burst in unannounced. I must have been a disturbing sight, standing six-foot three in what was left of my stockings, matted hair over my shoulders, grey beard bristling – Jehovah come to punish the world for its sins. After all I had frightened Emperors and Empresses, but these two young sinners rose

quietly, the young man offering me some bread whilst the
young girl poured water for me.

I told them why I was there and that I would not leave
until I had discovered the truth about them. They saw I was
determined so they asked me to sit on the only chair in the
room whilst they squatted on the floor in front of me and
told their story.

The young man spoke first. He said that their names
were Theophilus and Mary. I believed that, she looked like
a Mary – the Mary of the Gospel, but which Mary of the
Gospel – Magdalene or Mother of Christ? Each was an only
child of rich and noble families in the city of Antioch. They
were to be married. But one night when Theophilus was
fifteen he found a poor man in his father's stable, hiding in
the straw to keep warm. Around this poor man's mouth
and hands was a halo which only Theophilus could see and
which disappeared whenever the servants entered. This I
thought rather convenient, but I said nothing.

The holy man said his name was Procopius and he had
come from Rome. He had fled from his home on the day of
his wedding to escape marriage in order to serve God. He
then predicted the exact date of the death of Theophilus'
parents and also Mary's, which would be soon after. Mary
came to see him and he told the young couple that when
their parents died they were to sell everything they had and
give the money to the poor and live consecrated lives.

I was impressed but suspicious. Certain elements of their
story were familiar: children of a rich family, meeting a
holy stranger, in the stable – usually it was St Alexus –
giving away all their possessions to the poor. These were
the basic ingredients of legend. They could be true, but
they were familiar to all Christians.

Mary continued the story. They were instructed to live a
holy life consecrated to God but in disguise. No-one was to
know of it. So when their parents died on the date predicted,

they disguised themselves as Merry Andrews, Jumping
Mimus's and travelled throughout the East. They lived in
virginity together, whilst in the eyes of the world they
wallowed in sin – two shameful wantons, companions in
debauchery. I looked into Mary's beautiful face; could I
find the truth there? Were they saints, reviling, degrading
their flesh for the glory of God? Had these two beautiful
people reached the peak of asceticism? An ascetic who, by
means of prayer and fasting, was completely dead to the
temptation of the world had no longer to fear the world.
He or she need no longer run away, their inner cleansing
was so complete that they would give themselves up to
licentiousness without sin or risk, since they were no longer
subject to passion and so could indulge in wantonness.
They were ascetics beyond asceticism. Saint Salus, the
dissolute saint, drank, ate and was one day seen leaving a
prostitute's room looking furtively around him so as to
increase suspicion. Saints like that have so conquered
passion and so triumphed over nature that no glance or
touch can rouse them to any dishonourable action. The
Grace of God combined in them the most contrary elements
which otherwise would be incompatible. Could Theophilus
and Mary be of that breed? We solitaries had gone into the
desert to find purity, solitude and God, now the experiment
was turning full circle, with a return to the world. Who
would have thought these two performers, prostituting
themselves in the streets of Amin were saints?

I took Mary's face in my hands and looked for the truth
there. Yes, such beauty was saintlike. She told me the
degradation of her flesh was an offering to Christ. She sang
again, clear and true:

> By day my eyes, by night my soul desires thee
> Weary I lie alone
> Once in a dream it seemed you were beside me
> Oh if you would only come.

She explained the 'thee' was Christ. The song was a
desire for Christ's love to come to her.

We prayed together all night. I bearded, gnarled, hardened
by the sun, they bright and soft, with the beauty of youth. I
left in the morning and they continued performing in the
streets of Amin where their fame and mystery made them
even more popular; they attracted crowds wherever they
went.

When I was looking into the eyes of Mary, the truth
seemed obvious. As obvious as the truth always had been
to me. Later I had my doubts. But by that time they had
gone. They suddenly vanished. I never saw them again.
John of Ephesus met them once on the road to Byzantium
and I heard years later they bought a villa outside Antioch,
though another story had it they both took Holy Orders.

Were they telling the truth? Were they sinners for Christ?
Or just tricksters who knew our love of new and exotic
forms of worship? Was she a prostitute with a new perversion – sanctity? Or an ascetic with a new discipline –
fornication? And with these doubts came others. If I
couldn't divine the truth of a pair of common Merry
Andrews, how could I divine God's truth?

Earning a little money by making mats and baskets of
palm leaves, I built a hut and planted a garden. Men and
women still came to me, but I gave them food now instead
of advice. On the outbreak of the plague of '42, I looked
after the sick and forced the Emperor to help the victims
with food, clothes and shelter. There was work to do and
the days of my solitude were over. But not the endless war
between truth and lies, half-truths and half-lies, lies and
lies. In this world there's no break between truth and lies,
they are joined: did she lie by swearing she lay with men for
Christ's sake? And who was she lying to if she lied?

You'll say, reading this: 'Stupid holy fool – or just plain
old fool – of course they were lying. They tricked you.

You made them famous.'

Yes, that may be true. I'll soon know, absorbed into the universal mind of God who knows all things. It wouldn't surprise me to discover they were two tricksters, but I held her face in my hands and looked into her eyes . . . pretty picture . . . the light and the face, and the bright costumes in the flame . . . Of course I'll enter God's house, sit on His right hand, meet the disciples and the archangel Gabriel and bathe in everlasting light, but I confess above all I'm dying to know the truth about the Jumping Mimuses of Byzantium . . .

# THE THEORY AND PRACTICE OF BELLY-DANCING

*Slow eastern music and the sound of Alison dancing to it.*

ALISON: Six Travelling Hip Rolls, four Figure Eights, four
Camel Walks and repeat . . . I was just a ghost washing
clothes till I took up belly-dancing. Mention belly-dancing
and they all think of Greek restaurants, swirling skirts and
pop-eyed Sultans. But all over the country women're
signing up for belly-dancing classes in Y.M.C.A.'s recrea-
tion halls, Women's Guilds and Church social groups. I'm
thirty-four years old. I've had two pregnancies and my
stomach used to bulge like a football. Bellying got it back
into shape, improved my posture, made my hips supple,
tummy firm – no flab – and my circulation's one hundred
per cent. Socially I'm better too. When someone asks,
'What have you been doing?' Instead of mumbling, 'Kids,
house, same old thing,' I say, 'I've been belly-dancing.'
Their mouths drop. People look at you with new interest.
And it doesn't stop there, you can follow up with remarks
about Middle Eastern culture and the rest. I've known
women who went into belly-dancing for exercise and
ended up experts on Etruscan tomb sculpture and Turkish
cooking . . . Four Figure Eights, three Hip Circles –
mustn't forget to make the Hip Circles large, come down
on the right leg, up with the left hip into an up-and-down
Figure Eight Snake . . . But belly-dancing's more than just
exercise, it's an art. A marvellous physical and emotional
experience. It frees you from everyday. Your mind
wanders across the world when you're dancing and the
pavements disappear.

　　Ancient Egypt had bellies and in India you can still see
sculptures of belly-dancers like me in the old temples. The

Romans knew about it according to their poets. It's always been an expression of the peoples of the East, a part of their culture. Done right, it's not suggestive, sensual yes, but not sexy. When I'm dancing my hands never touch my body. Of course it has got certain overtones. When they danced it in harems they emphasised the pelvis movements, the same as they do in modern cabaret – but that's not classical bellying . . . Four backward Camel Walks, four Shoulder Shimmies . . . Glenda Fairclough said she started belly-dancing because she wasn't very athletic and couldn't keep up with her husband on the golf course. Now he'd rather watch her dance than break par. Gerald said I took it up for revenge. He's wrong. We used to be heavy with happiness, with his skin so cool against my skin in the morning and we looked babies in each other's eyes. But when you get no satisfaction from each other you go for it separately. We shared the same bed but not the same dreams. I had to manufacture out of nothing something to replace the song we had.

*The music becomes faster.*

. . . Eight Side to Side Hip Drops with a Scooting Shimmy, six Up and Down Shimmies and repeat . . . Looking after kids and a home, a woman gets a mental grey-out and the outlook's black. Your mind becomes blank. You can't concentrate on anything – it's sleepwalking in the day-time. Get up, breakfast, wash up, dress the children, take them to school, come back, make beds, clean, polish, shop, make lunch, collect children, serve lunch, take children back, wash up, laundry, collect children, prepare tea, Gerald comes home, cook, eat, wash up, put children to bed, watch television, bed and repeat and repeat. The needle gets stuck in the wax and you never get to the tune. Every day the same, it sucks you in. Everything level, no high achievements. Not monotonous exactly, just futile. Outside you do something and it's done, in the home it's never

done, today's clean floor is tomorrow's dirty floor and the
next day's clean floor and the next day's dirty floor – rat in
a cage, round and round, spin and spin. Nobody ever
writes 'the end' to it. It eats away your dreams. I wanted to
see my own reflection in the tables I polished just to make
sure I was still there. I held myself together but I was
gradually slipping away: a small shadow. There was
nobody, nothing. I took up belly-dancing because I wanted
to be something, have a value.

*The music slows down again.*

. . . Four Side Hip Thrusts, using two quick thrusts on each
side, Eight Hip Drops in place, Six Side to Side Hip Drops
and repeat . . . Once I knew what I wanted, then I lost it.
I'm happy now I know what I want. When I got into
bellying the music beat behind my forehead and fell into
my stomach. It demands tremendous dedication but I
drove myself mercilessly didn't I? Now the children are
older I can concentrate on what is important. When I found
that mirror I knew I was right. I took it as a sign. I'm sure
it's nineteenth century or even earlier, with all that gilt and
scrollwork round the edges, and the cherubs crowned with
laurel leaves in the corners.

Gerald hated it when I put it up in the dining room so I
could practise in front of it. He called it my 'Whorehouse
Mirror.' I know it doesn't quite go with the rest of the
furniture we got from Heals but I needed it for practising.
Gerald said I needed it like I needed a giraffe. I needed it! I
can see all of myself now. Six hours a day. That's the
minimum amount of practice, if you're serious. Bending,
stretching, sweating – Hip Thrusts! Hip Thrusts! I'll sometimes stop for a glass of water during a session, but that's
all. Must keep going; beyond the mountains there are more
mountains. I didn't care if we had friends round, if I hadn't
put in my six hours I'd practise in front of them. I am
trying to re-arrange my life, to escape, but without practice

the door remains bolted. That's what art is about isn't it? – sacrifice, sacrifice. Hip Thrusts! Hip Thrusts! Our friends sip their drinks politely and stare. I'd tell them to ignore my exercises, to carry on as if I wasn't there. They'd try, but all the time they'd be looking over at me. Hip Thrust! Hip Thrust! Gerald would always make some remark like 'She does it to bring the roses back to her elbows.' I'd let him make his remarks, I was making something for myself.

As a mother and wife I was a boney cage full of nothing, I was all kinds of people on demand – nurse, cleaner, psychiatrist, guard, cook, dustwoman. And I always had to smile. However I felt, I smiled. Phones used to ring, friends came over, the children ran around screaming and Gerald would grunt and glower and I was expected to patch things up – put Humpty Dumpty together again when he fell. So I smiled calmly and was hollow inside. Now I'm being fulfilled.

Gerald keeps complaining I only talk about belly-dancing. But it's what interests me. When I dance I know what's happening. I try to make him see the art of it, the beauty of the undulating movements which interpret the different moods of the music whether it's sad or happy, heavy or light.

Gerald doesn't understand what I'm talking about. I've tried to get him interested in the technical side of bellying which is really fascinating. Just the names themselves have a magic. Pelvic, Torso and Rib Cage Rolls, Forward and Backward Hip Shakes, Thigh Shimmies – which give you the same feeling as Scooting Shimmies – Backward Arm Circles, Head Slides, Serpentine Rolls and Sitting Cobras. I could talk all night about them . . . Serpentine Rolls and Sitting Cobras! But Gerald's eyes always glazed over. I could see he wasn't paying attention. Yet he expected me to pay attention to him when he talked about his world. And when I clicked my zills at him he just got up and left the room.

But a true belly-dancer must, *must* know how to click her finger cymbals if she wants to be a complete belly. They are very important to the dance but Gerald doesn't know, doesn't want to know . . . I'd better do some floor movements. A descent with a Body Roll, Four Serpentine Rolls, three Torso Circles and repeat . . . The world's meaner, harder, sicker than you think. I knew Gerald had a woman a long time before I started belly-dancing. I wasn't hurt because I did the same thing when I was younger. I never thought of it before but you grow old even when you're sleeping. You grow old sleeping. It's a shock growing old, suddenly finding yourself in corners full of memories. No, I wasn't hurt. Stop looking for comfort, there isn't any and if there were this life'd be for babies wouldn't it? Wouldn't it? There's no-one else. You pay so much for learning things like that. It's why I'm straining every muscle now.

Gerald says I've no right to complain as long as I'm taken care of financially. So I've got to make myself good enough to turn professional. I know Madam Constantine taught me pure classical belly-dancing that isn't the same as the cabaret style with all those pelvis thrusts and body-strokings and the audience putting coins in the dancer's bra and hip-band. But I wouldn't allow that. I'd insist I was paid a fee, no tips in bras. I'm going to get myself an agent and some good publicity photographs of myslf in oriental costume; that's the way it's done. I won't let them take photos of me performing without permission. You can be make to look very ugly when you're dancing if you're not careful. I know, I've seen myself in the mirror.

Madam Constantine wouldn't approve of me dancing in places like that. It's a compromise. But I think I could raise the whole level of belly-dancing. Show them a style they've never seen before, no bump and grind but pure bellying at its best.

I've got my act all worked out. Yes, I'm ready. I start with a medium fast musical introduction and enter with Travelling Steps, Hip Thrusts and Shimmies. A spin gets me into the slow section with Figure Eight Variations, Camel Walks, Abdomen Rolls plus Snake arm and veil movements. Then the musical tempo increases and I go into a fast section with Figure Eight Variations, Hip Thrusts and Shimmies all done to a faster beat. This section will finish with a spin and slow descent to the floor and then I'm naturally and smoothly into graceful floor movements, Cobras, Serpentine Rolls and the rest to a haunting accompaniment. The section ends with me rising and performing two standing slow movements which get me easily into position for another Fast Medium section – Travelling Hip Drops and Large Scooting Shimmies in circles. The music gets faster as I go into the finale – Fast Scooting Shimmies, Rapid Shimmies, Hip Thrusts and finishing with five fast spins and a fall. I rise slowly to take my bows. Oh when I'm dancing like that I can feel the ground tilt.

It's what I'm going to do, I'm not going to sit around here in a wet bathing costume for the rest of my life.

Gerald was the person I shared my life with when it wasn't worth sharing. Of course we were in love once, everybody's in love once, it's a condition. I remember his frayed cuffs and how pleased he was with his first silk handkerchief. He always brought flowers and was full of ideas and hope. Oh, life's harder than dancing. You're damn lucky if the past doesn't give you cause for regret. When you can't stand any more it's marked down on hospital charts. Heartbreaks must be taken care of. We should all try and make life seem useful and promising shouldn't we? Shouldn't we? At least I'm making the effort . . . Once more then, six Travelling Hip Rolls, four Figure Eights, four Camel Walks and repeat and repeat . . .

# THE END OF THE WORLD – AND AFTER

MILLER: Lord hear this, the last prayer of your servant William Miller of Low Hampton, New York State. You come with clouds – you rise up in anger and the dark angel's bright sickle cuts the vines – the sun is veiled and man hovers in the middle air – the earth reels – the world crumbles and ends. For ten years, Lord, I told them the world would end and this is the day, the hour, the last minutes before the earth is swallowed whole and time stops.

When I first knew I was too frightened of ridicule to speak out. But you gave me signs. I prophesied to the people and they cried, 'Let us sleep'. But I wouldn't let them sleep and raised an army of repentant sinners, fifty thousand strong. A host of Millerites wait outside whilst I pray alone in thy Tabernacle Lord. Thousands of others throughout America are on their knees, this night, sweating in fear. Trade has ceased, businesses are shut with notices which read: 'Closed in honour of the coming of the King of Kings'. And He will come, but the darkness will come first.

Lord I have commanded my followers to occupy themselves in good works and not to spend their last days in idleness, foolishness and worse – vain breath, vain breath. They tell me farmers have given away their land and livestock and you know Lord how hard it is for a farmer to give away anything. I myself saw a man fasten a pair of turkey wings to his shoulders, climb a tree and jump, expecting to fly straight to heaven. And a woman put all her valuables in a trunk and strapped it to her back so she could take it with her when she rose. Be merciful, Lord, be merciful with them as I am with the sceptics and jeerers.

You saw, Lord, how one of my followers stopped the philosopher Mr Waldo Emerson and his friend Mr Parker with the words: 'Gentlemen, don't you realize the world is coming to an end?' Mr Parker shrugged, 'It doesn't concern me, I live in Boston.' Boston?! Boston?! Even Boston will not be spared! By no means. And Mr Emerson too was unmoved saying, 'The end of the world doesn't bother me. I can get along without it.' No doubt. No doubt. We all could. But it is a fact that cannot be shrugged off with a quip.

All my calculations from the Book of Daniel pointd to the same conclusion that the world's end which precedes the Messianic age is now.

Daniel always speaks of 2300 days and has four important numbers: 1260 days, 1290 days, 1335 days and 70 weeks, which is 490 days. Each of these days I consider a year so 2300 days is 2300 years. My first calculation worked out thus – taking the life span of this world as 2300 we subtract 70 weeks which is 490 days which is 490 years which leaves 1810. Then we added the 33 years of the Saviour's life – because it postponed the end 33 years, added to 1810 leaves us with 1843. Other calculations came to the same conclusion. For example, again taking the life-span of the world as 2300 we subtract the date of the commandment to re-build Jerusalem 457 AD and we are left with 1843. I think everyone who listened Lord concluded that my calculations were irrefutable. Everything pointed to 1843.

I preached in all the Baptist Chapels in America. 'My friends, the Day of the Lord is at hand! And when it comes you and I shall pass into another state of being – a being of eternal torment and glory. Believe it! It comes suddenly. You are gazing at the sky – you are speaking to your wife and children – a thunder breaks – it is the Lord! – You are sleeping in your bed – you hear a crash – it is the Lord! – You feel the earth shaking under your feet – it is the Lord! Prepare.

*(singing)* There is a land of pure delight
Where saints immortal reign.
Infinite day excludes the night
And pleasures banish pain.

The sinners wept, fear gripped them by the threat. Outbreaks of lunacy trebled in Vermont, New Hampshire, Pennsylvania, Maine and New York – though there it was hardly noticed.

In the last year storms swept the country but we ran into the wet fields groaning and hymming. And the last night of the last year 1843 found us shivering in cold air waiting for the coming of the Bridegroom, all faces looking up at the dark sky, every eye strained to catch the first beam of the awful light piercing the clouds. I remember, Lord, I was so excited I left my false teeth on the kitchen table. What would you have said, Lord, if I had appeared before you without my teeth? I rushed back to get them as the last chimes struck . . . one . . . two . . . six . . . eight . . . ten . . . *midnight*. Oh Lord, Oh Lord, my teeth were in but where were the angels blowing the trumpets, bearing swords? Where was the final darkness, the glorious Resurrection . . .? Lord, Lord, nothing had changed. I wept in despair, there was no end. I staggered to my bed and pulled the blankets over my head. The fires of conviction were out.

Then – oh glorious then – Brothers Stor, Southard and Snow approached my bed and Stor whispered:

'Brother Miller your calculations are right.' Right?! Right?! I groaned under my blanket. 'How can they be right when we are all still alive and the earth still about us?'

'Your calculations are right but the year isn't' they insisted.

'But my calculations prophesied December 31st 1843 as the end. 1843 has passed!'

'The Christian year 1843 has but your prophesy applied to the Jewish year 1843. And the Jewish year ends on March 31st 1844!' they said.

*Eeeeekkkk.* I threw the blanket from my face. My heart leapt with joy, the destruction of the world was still possible. My faith in the Merciful Father was restored.

My powers increased, Lord, as the people saw my prophesy about to be fulfilled. Meteors streaked across the sky, mysterious lights were seen in heaven, there were plagues of frogs, toads and lizards, it rained blood and the Stock Market fell one hundred and fifty points.

And so the last day of March had come, the last day of the old Jewish Year, the last meeting, the last farewells, the last minutes of earthly life. Now, now move, move you ever moving spheres of heaven, that time may quicken and midnight come and William Miller will be blessed. Lord, stretch out Thy hand, suck up my soul. It flies from me and I am changed into angel-stuff. The end is here. It strikes the hour. *(He holds up his watch.) One* . . . *Two* . . . light stops . . . *three* . . . *four* . . . *five* . . . earth stops . . . *six* . . . *seven* . . . *eight* . . . time stops . . . *nine* . . . *ten* . . . *eleven* . . . I close my eyes. *Accept my soul Lord! . . .*

*(A long silence, then imperceptibly we hear the sound of Miller's watch ticking, then tentative singing.)*

> There is a land of pure delight
> Where saints immortal reign
> Infinite day excludes the night
> And pleasures banish pain . . .

It's dark but I can hear my own voice. Can you hear your own voice in heaven? Where are angel voices? And angel stuff? And angel light? If I open my eyes will I be blinded by angel light? Lord let me see you shining in glory. I open my eyes . . . *Ahh* . . . *Ahh* . . . *Ahh* this isn't heaven. Still in the cold world! No deliverance – no deliverance – and Christ not come . . . Oh not again Lord, I cannot be wrong again, but my flesh is warm, eyes open and the walls of the tabernacle still stand. Fool, fool, old fool. This time there's

no reprieve. The world survives and I can hear its laughter.
And my brethren outside – naked, lost in my word. They
wait for me to come out to them. *Ahh . . . Ahh . . .* is there
a hole deep enough for me?! The world shows no quarter to
failures and I've failed twice. Hide me! Someone hide me!
Lord leave me a little corner of darkness so I can hide.
Instead you hang me high on Golgotha, Christ, thy Son,
was pierced with thorns, spears and nails whilst I will be
hammered with laughter which digs deeper. I feel it tear me
now. Oh my bowels are wet *ahh . . .*

But Daniel always speaks of 2300 days and 1260 days and
1290 days and 1335 days and 70 weeks which leaves us 1810
add 33 years and we're left with this fixed day, this fixed
hour. I said Christ would come in his physical body rather
than in his spirit. Oh but I yearned to see you Lord in the
flesh to hear your voice with my own ears, to feel my heart
throb with the heavenly sound. I wanted to see Christ
dwelling again on an earth which would have resembled
the earth as it should be – green and new. My yearning was
for God but my words were all death and destruction. For
in the secret places of my heart I was happy at the thought
that they would be destroyed utterly and me and mine
would be in Paradise. Like Jonah I rubbed my hands in
satisfaction. Now it's their turn. When a man suffers he
ought not to say 'That's bad! That's bad!' Nothing God
imposes on a man is bad. But it's all right to say 'That's
bitter! That's bitter!'

I thought I'd done with pain but I groan under the
coming dog star of persecution. A hen prepared for the
table has to be plucked, gutted, washed, so it is with men
when God prepares us for justification. He uses the waters
of tribulation to cleanse the soul.

I predicted the greatest event in history and nothing
happened. And nothing comes of nothing they say. Yet
something always comes of nothing. The apology not

given, the love not shown, the word not spoken, the decision not taken, the battle not fought, the treaty not signed, the event that did not happen. Something has happened by not happening. All those nothings are effective messages and it's man who gives them meaning. I must try to find a meaning.

I knew I was right and rightness was a shield against doubt and chaos. And in this state of rightness I thought I was new-born and I knew without help of reason I had chosen the right path. So people came to me and I saw their suffering had nothing to do with their own weaknesses or the world but was part of a vast plan laid down in Heaven. Pride was the hunter. I sought honours and applause. I boasted of my goodness. I became a leader. I am rightly broken for it.

Well, now at least I stop my wanderings. I've tramped country roads and city streets for twenty years, now I can go home. But who'll remember me there? My wife Lucy'll remember the young soldier who asked for her hand and the farmer who worked in the fields, read at night, saw visions and raised a family in his vigour. Now my hair's white. Perhaps the east room is still kept ready for me? *(Singing)* 'There is a land of pure delight . . .'

Don't forsake me Lord as I will not forsake the vision. Yes, the Lord will still come. He is ever nigh unto the door, and there will be a new earth where the wicked are condemned, the good rewarded, the oppressors crushed and the people blessed. What a victory that will be.

Step out Brother Miller. You need your soldier's two a.m. courage now. A prophet whose prophecy has failed, who got it wrong, needs any kind of courage he can find. Step forward Brother Miller. Follow the vision, shout 'Victory!' Make the long walk to the door. One step at a time and you can cover continents. One foot in front of the other is the only way. First the right foot, then the left foot

. . . right, left, right, left . . . there! *(he stops walking)* All I have to do is open the door and step out. Is my beard tidy? Are my teeth in? Yes . . . yes . . . Try to stay with me Lord as I've tried to stay with you . . . *(low)* Courage Brother Miller. Courage . . .

*He opens the door of the tabernacle and steps out to shouts of abuse and laughter.*

# YESTERDAY'S NEWS

ANNA: Young man, if lobsters were just ten times bigger and carried guns, they'd be given respect instead of boiling water. I'm one hundred and thirteen years old and an O.B.E. I'm so old I have to be fumigated. That's why you're here isn't it? You want to get my story down on that machine. Sometimes sentences are just a noise to the old but I can still hold my water. I've got a personal maid and nurse. I can pay so I'm not treated like old rope. There's a lot of sad sights if you're old and the steam's running out. It's to do with the mind. But I'm different. I'm different, young man.

I've had congratulations from all over the world and a telegram from the Queen. She's coming to see me. If it's formal I'll wear my Marie Antoinette bonnet. She'll hear about Mrs Allen. I don't think the Queen knows much about her. And I'll tell her the wonder is not that such things should be, it's that they should be such things and not such other things.

Give me a drink. If it's wet I'll drink it when the mood's on me and the dancers in hobnail boots start thumping away in my head. I've drunk everything in my time. Once I even tried metal-polish and hard cider, that's a real thirst-quencher and better than having your arm cut off. It sent Percy McKellaway blind . . . or was it self-abuse? My memory isn't what it was when . . .

If you're old you lose your sense of time. You find yourself wondering what came first and what followed this and that and what happened when, how and why? It makes no difference. But the difference is what makes life worth living.

How can a little old lady like me fight the fading of memory? But I try, I try. I remember saying to my husband, George, 'I've a confession to make. I've been sleeping with another man.' And he said, 'Me too, turn over.' Oh I remember the horse-drawn buses and the Zeppelin raids and the Silvertown explosion and the long skirts and bustles and the ladies with lace handkerchiefs and lavender – now they tell me queers are running wild in Piccadilly.

I don't want to lie calmly in my grave and dream. I still like life with its sweet and bitter wonders. It's hard when your face is hairy and your teeth are out and your eyes have sunk into your head. It's better than having your body rot in a clean winding sheet but it's hard even if you've got charm. And I've got charm. Always have had. My mother said it's better to have charm than beauty and better to have money than anything.

My mother was a remarkable woman for her height. I owe everything to her. She taught me to always pay my way. I never owed anything to anyone, that's what puts years on your life.

I was an adventuress but I should've been an accountant. I've always liked working with figures. There's no hypocrisy there. Cheating, yes, but no hypocrisy. My mother set me up in business when I was about thirteen. I was gorgeous wasn't I? We took furnished rooms at 12 Lissom Grove. The landlady was passionately fond of me. My mother had lots of gentlemen callers and they looked at me like beggars at a sunbeam. But my mother said, 'God forbid my daughter should make the same mistakes I did. She's not going to sell herself cheap.'

Finally she dressed me in a white satin gown without sleeves to show off my arms and introduced me to an old man who kept rubbing his hands together when he looked at me: the rich know where the good wine lies.

He came to my room that night after paying the full price of admission – one hundred pounds: I wasn't being sold cheap. My mother told me to put up some kind of fuss. It was expected of a nice young lady. So I threw him out of the bed and broke two of his ribs – though he didn't notice at the time, except when he moved. I cried, 'Ooh, ooh, you'll split me in two.' The old man smiled proudly through his pain. With the help of cochineal and tomato ketchup I managed to re-sell my maidenhead at least twenty times before I was eighteen. There are no good girls only frightened men. I learnt very early that large sums of money are to be made in the love market but there are no rules because the price of love is governed by desire and nothing is more easy to manipulate than desire as I found out to my cost when I ran off with a singer from the chorus of *The Gondoliers*. I soon became pregnant and he lost his job. I was going to drown myself but I decided to wait for the warm weather. I've been rich and I've been poor – believe me rich is better. I'm not talking about the warm poverty of softies like you, young man, where you shelter under a leaky roof, on the edge of destitution because you temporarily lack money. I'm talking about the cold poverty of the poor where there's no bread for starving kids and the sick ones moan and there's no medicine for 'em and no help. That sort of poverty isn't just a lack of money, it's something positive, a disease more terrible than leprosy and the poor should be shunned like lepers. I had to cure myself before I rotted away. I abandoned my lover on Crewe station and my twin baby girls in the vestibule of a nearby church. I found out later they were taken to a Foundling Hospital where they died within a month of something called marasmus. Well, lessons have to be paid for and it's all yesterday's news.

When the world turns honest I'll take the veil. I went back to mother and met George. He was an eligible

bachelor – I forgot to ask eligible for what? He had a
receding chin and brain but he came from a good background. My mother said he had royal blood in his veins. I
didn't care if he had a royal flush in his kidneys. I married
him to please her though I knew insanity ravaged his family
from time to time.

He always carried a soap container in his pocket and
when he shook hands with someone he would go straight
out and wash them. In restaurants he drank coffee through
a straw so as not to touch the cup with his lips.

We had two good years until the money ran out and he
expected me to provide for both of us. 'What do you call a
man who is kept by his wife?' I asked. 'Lucky,' he replied.
He didn't think it wrong for a woman to prostitute herself
for her husband provided he approved. Neither did I but I
hated working for a sleeping partner. I had to be rid of him
but it was hard then, the scales were weighted against
women. Unfortunately for George his family had never
approved of divorce. I didn't want to leave him because he
could always return to me and my money. He had to leave
me. Luckily George's favourite meal was mushrooms. I
picked them myself. Somehow they got mixed with some
weed-killer. Now there are more efficient methods but in
those days we had to make do. Poor George, there's no
man so good that someone isn't delighted to be at his
deathbed.

There was talk, of course, about George's death. Yesterday's news. Murder's an ugly word – but bankruptcy is
uglier. I think I made the right choice. One's values remain
the same no matter how long you live; the hair on your
chin grows longer but your principles don't change. But I'll
admit my method with George had disadvantages. Killing
and such can have a bad effect on one's character if you're
not careful.

After a woman indulges herself, it can be downhill all the

way. From then on I thought nothing of lying, cheating, being lazy and rude. You start in a small way, wasting a wastrel and end up by being rude to your mother. And that's when I started drinking. Nothing to do with conscience, young man. I've managed to survive one hundred and thirteen years without a conscience. What's it for? Nobody's even been able to tell me. Can conscience put hot food in your stomach and money in your pocket? I don't believe in conscience.

A conscience wouldn't have helped us in two world wars.

*(Singing)* 'Goodbye Dolly I must leave you though it breaks my heart to go.'

They were good times for me. I bought and sold anything. I had lots of German friends and they paid well for information – it *was* the Germans we were fighting wasn't it, not the Czechs? Young man, the recruiting sergeant is always waiting at the corner trying to sell you a uniform or a flag. Don't buy!

The twenties were the best. I had the most exclusive house in London. Our prospectus listed sadism, masochism, voyeurism, fetishism, anal and oral intercourse and intercourse with mechanical instruments. It was good value for money but the overheads were high and profit margins slim so I had a sideline in white slavery and snow. I imported cocaine and exported girls to establishments in Cairo and Valparaiso.

They published stories of brutes raping virgins and shipping them to who-knows-where. But I can tell you those girls had been jumping for sovereigns with their legs spread out since the day they left school. Human beings are forced into sin as fish are forced into water. But everybody's against vice when they aren't practising it. I was the most notorious madame in London for a year or two. They called me a loose woman. I told them not to worry I'd be tight before the evening was over. But it's all yesterday's news. The truth was I kept a well-run house. We had our accidents, of course, like when Bishop Mallard was found asphyxiated in our Eastern room. He lay dead on the six inch Persian carpet with his trousers off beside the naked body of one of my girls. In the passion of the moment he'd accidentally kicked open a gas jet with his foot. He seemed happy enough. I don't know about the girl.

We catered for parties too, with special rates for Rotarians, Freemasons, Sales Conventions and the like. I tried to give them a good show. Once we had two naked girls running round a couch and some idiot we borrowed from a lunatic asylum in South Lambeth chasing them. The real idiots were down in the audience.

I had to be like a tiger. Young man, I think you are lovely. Greed was the motive that kept me going. They're always insulting greed. All I can say is God help the ungreedy – the poor, the blacks, the starving millions. I'm a grabber. When I grabbed I prospered. When I stopped grabbing I struck trouble.

Horatio Bottomly gave me some good advice. If you meet a man who wants to share his good fortune with you – run. He's a crook who's trying to swindle you out of your honest savings.

*(Singing)* Oh hear me sigh. I'm old, I'm old,
        Lie with me before I die.

Teddy was thirty years younger than me. It seems ever since I can remember everybody's been younger than me. Strapping chap. Very tall, well-shaped, dark skin, always in the best of humour – everybody's friend. I was fool enough to spend my money on him and he was smart enough to help me. The greatest chisler since Michaelangelo. Oh but his jingle jobs filled me to overflowing. He left and it was heartbreak hill for me. But the nice thing about tears is they come out in the wash. I had to start up again: gambling, abortion, blackmail, swindling – if there was a demand for it I was there.

Now I never give anything away. I'm a mean, selfish old mother-monster. But I'm still here because I've lived every day, every hour, every minute of my one hundred and thirteen years for myself alone.

You've got lovely hair, young man. I was going to tell the Queen the story of Mrs Allen wasn't I? She was a charlady in one of my brothels.

After her husband died, her neighbours said she'd come home drunk and was an unfit mother. So the authorities took away her little four-year-old girl and put her in a home. Some time after I gave Mrs Allen a hat of mine which she loved. She said her neighbours wanted to take the hat away too just because she loved it. So one evening she got hold of a hammer and nail, put on the hat, stood in front of a mirror, put the nail in the middle of her head and hammered it into her skull. They couldn't take the hat away from her as they took away her baby. It shows you shouldn't brood on yesterday's news; 'tisn't healthy. No I don't sit in the corner and worry. I'm still interested in myself. That's what keeps me going. You've got lovely hair, young man. The sentences are sounding like a lot of noise now. I'm tired. I want to be right for the Queen. You've got enough now haven't you? Prostitution, white slavery, drugs, abortion, murder, blackmail – passed like passing water. Now it's about as wicked as smoking a cigarette, as interesting as watching celery grow. Yesterday's news . . .

# GLORY

PEREGRINUS: All my life I've loved glory. Four years ago I promised I'd come to Olympia for the Olympic games of 165 to burn myself to death. My funeral pyre's over there. I built it myself. All that's left is for my friend Julius Theagenes here to light it . . . No, not yet Julius, not yet . . . I do not take my cremation lightly or coolly. Only nine days ago I was terrified because I caught a fever as I was sailing from Troad. I thought I was going to die – before my time and in an ordinary way. Like all sane men I'm afraid of death, yet now I run to it . . . No Julius, I'll tell you when to light up . . . First I shall deliver my own funeral oration. Hemlocked Socrates talked up to the last about himself; I claim the same privilege.

I'm certain most of you have heard of me. But for those who have had the misfortune to live outside the civilized world of Greece or Rome, I am Peregrinus, Peregrinus the Philosopher, *the* Peregrinus . . . hhhm, yes well . . . you might know me better as Proteus. It's a nickname I picked myself. I'm as changeable as a Proteus and it's an easier name to remember than Peregrinus.

Let me tell you about myself. I was born in Parium, a town whose only claim to fame will be that I was born there. They won't be grateful, people never are.

As a youth I studied and did things a young man is supposed to do. I had an affair with a married woman and had a horse-radish stuck up between my buttocks which was the penalty for adultery in that part of Greece. And I was caught with an Armenian boy. 'You'll pay for this!' his parents screamed. I did – three thousand drachmas which is extremely expensive for a boy, especially an Armenian.

But I recall Sophocles lost his expensive cloak squeezing an Armenian boy up against the city wall. The moral is, one should always stay well clear of Armenians. As you can see I had an ordinary youth, similar to most Greeks of my background and class. There was nothing at that time to mark me out.

My first taste of glory and controversy, for the two are never far from each other – was when I strangled my father. Ah, I see some of you remember me now. Yes I'm *that* Peregrinus . . . I would like to seize this opportunity of, once again, telling the whole truth of that memorable episode.

Certain writers who should know better have distorted the incident out of all proportion. The facts are these: my father craved respect as much as I craved fame. For him a life without the respect of others wasn't worth living. He was old and didn't want to decline into second childhood, for we are given little respect in our first childhood and none in our second. My father couldn't bear the thought of that so he asked me to kill him quietly after his sixtieth birthday.

Actually, he never asked, he ordered me to kill him: he was a difficult man, my father. As a dutiful son I obeyed but he didn't make it easy. No subtle poisons and such. He insisted I do it manually in the old Roman way. It was hard. My father was a strong man even at his age and could easily knock me to the floor if he was roused. Once I attempted to strangle him when he was asleep. As I bent over him trying to get the cord round his neck he opened one eye and stared into my face. 'Is this the best you can do?' he grunted. I felt a complete fool.

After a few more abortive efforts I finally caught my father dozing in front of a huge fire after a particularly fine dinner. This time I didn't fail him. *Uhg* . . . It was over in a few seconds. I believe he only pretended to be dozing just to help me.

Though I had only fulfilled my role as a dutiful son, there was an outcry in the town. Certain citizens, when they found out what had happened, wanted to drag me into court. It could have been difficult. Innocent or guilty, once you find yourself in the hands of lawyers you're lost. I had to avoid that calamity. Fortunately I was something of a philosopher even then. I knew human nature and the forces that move men. So I announced I would distribute my father's wealth to the people in the town. I was carried through the streets in triumph. Anyone who spoke of my father's death would've been strangled themselves. Money is important, without it you die unknown in your own backyard.

I had an income of my own, but one can never have too much. So, a little later I petitioned the Emperor, Marcus Aurelius, to restore my father's inheritance to me. He replied, 'A gift is a gift'. Not a very original observation coming from a philosopher of his inflated reputation. But it had the dubious virtue of being clear. I was to get no satisfaction from that quarter.

I left Parium and wandered from country to country according to my whim. I had acquired my first taste of glory. I was known as Peregrinus Patricide. It was not the reputation I particularly liked. True it was something to build on but I would've preferred something more substantial, the reputation of a patricide soon fades.

I needed something new. I found it in Syria. An old man with a white beard struck up an acquaintance with me. I was immediately suspicious of him because of his air of innocence and concern. I'd met cunning rogues like him before on my travels. My suspicions were confirmed when he said rather mysteriously he wanted me to make an investment of all the money and goods I had. I was to take a position in an organization he belonged to. The position was vague but I would be on call day and night. My reward was even vaguer – nothing now, but in the long term I would do very well indeed. You can see why I knew I was being cheated, particularly when he said I must act immediately. Tomorrow was too late. It's an axiom amongst swindlers and rogues that only the greedy can't wait and are ripe for plucking.

The old man said I was to do all this for their founder who had lived in some obscure Eastern province of the Empire some years before. I asked the name of this man. 'Jesus Christ' was the reply. Now I realized why I had thought the old man was a criminal. He was a Christian. It was a sign from the gods. This was indeed the new thing I craved. This Eastern religion was a rare novelty. And when I started talking to other Christian divines I realized they were children compared to me. Frankly they didn't have my intellect or education. I was converted. I became a Christian. I lectured on their books, confused and jumbled though they were, and I wrote a number myself.

Then I had a stroke of luck. I was arrested; injustice often comes in useful. Certain people put it about that I engineered the arrest myself. Liars! Damnable liars. I had nothing to do with it. It was the Governor of Syria. My arrest gave me great authority and earned me the reputation of having performed miracles. That's the way Christians are. Their religion is based on suffering in this world and the next. Their Jewish founder was crucified you know. So naturally they like others to follow his example. Martyrdom is in their blood. Perhaps that's where my idea for a fiery death began . . . Down Julius . . . down! . . . I was a great success in prison. Old men, women and orphans would come and visit me, bringing me food and comfort. Representatives of the Christian communities throughout Asia consoled me and promised help. Those were happy days.

Then I lost everything. With one vicious spin of the

wheel of fate, the Governor of Syria cast me down into the pits. He released me! In his damnable benevolence he set me free, deciding I wasn't even going to be punished: no rack, no maiming, not even a few lashes. I was no longer a miracle worker. The Christian community rejected me – this was no way for a true Christian to be treated. They suggested I had bribed the Governor to release me. I was frightened to face the fires of martyrdom. Me frightened! Liars! Mere liars! I am not afraid . . . No Julius will you please stay where you are. Don't be so *eager* . . . My authority was gone. The Christians were disillusioned with me. And, truth to tell, I was disillusioned with them. Their ideas, such as they were, were too muddled for a man who had been trained in logic. It's a well-meaning but fanatical sect, friends. I fear it will come to a bad end. My conversion, I realized, was a mistake, so I deconverted. That provoked a gratifying sensation for a few months and my name was on the lips of everyone that mattered.

But I took stock. I had been leading a full enough life it's true. I had loved, tasted the joys of belief and disbelief. I had known freedom and imprisonment, triumph and failure, fame and obscurity. Now I had to think of settling down, so I shaved my head and became a professional philosopher. Philosophy, not sodomy, is the Greek vice. The competition is fierce, not only from one's contemporaries, but also from the illustrious dead – Socrates, Plato, Aristotle and the rest. To make your mark, to leave your print in the sand, requires more than just talent. I went to Rome where I taught the concept that things are of no consequence. By way of illustration I broke eggs over my bald head and had myself beaten on the behind with a stick. I proclaimed the principle that the truth should never be left unspoken; that's the greatest crime against society. I abused Marcus Aurelius for pretending to be a philosopher as well as an Emperor. You cannot wield power and still claim to think. The Emperor never replied to my attack; he just had the Governor exile me from Rome.

I wandered again, but this time with a reputation. I was either loved or hated. My contemporary Aulus Gellius said I was 'a man serious in behaviour and instructive in conversation.' And then there is Lucius. Lucius hated me. He said I was always despised and treated with contempt. And he's here tonight waiting to spread lies about me. I know you're out there Lucius, skulking in the shadows, dripping poison! You can wait! And keep waiting! You too Julius . . .

Then one day the excitement of striving flagged and I plunged into melancholy. I faced the truth; a good part of my life was a failure. No, the truth should never be left unspoken. Nothing I did seemed to be taken seriously. They called me a fraud but if I am, I'm a genuine fraud.

They called my pride cruelty, my virtue stupidity, my eloquence bombast, my profundity fatuousness, my frankness arrogance. At sixty I had achieved notoriety but no glory, no true fame. It was too late.

But it wasn't, it wasn't. I wouldn't be defeated. If my life was a failure, my death would be a success. You can argue about a man's achievements, but you must approve if he dies for an idea, whatever it is. Only a little courage is needed and you are everlastingly in the right. A little courage . . . Yes . . . Yes . . . Julius stay where you are! . . . The Christians burn themselves to death for salvation, the Brahmins out of devout love of death. I burn to defeat death, to force fame to her knees and cry quarter. They'll raise altars to me, my disciples promised to build a temple on this site. Golden statues will be erected in my memory, poets will sing of me, I'll be immortal! You can think about lighting your torch now, Julius . . . But what if they don't, what if they don't raise altars and statues? The real monuments of the dead are in the hearts of the living. What if I'm forgotten and all my courage is for nothing. What a waste

of a life and all that wood. Friends, I'm not backing out of
burning. I'd only do that if you begged me to spare myself.
If you said, 'Stay alive for the sake of Greece!' Then I
might. But of course you won't say that. You wouldn't
spit in my mouth if my throat was on fire. It's because you
don't like me isn't it?! You've never liked me. None of you.
I've never been *nice* . . . Julius, light your torch now . . .
Julius . . . That was quick. You're very quick Julius. Very.
Now stay, don't go over to the pile till I tell you . . . I know
what you're saying out there. I see it on your faces. 'Why
doesn't he get on with the roasting?' The only reason you
came out here in the middle of the night was to see me
roast. I'm Proteus you know. I should change my mind
just to spite you.

*The crowd is heard growling.*

But I won't. I've always been imprisoned by other people's
opinion of me. I look out into the shadows and know I'm
sacrificing years of living to win the praises of people like
*you*. You don't deserve me . . .! Julius, go light it! Light it
Julius!

**Julius** *is heard walking over to the pile.*

I'm cold . . . but soon I'll be warm enough . . . Let it burn
Julius, let it burn . . .

*The fire is heard burning.*

My enemies will say death was just an excuse for not living.
They won't be defeated by what I do and posterity won't
care. In a few years' time they won't know who I am –
Peregrinus who? Why should they remember the name of a
man who died voluntarily in the service of a cause he didn't
even believe in.

*He starts moving towards the fire.*

I'm coming Julius, it's getting late . . . I stumble into this
last darkness knowing I'll gain no reward in this world or
the next. There's no point to it now, no reason, useless . . .

*He stops in front of the fire.*

But perhaps there is a kind of glory there – to do it knowing it's useless . . . and after all, as that Imperial idiot said, a gift is a gift . . . I just hope you're satisfied that's all!

*He steps forward. The fire roars and consumes him.*

# ROSA

*Sound of tape-recorder being switched on.*

DR ROSA HAMILTON: Rough draft memo to the North-East London Area Health Board from Dr Rosa Hamilton. I have completed investigations, accompanied by Welfare Officer Gannon, of the three outstanding applications for admission to Residential Council Homes.

Case Number 276/3 – Mrs Hoggart, lives with her daughter Muriel in a council flat in Aldgate. She is a widow of eighty-five, slightly deaf, with bad teeth, thrombosis of the right leg and avitaminosis resulting from a Vitamin A deficiency. She sat all through the interview staring at the china ducks on the wall opposite. We were told she had fallen out of bed two days previously and she did have discolourations round her eyes. I offered to examine her but she had already been seen by her own doctor. Her daughter, Muriel, complained that she couldn't do much for herself now. 'She keeps wetting the bed and does the other thing too if she can't get up in time. And I always leave a pot there. I'm out working all day but my daughter, Emily, hasn't got a job yet so she helps her, but that can't be for always. She'll get a job soon and then what? My husband's gone and my eldest daughter's in hospital. I don't want to send Mum away but I work hard. I see the factory and this place. If I don't get a break I'll really lose my temper with her one day.'

Muriel's youngest daughter, Emily, came in whilst the old lady was signing an A1/7/84 form. Emily looked furiously at her mother. As we left an argument broke out between them. Emily accused her mother of getting rid of granny. 'You're sending her off to die!' she shouted.

'I don't know what else to do,' her mother shouted back. 'It's for the best, isn't it Mother? Isn't it Mother?' Muriel appealed for reassurance to the old lady who just sat there.

Recommendation: Mrs Hoggart be taken into a residential Home.

Case 294/15 – Eighty-year-old Mr Trevor lives with his seventy-four-year-old sister, Dora, in a council house in Whitechapel. He was sitting in his bedroom when we arrived. It was a bare room with a bed and a few clothes hanging on the wall. Mr Trevor's jacket and trousers were stained with food. Mr Trevor has a paralysed left arm and has great difficulty pulling himself up the stairs from the ground floor to his bedroom. 'By the time I get up here I'm gone,' he said.

He used to be a dustman but does not qualify for either contributory or disability pensions. Dora told us that he had a son who was in prison and had tried to commit suicide twice.

Mr Trevor had asked to go into a residential Home because he was becoming a burden to his sister. 'Darkness has got into my head. I can't even put on my socks myself and I suffer from convulsions because of my chest.' He is being treated for bronchiectasis.

Dora would like him to stay with her because she said that he was a good son to their mother and father all the years she could remember. But she finds it hard now to look after herself and her brother. She is afraid to leave the house.

Mr Trevor said that he missed not being able to go to the park. He couldn't go alone. It would be nice if some strong young chap would help. He could lean on him. Mr Gannon agreed it would be best if someone could call round but there was nobody available.

Recommendation: Mr Trevor to be taken into a residential Home.

Case 304/79 – Mr Forbes is a widower of seventy-three who lives with Mrs James, a widow of seventy in a one-room terraced house in Aldgate East. They have a number of plants in pots and a carpet which was sticky under our feet. 'It smells terrible in the summer,' a neighbour told us.

Mr Forbes has severe and crippling osteoarthritis of the knee joints and has great difficulty moving. He lost his wife ten years ago and has a married daughter, Vivian, who lives nearby. We did not see her but the son-in-law, John, turned up to explain that Vivian was ill. This may have been true or just an excuse. Vivian and John were moving up North and would not be able to look in to see the old couple. 'You've done enough,' Mr Forbes muttered. 'He's done enough hasn't he Mrs James? We've had our time. We're going to be out of it, out of next winter and those prices and the debts and the rest.'

Mr Forbes had been a clerk but does not qualify for a full pension. He said that he did not want to be a nuisance but was there any chance of him and Mrs James being put in the same Home?

The Welfare Officer could not promise anything. It was difficult enough keeping legally married couples together, but he would try. 'Thank you, sir, thank you,' said Mr Forbes.

Mrs James nodded vaguely when Mr Forbes told her the news. She is a partly blind person and has Paget's disease of the bone. She has one son living in Wapping, whom she has not seen for a year. Though she would not talk about him, it is possible he disapproves of her living with a man.

Mrs James trembled during the interview. Mr Forbes tried to get her to tell us if she wanted to go into a Home or not, but she kept pulling her stockings up and down.

Recommendation: Mr Forbes and Mrs James to be taken into a residential Home.

It is no wonder these old people want to leave. They live

in a part of the East End of London which looks as though it has been dismembered and the dead pieces left lying about. Living there is like living in a corpse. They feel that our Homes would be an improvement – I have sad news for them . . . You can't say that Rosa. By objective. I can't. I'm riding round and round, it's like going somewhere just to come back from nowhere. I need a drink. I've always been full of pep – well full anyway. By objective Rosa. No, I've been objective enough for one day . . . They all damn well know our Homes are waiting rooms for death. But they're poor; they have nowhere else. It's not how much money you make in your life that counts, but how much you're got when you quit. Our Homes answer the question, 'Is there life before death?' with a resounding 'No.' You find the old sitting in Day Rooms counting the window panes. All they see are strangers, all they want is their own . . . That's unfair Rosa. I want to be unfair. I want to be angry . . .

Some of our places have single rooms, wardrobes and dressing-tables, but the corridors are still long and draughty. It's because Health Boards like ours still cling to the idea we mustn't make it too good for them; the public must be protected from the undeserving poor. Of course they're undeserving if they end their days in Homes supported by us. The terrible thing is the old people believe it too. They feel they don't deserve any better and their misery has no meaning. They've known failure for so long they wither and become ugly. Beauty needs a measure of success and happiness. I asked one old man why he was crying. 'I'm not crying,' he said, 'These are just tears.'

I'm resigning, gentlemen. Don't cheer please. How did you ever come to engage me in the first place? You never liked women – well, only with mustard. I'm resigning because I've lost my ability to hate: one's last defence against death and despair is hatred.

And I'm growing tired. After twenty years of it, Dr Rosa is tired of seeing old men and women wrapped in blankets staring up at the ceiling and turning yellow – tired of that bloody smell of urine, spit, stale cabbage, disinfectant and defeat – tired of human beings not living and functioning, but dying in a chair, on their backs – tired of men so lousy no-one can go near them till they've been scrubbed with a long-handled brush – tired of coronaries, arthritis, bronchitis and the rest – tired of old women with thin arms, legs, flat chests, sagging bellies and old men lying with the sheets pulled up over their faces – tired of old kidneys, lungs, bowels, deafness, blindness, old age.

I never felt this way before. I had energy. I needed it to get away from home and through medical school. I remember my father telling me to make a go of it. He was a handsome and intelligent man, but all his life he was dissatisfied and unfulfilled. Although nature had generously endowed him for something fine and noble, he spent his days in a bank, counting other people's money. At least he died without posing – he just fell down one day and hiccoughed. My mother was as neat and careful in death as she was in life. That's all she seemed to care about.

Well, I guess I made a go of it, though as a woman it was double-hard. I needed all my anger to win through. When I was studying there were quite a few brilliant women students who got frightened their careers might hinder their marriage prospects. So they stopped themselves. Idiots! I didn't, though I fell in love. Funny how he immediately expected me to find a deep fulfilment in marriage and motherhood: after qualifying as a doctor, my life was to be filled with such after-hours stupidities. A man trains to be successful in life, a woman is trained in case she's a failure and doesn't get married. The bloody waste of it! And then there was Dr Mark Summers. He wanted to marry me but he wouldn't get a divorce from his mother.

I've had offers. But one's better alone . . . What's all this to do with the price of onions, Rosa? Nothing – I'm just not being objective, that's all . . . I specialized in geriatrics because all the heroic diseases like tuberculosis, smallpox and plague were more or less beaten. But the last disease, old age, was still with us. The fight against it was hard and it was one you could never win. But I thought you could gain small victories. I fought with all the enthusiasm of youth. When I first took this job I could wear anything, now I usually do. I look like a burlap bag. I eat when I can, sleep where I can – usually on the office sofa. I have four residential Homes, six hundred patients submerged under a mountain of paper: form AC 2/4/2, form BD/42, form K/37 . . . It seems I've barely had enough time to look round before a half-century vanished as if were a single day. And I thought I'd done so much.

I've suffered half-a-dozen Area Health Boards in my time: fought them all for more money, more Homes, better conditions. All any of them ever wanted was to rest in peace – but that's for tombstones! Nothing irritates official minds more than human diversities and differences. All kinds of trouble are to be found in the murky byways of individualism.

I had heroic battles. I told one Board Chairman – the Reverend Hutchinson – to stop prattling on about the ennobling qualities of suffering and try to do something to eliminate it instead. I asked another – he was the one with the money-bags under his eyes – if I could rent him to haunt a house. A third was so crooked he would steal two left shoes. He was easily the best. Heroic times. I shouted, got suspended with and without pay, vilified and reprimanded. Now, unfortunately, I've mellowed. What's worse, I'm accepted. I'm that 'game old bird' – or 'bag' – Dr Rosa Hamilton, the grubby Nightingale of the East End, raincoat flapping in the breeze, cigarette dangling from the corner of her mouth, the smell of drink on her breath. It gets harder each year to find the anger to get things changed. Oh, I've managed to get a few over the years, to make life a little better for the old and sick. But such individual acts of goodness only institutionalize the injustice and therefore make it permanent. I'll end my time making conditions worse by making them better. You don't change the bitter seas of this system by pouring the odd bottle of social reform into it. There's a wall of indifference between the old and the rest of society. Chipping away a few bricks is useless. Only hammer blows will break it down.

I believe the organization of our bodies is such a marvel that the soul must surely have great difficulty in separating itself from the body it has inhabited for years. Death is a disaster for the soul, for the death of the body diminishes it, destroys its home. Our Homes degrade bodies so the soul leaves thankfully. We let our people shrink, see them cut off one feeling after another, block every life-giving contact so they grow weary of everything; they don't live, they linger. Eskimos leave their old people out on ice floes when they are no longer useful. They leave them to drift out to sea and freeze to death. We leave ours in Homes where they drift away to die too.

If only the old would re-discover rage. If only they'd turn their last sunsets into bloody ones. God, I'd like to lead an army of the old and poor, an army of Mr Trevors and Mrs James'; battalions of decrepit bodies, firing from deformed hips; bomb-throwing squads of deaf and blind; swarms of asthmatics and incontinents, rocket attacks from speeding wheelchairs; a Geriatric Terrorist Army! If you want revolution in our time you must have slaughter on your mind. That would punch a hole through the wall – *whoom, boom, bang* . . . Bomb-throwing geriatrics?! *Never* . . . Why do I get into this state? One reason, I hate the waste of it. Old people surely should be our best guides. They have more experience, observed more because they've lived. They should still be of use . . . Oh this won't do, won't do at all. Certainly not for an Area Health Board. Take out all the rage and passion. You should know better by now. You started off cool and objective, keep it that way. It's a report, woman – facts, be objective – scrub out the rest . . .

It's the end, so we go on a little longer. Wipe and re-draft, then you can give yourself that drink . . .

*The tape is run back and wiped, then stopped and run forward.*

Rough draft of memo to the North-East London Area Health Board from Dr Rosa Hamilton .˙. .